Understanding China

More information about this series at http://www.springer.com/series/11772

Yunmei Wu

Compliance Ethnography

How Small Businesses Respond to the Law in China

 Springer

Yunmei Wu
Research Innovation Team of Yunnan Social
Construction Key Issues at the New Development
Stage, Yunnan Academy of Social Sciences
Kunming, China

In addition to the fund of Research Innovation Team of Yunnan Social Construction
Key Issues at the New Development Stage, the research of this book also received
financial assistance from the VENI project "Reorienting Global Risk Regulation:
Matching Regulatory Instruments and Enforcement Capacity in Emerging Market
Contexts" in 2009.

ISSN 2196-3134   ISSN 2196-3142 (electronic)
Understanding China
ISBN 978-981-16-2886-3   ISBN 978-981-16-2884-9 (eBook)
https://doi.org/10.1007/978-981-16-2884-9

To My Family

Contents

1   **Introduction** 1
   1.1   The Problem of Compliance 1
   1.2   Existing Approaches to Study Compliance 3
       1.2.1   The Endogenous Approach and its Limits 4
       1.2.2   The Exogenous Approach and its Limits 5
       1.2.3   The Process Approach and its Limits 10
   1.3   An Ethnographic Approach and Methodology 11
   1.4   A Three-Process Scheme 13
   1.5   Case Selection and Data Collection 15
   References 18

Part I   Descriptive Analysis of Compliance Behaviors

2   **Descriptive Analysis of Compliance Behaviors** 25
   2.1   Describing Compliance Behaviors 25
       2.1.1   Process Perspective 26
       2.1.2   A Subjective Perspective 28
   2.2   Classifying Compliance Behaviors 29
   2.3   Characterizing the Subject of Compliance Behaviors 34
   2.4   Structure of the Case Description 38
   References 38

3   **An Idealistic Restaurant** 41
   3.1   Introduction 41
   3.2   A Different Restaurant 42
   3.3   Meet the Owner 44
   3.4   Getting Ready to the Business 45
   3.5   Learning to Play the Game 47
       3.5.1   Business License 50
       3.5.2   Catering Service License 50

	3.5.3	Fire License	51
	3.5.4	Drainage License	52
	3.5.5	Decoration License	53
	3.5.6	Environmental License	54
	3.5.7	Compliance as Clarification Process for Opening Licenses	54
3.6	Daily Operation		56
	3.6.1	Pork and Chicken	56
	3.6.2	Dishware Disinfection	58
	3.6.3	Health Certificate	60
	3.6.4	Handwashing	60
	3.6.5	Keeping Nails Short	62
	3.6.6	"*Fapiao*" Receipts	63
	3.6.7	Compliance as Interactive Process of Restaurant Ideology and Legal Requirements in Daily Operation Norms	65
3.7	Discussion		66
	3.7.1	Classifying Compliance Behaviors at the Idealistic Restaurant	66
	3.7.2	Characterizing the Subject of Compliance at the Idealistic Restaurant	70
References			73

4 A Profit-Maximizing Restaurant .... | | | 75
4.1	Introduction		75
4.2	A Small but Profitable Restaurant		76
4.3	Meet the Owner		77
4.4	Learning to Dance with the Law		79
	4.4.1	Environmental License	79
	4.4.2	Catering Services License	80
	4.4.3	Fire License	81
	4.4.4	Business License	81
	4.4.5	Taxation License	81
	4.4.6	Opening License Renewal	82
	4.4.7	Compliance Process as Learning Practice Rule in Opening Licenses	84
4.5	Daily Operation		85
	4.5.1	Dishware Disinfection	86
	4.5.2	Health Certificate	88
	4.5.3	*Fapiao* Receipts	89
	4.5.4	Washing Hands and Cutting Fingernails	91
	4.5.5	Learning Process in Daily Operation (Non)Compliance Behaviors	93
4.6	Discussion		94

4.6.1 Classifying Compliance Behaviors
at the Profit-Maximizing Restaurant 94
4.6.2 Characterizing the Subject of Compliance
at the Profit-Maximizing Restaurant 98
References 103

5   **Compliance Pluralism** 105
5.1 Introduction 105
5.2 Compliance Pluralism 106
5.3 Compliance Processes 111
5.4 Characterizing Compliance Subjects 114
5.5 Conclusion 116
References 117

Part II   Explaining Compliance Behaviors

6   **Metamorphosis of Legal Knowledge: How Did the Laws Arrive
at the Restaurants?** 121
6.1 Introduction 121
6.2 The Process of Legal Knowledge Formation 122
6.2.1 Definition of Legal Knowledge 123
6.2.2 Methods of Acquiring Legal Knowledge 124
6.3 Legal Knowledge in Restaurants 126
6.3.1 Limited Doctrinal Legal Knowledge 126
6.3.2 Abundant Legal Practice Knowledge 128
6.3.3 Sources of Legal Knowledge in Restaurants 128
6.3.4 Comprehensive Legal Knowledge 133
6.4 Effects of Enforcement Encounters 134
6.5 Conclusion 139
References 141

7   **Toxic Culture: How Did Organizational Norms Mediate
the Transition of Laws?** 143
7.1 Introduction 143
7.2 Organizational Norms and Compliance 144
7.2.1 Organizational and Social Norms 144
7.2.2 How Social Norms Influence Compliance 146
7.2.3 Competition Between and Activation
of Organizational and Legal Norms 147
7.2.4 The Formation of Organizational Norms 149
7.2.5 Organizational Socialization and Management
Processes 152
7.3 Socialization and Management Processes in Restaurants 153
7.3.1 Hiring 154
7.3.2 Training 156
7.3.3 Monitoring 160

7.3.4   Evaluating and Rewarding 163
7.3.5   Problem Resolution 164
7.4   Organizational Norms in Restaurants and Compliance
Behaviors 166
7.4.1   Organizational Norms at the Idealistic Restaurant 166
7.4.2   Organizational Norms at the Profit-Maximizing
Restaurant 173
7.4.3   Organizational Norms and Compliance Behaviors 176
7.5   Interaction Between Legal Norms and Organizational Norms 179
7.5.1   Activation 179
7.5.2   Competition 180
7.6   Conclusion 182
References 185

**8   The Individuals: How Did Individuals Make Compliance
Decision?** 189
8.1   Introduction 189
8.2   Compliance Variables in Theory 191
8.2.1   Plural Subjective Deterrence 192
8.2.2   Personal Norms 194
8.2.3   Descriptive Social Norms 195
8.2.4   Perceived Obligation to Obey the Law 196
8.2.5   Capacity 197
8.3   Dialogue Interview Method 199
8.4   Measurement of Compliance Behaviors 201
8.5   Subjective Explanations of Compliance Behavior 202
8.5.1   For Compliance Behaviors 202
8.5.2   For Violation Behaviors 205
8.5.3   Operational Benefit and not Being Responsible 208
8.6   Interviewees' Understanding and Perceptions of Each Variable 210
8.6.1   Plural Subjective Deterrence 210
8.6.2   Perceived Obligation to Obey the Law 214
8.6.3   Descriptive Social Norms 217
8.6.4   Personal Norms 219
8.6.5   Capacity 222
8.7   Association Analysis of Compliance Behaviors and Influential
Variables 225
8.8   Comparison Between Subjective Self-Explanation
and Variable Association Analysis 227
8.9   Conclusion 228
References 230

9   Conclusion 235
  9.1   Introduction 235
  9.2   Summary Findings 237
  9.3   An Integrated Model 241
  9.4   Methodological Implications 246
  9.5   Implications for Regulatory Strategies 248
  9.6   Implications for Addressing Compliance Challenge 250
  References 251

Appendix A: Laws Concerning Restaurants Involved in This Book 253

Appendix B: The Methodology of Case Study 259

Appendix C: Supplemental Cases 263

Uncited References 271

Acronyms and Abbreviations

CDC   Centers for Disease Control
CMD   City Management Department
CNY   Chinese Yuan
CSA   Community Supporting Agriculture
EEO   Equal Employment Opportunity Law
FDA   Food and Drug Administration Bureau
GDP   Gross Domestic Product
ICA   Industrial and Commercial Administration Bureau
MSG   Monosodium Glutamate
NGO   Nongovernmental Organization
NPC   National People's Congress
OECD   The Organisation for Economic Cooperation and Development
POOL   Perceived Obligation to Obey the Law
SAT   State Administration of Taxation

List of Tables

Table 1.1   Summary of restaurants studied 16

Table 3.1   A summary of the opening licenses required
for restaurants 49

Table 3.2   Variations of compliance and noncompliance
at the idealistic restaurant 67

Table 3.3   Motivational postures at the idealistic restaurant 72

Table 4.1   Variations of compliance and noncompliance
at the Profit-Maximizing restaurant 96

Table 4.2   Motivational postures at the Profit-Maximizing restaurant 100

Table 6.1   Clusters of legal practice knowledge at the idealistic
restaurant and the Profit-Maximizing restaurant 129

Table 7.1   Organizational norms and compliance behaviors 177

Table 8.1   Variables at individual level 198

Table 8.2   Number of interviewees and behaviors identified 199

Table 8.3   Frequency of compliance behaviors 202

Table 8.4   Factors identified in the subjective explanation of positive
compliance behaviors 205

Table 8.5   Factors identified in the subjective explanation
of violation behaviors 208

Table 8.6   Frequency of plural subjective deterrence 211

Table 8.7   Frequency of perceived obligation to obey the law 214

Table 8.8   Frequency of descriptive norms 218

Table 8.9   Frequency of personal norms 219

Table 8.10   Frequency of recognition of legal requirements
in trichotomy 222

Table 8.11   Frequency of recognition of legal requirements
in dichotomy 223

Table 8.12   Frequency of practical constraints 225

Table 8.13   Cross Tabulation of Compliance Behaviors and Variables 225

Table C.1   Compliance behaviors, motivational postures, and
management styles in the three restaurants 269

Chapter 1
Introduction

1.1 The Problem of Compliance

Since opening to trade and undergoing economic reform in the 1980s, China has experienced remarkable economic growth and the development of a market economy. In 1992, following a speech by Deng Xiaoping,[1] China further made an important strategic decision to establish a socialist market economy, which required the creation of a new regulatory system that differed from the previous system of commands coupled with a planned economy. Consequently, China has been developing an increasingly comprehensive system of regulatory laws and institutions, and has been attempting to implement legislation to regulate the rapidly emerging market actors and processes. Hundreds of laws and regulations have been enacted to regulate various domains in the swiftly developing socialist market economy, such as environmental protection, food safety, product quality, public auctions, occupational health and safety, enterprise registration, and land usage.

By the end of August 2011, the Chinese Communist Party concluded that the socialist system of laws with Chinese characteristics has been set up, noting that

> all legal branches have been set up, covering all aspects of social relations; basic and major laws of each branch have been made; related administrative regulations and local regulations are fairly complete; and the whole legal system is scientific and consistent. A socialist system of laws with Chinese characteristics has been solidly put into place.[2]

The pace of legislation has not slowed down since. From the end of August 2011 to the end of September 2014, the number of administrative regulations has increased

---

[1]On January 17, 1986, Deng Xiaoping, a former Chinese leader, spoke at the meeting of the Central Politburo Standing Committee of the Communist Party of China (PSC) and proposed that it is necessary to use "two hands" to achieve the "four modernizations," with one hand developing the economy and the other strengthening the legal system.

[2]http://www.scio.gov.cn/ztk/dtzt/65/12/Document/1060811/1060811.htm.

Y. Wu, *Compliance Ethnography*, Understanding China,
https://doi.org/10.1007/978-981-16-2884-9_1

from 706 to 737, and that of local regulations has increased from 8600 to 8909.[3] In 2015, the NPC standing committee further enacted five laws and amended 37 laws.[4]

However, while China has achieved great success in enacting laws, it does not automatically mean these laws have successfully prevented and controlled the ecological, financial, and health risks that inevitably came with China's massive economic growth and industrialization. Having a law is but a first step in changing risky behavior. Simply stating that certain behavior is not allowed, or instituting penalties or even rewards to incentivize less risky behavior, does not automatically lead to a change in practice. For that to happen, the actors the law addresses should actually comply with the legal rules established.

In fact, China is experiencing a compliance crisis. Frequent violations are common in many areas of law, and these violations cause great risk and harm to the natural environment, public health and security, the market economy order, the credibility of government authority, and even the credibility of legal authority. A core question is thus, how can regulatory bodies ensure compliance? Consider, for instance, the following examples. In terms of food safety, in 2008, a large and well-known Chinese milk producer, Sanlu, produced milk powder for infants that contained Melamine, a kind of inedible additive, and caused urinary system problems in babies and children. In 2005, several large food producers, including KFC and Heinz, were exposed to magdala red, an illegal additive that may cause cancer, in various widely consumed foods.

In addition, in terms of environmental pollution, in 2007, Taihu Lake in Jiangsu province, which is the main source of drinking water for Wuxi, a city near Shanghai, was polluted severely with algae due to serious industrial pollution from nearby factories. Moreover, an explosion in the hazardous article storage area of an international logistics company in Tianjin in 2015 exposed the prevalent problems of fraudulent environmental assessment reports and other problematic licensing practices in construction.

Similar problems have arisen in the field of occupational health. In 2009, Zhang Haichao, a Henan farmer worker, was diagnosed with pneumoconiosis, locally known as "dust lung." This occupational disease, caused by the inhalation of dust, is prevalent in workers doing mining-, excavating-, smashing-, and polishing-related work in the mining, machine manufacturing, construction material, and road construction industries. By making his condition known, he exposed common violations of occupation health and safety regulations that occurred nationwide.

In addition to the serious events caused by the violation of laws, less significant, yet still dangerous, violations occur in everyday life. The "Chinese way to cross the road" describes the general phenomenon of people crossing the road while the

---

[3]See http://www.china.com.cn/zhibo/zhuanti/ch-xinwen/2014-11/06/content_33986113.htm and http://www.scio.gov.cn/ztk/dtzt/65/12/Document/1060811/1060811_1.htm.

[4]http://www.npc.gov.cn/npc/xinwen/2016-03/10/content_1975326.htm.

crossing lights are red. Despite legal restrictions, fake *Fapiao* receipts, the official proof of tax payments in China, have repeatedly emerged. Furthermore, corruption scandals involving government officials keep being exposed, despite China having some of the world's most stringent anticorruption laws. Overall, compliance is a severe challenge for China on the way to "building a nation of laws."

1.2 Existing Approaches to Study Compliance

Compliance has been a growing field in regulatory research and has led to the development of two mainstream approaches. The first approach considers the concept of compliance changeable and dynamic. Multiple meanings of compliance exist among key actors in the regulatory field, and in certain situations, those key actors negotiate and construct the very meaning of compliance. Therefore, the concept of compliance becomes the research object, with researchers attempting to discover how compliance is understood and conceptualized. In their comprehensive review, Parker and Nielson (2009) categorized this kind of research as endogenous-approach research.

The second mainstream approach is the exogenous approach as Parker and Nielson (2009) named, which treats the understanding of compliance as exogenous to the research, that is, produced from or derived from external sources. This kind of research takes the concept of compliance as predefined and uses it as either a dependent or independent variable to discover the causal relationships between compliance and other variables. Its interests are pragmatic, aiming to explain the causes or effects of compliance.

A third, less-known approach to the study of compliance combines the endogenous and exogenous approaches to a certain extent. This approach, the process approach, focuses on identifying the steps and processes of how legal norms become the actual behaviors required by these norms, and exposes factors influencing these steps and processes (Henson and Heasman 1998; Fairman and Yapp 2004; Chemnitz 2012; Van Rooij 2013b). By dividing compliance into steps and processes, which allows researchers to study and evaluate compliance based on steps and processes, it overcomes the limits of compliance evaluation in the endogenous approach. By tracing the compliance process, it facilitates the study of how compliance is constructed, which is lacking in the exogenous approach.

While each approach gets its strength in understanding one aspect of compliance phenomenon in real life, it also has limitations. Being caution about these limitations will help researchers choose appropriate approach and know the limits of different research.

1.2.1   The Endogenous Approach and its Limits

The endogenous approach takes the concept of compliance as the research object (e.g., Lange 1999; Fairman and Yapp 2005; Edelman et al. 1991; Edelman and Talesh 2011). The purpose of this approach is to discover multiple meanings of compliance among different actors and to uncover the social construction processes that create understandings of compliance and the power relations between the actors involved. In this approach, the concept of compliance is not seen as static according to its formal definition—"the state or fact of according with or meeting rules or standards"[5]—but as dynamic and changeable. To define compliance requires addressing the corresponding legal norm. However, as many studies shown, legal norms are seldom clear enough to verify behavior but rely on interpretation in specific situations.

For example, Huising and Silbey (2011), in a study of the safety regulations at a university, indicated that what constitutes a clear corridor is never clarified in the regulations, and what constitutes a clear corridor had to be specified in every situation. Because different actors interpret the meaning of legal norms and the behavior considered compliance with these norms in different ways that favor their interests, no uniform meaning of the concept of compliance exists among key actors in the regulatory field. Furthermore, other parties influence actors' understanding of compliance. For instance, a regulated company may influence a regulator's definition of compliance. Talesh (2009), in a study on consumer protection law, revealed that a manufacturer developed its own dispute resolution institution for resolving consumer complaints, and later, it successfully persuaded the regulator to accept its institution and change its definition of whether the manufacturer complied with the legislation. Therefore, the meaning of compliance is socially constructed.

Lange's (1999) research on a waste management site supports this view. Lange spent six months on a waste management site conducting participant observation and interviews to gain an understanding of how regulations were implemented in practice. Taking the endogenous approach, he focused on how the regulator and regulated communicated about and negotiated behaviors that could be accepted as compliance with legal guidelines. He found that the conditions for site licensing usually were not imposed by the regulatory authority upon the regulated but were negotiated when the inspector visited the site based on the real conditions. Onsite inspection provided information about working routines and factors that was more detailed than the site license prescribed, which left space for negotiation. Thus, operational rules related to the completion of work may arise out of social practices or social relationships, and compliance can be constructed on levels of both the routing behavior practice and the interpretation of the meaning of legal rules. In this endogenous approach, compliance was not static and predefined by the regulator with reference to established legal norms, but fluid and constructed during the interaction and negotiations between the regulator and the regulated. As Lange argued, compliance here is thought to be a "link concept" addressing the relationship between rules and social practices (Lange 1999).

---

[5]https://en.oxforddictionaries.com/definition/compliance.

Focusing on the discussion of the concept of compliance and its construction, the endogenous approach has a broader ambition that provides a better understanding of the fundamental questions about the nature of law and compliance with it. It draws attention to the multiple meanings and understandings of compliance, and provides understanding to those who are the objects of regulation in terms of how they view the regulatory requirements and compliance behavior. By considering the perception and understanding of different actors and learning how compliance is negotiated and constructed, it opens the discussion of ways to improve regulation and society. For instance, transparent information exchange between the regulated and regulator may improve regulation (Lange 1999).

Nevertheless, the endogenous approach faces great limits. Because the definition of compliance for endogenous researchers is fluid, there is no standpoint against which actual behavior and its outcomes can be evaluated and analyzed (Parker and Nielson 2009). Therefore, the endogenous approach is not helpful for answering the crucial practical question of how to improve compliance, which is important for anyone who seeks to understand how regulation can become more effective in reducing and controlling the risks it sets out to address. When we understand, as the endogenous approach seeks to do, what the meaning of law is, we do not yet know how such law can successfully achieve its goals and actually improve behavior as intended with the implementation of the law. While the endogenous approach is attractive for understanding how regulatory interactions shape the meaning of law and compliance itself, it does not directly offer practical support for those seeking to overcome China's immense compliance problems and the resultant failure of regulatory law to deal with the risks and dangers caused by the country's rapid industrial and economic development.

1.2.2 The Exogenous Approach and its Limits

The exogenous approach takes the definition of compliance as predefined in research, but questions what influences compliance and how to improve compliance. In this approach, compliance is not a core conceptual object of study needing to be explored and interpreted; it is either a dependent or independent variable used to discover causal relations between compliance and other variables. This approach is useful for discussing ways to improve compliance.

For example, Fairman and Yapp (2004) attempted to study the effects of enforcement on business compliance performance. To identify the relationship between enforcement styles and compliance performance, they predefined compliance as subjects' fulfillment of prescriptive requirements assessed by a professional inspector, thus reflecting the formal concept of compliance. Furthermore, they measured the enforcement styles of the district enforcers. Subsequently, they analyzed the effects of enforcement on the level of formal compliance with the law using quantitative correlation analysis. This approach was oriented toward the practical aspects of compliance with the ambition to determine what kind of enforcement style would improve compliance rate.

The exogenous approach seems more fitting for dealing with China's problems, as it helps researchers to understand what factors are at play in compliance, and can enable regulators to test different approaches to improving compliance. However, there are several major criticisms of the exogenous approach. Most crucial of these are problems of operationalizing compliance and collecting data. In existing exogenous studies, compliance was usually operationalized by reference to the compliance motivations and attitudes of the regulated actors, or policy goals, in terms of whether businesses meet certain substantive goals. Operationalizing compliance in different ways serves different research aims. These studies operationalizing compliance by reference to the motivations and attitudes include the work of Braithwaite et al. (1994) and Braithwaite et al. (2007) on motivational postures, Winter and May's (2001) studies of various motivations for compliance among Danish farmers in relation to environmental regulations, and May's study of U.S. marine facilities in relation to water quality (May 2005). For example, Braithwaite et al. (1994) discussed four motivational postures the regulated may take when facing regulation, defined based on their perception of and attitude toward the regulatory community in terms of regulatory goals and means. Compliance attitudes and motivations are worth studying in their own right, but it is important to remember they will not always translate into compliance action (Parker and Nielson 2009).

Another common method of operationalization is to operationalize compliance by reference to policy goals, which means studying compliance by focusing on whether a business meets certain substantive goals. These goals include environmental emissions (Andrews 2003; Berkhout and Hertin 2001; Johnston 2006; Winter and May 2001, 2002), greater employment of women or racial minorities (Braithwaite 1993), and fewer worker injuries and fatalities (Mendeloff and Gray 2005). The approach of operationalizing compliance in terms of policy goals is useful if the aim of the research is to evaluate policy implementation. However, this approach of operationalization examines compliance with a substantive objective the rule is expected to serve, but not the behavioral compliance with a rule, and it cannot say whether it is compliance that delivers the outcome or not (Parker and Nielson 2009).

As Parker and Nielson (2009) noted, compliance researchers ultimately want to evaluate whether people comply with regulations and whether this leads to achieving substantive goals. Logically, it is important for both policy evaluation and theory testing to be able to explain which regulatory interventions prompt which behavioral responses and whether these behaviors lead to the desired goal. To do so, compliance should be operationalized as compliance behavior, or the behavioral response to legal requirements that adheres to the law and that is accepted by the regulator as compliance.

Nevertheless, to operationalize compliance as compliance behavior is difficult, and researchers face two significant challenges. The first is that researchers have to find a standpoint from which to evaluate compliance behavior. Whether or not certain behavior can be defined as compliance needs to be clarified and predefined.

In doing so, the researcher becomes part of the process of constructing the meaning of compliance, as it is impossible to choose an evaluation standard without implicit or explicit use of norms and values. This carries a heavy moral responsibility, and researchers have to carefully consider their own positions in defining the meaning of compliance.

The second challenge relates to collecting data about compliance behavior. To operationalize compliance as compliance behavior is usually constrained by the available sources of data on compliance behavior. Finding a way to collect reliable and valid data that measures compliance behavior is crucial. In the existing compliance literature, self-reports and official reports are the most popular data collection methods, and the experimental method is less common. While each of these three data collection methods has its own strengths, they also have many restrictions.

When using the experimental method, researchers manipulate an environment in which people perform the behavior under study and observe that behavior before drawing appropriate conclusions based on various controlled variables (e.g., Köbis et al. 2015). The major advantage of this method is that researchers can isolate the variables of interest and study the effects of researchers' manipulations, and this method is effective in the study of the psychological processes engaged in the real-world counterpart of the situation an experiment manipulates. However, it has several clear disadvantages. First of all, external validity is questionable. If the purpose of the experiment is obvious to the subjects, it affects whether the subjects react in their usual ways (Webley and Halstead 1986). In addition, an experiment is artificially designed—no matter how sophisticated the design, it cannot replace the real situation that involves numerous variables and changeable possibilities that researchers cannot fully involve in the experiment. Hence, although an experiment can manipulate and study some cause–effect relationship using controlled variables, it is less capable of explaining the situation when new variables arise. In a regulatory experiment, participants usually are not the real regulatory objects, and participants are placed in an environment that may be unknown to them. Therefore, the elicited behavior may be partly hypothetical in this respect. Carrying out an experiment in a real-life situation, for example, by randomly assigning a large number of businesses to a more lenient, cooperative inspection regime and a similar number to a stricter, punitive regime, has obvious ethical and political problems (Parker and Nielson 2009). It is likely to take an unusually persuasive researcher and a visionary regulator to achieve this sort of experimental design.

Compared to the experimental method, reviewing government records is a common way of collecting data for compliance behavior. Based on the judgment of regulatory officers, regulatees are classified as in compliance or in violation. In this scenario, compliance depends on to the formal concept of compliance from the perspective of regulatory officials. Yet this method also faces several challenges. First, official records are unreliable because they do not account for violation that go undetected or unreported (Coleman and Moynihan 1996; Jupp 1989; Shover and Hochstetler 2006), and many business violations are never officially discovered or recorded. Organizations may hide breaches on purpose (e.g., secret illegal dumping of pollution in a river; Parker and Nielson 2009). Due to their heavy workload, regulators are less likely to monitor regulated business at ideal intervals. Even proactive regulators that actively monitor compliance through inspections or audits miss many violations that come and go during the intervals between inspections and rarely discover all violations even at the time of inspection (Parker and Nielson 2009). This is especially true for small and medium-sized enterprises in China, which may be inspected only once since established or once a year. Of the violations detected, not all are recorded because of inattention, discretionary leniency, or even corruption (see Hill et al. 1992; Weil 1996). Moreover, because of regulators' discretion, the data they record about compliance and noncompliance are likely to be normatively biased (Parker and Nielson 2009), and social, political, and economic factors may influence official enforcement decisions regarding what should be considered compliance. Furthermore, regulated businesses may negotiate with regulators and influence regulators' understanding and recording of compliance. The unreliable and biased data from regulatory records are problematic not only because they are biased but also because the bias and its criteria are not transparent. Researchers usually have access to only part of official enforcement statistics that are the outcome of a range of subjective assessments of behavior unknown to the researchers. Additionally, the filtering processes and criteria regulatory agencies use to determine compliance are often unconscious, ambiguous, and therefore unknown. Therefore, researchers cannot explain the data bias.

Self-reporting is a common method of collecting data on compliance behavior. For this method, respondents are required to complete questionnaires or participate in interviews to answer questions about their actions and reactions to certain legal norms (Elffers et al. 1992). Their answers to the questions posed constitute the data on compliance behavior. Answers can be a simple "yes" or "no," or respondents can be asked to rate responses on a Likert-type scale to questions or statements such as "Did you try to under declare your income or overstate your deductions in 1986?" "To what extent do you agree with the following statement?" and "I did not under declare my income or deductions in 1986." Consequently, the data on compliance behavior used for analysis relies entirely on the self-reported information derived from the people who engage in these behaviors. Generally, the respondents themselves are the most knowledgeable about their own history of compliance with the law. When assured of their anonymity and of confidentiality, respondents may report low-level criminal activity more readily and completely than would be captured in official data.

Nevertheless, that the reliability of self-reported data on compliance behavior is lacking has been well documented in the literature (see Elffers et al. 1992: 550; Zimring and Hawkins 1973: 321–327; Wilson and Herrnstein 1985: 37–38; Hessing et al. 1988). Memory problems are the most common cause of unreliable information in self-reporting. Criminological studies have shown that under or over reporting of crime is common because of memory lapses or more complex tricks of memory such as remembering the wrong time or forgetting certain activities. Similarly, self-presentational concerns lead to unreliability when using this method. Generally, people like to pretend to be good citizens that comply with the law. Therefore, they are more likely (either deliberately or subconsciously) to interpret and report events in a way that exaggerates their compliance with the law and underplays or excuses noncompliance (Jupp 1989: 102).

Researchers usually seek to overcome such social desirability bias by guaranteeing anonymity, by framing questions about illegal activity in neutral and factual ways (e.g., Winter and May 2002: 126), and by providing respondents with a range of apparently socially acceptable ways to confess noncompliance. For instance, instead of asking respondents to answer "comply" or "not comply," which may provoke the feelings of guilt and shame and result in false answers, researchers offered respondents several ranks, that is, "definitely did," "probably did," "probably did not," and "definitely did not," to reduce the pressure of confessing their behavior (Scholz and Lubell 1998: 402–403). In addition, building trust with respondents and better understanding how respondents think and behave helps to reduce the social desirability bias of the self-reporting method. When researchers have a good relationship with respondents and respondents believe researchers will not reveal their illegal behavior to anyone who may harm them, respondents are more likely to report low-level criminal activity. Moreover, if researchers understand how respondents think and behave, and the values and norms respondents care about, the researchers can evaluate the bias of self-reported data. However, doing so involves a great deal of work and requires spending a long time with respondents.

When the research objects are business firms and the topic is regulatory compliance, memory problems and social desirability bias in the self-reporting method are more complex than with individual criminal activity (Parker and Nielson 2009). Ideally, all individuals in the section of the organization where the relevant illegal activity might have occurred should be asked to respond to researchers (e.g., Weaver and Trevino 1999; Key 1999). Yet this might be impractical for reasons of access or cost. Instead, researchers have to choose only one or a few individuals to obtain data, which means individual respondents will be required to not only remember and report their own behavior but also that of others or organizational behavior. Because individual respondents may not know enough or clearly remember events that occurred in the organization to report accurately on organizational compliance, this increases the possibility of unreliable information caused by memory problems. Furthermore, researchers may gain access to corporate records that document the compliance behavior of the organization, for example, regarding emissions or customer complaints. Nevertheless, organizational records of compliance are institutionally created, and they may involve considerable social desirability bias. Business firms may be intentionally organized so that information about noncompliance is hidden. Before using these records, researchers must evaluate the value of the information offered, which requires understanding the internal processes of record creation and the knowledge and values on which the records are based.

Because of the restrictions of the three conventional methods of collecting data on compliance behavior, several researchers developed sophisticated designs to reduce these restrictions to a certain extent (e.g., Webley and Halstead 1986; Elffers et al. 1992). For instance, they added confrontational questions when using the self-reporting method to overcome memory problems associated with this method and to reduce the effect of self-presentational concern by manipulating the desire to uphold a coherent image before the interviewer. Moreover, researchers added two steps, namely reassessment and expert assessment, to the first assessment to gain the cooperation of and build confidential relationship with officers to reduce measurement errors and increase reliability. In the experimental method, researchers hid the purpose of the experiments by using a sophisticated experiment design.

However, Elffers et al. (1992) found that despite the ability of sophisticated design to reduce the restrictions discussed to a certain extent, using the three data collection methods still involve significant challenges when measuring compliance behavior. Employing the three methods when measuring compliance in a tax evasion study yielded different results, with a lack of association between the three kinds of results. Elffers et al. argued that the existing measurement error cannot explain the lack of association between the three behavioral measures. The most probable explanation is that tax evasion behaviors may consist of at least three independent conceptual aspects, and the three unrelated aspects were addressed by the three data collection methods. Consequently, they called for further studies to gain a better understanding of real-life tax-evasion behaviors. To date, no research has been produced in other regulatory fields to test or support this argument. Nevertheless, the concerns of Elffers et al. are notable and should be considered when collecting data on compliance behaviors. Later in the book, I will show how my findings respond to their question and proposition.

In a short summary, the exogenous approach is useful in discussing China's compliance challenge, and to operationalize compliance as actual compliance behaviors is especially attractive, as one of the aims of this book was to discover causes for compliance. However, there are many restrictions for data collection. Collecting data of compliance behaviors in a real-life situation with experiment method is almost impossible. Survey and governmental data are challenging not only because of those limits mentioned above, but also because noncompliance in China being a sensitive subject, respondents may provide biased answers that inflate the level of compliance, and governmental data may be of poor quality due to weak enforcement capacity, biased toward compliance, and inaccessible to researchers.

1.2.3   The Process Approach and its Limits

The less-known Process approach, focuses on identifying the steps and processes of how legal norms become the actual behaviors required by these norms, and exposes factors influencing this process (Henson and Heasman 1998; Fairman and Yapp 2004; Chemnitz 2012; Van Rooij 2013b). Henson and Heasman (1998) proposed a compliance process composed of several steps, namely identifying the regulation, interpreting the regulation, identifying change, making the compliance decision, specifying the method of compliance, communication, implementation, and evaluation or monitoring. Chemnitz (2012) discussed the compliance process by integrating a decision process model and diffusion theory and identified several stages of the decision model: the knowledge, attitude, decision, implementation, and moni-toring stages. Van Rooij (2013b) defined compliance as a set of recurring, nonlinear processes through which legal norms enter into the operations and perceptions of the regulated actors at different stages of the production chain, including learning, negotiation, dissemination and translation, operational, verification (and simulation), and institutionalization and internalization processes.

This approach shows how compliance finally comes about during a series of steps or a process, and researchers can study the compliance process instead of compliance based on a static point and view. It is promising for addressing some of the limitations of the endogenous and exogenous approaches. By dividing compliance into steps and processes, and focusing on the process instead of the outcome, it allows researchers to get out of the entangled issues on how to measure compliance outcomes. Instead, it can benefit from the process it is tracing that helps to zoom in understanding compliance as it occurs and facilitates the study of how compliance is constructed, while keeping analysis of factors of influence confined to parts of the process in stead of on the whole, decreasing challenges of causation (Van Rooij 2013b).

Nonetheless, the Process approach always tend to set legal norm as the start point and compliance behavior as the termination, try to exhaust the steps the process involves, and imply a one-dimensional process from legal norms to compliance behavior. These steps and process are theoretically integrated, but too simple to explain the compliance behaviors in real world, as Kim (1999) has found that the regulated actors comply with legal norms without knowing them is quite common in real life.

1.3 An Ethnographic Approach and Methodology

This book offers an ethnographic approach to capture compliance as behavioral response to laws that occurs on a daily basis within regulated businesses, sees how compliance behaviors emerges within businesses, explores what factors influencing compliance behaviors and how compliance can be improved.

It draws the ethnographic method, namely participant observation and deep immersion into the interactions that occur during compliance, from the endogenous approach and draws the central goals, namely to understand what factors contribute to compliance and noncompliance, from the exogenous approach. Further, it draws the perspective from the Process approach, namely examining processes as they occur over time. However, it will be used in a different way than described above. It was not intended to exhaust all steps the process may involve but using the process tracing methodology. By doing so, I intended to zoom in on understanding compli-ance behavior as it occurs and develops instead of measuring the behavior at a static point. Thus, the measurement of compliance behavior became a series of obser-vations and data collections instead of a single judgment at a certain point, which made it contextual and situational in a specific context. It reduced the risk associated with measuring compliance at a static point and the risk that compliance equals the outcome of regulation and negotiation as traditional compliance measurements, such as self-report survey and governmental inspection data face with. As it will show in this book, ethnographic approach provides sufficient detail to capture the reality of compliance in practice which is missing in traditional measurement and challenges the static and decontextual understanding of compliance. It also allows to understand how the process progressed and to capture the features of the process, which is helpful in discussing factors influencing compliance behavior and mechanisms that influence the establishment of compliance behaviors.

Ethnographic approach asks for describing compliance behavior in its every day practice. To do so, it should first of all operationalize compliance as compliance behavior, which is predefined as the behavioral response to the legal requirements in accordance with the law and accepted by the regulator as compliance, and second trace the process of how compliance behavior comes into being. It allows researchers to see evolving real-life compliance behavior in its contexts. In addition, it raises the possibility of investigating what the comprehensive conceptual sets of compliance behavior are (as requested by Elffers et al. 1992), and what factors influence the process of the development of compliance behavior.

Rather than isolating a single type of rule, as has been done in most compliance studies, this book tries to understand how a business responds to a combination of legal rules that seek to shape behavior. The endogenous and exogenous approaches to studying compliance have one common problem: they study compliance using one rule at a time and at one moment in time, which does not reflect real-world conditions for regulated actors, especially businesses. In reality, businesses must comply with a multitude of laws, ranging from registration to taxation, from accounting to environment protection. According to one estimate in early 1990s, US companies have to comply with 300,000 rules, backed up by criminal enforcement (see Coffee 1991: 216). The business studied in this book has to get five to ten opening licenses that are backed up by laws when starting up. In addition, compliance is interactive, as compliance with one law can affect compliance with another law. When a regulated firm interacts with a regulator from one regulatory system, it is influenced by its experience with other regulators from other regulatory systems. Thus, each new regulatory encounter exerts influence on future interactions with other regulators. So, the reality of business compliance is one of legal pluralism where organizations have to respond to a multitude of rules and regulatory process can be interactive, and this book seeks to reflect such pluralism and interaction by involving multiple legal rules that a business faces in reality.

As to the process, the book not only looks at the process that how compliance behavior arose, developed, settled and presented, but also includes the course of business cycle, both during the initial start-up phase, as well as during daily operations, as the regulatory environment (especially the types of inspections and oversight) changed during different phases, and that this directly affected compliance behavior.

Moreover, this book combines both organizational and individual levels. Much of the existing research on regulatory compliance, especially the exogenous work that has great practical relevance, tends to focus on either the regulated individual or the regulated organization as an entity, rather than combing the two levels (for an exception, see Parker and Gilad 2011).[6] The organizational behaviors the law aims to regulate ultimately consist of the actions of individuals within such organizations. At the same time, organizational behavior is not a pure aggregation of individual behaviors—it implies certain kinds of unification of individual behaviors. Individual behaviors are inevitably influenced by the characteristics of the same organization, that is, organizational structure, culture, and norms. One individual's behavior influences and is influenced by the behavior of others in the same organization. For instance, when food safety laws require restaurants to safeguard food safety by workers washing their hands before processing food, workers rather than restaurants as entities ultimately take the action of washing hands. When every worker washes his or her hands according to the rules when he or she works in one restaurant (individual compliance), this restaurant complies with the handwashing rule (organizational compliance). Nevertheless, the workers that do not comply with the handwashing rule in one restaurant may comply with the rule in another restaurant. Therefore, studying compliance behavior at individual level may not satisfactorily explain organizational compliance. Organizational compliance and individual compliance are interrelated but different in reality, and combining the two levels would generate valuable insight into compliance.

Many researchers have found that organizational characteristics, such as organization scale (Shadbegian and Gray 2005), organizational culture (Gherardi and Nicolini 2002), managerial incentives, and organizational identity (Howard-Grenville 2006; Howard-Grenville et al. 2008) influence compliance. However, the reality is that members in an organization contribute at least partly to organizational characteristics and culture. The organization and individual in the organization have mutual influence, and both the organization as a whole and individuals in that organization construct compliance and present compliance. Many studies on compliance failed to involve such a dynamic construction. So, this book intends to reveal the dynamic construction between organizations and individuals through discussion of the formation of organizational norms.

As such, this book, using ethnographic method, will capture the behavioral responses at both organizational and individual level to a multitude of legal rules as they occur over a prolonged period of time.

1.4 A Three-Process Scheme

This book aims to explore what factors influencing compliance behavior and gives insights to how compliance can be improved. After capturing the behavioral

---

[6]Parker and Gilad (2011) focused on corporate compliance management systems and claimed to understand these systems in terms of the interaction between structure (adoption of formal compliance systems) and agency (perceptions, motivations, and strategies of individuals at all levels of the organization) through culture (local norms and habituated practices). They showed how structure and agency interact through culture at three nodes of implementation of the compliance system.

responses to legal rules, it tries to understand the causes of the variations in compliance behavior found. To do so, compliance was theoretically viewed as an interaction between legal norms and individual behavior, which can be expressed as Law $\longleftrightarrow$ Behavior (Van Rooij 2011). Compliance exists when the behavior somehow comes to align with the law.

This book begins with the law itself in the basis scheme of Law $\longleftrightarrow$ Behavior, specifically with an analysis of how the law arrived at the restaurants. As detailed in Chap. 6, it analyzes both the comprehensive legal knowledge formation of business and the transmission of legal norms through law enforcement encounters.

Then it looks at the organizational facet, to see how restaurants respond to legal norms. As detailed in Chap. 7, I follow insights form Moore (1973) and Heimer (1999) that the law competes with organizational norms in shaping behavior. The scheme becomes Law $\longleftrightarrow$ Organization $\longleftrightarrow$ Behavior. I identify the relevant organizational norms, discuss how legal norms transmitted to workers during socialization and management processes including hiring, training, evaluation, and problem resolution, and how organizational norms activate or compete with legal norms and shape compliance behaviors.

Behaviors ultimately take place at individual level. Compliance may be shaped by both legal norms and organizational norms, but finally comes out from individual decisions-making process, as individuals do the actual acting. So the scheme becomes Law $\longleftrightarrow$ Organization $\longleftrightarrow$ Individual $\longleftrightarrow$ Behavior. To understand individual-level decision making, as detailed in Chap. 8, I use two approaches. First, I examine how individual employees in the restaurants explained their own compliance or violation behaviors, which elucidates individual compliance motivations inductively and subjectively. Second, I consider key individual motivations for compliance at the individual level by studying six key variables identified in the existing compliance literature, namely plural subjective deterrence, personal norms, descriptive social norms, perceived obligation to obey the law, recognition of legal requirements and practical constraints. These variables also are explained in more detail in Chap. 8.

As a result, the explanation of compliance behaviors is categorized into three levels: regulatory, organizational, and individual. The discussion of legal knowledge formation process and of how laws arrive at restaurants is on the regulatory level, the analysis of the interaction between legal norms and organizational norms is on the organizational level, and subjective explanation and variable association analysis is on individual level. The three levels reflect three core processes through which compliance behaviors may take place: regulatory, organizational, and individual processes. The regulatory process refers to the interaction process between the regulator and the regulated actors, the organizational process refers to the internal organizational institutions through which the law is transmitting to regulate organizational compliance behavior, and the individual process is the personal decision-making process involved in compliance behaviors. By discussing the focuses in each process, mechanisms are revealed through which compliance behaviors take place. I do not claim to study those processes fully, in terms of how compliance behaviors take place within the three processes, but examine some core concepts in each process in the light of the compliance concept model.

1.5 Case Selection and Data Collection

This book aims to offer a unique new empirical study of compliance in China, which seeks to understand the variation in compliance behaviors as they exist for different legal norms and change over time in one particular organizational setting. It allows both an endogenous understanding of what compliance means and an exogenous exploration of compliance, as well as a processual dynamic understanding of how compliance varies and changes, and, ultimately, of what explains such variations. This is achieved through in-depth case studies that allows comprehensive qualitative research and poses "how" and "why" questions related to compliance as they play out in particular businesses. The case study method allows the researcher to focus on the selected regulated entities in depth, discuss various variables that appear, and examine causality to explore how various compliance behaviors manifest and how those compliance behaviors can be explained.

To perform the case studies, a type of business had to be chosen. Criteria included that it was readily accessible, especially for participant observation, one of the core methods used; that compliance behavior was observable to overcome some of the methodological problems of survey-based compliance research; and that a multitude of legal rules applied, which could be studied over time. Restaurants fit these categories. I was permitted to pose as a server in restaurants, which enabled me to conduct day-to-day observations on compliance behaviors in restaurants and have in-depth discussions with workers, managers, and owners. In addition, restaurants are legal microcosms where a variety of rules applies that can be observed in everyday behavior.

Moreover, studying restaurants has an important practical purpose and significance. Restaurants are a prime example of a small business regulated by a range of legal norms, from environmental protection to food safety, from fire regulation to taxation, and from business registration to city management. A deep ethnographic case study at a restaurant thus offers a microcosm of compliance processes, many of which are observable and discussable.

To describe compliance behavior and capture the complexity of the processes of compliance behavior, the diverse cases technique was used to select cases. Diverse cases encompass maximum variance along relevant dimensions (Seawright and Gerring 2008). During the pilot study, cases were chosen based on their size and consumption levels, which are clearly diverse. I accessed six restaurants (see Table 1.1). Based on the pilot study, two extreme different restaurants were chosen to exemplify how compliance behavior takes place. As the review of the three classification methods of compliance behavior suggests (see Chap. 2), the nature or ideology of the actors, the attitudinal factor, and the commitment to regulation are useful elements in understanding and classifying compliance behavior. The two restaurants chosen had different operation ideologies. One was health oriented, the owner of which cares about food safety and the environment, claiming that provides only healthy food and rejects unhealthy ingredients and cooking methods. This health-oriented ideology aligns with the purpose of food safety laws restaurants have to obey. During the pilot

Table 1.1 Summary of restaurants studied

Restaurant	Features	Study depth	Data in this book
The idealistic restaurant	Small[a], middle consumption[b]	Comprehensive Extended participant observation in restaurant In-depth interviews with owners and employees	Core case and source of individual data
The profit-maximizing restaurant	Small, low consumption	Comprehensive Extended participant observation in restaurant In-depth interviews with owner and employees	Core case and source of individual data
L restaurant	Small, low consumption	Less comprehensive Short observation in the restaurant In-depth interview with owner	Complementary case and source of individual data
W restaurant	Small, low consumption	Less comprehensive Short observation in the restaurant Mid-depth interview with managers	Complementary case
H restaurant	Medium, low consumption	Mid-depth Two weeks' participant observation in restaurant Mid-depth interviews with manager and employees	Complementary case
S restaurant	Medium, but part of a big catering group brand, High consumption	Mid-depth In-depth interviews with 14 people, including top manager and employees	Complementary case and source of individual data

[a]Restaurant size classification was based on the classification standard defined in the national FDA regulation on the catering service industry (See "Catering service food safety operational norms," August 22, 2011, http://www.foodmate.net/law/shipin/173257.html). A small restaurant has floor space up to 150 m^2 or up to 75 service seats, while medium-sized restaurants cover 150–500 m^2 or feature 75–250 service seats.

[b]There is no standard classification of restaurant consumption; thus, in this study, restaurants were classified as high consumption (consumption per customer of 100 CNY and higher), middle consumption (consumption per customer of 50–100 CNY), and low consumption (consumption per customer of 50 CNY or less).

study, it was found that this restaurant satisfied most legal requirements. The second restaurant was economy oriented, the owner of which always looks for ways to cut costs and maximize profit. It used various, sometimes dishonest, strategies to satisfy legal requirements. This book labels the first restaurant the Idealistic restaurant and the second one the Profit-Maximizing restaurant to makes it easier for readers to distinguish the two restaurants and the two business orientations that gave rise to them. In addition to the two core restaurants, data from other four restaurants was included to add complementary information and dimensions.

To do ethnographic case study requires extensive participant observation and interviews, and close contact with the regulated, which allows researchers to trace back or follow the process and capture the characteristics of the regulated to understand their behavior. I conducted extensive participant observation by working as a waitress, with the explicit permission of the owner and workers to do so while conducting research, and did in-depth interviews with owners and workers. During the extensive period of study, over three years, from May 2011 to September 2013, I was able to observe in depth how different rules entered the business over a prolonged period of time and how owners, managers and employees interacted with each other and with regulators in responding to these rules.

When I worked as a server during participant observation, I did not take field notes. Instead, every day after work and after leaving the restaurants, I noted what I had observed and found based on memory. Furthermore, I used a digital recorder to record conversations with restaurant owners and workers that I initiated on purpose, later transcribing these conversations.

The method of participant observation is vital here though its use has been limited in compliance research (for exceptions, see Gray 2002, 2006). Participant observation is "a method in which an observer takes part in the daily activities, rituals, interactions, and events of the people being studied as one of the means of learning the explicit and tacit aspects of their culture" (Musante and Dewalt 2010: 260). Using the method of participant observation has several benefits. First, the topic of compliance with laws is always sensitive, which motivates people to disguise their violation behaviors or intentions and show compliance when facing a researcher who suddenly appears to observe or question them. However, by consistently participating in people's lives and building trust in the process, the researcher gradually ceases to be a disturbing element, which allows the person to observe the real-life situations and behaviors to the utmost extent. Second, an important purpose of compliance research is to discover the rule in action, compare behaviors with the rule in book, and find ways to improve the law system. To do this, researchers need to be open to discovering unexpected information instead of selectively learning information. Participant observation allows researchers to acquire information in an open-ended fashion and learn the unexpected. Moreover, researchers participating in and observing a life situation develop a tacit understanding of people and their behaviors they may not be able to explicitly express.

Semi-structured dialogue interview was used to obtain data for the individual level analysis. Through 35 in-depth interviews, structured as dialogues (cf. Van Rooij 2016), I was able to study all six individual variables and examine 108 cases of compliance behavior. The 35 interviewees included 20 owners and employees at the two core restaurants, that is, the Idealistic restaurant and the Profit-Maximizing restaurant; 14 managers and workers at S restaurant; and one owner at L restaurant. The sampling and operationalization are elaborated in Chap 8. In addition, all formal interviews were recorded and transcribed. Participants were not aware of the recordings during formal and informal conversations.

The method of dialogue interview is also important (Van Rooij 2016; Yan 2014). It was employed in this research to unearth the regulated actors' subjective explanations of their behavior and perceptions of each variable. For details on the application of this method, refer to Chap. 8. Nevertheless, it is worth underscoring its value here in terms of methodology. Compliance with laws is a delicate topic. Therefore, it is difficult to obtain reliable data from self-reporting, as several researchers have noted (e.g., Elffers et al. 1992). The method of participant observation is one way to reduce sensitivity and increase the reliability of field data, although it carries risk of bias. Other strategies include maintaining extended, sometimes private, contact with the regulated actors, involving oneself in more aspects of life than the research focus, avoiding commenting on or criticizing their behavior, respecting research subjects no matter what comes to light, and so forth. They do not provide much data and instead act as methods to build trust and prepare for the final dialogue interview. The dialogue interview is the core of obtaining reliable data related to the regulated actors' subjective perceptions, which is critical in explaining their behaviors.

A dialogue interview helps to create a comfortable and fluent dialogue environment within which the regulated actors are more likely to offer their true opinions and considerations. The conversation usually begins with regulated actors' life or work situations, with research questions inserted in this dialogue. Sensitive questions and neutral questions are combined in a way that does not easily arouse the alertness of the regulated actors. Both open-ended and close-ended questions are used and combined to create a comfortable and natural conversation that resembles a dialogue between equals and to prevent the regulated actors from feeling being pushed. Follow-up questions are often used to obtain information that is more precise and detailed. Sometimes, the interviewer's moderate self-exposure, that is, life experience or feelings, is necessary. Comparing to the general interview method, the dialogue interview does not address the research question as quickly, directly, and intensively as the general interview does. It allows a causal, relaxed conversation to take place more slowly, but it does require more time. For instance, one dialogue interview may take more than two hours.

References

Andrews, R. 2003. Environmental Management Systems: Do They Improve Performance? *National Database on Environmental Management Systems.* Chapel Hill: University of North Carolina. http://ndems.cas.unc.edu.

Berkhout, F., and J. Hertin. 2001. *Towards Environmental Performance Management*. Brighton: University of Sussex, Science Policy Research Unit.

Braithwaite, Valerie. 1993. The Australian Government's Affirmative Action Legislation: Achieving Social Change Through Human Resource Management. *Law Policy* 15: 327–354.

Braithwaite, Valerie, John Braithwaite, Diane Gibson, and Toni Makkai. 1994. Regulatory Styles Motivational Postures and Nursing Home Compliance. *Law & Policy*, 16(4): 363–394.

Braithwaite, John, Cary Coglianese, and David Levi-Faur. 2007. Can Regulation and Governance Make a Difference? *Regulation & Governance*, 1(1): 1–7.

Chemnitz, C. 2012. *The Impact of Food Safety and Quality Standards on Developing Countries Agricultural Producers and Exports*. Doctoral dissertation, Humboldt-Universität zu Berlin, Landwirtschaftlich-Gärtnerische Fakultät.

Coffee Jr, John C. 1991. Does Unlawful Mean Criminal: Reflections on the Disappearing Tort/Crime Distinction in American Law. *Bulletin Review*, 71: 193.

Coleman, C., and J. Moynihan. 1996. *Understanding Crime Data: Haunted by the Dark Figure*. Buckingham, UK: Open University Press.

Edelman, Lauren B., and Shauhin A. Talesh. 2011. To Comply or not to Comply—That isn't the Question: How Organizations Construct the Meaning of Compliance. In *Explaining Compliance: Business Responses to Regulation*, ed. Christine Parker and Vibeke Lehmann Nielsen, 103–122. Cheltenham: Edward Elgar.

Edelman, Lauren B., Stephen Petterson, Elizabeth Chambliss, and Howard S. Erlanger. 1991. Legal Ambiguity and the Politics of Compliance: Affirmative Action Officers' Dilemma. *Law & Policy*, 13(1): 73–97.

Elffers, Henk, Henry S. J. Robben, and Dick J. Hessing. 1992. On Measuring Tax Evasion. *Journal of Economic Psychology* 13 (4): 545–567.

Fairman, R., and C. Yapp. 2004. Compliance with Food Safety Legislation in Small and Micro-businesses: Enforcement as an External Motivator. *Journal of Environmental Health Research* 3: 44–52.

Fairman, R., and C. Yapp. 2005. Enforced Self-regulation, Prescription, and Conceptions of Compliance Within Small Businesses: The Impact of Enforcement. *Law & Policy*, 27(4): 491–519.

Gherardi, S., and D. Nicolini. 2002. Learning the Trade: A Culture of Safety in Practice. *Organization* 9: 191–223.

Gray, Garry C. 2002. A Socio-legal Ethnography of the Right to Refuse Dangerous Work. *Studies in Law, Politics, and Society* 24: 133–169.

Gray, Garry C. 2006. The Regulation of Corporate Violations: Punishment, Compliance and the Blurring of Responsibility. *British Journal of Criminology* 46 (5): 875–892.

Heimer, Carol A. 1999. Competing Institutions: Law, Medicine, and Family in Neonatal Intensive Care. *Law & Society Review* 33 (1): 17–66.

Henson, S., and M. Heasman. 1998. Food Safety Regulation and the Firm: Understanding the Compliance Process. *Food Policy* 23 (1): 9–23.

Hessing, Dick J., Henk Elffers, and Russell H. Weigel. 1988. Exploring the Limits of Self-reports and Reasoned Action: An Investigation of the Psychology of Tax Evasion Behavior. *Journal of Personality and Social Psychology* 54: 405–414.

Hill, C., P. Kelley, B. Agle, M. Hitt, and R. Hoskisson. 1992. An Empirical Examination of the Causes of Corporate Wrongdoing in the United States. *Human Relations* 45: 1055–1077.

Howard-Grenville, Jennifer A. 2006. Inside the 'Black Box': How Organizational Culture and Subcultures Inform Interpretations and Actions on Environmental Issues. *Organization and Environment* 19 (1): 46–73.

Howard-Grenville, Jennifer, Jennifer Nash, and Cary Coglianese. 2008. Constructing the License to Operate: Internal Factors and Their Influence on Corporate Environmental Decisions. *Law & Policy* 30: 73–107.

Huising, Ruthanne, and Susan S. Silbey. 2011. Governing the Gap: Forging Safe Science Through Relational Regulation. *Regulation and Governance* 5: 14–42.

Johnston, J. 2006. The Promise and Limits of Voluntary Management-Based Regulatory Reform: An Analysis of EPA's Strategic Goals Program. In *Leveraging the Private Sector: Management-Based Strategies for Improving Environmental Performance*, ed. Cary Coglianese and Jennifer Nash, 167–200. Washington, DC: Resources for the Future.

Jupp, V. 1989. *Methods of Criminological Research*. London: Unwin Hyman.

Key, S. 1999. Organizational Ethical Culture: Real or Imagined? *Journal of Business Ethics* 20: 217–225.

Kim, Pauline T. 1999. Norms, Learning, and Law: Exploring the Influences on Workers' Legal Knowledge. *University of Illinois Law Review* 2: 447–516.

Köbis, N.C., J.-W. van Prooijen, F. Righetti, and P.A. van Lange. 2015. 'Who Doesn't?'—The Impact of Descriptive Norms on Corruption. *PLoS ONE* 10 (6): e0131830. https://doi.org/10.1371/journal.pone.0131830.

Lange, B. 1999. Compliance Construction in the Context of Environmental Regulation. *Social & Legal Studies* 8 (4): 549–567.

May, P.J. 2005. Compliance Motivations: Perspectives of Farmers, Homebuilders, and Marine Facilities. *Law & Policy* 27 (2): 317–347.

Mendeloff, John, and Wayne B. Gray. 2005. Inside the Black Box: How do OSHA Inspections Lead to Reductions in Workplace Injuries? *Law & Policy* 27: 219–237.

Moore, Sally Falk. 1973. Law and Social Change: The Semi-autonomous Social Field as an Appropriate Subject of Study. *Law & Society Review* 7 (4): 719–746.

Musante, K., and B.R. DeWalt. 2010. *Participant Observation: A Guide for Fieldworkers*. Lanham, Md.: Rowman & Littlefield.

Parker, C., and Sharon Gilad. 2011. Internal Corporate Compliance Management Systems: Structure, Culture and Agency. In *Explaining Compliance: Business Responses to Regulation*, ed. Christine Parker and Vibeke Lehmann Nielsen, 170–195. Cheltenham, UK: Edward Elgar.

Parker, C., and V. Nielsen. 2009. The Challenge of Empirical Research on Business Compliance in Regulatory Capitalism. *Annual Review of Law and Social Science* 5: 45–70.

Van Rooij, Benjamin. 2011. Compliance: A Concept Note. On file with the author.

Van Rooij, Benjamin. 2013b. Compliance as Process: A Micro Approach to Regulatory Implementation. On file with the author.

Van Rooij, Benjamin. 2016. Weak Enforcement Strong Deterrence: Dialogues with Chinese Lawyers About Tax Evasion and Compliance. *Law and Social Inquiry*, 41(2): 288–310.

Scholz, John T., and M. Lubell. 1998. Trust and Taxpaying: Testing the Heuristic Approach to Collective Action. *American Journal of Political Science* 42: 398–417.

Seawright, Jason, and John Gerring. 2008. Case Selection Techniques in Case Study Research: A Menu of Qualitative and Quantitative Options. *Political Research Quarterly* 61 (2): 294–308.

Shadbegian, R.J., and W.B. Gray. 2005. Pollution Abatement Expenditures and Plant-Level Productivity: A Production Function Approach. *Ecological Economics* 54: 196–208.

Shover, N., and A. Hochstetler. 2006. *Choosing White-Collar Crime*. Cambridge, UK: Cambridge University Press.

Talesh, Shauhin. 2009. The Privatization of Public Legal Rights: How Manufacturers Construct the Meaning of Consumer Law. *Law & Society Review* 43 (3): 527–562.

Weaver, G., and L.K. Trevino. 1999. Compliance and Values-Oriented Ethics Programs: Influences on Employees' Attitudes and Behavior. *Business Ethics Quarterly* 9: 315–335.

Webley, Paul, and Steve Halstead. 1986. Tax Evasion on the Micro: Significant Simulations or Expedient Experiments? *Journal of Interdisciplinary Economics* 1 (2): 87–100.

Weil, D. 1996. If OSHA is so Bad, Why is Compliance so Good? *RAND Journal of Economics* 27: 618–640.

Wilson, J.Q., and R.J. Herrnstein. 1985. *Crime & Human Behavior: The Definitive Study on the Causes of Crime*. New York: Simon and Schuster.

Winter, Soren C., and Peter J. May. 2001. Motivation for Compliance with Environmental Regulations. *Journal of Policy Analysis and Management* 20 (4): 675–698.

Winter, Soren C., and Peter J. May. 2002. Information, Interests, and Environmental Regulation. *Journal of Comparative Policy Analysis*, 4(2): 115–142.

Yan, Huiqi. 2014. *Why Chinese Farmers Obey the Law: Pesticide Compliance in Hunan Province, China.* Doctoral dissertation, Amsterdam University.

Zimring, F.E., and G.J. Hawkins. 1973. *Deterrence: The Legal Threat in Crime Control.* Chicago, IL: The University of Chicago Press.

Part I
Descriptive Analysis of Compliance Behaviors

Chapter 2
Descriptive Analysis of Compliance Behaviors

To provide detailed insight into the processes of real-life compliance behavior, yet without addressing what influences or explains such behavior, the ethnographic approach, descriptive analysis of compliance behaviors, was employed. This involves describing how restaurants respond to various legal rules that apply to them both during the start-up phase and during regular operations. Such behaviors are characterized in an attempt to move beyond the simple compliance–violation dichotomy.

When we describe various compliance behaviors and how they take place, the classification of such behavior soon become highly complex, and it cannot be simplified as compliant or noncompliant, but need to look for some nuanced classification. Furthermore, the regulated are always assessed using certain models to predict and understand their behaviors. For instance, Kagan and Scholz (1984) proposed three categories of noncompliers: amoral calculators, political citizens, and incompetent entities. Models of noncompliers or compliers are seemed useful for the regulator predicting the behaviors of the regulated. So, I will review the existing literature about the classification of compliance behaviors and characterizing the actors in this chapter which will serve as the first normative framework to analyze the compliance practices further analyzed in subsequent sections.

2.1 Describing Compliance Behaviors

Te approach of descriptive analysis of compliance behavior, aims to understand how the compliance process progressed and to capture the features of the process, which would be helpful in discussing factors influencing compliance behavior and mechanisms that influence the establishment of compliance behaviors. While it draws the central goals, namely to understand what factors contribute to compliance and noncompliance, from the exogenous approach, it draws the data collection method and constructive perspective from endogenous. According to the endogenous

Y. Wu, *Compliance Ethnography*, Understanding China,
https://doi.org/10.1007/978-981-16-2884-9_2

approach, final compliance behavior is socially constructed, and different actors have different understandings of compliance behavior. Moreover, it draws process perspective from the process approach, which provides an alternative means of measuring and studying compliance behavior. Consequently, in order to describe compliance behavior, the endogenous way of thinking was followed to learn the construction process of compliance behavior, but not to analyze the construction of the compliance concept. Instead, the process approach was employed to analyze how the behavior developed. The focus was not on the notion or concept of compliance but the compliance behavior that could be observed and described as present and past actions. To describe compliance behavior, researchers must employ the process and "other side" subjective perspectives.

2.1.1 Process Perspective

Although the process approach is rare in compliance research, it has been used in several studies, generally to identify process steps and construct a universal process model. For instance, Henson and Heasman (1998) proposed that the compliance process by which food businesses comply with legal requirement involves several steps, namely identifying the regulation, interpreting the regulation, identifying the change, making the compliance decision, specifying the method of compliance, communication, implementation, and evaluation or monitoring. Through a discussion of these steps, they found that business size causes the differences in the manner in which individual businesses comply with new regulations (Henson and Heasman 1998). Fairman and Yapp (2004) developed a compliance process model based on Henson and Heasman's (1998) model.

Chemnitz (2012) examined the compliance process by integrating a decision-process model and diffusion theory and identified several stages of the decision model, namely the knowledge, attitude, decision, implementation, and monitoring stages. Through a discussion of these stages as they apply to the compliance process, factors such as size and vertical information flow were found to play important roles in farmers' compliance. Moreover, Van Rooij (2013b) defined compliance as a set of recurring, nonlinear processes through which legal norms enter into the operations and perceptions of the regulated actors at different stages of the production chain, including learning, negotiation, dissemination and translation, operational, verification (and simulation), and institutionalization and internalization processes.

There is an underlying similar logic to existing studies using the process approach—researchers attempt to illustrate the entire compliance process, from external legal norms to regulated behavior or even internal norms. Although this illustration is logical, it is oversimplified, and it fails to reflect the real situation. Compliance behavior can be motivated at different steps and does not necessarily follow the same logic from acknowledging a legal norm to developing a compliance behavior. Compliance behavior may arise from internal values and norms without actors noting corresponding legal norms. Thus, the existing process approach over-simplifies the actor who undergoes the compliance process as an individual, and it reduces the business organization to a representative individual with the sole role of receiving information regarding a legal norm and responding to that information. It dismisses the internal organizational structure and business employees. In reality, the regulated can be both individuals and organizations that experience different compliance processes and play different roles in those processes. Therefore, the process involves considerable variations and layers. Yet if all variations are considered, the compliance process model becomes enormous and too complex to understand. Hence, in this research, a modified version of the process approach was used to study and measure compliance behavior.

First, instead of discussing compliance behavior using a universal process model that moves from legal norm to behavior, I attempted to describe the tracing process related to how the compliance behavior takes place. Thus, the steps that form the process model were not described; instead, each compliance behavior was viewed separately, and I am going to describe how the behavior arose, developed, and settled and presented. For example, restaurants are legally required to obtain a number of licenses before opening. I traced the process the restaurants followed to obtain their licenses.

Second, compliance behavior is described in the research using the insights derived from three core processes. Although compliance behavior may originate and develop from several processes or contexts, it inevitably goes through three core processes. The first is the compliance process at regulatory level. As many compliance studies, especially endogenous research, show, compliance is negotiated and constructed through interaction between the regulator and the regulated. Accordingly, interaction between the regulator and the regulated must be one of the core processes. The second is the compliance process at organizational level. An organization is a semiautonomous social field (Moore 1973). It can generate rules, customs, and symbols internally, but it is also vulnerable to rules, decisions, and other forces emanating from the external environment. Thus, compliance behavior may arise from the organizations' own rules or from the negotiation between the internal rules and external forces, such as legal norms implemented by the government. The third is the compliance process at the individual level. Ultimately, an individual must perform compliance behavior, and compliance can occur only when someone carries out certain required behavior. The one tasked with performing the compliance action decides to engage in the required behavior. Consequently, the personal decision-making process becomes the third core process out of which compliance behavior arises.

Accordingly, how compliance behavior takes place was described using insights drawn from the three core processes: the regulatory process, or the interaction between the regulator and regulated; the organizational process, or the evolution of compliance behavior from the organizational culture and characteristics or from negotiation between internal and external forces; and the individual process, or individual decision making. The three levels show a successive order for the development of compliance behaviors. Although the individual level is the core, an individual in an organization is influenced by the organizational level of the process. At the same time, the organizational level is influenced by the regulatory level of the process. However, the final compliance behaviors do not necessarily go through all three process levels. From the perspective of the regulated, the individual level is the core, and it determines the final process of making the decision of compliance, while the organizational and regulatory levels provide a context for making this decision.

While tracing back compliance behavior, the process perspective demands that the researcher focus on the actor of compliance behavior to consider how the actor perceives, acts, and makes decision. This leads to the second element of describing compliance behavior, the "other side" subjective perspective.

It is important to note that the process approach is similar to the method of causal process tracing (CPT), which has received increasing attention in social science research recently in terms of developing a "comprehensive storyline" related to a delineated social fact and searching for cog and wheel of the mechanism that produced the outcome discussed (Bennett and Checkel, forthcoming; Hestrom and Bearman 2009; Mahoney 2015). However, it differs from CPT in several ways. Describing compliance behavior is a way to operationalize and collect data on the explanandum, compliance behaviors. In contrast, the explanandum researched using CPT is always definite, with clear social outcomes, such as U.S. decision making regarding the 2003 intervention in Iraq (Lake 2011). Hence, CPT is not a method used to operationalize the explanandum. Furthermore, besides extensive storytelling and history tracing, CPT involves a cluster of techniques of proposing hypotheses and conducting four kinds of tests to precisely and clearly explain the mechanism that produces the outcome discussed. However, describing compliance behavior using the novel approach proposed in this book does not involve such well-developed techniques. Although extensively describing the process of how compliance behaviors emerge provides opportunities to identify mechanisms that produce and explain these behaviors, it serves not as an explanation method but as a research approach to the explanandum.

2.1.2 A Subjective Perspective

Tracing compliance behavior by following the actor in three core processes demands consideration of the "other side" subjective perspective. In most studies, the regulated is viewed as passively responding to the legal norms. When discussing compliance, most researchers explicitly or implicitly take the perspective of the regulator to examine why the regulated comply and to determine how to spur compliance. As a result, researchers discussed the regulatees' motives for complying, their perceptions of enforcement style, and their motivational attitudes toward inspectors from an objective point of view, but failed to consider the actor who engages in the compliance behavior as an enabled actor situated in certain social contexts. The regulated are enabled actors, and the compliance behavior in which they engage is only one aspect of their daily life. How the compliance behavior occurs is deeply embedded in the social context in which the actors are situated. To describe compliance behavior, the researcher must focus on the actors, and they must be viewed as subjects rather than as objects. Seen from a subjective point of view, the actors reveal a real-life picture of how compliance behavior occurs in their lives, which may improve the understanding of compliance behavior.

Furthermore, actors in organizations who are subject to compliance are stratified, not homogenous. As Gray and Silbey (2011) argued, when research examines "the other side of the compliance relationship," it is often limited to the interactions between regulators and high-level figures inside organizations. The frontline workers, whose activities most often produce violations or compliance, have not been systematically incorporated into the literature. The organization is depicted as a unified corporate person represented by only the manager, instead of as a set of persons, actions, resources, spaces, and times coordinated to achieve a recognized purpose and set of interests. Therefore, in their research, Gray and Silbey explicitly applied an "other side" perspective to study how the workers, not the managers, who enact compliance during daily operations actually interpret and respond to regulations (Gray 2002, 2006; Gray and Silbey 2011; Gray and Silbey 2014). Garry Gray worked in a factory for five months to investigate how safety rights in law are translated into practice (compliance behavior) for individual workers at the local level (Gray 2002, 2006). By studying the compliance behavior that actually occurred through participant observation and personal narratives, he discovered three ways in which workers refused to perform unsafe work (and thus engaged in compliance behavior). Based on the discussion of how the compliance behavior took place, he showed how individual workers' personal experience plays a role in refusing unsafe work, and how the individual responsibilization strategies used in work safety regulation neglected the social context of the worker and potentially encouraged noncompliance behaviors.

The research process used in this study aligns with that employed by Garry Gray—studying compliance behaviors directly from the perspective of the regulated. As Braithwaite et al. (1994) suggested by taking the perspective of those regulated rather than the perspective of the law enforcers, this approach improves the understanding of the different sets of considerations that shapes regulatory behaviors. Therefore, in this study, the focus was on the main actors in the three core processes that produce compliance behavior. As they were subjects of compliance behavior, their experience of compliance and their perceptions and considerations were studied along with the social contexts in which they were situated. Because of the focus on the regulated, the regulatory process level was discussed from mainly the restaurant owners' point of view. On the organizational and individual process levels, both restaurant employees and restaurant owners as the main actors were studied and discussed.

2.2 Classifying Compliance Behaviors

Describing compliance behavior in detail and examining various compliance processes yielded a complicated array of different behaviors. To make sense of this complex array of behaviors required classification of the compliance behaviors identified. Simply using compliance and noncompliance is inadequate, as several studies have shown (Edelman and Talesh 2011), and it may invite the problem of constructing the definition of compliance (Parker and Nielson 2009). To maximize the number of characteristics of compliance behavior captured, I turned to the existing literature, which provided several typologies to capture the characteristic of compliance behaviors.

One classification method is based on an assessment of the extent to which regulated behaviors correspond with legal norms. The extent can be assessed in both width and depth. In terms of width of compliance, regulated behavior may partly (ranging from none to partial, and to fully) accord with legal norms. For compliance with food standards, Henson and Heasman (1998) explored compliance using a scale ranging from noncompliance to partial compliance and, finally, to full compliance. Instead of a binary classification of compliance and noncompliance, the width of compliance provides a more complex and positive perspective on compliance behaviors. It acknowledges and appraises partial compliance and allows a discussion of reasons for partial rather than full compliance, which focuses attention on efforts to expand compliance and reduce noncompliance.

From a point of view of depth instead of width, Van Rooij (2011) proposed a scale of the depth of compliance ranging from shallow compliance to deep compliance, and further to ultra-deep compliance. This change from width to depth of compliance draws attention to why certain regulated firms or individuals are more likely to repeat compliance behavior but others are not. Shallow compliance is a compliance process where the regulated actors respond by doing exactly what is they are told and motivated to do by certain external motivators without institutionalizing the actions into their internal personal, working, or social norms. Shallow compliance easily decreases after the external motivation diminishes, and the compliance process lacks continuity and demands continued pressure from external motivations to ensure behavior occurs in accordance with the legal norms.

In contrast, deep compliance means the institutionalization of legal norms into the personal, working, or social norms of the regulated actor has taken place, and the behavior of the regulated actor is shaped by those internal norms rather than solely by the external motivation, for example, external enforcement, that reflects the legal norm. Ultra-deep compliance occurs when legal norms and the goals of specific legal norms become internalized into the morals of the regulated (Vandenbergh 2003). Actors voluntarily comply with legal norms, or even creatively comply with the goals of legal norms, regardless of whether there are external pressures or incentives to do so. The deeper the compliance, the less external action is needed to sustain the behavioral change sought and the less need there is for the legal norms to exist.

If the depth and width methods view compliance from a quantitative perspective, that is, less compliance or more compliance, shallow compliance or deep compliance, compliance can be viewed from a qualitative perspective as, for example, negotiated compliance, voluntary compliance, enforced compliance, over-compliance, creative compliance, symbolic compliance, fake compliance, conflictive compliance, coincidental compliance, and delayed compliance.

Compliance is not determined by the regulated alone, but always arises from a negotiation between the regulator and regulated. Therefore, negotiated compliance was the first form of compliance widely discussed during the 1980s. Langbein and Kerwin (1985) suggested that final compliance is determined by the negotiations between agencies and affected parties due to the ambiguous and broad laws and the quasilegislative processes in agencies. Negotiated compliance, according to Langbein and Kerwin (1985), refers to the eventual compliance with a negotiated version of the original standard, or a finding of noncompliance and payment of a possibly negotiated penalty. To discuss the concept of negotiated compliance, the authors slightly modified the term "noncompliance," which, compared to negotiated compliance that develops after a negotiation process, "refers only to noncompliance just or soon after the time the standard or penalty is promulgated" (Langbein and Kerwin 1985: 859). In other words, negotiated compliance is more longitudinal and may include initial noncompliance, but the result is a status of compliance accepted by the regulators. Negotiated compliance may alter the substance of the standard, which may reduce the cost of compliance.

Negotiated compliance is closely linked to delayed compliance, a term used by Langbein and Kerwin (1985) to describe the possible outcome of initial noncompliance in the compliance process. It refers to the situation where the regulated party consciously or unconsciously delays compliance with the law. Sometimes the delay itself is its own reward for the regulated party, and the delayed is deliberate. However, sometimes the regulated party delays compliance due to ignorance of its responsibility. Delayed compliance may become negotiated compliance during the process of delaying and negotiation, and initial noncompliance may change into other forms of compliance. Often, compliance results from negotiation between the regulator and the regulated, as negotiated compliance implies; nevertheless, the terms "delayed compliance" and "negotiated compliance" are too broad to be useful to discuss the complexity of compliance behaviors.

Other kinds of compliance, seen from the qualitative perspective and from the view of the subject of the compliance behavior, are more useful for capturing the characteristics of complex compliance behaviors in restaurants. Voluntary and forced compliance are based on incentives and the willingness of the regulated to adhere to the law. Voluntary compliance refers to the situation where the regulated are cooperative and willing to meet the regulatory standards, and the core of voluntary compliance is the "willingness to obey the law" and the "good faith" of the regulated (Scholz 1984). Enforced compliance is the opposite of voluntary compliance, where the regulated comply only under the threat of punishment. The regulated and regulator are in an antagonistic climate characterized by a "cops and robbers" attitude on both sides (Kirchler et al. 2008). In cases of enforced compliance, the regulated is always inclined to calculate the cost and benefit of evading and prefers to evade compliance whenever possible.

Over-compliance refers to the situation where the regulated achieved the regulatory goals to a greater extent than required by existing regulations. Over-compliance alone is mainly a quantitative view of compliance, which is similar to partial and full compliance. However, it implies a qualitative difference. Based on the intention of the regulated, there is voluntary over-compliance (Arora and Gangopadhyay 1995), and passive over-compliance. For passive over-compliance, the regulated seeks to only comply with the law, but due to technological indivisibilities, delivers more than the legal requirements (Prakash 2001). In contrast, for voluntary over-compliance, also called beyond compliance, the regulated may adopt compliance polices specially intend to exceed the extant requirements of laws (Prakash 2001), may provide environmental public goods with standards higher than those required by law, or follow more stringent policies than extant laws (Reinhardt 1999; Prakash 2001; Gunningham et al. 2004). Therefore, they may modify physical aspects of value-addition processes or adopt new management systems (Prakash 2001).

Creative compliance is based on differentiation between the letter of the law and the spirit of law, which refers to the slippage of one part, either the letter or the spirit of the law, while conforming to another part of law. Consequently, there are two kinds of creative compliance. One is negative regarding the spirit of the law, referring to a situation where the regulated uses legal forms that hide the reality of what the law substantially aims to regulate (McBarnet and Whelan 1991). This kind of creative compliance partly originates from legal formalism and regulators' legalism, that is, to emphasize conforming to the letter of the law results in purposely manipulating the legal norm to disguise substantially violating the spirit of law. This is especially prevalent in accounting compliance. The second form of creative compliance, which is positive regarding the spirit of the law, is known as affirmative slippage of the legal requirements (Farber 1999). In this case, the regulator and regulated may collaborate to reinvent the regulation, and such positive creative compliance behaviors may be later partially ratified by the legislature. For instance, the penalties that should have been paid to government under the Clean Water Act are in reality used for mitigation projects. This creative compliance was partially ratified by Congress in the citizen suit provision of the Clean Air Act.

In contrast to negative creative compliance, where the regulated manipulate the law to circumvent or undermine the purpose of the regulation, symbolic or cosmetic compliance involves the regulated responding to an ambiguous law by creating a visible commitment to the law that does not serve the substantial goal of the law (Edelman et al. 1991; Edelman 1992; Grossman 2003; Krawiec 2003; Krieger et al. 2015). For instance, an organization may establish some internal structure to respond to equal employment opportunity (EEO) or sexual harassment laws. These internal structures act as window-dressing or symbols of their attention to law. The normative value of these internal structures is not their substantial contribution to reducing discrimination within employment or preventing sexual harassment, but endorsing the legitimacy of the organization. Correspondingly, regulators view and accept these internal structures as evidence of ensuring EEO implementation or preventing sexual harassment.

While symbolic compliance may potentially lead to true compliance, fake compliance,[1] or Potemkin Village[2] compliance, involves clear dishonesty and does not potentially lead to real compliance. In fake compliance, the regulated actors falsify a situation to seem in compliance for the sake of regulators, who believe this to be the case. However, this is only a façade, and the regulated are not in compliance. As the purpose-built replica of a pleasant peasant village in the story of Potemkin Village (Gray 2006) showed, the purpose of the compliance behavior was to disguise the unpleasant realities of country life. Gray found that the workplace suddenly would be cleaned and legal requirements for a safe working environment would be followed, but that this was simply a short-lived disguise for an upcoming inspection tour. After the inspection tour, everything would return to normal, and the unsafe working environment would persist.

In some cases, the regulated comply with the spirit of the law, but they do so unintentionally, which is known as coincidental compliance. Here, compliance behaviors may occur for reasons entirely exogenous to the legal process (Raustiala 2000) or may not be induced by legal rules (Mitchell 1994). Mitchell (1994) proposed the term "coincidental compliance" when discussing compliance with the international treaty on oil pollution, referring to compliance behaviors that conform to an explicit treaty provision but that would have occurred even without the treaty rules (Mitchell 1994: 429). Mitchell (1994) noted that the oil discharge of a company decreased largely due to economic considerations and that the compliance behavior was not intentionally pursued but coincidentally adhered to international discharge limits.

---

[1] Noutcheva (2006, 2009) also used the term "fake compliance" when researching the compliance patterns of Balkan states in light of the European Union's conditional offer of membership. I identified fake compliance as one of four compliance propensities: genuine compliance, conditionality-driven compliance, socialization-driven compliance, and fake compliance. Noutcheva's definition of fake compliance differs from the definition used in this study. Noutcheva used two dimensions to build a model to identify the four compliance propensities, namely legitimacy and cost/benefit analysis. According to the author, fake compliance occurs when the legitimacy of EU conditions is low and the cost exceeds the benefit in the long term; furthermore, the cost of total refusal to comply is even higher. In practical terms, fake compliance may include some compliance behaviors such as setting up "institutions in response to EU conditionality, but these institutions remain empty shells and exist more on paper than in reality." In this study, Noutcheva's definition of fake compliance aligns more closely with symbolic compliance.

[2] The saying of "Potemkin Village" comes from a story. "The Empress Catherine the Great, who was quite near-sighted, had arranged a boat tour [of the Ukraine and Crimea] for a group of visiting European royalty. She wanted to show them the prosperous countryside with its happy peasants. Her chief advisor, Gregory Potemkin, knew that this wasn't the reality the visitors were going to see. To avoid embarrassing the Tsarina, he ordered the construction of the facades of peasant villages along the river route. As the boat passed by, Catherine imagined she was showing her guests a pleasant pastoral scene. The visitors, however, saw only the attempt to hide the unpleasant realities of life" (Tager and Phelps 2004). So, Potemkin Village is used as an analogy in some compliance research to reflect the local culture of health and safety reactions to inspection enforcement. In this culture, legal norms are strictly complied with when there is a health and safety inspection tour. However, after the inspection tour, all kinds of violation reappear. People become accustomed to this kind of performance when inspections happen. See more in Garry Gary's "The Regulation of Corporate Violations" (2006).

Due to the complexity of the legal system, conflictive compliance exists, where "satisfying one demand may require violating others" (Pfeffer and Salancik 1978). The conflict may arise from different legal requirements regulating the same behaviors (Maxwell et al. 2011), or from different demands from regulative, normative, and cognitive systems (Pache and Santos 2010), as requirements from these institutions may compete with each other (Heimer 1999).

While the kinds of compliance examined in this section have been discussed in regulatory and compliance literature, they by no means describe all kinds of compliance. Dimensions that define or differentiate those compliance types, such as whether the regulated intend to comply, whether the regulated comply with the letter or the spirit of the law, whether the compliance behavior is a disguise or a reflection of reality, and whether compliance with one legal norm will violate another legal norm or norms from another system, may exist. However, to date no unified classification system has been developed that incorporate all of them. In addition, it was not the aim of this research to create an exhaustive list of compliance behaviors and build a comprehensive classification system. Instead, the different kinds of compliance were introduced to guide the descriptions and capture the complexity of restaurant behaviors described in chapters that follow.

2.3 Characterizing the Subject of Compliance Behaviors

The review of compliance behavior raises important questions about understanding the complex compliance behaviors in restaurants, and the reasons for the complexity of these behaviors. As shown in the literature, the regulated are always assessed using certain models to predict and understand their behaviors (Kagan and Scholz 1984; Braithwaite et al. 1994; Kagan et al. 2003). In this section, three influential works on understanding the subject of complex compliance behaviors are outlined, two of which subsequently were used in the analysis of restaurants and their compliance behaviors.

Kagan and Scholz (1984) proposed three categories of noncompliers that address the reasons for compliance behavior: amoral calculators, political citizens, and incompetent entities. Amoral calculators are motivated entirely by profit seeking and always make rational choices that benefit them most. They will violate the law when the profits and costs of breaking the law exceed the perceived costs and benefits of abiding by the law. Political citizens are inclined to comply with the law if they believe the law is reasonable, but fail to comply if they believe it is unreasonable. Incompetent entities are inclined to obey the law, but fail to do so because of organizational incompetence.

These three categories were built on the premise that to fail to comply means there is a good reason for noncompliance based on the nature of the regulated. Thus, noncompliance is closely related to the nature of the regulated, whether the regulated is an amoral calculator, a political citizen, or an incompetent entity. For amoral calculators, the regulator should behave like the police to deter violations and increase the threat of higher costs if they do not comply with the law. For political citizens, the regulator should act as a politician who persuades them that the legal norms are good for most people and compliance is the right thing to do. For incompetent entities, the regulator should educate and help them find ways to comply. Classifying compliance behavior in this way is in fact classifying the nature of actor.

Braithwaite et al. (1994), in a study conducted in a nursing home in Australia, demonstrated that regulators cannot systematically analyze the motives of the regulated or clearly identify whether they are amoral calculators, political citizens, or incompetent entities, nor can Kagan and Scholz's (1984) three categories predict compliance behaviors. In contrast, Braithwaite et al. (1994) suggested influencing compliance behavior through motivational postures expressed during the regulatory encounter. Instead of classifying the motives and nature of actors, motivational posture classifies the actors' attitudes to and interactions with the regulatory team. Braithwaite et al. (1994) contended that the interaction between the regulator and the regulated is more important than pure motives and argued that using the behavioral-decision model to analyze compliance behavior requires greater consideration of the social contexts in which the behaviors take place. The concept of motivational postures captures the overall attitude of the regulated and reflects the level of social distance the regulated place between themselves and an authority. This social distance is developed upon evaluations of how authorities and their laws perform, what they stand for, whether they pose a threat to an individual's goals, and whether they align with the value system of the regulated (Murphy 2014). Braithwaite et al. (1994) viewed this system as a better predictor of future compliance behaviors.

Braithwaite et al. (1994) identified four motivational postures in their study of nursing home directors: resistance, disengagement, managerial accommodation, and capture. Resistance is hostile to and involves confrontation of the regulatory goal and inspectors' way of working, while disengagement reflects negativity toward the regulatory goal and regulatory community, with the disengaged regulated being disinterested in regulation and attempting to avoid it. Managerial accommodation, on the other hand, is cooperative, with managers accepting responsibility for the implementation of regulation, participating in the regulatory process, and doing what is expected of them. Furthermore, they have their own managerial plans to realize regulatory goals. Those classified as captured align with the enforcers and show high identification with the standards monitoring process. They accept the regulatory goals and the means for achieving these goals. This typology is based on Merton's (1968) modes of adaptation to a normative order, which constitutes five modes of adaptations considering the subjects' attitudes toward the goal and institutionalized means of the normative order.

Subsequently, Braithwaite included the concept of game playing as the fifth posture, which emerged from a discussion about posturing between tax officials and taxpayers proposed by McBarnet (1992). Game playing refers to "a particular kind of attitude to law: Law is seen as something to be moulded to suit one's purposes rather than as something to be respected as defining the limits of acceptable activity" (Braithewaite 2003: 18–19). The five modified motivational postures are game playing, disengagement, resistance, capitulation (previously managerial accommodation), and commitment. Commitment and capitulation reflect a general positive orientation and close relationship with authority. The regulated with the motivational posture of commitment believe the enforcement system to be desirable and feel morally obliged to act to obey the law with good will. Those with the capitulation posture accept the enforcement authority as legitimate and feel that the enforcement authority is a benign power, provided they act properly and defer to its authority.

In contrast to the two positive postures, the remaining three are negative and defiant. The regulated with the resistance posture doubt the intention of the enforcement system to behave cooperatively and benignly toward those it dominates. They are inclined to fight for their rights and to curb the power of enforcement authorities. The disengagement posture also communicates resistance, but the disenchantment within it is more widespread. Those with disengagement posture do not see any point in challenging the authorities and are not interested in changing or improving the enforcement system. Their main objective is to keep themselves and the authority socially distant and blocked from view. Game playing posture shows a particular kind of attitude toward the law, which is seen as something to be molded to suit one's purposes rather than as something to be respected as defining the limits of acceptable activity. Those with game playing posture consciously attempt to find loopholes in the law and operate in the gray area of the law to minimize the cost of obeying the law. Moreover, the five motivational postures may overlap or be related. Commitment and capitulation are compatible, while disengagement may be compatible with resistance and game playing. In other words, the regulated may demonstrate more than one posture in any specific encounter.

Nevertheless, Braithwaite (2003) claimed that motivational posture is as an indicator of the degree to which an individual consents to the authority but not necessarily a sign of obedience or disobedience. The relationships between motivational postures and compliance-related activities exist in the expected direction. Those who express postures of commitment and capitulation to the tax system are more likely not to attempt tax evasion and tax avoidance, while those who express postures of resistance to, disengagement from, and game playing with the tax system are more likely to attempt tax evasion and tax avoidance. However, the correlation between motivational posture and compliance behavior is uniformly low, possibly because noncompliant actions may be initiated for a number of reasons and the motivational posture reflecting only the attitudinal factors. Consenting to authority is important for showing compliance, but consenting differs from obeying a request from a legally designed authority. As Elffers et al. (1992) demonstrated, compliance behaviors might consist of several conceptual aspects. Motivational posture may reflect only one of them, which is more attitudinal.

Kagan et al. (2003) composed the third typology of compliance actors in a discussion on environmental management. They identified five ideal types of environmental compliance actor, or "environmental management style": environmental laggards, reluctant compliers, committed compliers, environmental strategists, and true believers. Environmental laggards, who are on the lowest level of compliance, have a negative attitude toward regulatory requirements and comply only to avoid costly enforcement actions. Reluctant compliers are more willing to keep up with regulatory requirements but seek to meet only the minimum standards prescribed by regulations. Committed compliers are more cooperative with regulators, but comply mainly to show they are compliers to gain legal and social license. Environmental strategists have a more future-oriented conception of environmental objectives and believe that environmental improvements can lead to improved economic performance. They often take environmental measures that go well beyond legal compliance. True believers explain their decisions on environmental issues not purely in pragmatic terms but also in terms of principle, as "the right thing to do." They are more inclined to invest in environmental measures for over-compliance as "good business decisions," even if the numerical payoff cannot be calculated ex ante.

These five types of compliance actors show five combinations of managerial attitudes and actions that mark the intensity and character of each management team's commitment to meeting environmental responsibilities. The attitude here refers to managers' attitudes toward environmental problems. Actions refer to managers' actions and implementation efforts to meet specific economic, regulatory, and community challenges. This involves three related dimensions of commitment: the intensity of managerial scanning for environmentally relevant information, management's degree of responsiveness to environmentally relevant information, and the assiduousness with which the company had institutionalized implementing routines to ensure high levels of environmental consciousness and control capacity.

Similar to Braithwaite et al. (1994) classification of motivational postures, this method of compliance actor classification rests on two aspects: the attitude of the compliance actor toward the environmental requirements (negative, good when better related to business goal, good and moral thing to do), and the willingness of regulatory commitment (not willing, willing to minimum standards, willing to beyond-compliance). These ideal types of compliance actors affect how firms respond to pressures from regulatory regimes and economic constraints. Successive ideal type displaying greater commitment predicts better environment performance and deeper environment compliance.

The three classifications evolved from the motives or nature of the actors, to attitudinal motivational posture, to attitude combined with commitment. Each classification system provides unique insights into the characteristics of the subject of compliance and its compliance behavior. They emphasize the importance of the nature or ideology of the actors, the attitudinal element compliance behavior reflects, and commitment to regulation in understanding compliance behavior. This research borrowed ideas from the latter two typologies of compliance to characterize the rich and varied compliance behavior observed in restaurants.

2.4 Structure of the Case Description

The next two chapters outline the legally relevant compliance behaviors in the two core cases, namely the health-oriented restaurant and the economy-oriented restaurant. While they are situated in their social, organizational, and personal contexts and both cases and the relevant compliance behaviors are described in great detail, no analysis or explanation occurs in this section.

The two cases and their compliance behaviors are framed using a five-step structure:

1. The main characteristics of the two restaurants are described to show how they differ.
2. The history of the establishment of each restaurant is described to show the social context and social support system of the owner, which situates the restaurant in a specific context. The restaurants' compliance behaviors are deeply embedded in these social contexts.
3. The owners' personalities and leadership styles are described. Leadership is critical for any organization, and it can be a decisive factor in the functioning and success of the business.
4. Various behaviors related to legal norms in both the process of applying for opening licenses and daily operation are described to illustrate the processes taking place and their complexities.
5. The information is placed within the three typologies reviewed in this chapter to critically assess how the various compliance and noncompliance behaviors in these two cases can be qualified.

References

Arora, Seema, and Shubhashis Gangopadhyay. 1995. Toward a Theoretical Model of Voluntary Overcompliance. *Journal of Economic Behavior and Organization* 28 (1995): 289–309.

Bennett, Andrew, and Jeffrey T. Checkel. (forthcoming). Process Tracing: From Philosophical Roots to Best Practices. In *Process Tracing in the Social Sciences: From Metaphor to Analytical* Tool, ed. Andrew Bennett and Jeffrey T. Checkel.

Braithwaite, Valerie. 2003. Dancing with Tax Authorities: Motivational Postures and Non-compliant Actions. In *Taxing Democracy: Understanding Tax Avoidance and Evasion*, ed. Valerie Braithwaite, 15–39. Ashgate

Braithwaite, Valerie., John Braithwaite, Diane Gibson, and Toni Makkai. 1994. Regulatory Styles Motivational Postures and Nursing Home Compliance. *Law & Policy* 16(4): 363–394.

Chemnitz, C. 2012. The impact of food safety and quality standards on developing countries agricultural producers and exports. Doctoral dissertation, Humboldt-Universität zu Berlin, Landwirtschaftlich-Gärtnerische Fakultät.

Edelman, Lauren B. 1992. Legal Ambiguity and Symbolic Structures: Organizational Mediation of Civil Rights Law. *American Journal of Sociology* 97 (6): 1531–1576.

Edelman, Lauren B., and Shauhin A. Talesh. 2011. To Comply or not to Comply—That isn't the Question: How Organizations Construct the Meaning of Compliance. In *Explaining Compliance:*

Business Responses to Regulation, ed. Christine Parker and Vibeke Lehmann Nielsen, 103–122.Cheltenham: Edward Elgar.

Edelman, Lauren B., Stephen Petterson, Elizabeth Chambliss, and Howard S. Erlanger. 1991. Legal Ambiguity and the Politics of Compliance: Affirmative Action Officers' Dilemma. *Law & Policy* 13(1): 73–97.

Elffers, Henk, Henry S. J. Robben, and Dick J. Hessing. 1992. On Measuring Tax Evasion. *Journal of Economic Psychology* 13 (4): 545–567.

Fairman, R., and C. Yapp. 2004. Compliance with Food Safety Legislation in Small and Micro-businesses: Enforcement as an External Motivator. *Journal of Environmental Health Research* 3: 44–52.

Farber, Daniel. A. 1999. Taking Slippage Seriously: Noncompliance and Creative Compliance in Environmental Law. *Harvard Environmental Law Review* 23: 297–325

Gray, Garry C. 2002. A Socio-legal Ethnography of the Right to Refuse Dangerous Work. *Studies in Law, Politics, and Society* 24: 133–169.

Gray, Garry C. 2006. The Regulation of Corporate Violations: Punishment, Compliance and the Blurring of Responsibility. *British Journal of Criminology* 46(5): 875–892.

Gray, Garry C., and Susan S. Silbey. 2011. The Other Side of the Compliance Relationship. In *Explaining Compliance: Business Responses to Regulation*, ed. Christine Parker and Vibeke Lehmann Nielsen, 123–138. Cheltenham: Edward Elgar.

Gray, Garry C., and Susan S. Silbey. 2014. Governing Inside the Organization: Interpreting Regulation and Compliance. *American Journal of Sociology* 120(1): 96–145.

Grossman, Joanna L. 2003. The Culture of Compliance: The Final Triumph of Form over Substance in Sexual Harassment Law. *Harvard Women's Law Journal* 26 (3): 3–75.

Gunningham, Robert A. Kagan, and Dorothy Thornton. 2004. Social License and Environmental Protection: Why Businesses Go Beyond Compliance. *Law & Social Inquiry* 29(2): 307–341.

Hedstrom, Peter, and Peter Bearman. 2009. *The Oxford Handbook of Analytical Sociology*. Oxford: Oxford University Press.

Heimer, Carol A. 1999. Competing Institutions: Law, Medicine, and Family in Neonatal Intensive Care. *Law & Society Review* 33 (1): 17–66.

Henson, S., and M. Heasman. 1998. Food Safety Regulation and the Firm: Understanding the Compliance Process. *Food Policy* 23 (1): 9–23.

Kagan, R. A., and J. T. Scholz. 1984. The "Criminology of the Corporation" and Regulatory Enforcement Strategies. In *Regulatory Enforcement*, ed. K. Hawkins and J. M. Thomas, 67–95. Boston: Kluwer-Nijhoff Publishing.

Kagan, R.A., N. Gunningham, and D. Thornton. 2003. Explaining Corporate Environmental Performance: How Does Regulation Matter? *Law & Society Review* 37: 51–90. https://doi.org/10.1111/1540-5893.3701002.

Kirchler, Erich, Erik Hoelzl, and Ingrid Wahl. 2008. Enforced Versus Voluntary Tax Compliance: The 'Slippery Slope' Framework. *Journal of Economic Psychology* 29: 210–225.

Krawiec, Kimberly D. 2003. Cosmetic Compliance and the Failure of Negotiated Governance. *Washington University Law Quarterly* 81: 487–544.

Krieger, Linda Hamilton, Rachel Kahn Best, and Lauren B. Edelman. 2015. When 'Best Practices' Win, Employees Lose: Symbolic Compliance and Judicial Inference in Federal Equal Employment Opportunity Cases. *Law & Social Inquiry* 40 (4): 1–37.

Lake, David. 2011. Two Cheers for Bargaining Theory: Assessing Rationalist Explanations for the Iraq War. *International Security* 35 (3): 7–52.

Langbein, L., and C.M. Kerwin. 1985. Implementation, Negotiation and Compliance in Environmental and Safety Legislation. *Journal of Politics* 47 (3): 854–880.

Mahoney, James. 2015. Process Tracing and Historical Explanation. *Security Studies* 24 (2): 200–218. https://doi.org/10.1080/09636412.2015.1036610.

Maxwell, Jeremy, Annie I. Anton, and Peter Swire. 2011. A Legal Cross-References Taxonomy for Identifying Conflicting Software Requirements. Research paper presented in 2011 at the *IEEE 19th International Requirements Engineering Conference*, 197–206.

McBarnet, Doreen. 1992. Legitimate Rackets: Tax Evasion, Tax Avoidance, and the Boundaries of Legality. *The Journal of Human Justice* 3 (2): 56–74.

McBarnet, Doreen, and Christopher Whelan. 1991. The Elusive Spirit of the Law: Formalism and the Struggle for Legal Control. *Modern Law Review*, 54: 848–873.

Merton, Robert K. 1968. *Social Theory and Social Structure*. New York: Free Press.

Mitchell, Ronald B. 1994. Regime Design Matters: Intentional Oil Pollution and Treaty Compliance. *International Organization* 48 (3): 425–458.

Moore, Sally Falk. 1973. Law and Social Change: The Semi-autonomous Social Field as an Appropriate Subject of Study. *Law & Society Review* 7 (4): 719–746.

Murphy, Kristina. 2014. Turning Defiance into Compliance with Procedural Justice: Understanding Reactions to Regulatory Encounters through Motivational Posturing. *Regulation & Governance* 10 (1): 93–109.

Noutcheva, Gergana. 2006. EU Conditionality, State Sovereignty and the Compliance Patterns of Balkan States. In Conference Paper for the *3rd Pan-European Conference on EU Politics*, Bilgi University, Istanbul, September 21–23, 2006.

Noutcheva, Gergana. 2009. Fake, Partial and Imposed Compliance: The Limits of the EU's Normative Power in the Western Balkans. *Journal of European Public Policy* 16(7): 1065–1084. https://doi.org/10.1080/13501760903226872

Pache, Anne-Claire., and Filipe Santos. 2010. When Worlds Collide: The Internal Dynamics of Organizational Responses to Conflicting Institutional Demands. *Academy of Management Review* 35 (3): 455–476.

Parker, C., and V. Nielsen. 2009. The Challenge of Empirical Research on Business Compliance in Regulatory Capitalism. *Annual Review of Law and Social Science* 5: 45–70.

Pfeffer, J., and G.R. Salancik. 1978. *The External Control of Organizations: A Resource Dependence Perspective*. New York: Harper & Row.

Prakash, Aseem. 2001. Why do Firms Adopt 'Beyond-Compliance' Environmental Policies? *Business Strategy and the Environment* 10: 286–299.

Raustiala, Kal. 2000. Compliance and Effectiveness in International Regulatory Cooperation. *Case Western Reserve Journal of International Law* 32 (3): 387–440.

Reinhardt, Forest. 1999. Economic Rationales for 'Beyond Compliance' Behavior. *Journal of Industrial Ecology* 3 (1): 9–21.

Van Rooij. 2011. Compliance: A Concept Note. On file with the author.

Van Rooij. 2013b. Compliance as Process: A Micro Approach to Regulatory Implementation. On file with the author.

Scholz, John T. 1984. Voluntary Compliance and Regulatory Enforcement. *Law & Policy* 6 (4): 385–404.

Tager, J., and Phelps, B. 2004. A Critique of the Gene Technology Act and its Implementation. www.non-gm-farmers.com/news_details.asp?ID=1752.

Vandenbergh, M. 2003. Beyond Elegance: A Testable Typology of Social Norms in Corporate Environmental Compliance. *Stanford Environmental Law Journal* 22: 55–144.

Chapter 3
An Idealistic Restaurant

3.1 Introduction

In this chapter, an extended case study is described to exemplify the study of the compliance process by illustrating compliance behaviors and explaining how the method of describing behaviors contributes to the understanding of compliance. The chapter focuses on the case of the Idealistic restaurant.

Although many beyond compliance behaviors, such as purchasing ingredients of higher quality than legally required, were evident at the Idealistic restaurant, some violations occurred, including falsification of the disinfection log and failure to disinfect all tableware. Furthermore, the business attempted to achieve certain compliance behaviors by practicing fraudulent or even illegal behaviors. For example, the Idealistic restaurant bought counterfeit certificates for their traditionally slaughtered pigs to prove the pork was safe, despite providing organic pork that was of higher quality than certified pork. In addition, acquiring a drainage license required bribery and fraudulent conduct. This supports the views that compliance is complex and that various kinds of compliance, such as beyond compliance, symbolic compliance, fake compliance, fraudulent compliance, and conflict compliance coexist in one case.

Moreover, the case demonstrates the difficulty of assessing compliance based on a static point and highlights the importance of tracing back compliance processes. The tracing process shows how the Idealistic restaurant learned the legal requirements, competed with the legal requirements, and constructed its compliance behaviors. Furthermore, the subject of these compliance behaviors are characterized and linked to the complex forms of compliance described previously. This enabled to connect the case study to the literature discussed in Chap. 2 and to identify factors affecting compliance behavior.

In following sections, the context and background of the Idealistic restaurant, including the main features, the owner, and the process of establishing the restaurant, are described to provide an overview for understanding the context of compliance behaviors. Additionally, as shown in Chap. 7, the restaurant leadership and employee components have a significant influence on the compliance of the restaurant.

© The Author(s), under exclusive license to Springer Nature Singapore Pte Ltd. 2021
Y. Wu, *Compliance Ethnography*, Understanding China,
https://doi.org/10.1007/978-981-16-2884-9_3

Next, various compliance behaviors are examined in detail, beginning with the opening licenses, the first legal requirements a restaurant faces. The case shows how a novice in the catering industry encounters various legal hurdles, and how she learns to deal with them. Seen from the three core processes on which the research focuses, the compliance behaviors regarding the opening license exemplify mainly the regulatory process, that is, the interaction between regulators and the restaurant.

Subsequently, the daily operation legal requirements are investigated. These differ from the once-off opening licenses, as they require daily compliance. They cannot be assessed at a static point, as they rely on daily action, which implies that a process perspective is required to understand compliance behavior in this context. Furthermore, in terms of daily operation compliance, both restaurant workers and owners become the compliance actors on which the study must focus.

3.2 A Different Restaurant

Pig Slaughtering Notice

On May 27, our restaurant will get an organic pig from Wang Shihua in Baipo Village. The organic pig is fed traditionally without manufactured feed. You are welcome to have a taste.

Notices like these appeared on the board outside the Idealistic restaurant regularly, usually every several days. Just outside the door of the restaurant, several slogans were displayed: "Plant vegetables without using chemical fertilizers and pesticides," "Cook food without MSG and chicken bouillon powder," and "Learn from tradition." The main wooden door of the restaurant bore two traditional pictures of the door god and a pair of antithetical couplets, written in a beautiful script: "Don't mind ordinary food, it is not so delicious," and "Don't you know no poison is the best for your body?".

So is this just a gimmick? China is in the midst of a food crisis. Restaurants have been caught selling fake beef,[1] and there is widespread concern about gutter oil.[2] Massive amounts of inedible additives are used illegally,[3] and some fruit juice contains little fruit but large amounts of chemical additives. The endless increase in food safety problems is frustrating; therefore, there must surely be a market for safe

---

[1] Since 2010, fake beef has been discovered in some small restaurants and factories in China. The "beef" was actually made from pork (which is considerably cheaper than beef) that had been treated with chemical additives to make it look like beef.

[2] "Gutter oil" is a term used in China to describe illegally recycled waste oil collected from sources such as restaurant fryers, sewer drains, grease traps, and slaughterhouse waste. It has been a great concern and focus in the food safety crisis in recent years.

[3] Some news outlets have reported the use of industrial chemicals in food processing. For instance, chicken claws are soaked in industrial caustic soda, squid is soaked in formalin.

food. Indeed, many restaurants have taken to advertising the safety of their food.[4] Nevertheless, after eating there once, most customers tell a different tale.

At the Idealistic restaurant, only vegetables in season were served. This limited menu options, as, for example, winter vegetables such as radishes would be unavailable in summer, and summer vegetables such as eggplant would be unavailable in winter. The menu written on the blackboard often noted that only one or two portions of certain dishes would be available, which might have left first-time customers disappointed at the lack of variety. However, returning customers were satisfied with whatever was supplied.[5]

Moreover, the restaurant clearly indicated the origin of each food ingredient used and showed which farmer had grown it. The names of the villages of origin and of the farmers who supplied the products were displayed prominently. For example, sugar was bought from Brother Qiu in G province, who planted the sugar cane and manufactured the black sugar, while the skin of Tofu was made by Uncle Wu in L county. Rice was planted by the Family Liu in Q county, and the tomatoes were planted by the Family Yang in Q county. Not only the food materials but also all dishes, cups, and tables could be traced back to the manufacturers. For example, the dishes were made locally, and the cups in M county.

The restaurant indicated the origins of its food and materials to show its commitment to organic food production and its concern about food producers. The underlying ideology of this restaurant was to create an economic partnership between food consumers and producers. Consumers supported food producers with their purchase behaviors to encourage organic, seasonal, regional production. Although these products were not as aesthetically pleasing or diverse as commercially gown products, they were healthy and environmentally friendly. Thus, food consumers partially shared the production risks of food producers through purchases promises.

All the farmers who supplied the restaurant were reliable supporters of traditional agriculture and livestock cultivation who farmed without using chemical fertilizers, pesticides, and manufactured feeds or trusty suppliers of processed products that did not contain harmful artificial additives. Therefore, instead of simply claiming that the food supplied is generally safe and free of illegal additives or counterfeit products, the restaurant went to great lengths to prove its commitment to healthy food. It probably exceeded what most customers, who simply want safe food, would even want or demand. The restaurant did so not to attract customers but out of idealism.

---

[4]Faced with the increasing social concerns about food safety, many restaurants have developed strategies to claim the food they provide is safe. For example, some restaurants note on their menus that they do not use gutter oil, while other place bottles of oil along the stairs to show they use good oil. Furthermore, some restaurants photograph the flavorings used in their food to support their claim that they use only safe additive, and others claim to produce certain food materials, such as tofu and flour themselves, or that they grow their own vegetables and bean sprouts.

See http://news.shangdu.com/101/2009/04/08/2009-04-08_26411_101.shtml.

[5]During observation in the restaurant, several customers were briefly interviewed to determine why they chose this restaurant. For example, Mrs. Guo from a nearby university, who was a frequent customer, claimed that "it is good to just eat vegetable in season" and that "vegetable has its own season to grow." She further stated that "all vegetable not in its season is planted with lots of chemical fertilizer and pesticides" and that "it is better to eat healthier food than special dishes.".

The Idealistic restaurant moved beyond providing safe food in an effort to provide good food. Food that will not cause illness in the short or long term is considered safe, but good food benefits not only the health of consumers but also the ecosystem, in which people form part of the entire food chain. Food that is good for people should also be ethically sourced and good for the environment.[6] Eventually, what is good for the environment is good for people, and for human health. The organic, seasonal, regional production encouraged by the Idealistic restaurant was obviously good for the local fauna, flora, and environment, the producer, and consumers. Hence, advertising of the Idealistic restaurant claims that good food surpasses safe food implies superior food safety in the entire ecosystem.

Nevertheless, supplying food in this was is costly and difficult, and finding reliable, trustworthy suppliers is particularly challenging. Sourcing suppliers involves identifying them, communicating and negotiating with them, and sometimes fostering them through one-on-one personal contact to ensure the products they provide are grown or made without prohibited ingredients. In addition, this is time consuming. According to the owner of the Idealistic restaurant, the two main aspects of operating her restaurant were finding food materials and managing the employees. It seems this restaurant did not benefit from market efficiency,[7] as the restaurant had to source its products from suppliers in different village. Neither efficiency nor profit is a priority of the Idealistic restaurant, as indicated by the operation of this restaurant.

3.3 Meet the Owner

The owner of the Idealistic restaurant, born in 1980, had never dreamed she would one day become the owner of a restaurant, as she began her career on a very different path. She earned a Bachelor of Arts in computer science, after which she struggled for three years to earn a living in the city, like most of her classmates. However, she began to develop a growing feeling that this was not how she wanted to live and soon found a volunteer job at a non-governmental organization (NGO).[8] As part

---

[6]Michael Pollan expressed the concept of good food well in *The Omnivore's Dilemma* and *In Defense of Food*. In the former, he returns humans to the food chain and argues that people should ethically sourced food cultivated in an environmentally friendly manner. In the latter, he attempts to draw the reader back to the tradition, culture, and happiness of eating, which have become confused by nutritionism.

[7]Here, the narrow definition of market applies, that is, an open place or a covered building where buyers and sellers convene for the sale of goods. Like the fresh market, the wholesale market influences daily life. For a broader definition, see http://dictionary.reference.com/browse/market.

[8]This NGO was established by several local urban youths who pursue healthy and good food products. For them, this means products produced in the traditional manner without modern ingredients that change the natural growth of food materials, such as chemical fertilizers, pesticides, chemical additives, and manufactured feeds. These products benefit people and the environment, but producing them is often costly and requires hard work. Thus, this NGO encourages villagers to produce good food by gaining support from consumers, and attempts to convince consumers to support good food production by buying good food, which costs more than ordinary food. To do

of her nonprofit work, she interned at a restaurant. That restaurant, established by the NGO, encouraged organic and traditional agriculture and livestock cultivation by connecting small farmers to consumers in cities. The concept underlying this restaurant was community-supporting agriculture (CSA). She worked there as an intern being a server and community participation promoter. The job introduced her to a new world, and she loved her work, particularly earning a living while providing safe food. Yet at that time, she never thought she would one day become a restaurant owner. She continued doing one volunteer job after another, and she enjoyed her work for the NGO, which mainly involved communicating with villagers to promote community participation and community-supported agriculture.

The idea of opening her own restaurant came after the birth of her daughter. She did the same community promoter job after she gave birth, but found that she spent too little time with her daughter. When her daughter was several months old, she returned from a long fieldtrip, only to have her daughter push her away when she tried to hug her. It was heartbreaking, and it took a long time to repair her relationship with her daughter. This increased her need to spend more time with her daughter while earning a living, and finally, she came up with the idea of opening her own restaurant just like the one where she did her internship. She loved to work with the villagers and the land as she did while working for the NGOs, but she also wanted to stay with her little daughter and make a living. Her previous pleasant experience in the restaurant industry showed she could combine the two by opening a similar restaurant. She soon gained the support of her husband. To be prudent, she organized several organic pig slaughtering activities and happily found that she could sell all the pork. It built up her confidence for this unexpected venture.

However, being a restaurant owner went against her parents' expectation for their daughter. As is common with rural parents, they hoped their daughter would find a stable job with a good salary in the city. Opening a restaurant is costly and risky, so the owner's parents initially disagreed with her idea. To persuade her parents, she talked about her unhappiness in previous jobs, the internship experience in that restaurant, her concerns about the current food safety problem, the life she would prefer to live, and so forth. She finally asked her parents, "What kind of life do you want your daughter live? Doing high-paid work or being healthy and happy?" Her parents consented and provided great support for her business.

3.4 Getting Ready to the Business

Opening her dream organic restaurant that fulfilled the concept of the community supporting agriculture was challenging. The first hurdle was finding a trustworthy and capable cook who believed in the concept of organic food and who could cook

so, the NGO opened a restaurant that acts as a platform for consumers to taste good food and as a bridge to connect consumers to food producers. The restaurant also funded the daily operation of this NGO.

without using the artificial additives that have become popular.[9] The owner turned to her young brother who had been a cook for over four years. However, initially, he was reluctant to accept his sister's offer, as he had become bored with the food industry. Nevertheless, the owner managed to convince him to intern at the restaurant she used to intern, and after six months, he began to accept and enjoy the lifestyle the restaurant advocated and felt it working there was a worthy way to earn a living:

> Firstly, there are several investment partners but only one of them to manage the restaurant. You only need to invest a small amount of money that you can afford. Small restaurant is easily to survive. Or even if it fails, you still can bear the loss, and don't need to jump to death.[10]

For him, earning a living was his most important concern in the beginning. He had been thinking about opening his own rice noodle restaurant, but did not do so for various reasons. Thus, the idea of opening a restaurant together provided a good opportunity, and his intrinsic concern about health also motivated him to join his sister's business. He was particular about food, and, for example, he would refuse to eat food if he found a hair in the dish. The idea of organic, healthy food aligned with his intrinsic pursuit of health, and the natural match between him and the restaurant afforded him the opportunity to make the most of his character as a manager and benefitted the restaurant.

Finding other staff also was challenging. Finding servers and kitchen workers was not as easy as the owner imagined.[11] Apart from the common phenomenon of labor shortage in the catering industry, the Idealistic restaurant's ideology of cooking caused some difficulties. They searched the job market for kitchen workers, but those who came to enquire did not believe the Idealistic restaurant would cook dishes without MSG and chicken bouillon powder, and they thought she was lying and did not intend to recruit workers. Some candidates responded to her statement by saying, "I don't even use a heater when I cook,"[12] which was a sarcastic response to the notion of cooking without MSG and chicken bouillon powder. Therefore, the

---

[9]I learned a new phrase, "*Tiaoliao* cook," that was to name a kind of cook, from an informant in F restaurant. F restaurant is not included in this book because of insufficient data. *Tiaoliao* cooks, meaning additive cooks, do not know how to use and master the original taste and properties of various foods to make delicious and beautiful dishes but rely greatly on multiple additives to add flavors and colors. The informant, who had been a cook for 18 years, claimed those *Tiaoliao* cooks are usually young and eager to become real cooks after studying cooking as trainees for one or two years (male, 34, interview on Feb. 16, 2014).

[10]Interview with the head chef of the Idealistic restaurant, May 24, 2013.

[11]Difficulty finding servers and restaurant workers is a common phenomenon, despite China's large migrant population, which reached 236 million in 2012. Migrants often fill these jobs. This phenomenon has social and economic causes, including low salaries and constraint of the household system. This kind of labor shortage is not a gross shortage of labor but a structural shortage. This "labor shortage" in the catering industry has been discussed by numerous researchers, including Zhao and Ran, who analyzed the phenomenon and reported their findings in "Reasons and suggestions to the 'labor shortage' in Catering industry," Economic Research, 2011(31).

[12]Interview with the owner's husband on May 22, 2014.

Idealistic restaurant relied on its large social network to recruit workers from a pool of relatives, friends, villagers, and previous employees.[13]

After resolving her staffing problems, the owner had to find food. This was challenging because she could not buy food products from the market but had to find reliable farmers to grow vegetables without using chemical fertilizers and pesticide to raise chickens, pigs, and cattle without using manufactured feed. Many farmers use nonorganic commercial products and do not believe organic farming is effective.[14] Moreover, dishonest farmers may secretly use chemicals or pesticides despite assurances that they would not. Therefore, reliable farmers who rigidly follow the principles of organic farming need to be fostered in the long term. Initially, the owner had to persuade her parents, who farmed small plots of land and would adhere to the principles of organic farming, to produce food for her restaurant. They agreed to grow vegetables and raise livestock to support her restaurant, and they mobilize several relatives to assist them.

In addition to the staff and food, the owner had to raise start-up capital. With the support of the mother restaurant operated by the NGO, where she previously worked and benefit from its money raising methods, she received the opening fund of 360,000 CNY[15] from more than a dozen of shareholders. These shareholders included the mother restaurant, the owner, the owner's husband, the owner's young brother, and friends of the owner's husband. Each shareholder contributed a different amount of money, as little as 10,000 CNY or as much as 50,000 CNY.[16] Shareholders, except the owner's husband and young brother, were not involved in the operation and daily management of the restaurant, and she retained full responsibility for operating the restaurant. These investments were based on friendship or supporting the concept of CSA rather than on profit.

3.5 Learning to Play the Game

The owner's real difficulties with opening a restaurant would begin when applying for opening licenses. She felt she was not suited for business, and this seemed to be

---

[13] Although many platforms provide opportunities to find workers, such as online advertisements, onsite advertisements, and the formal labor market, social networks, or in another word Guanxi networks, still have an important function in finding employment or staff in China. To learn more about the role of social networks in occupational processes, refer to Yanjie Bian, "Chinese social stratification and social mobility," *Annual Review of Sociology*, 2002(28): 91–116.

[14] Chemical fertilizers became popular when China's markets opened in the late 1980s. The opening and reform sparked mass, lasting migration from rural areas to cities, which created labor shortages for farmers. Chemical fertilizer soon became popular due to the significant increase in yield and the labor savings they bring about. For more information about the history of chemical fertilizer in China, read Hui Fuping and Guo Ciming's 2012 paper.

[15] About 45,000 euro at 1 Euro = 8 CNY.

[16] Interview with the owner's husband, April 6, 2013.

the case as she navigated satisfying the numerous regulatory demands for starting her restaurant.

Before opening, a restaurant requires several opening licenses. Every individual business in China requires a business license, according to the "Individual Business Registration Regulation" issued by the State Administration for Industry and Commerce of the People's Republic of China.[17] In addition, for a restaurant, a special catering service license is required, according to Article 29 of the Food Safety Law of the People's Republic of China,[18] which states, "The State implements a licensing system for food production and trading. Any organization or individual shall obtain ... [a] catering service license according to law before engaging in ... catering service." Furthermore, an environmental license is required, as restaurants are considered environment polluters because they release cooking fumes and oily wastewater, and cause noise pollution, according to the Regulation for Administration of Pollutant Discharge License[19] issued by the Ministry of Environmental Protection of the People's Republic of China.

Because it is a public gathering place, a restaurant requires a fire license, according to article 15 of the Fire Control Law[20] of 2008, and a tax registration license[21] is required according to the Administration Regulation of Taxation Registration issued by the State Administration of Taxation. Moreover, a drainage license is required according to the 2006 Administration Regulation of City Water Discharge[22] issued by the Ministry of Housing and Urban–Rural Development. Additionally, a decoration license is needed if the restaurant wants to add structures such as awnings or lightboxes outside the building, and a liquor license[23] and tobacco selling license[24] are required if the restaurant intends to sell alcohol and tobacco. Finally, if cultural performances are planned for the restaurant, a Cultural Performance License is also required. Thus, five to ten licenses are required, which means the restaurant must deal with five to ten government administration departments.

Some of these licenses have to be obtained before the operation of the business, specifically the business license, environment license, catering services license, and decoration license, while some, that is, the fire license, tax registration license, drainage license, and liquor license, can be obtained after opening. According to

---

[17] http://www.saic.gov.cn/zcfg/xzgzjgfxwj/xxb/201403/t20140303_142668.html.

[18] For the English version of the food safety law, refer to http://www.lawinfochina.com/display.aspx?lib=law&id=7344&CGid=.

[19] This regulation is an exposure draft. There is no officially issued national regulation on pollutant discharge. However, many provinces, such as Yunnan, Guangdong, Jiangsu, and Zhejiang, have created their own provincial regulations.

[20] http://www.china.com.cn/policy/txt/2008-10/29/content_16680891.htm.

[21] http://www.chinatax.gov.cn/n480462/n4273674/n4273693/n4273747/n4329302/11214901.html.

[22] http://www.mohurd.gov.cn/zcfg/jsbgz/200701/t20070122_159090.html.

[23] See "Regulation Rule of Alcohol Circulation" issued by Ministry of Commerce in 2005. http://www.mofcom.gov.cn/aarticle/b/d/200511/20051100748397.html.

[24] See "Law of Tobacco Monopoly" issued by the NPC Standing Committee in 1991. http://www.tobacco.gov.cn/html/27/2701/270101/765012_n.html.

regulations, a restaurant must obtain the first four licenses before operation, but this is not strictly enforced in practice. Because applying for licenses takes time, restaurants are allowed to operate for several months before obtaining those licenses. For a summary of the licenses required, see Table 3.1.

Soon after she began applying for licenses, the owner of the Idealistic restaurant learned how difficult it was in practice to comply with the opening license requirements. She found it so difficult that she would later complain, "We just want to run the business honestly and do something good. But why do we always meet various obstacles and why do those government officers create obstacles like that?" To be in compliance, the first step is understanding the requirements and knowing what to do. However, for her, knowing the requirements seemed difficult and involved a great deal of interaction with inspectors and enforcement department officers.

Table 3.1 A summary of the opening licenses required for restaurants

Name of license	Law	Regulator	Application Interval
Business	Individual Business Registration Regulation	State Administration for Industry and Commerce	Before operation
Decoration	Regulation for Administration of City Road	City Management Department	Before starting decoration
Environmental	Regulation for Administration of Pollutant Discharge License	Ministry of Environmental Protection	Before obtaining business license
Catering services	Food Safety Law	Food and Drug Inspection and Administration Bureau	Before obtaining business license
Tax registration	Administration Regulation of Taxation Registration	State Administration of Taxation	After obtaining business license
Fire	Fire Control Law	Fire Control Bureau under the Ministry of Public Security	Before obtaining business license
Drainage	Administration Regulation of City Water Discharge	Drainage Department	After obtaining business license
Liquor	Regulation Rule of Alcohol Circulation	Alcohol Circulation Regulation Bureau under the Ministry of Commerce	After obtaining business license
Tobacco	Law of Tobacco Monopoly	National Tobacco Monopoly Bureau	After obtaining business license
Cultural performance		Ministry of Culture	After obtaining business license

The subsections that follow contain a description of the process of obtaining each license that shows how the Idealistic restaurant interacted with regulatory authorities, first to determine the requirements and then to ensure compliance.

3.5.1   Business License

The business license is the first opening license for which the restaurant needed to apply. According to article 14 of the Individual Business Registration Regulation, only four documents need to be submitted for a new registration. These are the registration application signed by the applicant, the applicant's identity certificate, the certificate of the business site, and other documents required by the State Administration for Industry and Commerce. Although the requirements look simple, they are far from clear regarding the format and exact content of those documents. The owner of the Idealistic restaurant visited to the Industrial and Commercial Administration Office (ICAO) more than seven times before all documents exactly met the requirements. For instance, the house rental contract would be checked as the certificate of the business site. However, several problems were found in this contract at different times. One problem was that the contract did not explicitly state that the house would be used as a restaurant, while another was that only one tenant should sign the document. Other problems included the name of the homeowner, the maximum rental period, and a lack of community permit certificate for opening a restaurant.

Every time the owner went to ICAO to submit her documents, the officer would point out a problem and ask her to correct it or to obtain additional certificates. After correcting the previous problem and submitting new documents, more problems would be pointed out, and she had to return. It seems the ICAO officers never inform applicants of the full requirements at once, or the government officers were unaware of the full requirements, as the leader raised questions after customer-facing staff submitted documents to him or her for the official stamp.

3.5.2   Catering Service License

The same lack of transparency appeared in the application process for a catering services license, which took four months to obtain. This time, fulfilling the requirements brought a moral dilemma for the owner of the Idealistic restaurant, as she could either engage in corruption and ensure the legal status of her restaurant or avoid corruption but face sanctions for running an illegal restaurant. She was confronted by both her idealistic nature and some government departments' pervasive corruption.

To obtain a catering services license, an onsite inspection is required to assess the condition of the kitchen equipment. However, the inspectors never pointed out all the problems during a single visit. They inspected the restaurant multiple times in four months, and every time, they would point out one problem. For instance, once they noticed that each cabinet containing dishware was labeled with hand-written paper, and they claimed that this was inadequate, as cupboards require printed labels. After correcting this, the owner called the inspectors to inform them that the correction had been made. Two weeks later, the inspectors visited again, and this time pointed out that the window between the kitchen and the hall for passing dishes was open without a shield. They claimed there should be an oil shield on the window. She installed the oil shield and reported back, but after another two weeks, they returned and noted that the kitchen required additional sinks. Although it had two sinks in the kitchen, they claimed that the restaurant should have at least three. One problem was pointed out after another, and each problem cost her half a month. Three months passed, but the inspectors still seemed dissatisfied with the restaurant's equipment and facilities, and denied the business a catering service license.

Friends reminded her that she should give the inspectors some *hongbao*,[25] or money in the red envelope, which is a euphemism for a bribe. To give *hongbao* seems an open secret for those running restaurants, but she found the practice immoral, saying, "Someone mentioned that to me. But I just do not want to do that, you know, to encourage such unhealthy and evil phenomena."[26] Nevertheless, she saw no option but had to give *hongbao* this time to obtain the catering service license. She felt forced to offer a bribe, although she provided the inspectors with gifts rather than cash. During their last visit, the inspectors arrived at lunchtime. She invited them for lunch and again introduced their restaurant to them. After lunch, each inspector received some gifts. During that lunch, the inspectors pointed out all other requirements, and soon after, she made the necessary changes and finally received the catering services license.

3.5.3 Fire License

Before applying for the fire license, the owner's friends and other restaurant owners warned her that this would be the most difficult license to obtain because the army is responsible for this license, and they claimed that the inspectors have a big appetite (*Weikou Da*), which means they demand large bribes. A friend's restaurant in another province was fined 20,000 CNY for not having a fire license. Another friend, who was serving in the army, told her that this time she also should give inspectors *hongbao* and promised to look for acquaintances in the army to help her pass on *hongbao*.

---

[25]In China, *hongbao* is based partly on folklore. It originally referred to money placed in a red envelope and offered as greeting gifts during certain festivals, such as Spring Festival; on special celebratory occasions, such as birthdays; or to express appreciation to someone, such as the money the groom gives the bridesmaid as a sign of appreciation for accompanying the bride. However, currently this word has a broader use, as it also refers to money and benefits in exchange for receiving benefits. For example, a patient would give a doctor *hongbao* in the hope that the doctor moves him up the surgery schedule. Xianghong Zhou and Li Tian analyzed the phenomenon of *hongbao* in hospitals in "Analyzing *hongbao* in hospital," Society, 2001(10).

[26]Interview with the owner of the Idealistic restaurant on May 30, 2012.

This time, scared by the advice she receive, she agreed to offer *hongbao* in exchange for a fire license.

While both psychological and physical prepared for giving *Hongbao* this time, the owner experienced a dramatic shift regarding bribes. Although prepared to give *Hongbao*, the Idealistic restaurant satisfied and even exceed the requirements set out by the Fire Control Administration Department. She had bought more fire extinguishers than required because her restaurant needed more. Several days after launching her application, the inspectors came. The owner's husband, tried to hand each inspector *hongbao* that was prepared in advance, an envelope containing 500 CNY, but he was refused! Moreover, the inspectors pointed out only one problem— the door. The main door in the Idealistic restaurant opened inward instead of outward, as required. She changed the door and reported the change to the inspector by phone. She was surprised to learn that without additional inspections or needing to submit photographic evidence, the license was ready for collection after paying the training fee of 1200 CNY. The only time they were prepared to give *hongbao*, it was not required. She never knew why inspectors refused the *hongbao* they offered, and it was ascribed to their incapability to deal with such matters. As the chef and manager, the owner's brother, explained, "We do not know how to make contact with them [inspectors]. Even if we want to give them *Hongbao*, we don't know how to do it in the right way. We just cannot make it."[27]

3.5.4   Drainage License

The most significant problem with the drainage license was not meeting the requirements but having the required personnel check the equipment. Unlike the catering services license that is an essential opening license for a restaurant and a prerequisite for the business license, the drainage license can be obtained after the restaurant has opened. The owner of the Idealistic restaurant was not aware of this license before inspectors from the Drainage Department came to check her restaurant. When the inspectors first came, the head chef claimed they commented on the restaurant's drainage facilities and wastewater equipment with "it is acceptable and qualifies" and "the water is clean" when walking through the restaurant and checking the kitchen. However, later, while filling in the form, the inspectors noted that "grease has not been segregated completely."[28] They demanded that the Idealistic restaurant obtain a drainage license by the conclusion of the meeting. The owner thought little of it and visited the Drainage Department offices to begin the application. She began to prepare the materials needed by following the instruction, as she did previously for other licenses. Nevertheless, she did not realize what was taking place behind the scenes.

---

[27]Interview with the head chef of the Idealistic restaurant on May 22, 2013.

[28]Interview with the owner of the Idealistic restaurant, on May 30, 2012, and interview with the head chef of the Idealistic restaurant, on May 22, 2013.

One day, the owner received a call from the inspector who had checked the drainage system, and he informed her they would collect the required materials the next evening. Following her catering services license experience, she knew to prepare dinner for them, but she was still not familiar with the underlying rules. During dinner, she handed the inspectors all materials they had mentioned on the phone, and then the inspector asked, "Nothing else?" and she answered, "Nothing." She did not realize what the question meant until several days later.

After dinner, the inspectors left her a telephone number and asked her to call someone to examine the wastewater system, but the person who answered always claimed to be too busy to come, and the inspector who gave her the number never returned. Her friend reminded her that the inspector might have been asking for *hongbao* when he asked, "Nothing else?" After almost a year, no one had come to examine the wastewater system. During this period, someone who claimed to be from the same government department came to the restaurant and was invited to have dinner twice, but instead of helping them complete the application procedure, the person suggested abandoning their application. However, the owner stressed, "We want to get the license. We surely want to."[29]

The owner of the Idealistic restaurant finally obtained the Drainage License with the help of a friend who had an acquaintance who worked in the relevant Drainage Department. The acquaintance helped them to contact a water quality testing station, and the station staff asked the owner to bring some wastewater to the station for examination. Before she took the water, the acquaintance advised her not to take the real wastewater but to take cleaner water. What is surprising is that the owner and her brother (the chef) intended to take pure tap water because they was afraid other water would not pass the test.[30] At the suggestion of that friend, they added a small amount of water in which vegetables had been washed. They obtained the license six days later.

3.5.5 Decoration License

Compared to the subtlety employed by other departments, the city management department (Chengguan) brazenly asked for *Hongbao*. The owner spent 1000 CNY while decorating the restaurant for dealing with inspectors from this department. One day while workers were constructing decorative structures, inspectors from the city management department performed an inspection and informed the owner that she did not have a decoration license. These inspectors went on to ask the owner whether she wanted to follow the formal procedures of sanctions or deal with it in private. They explained, although the owner felt they threatened her, that if she dealt with

---

[29]Interview with the owner of the Idealistic restaurant on April 16, 2013.

[30]The owner's brother observed the same inspectors taking pure tap water from the neighboring restaurant, and that restaurant received its drainage license soon after. Interview with the owner's brother on April 16, 2013.

it in private, she would simply give them money and receive a receipt. Afterward, she could carry on with the fitment construction. If she wanted to follow the formal procedure of sanctions, all machines and materials used for decoration would be confiscated and the decoration would have to cease. Moreover, the formal procedure would take 10–15 days. Feeling threatened, the owner answered that they chose to deal with it in private.[31] After giving them 1000 CNY, without making any changes, the owner continued with the decoration construction.

3.5.6   Environmental License

After obtaining all the licenses that tested her intelligence, emotions, social skills, and morality, the owner found the application process for the environmental license surprisingly easy. She asked a company specializing in this field to install all the required equipment. The environmental inspector visited once, took some photographs, and did not point out any problems. It took seven working days to obtain the license. The owner attributed this to the fulfillment of the licensing requirements, stating, "[The] environmental license is easy because we satisfied all of their requirements, and the purify capacity of the equipment even exceed what the license required."[32]

3.5.7   Compliance as Clarification Process for Opening Licenses

The processes of obtaining the opening licenses shows how the Idealistic restaurant interacted with the enforcement departments and inspectors to clarify the exact requirements that needed to be met to comply with legislations. This differs from the negotiation process, as indicated in several endogenous studies, where the legal norm is vague and requires clarification according to the situation on site. For example, Huising and Silbey's (2011) study of the safety regulation at a university showed that what is considered a clear corridor differs from site to site and needs to be specified and negotiated on each site. On each site, a level of "clear enough" for safety considerations was specified depending on the corridors, inhabitants, activities, buildings, and sometimes even the city block. Both the regulator and the regulated are involved in negotiating the acceptable situation with which the regulated should comply.

Lange (1999) studied license compliance on waste sites and found the conditions for the license usually were not imposed by the regulatory authority upon the regulated but were negotiated. For example, the volume of waste that can be contained on one waste site may be adjusted based on the specific conditions on the waste

---

[31] Interview with the owner of the Idealistic restaurant on May 30, 2012.

[32] Interview with the owner of the Idealistic restaurant on May 30, 2012.

site rather than according to the standard numbers listed on the license. If the waste control officer felt that the amount of waste handled on a site, despite being well within the volume allowed by the site license, caused other operational problems, the officer would negotiate with the site owner to reduce the volume of waste on the license. Conversely, on another site, when the waste control officer found that the site owner was storing more waste than the license allowed but that it caused no further problems, the officer suggested amending the license to allow the site store more waste.

However, in the case of the Idealistic restaurant, in terms of the requirements of a kitchen and contract that meet requirements, these requirements were not negotiated bilaterally. Instead, the regulator issued demands that the regulated met. During the business license application, to comply with the requirements of the rental contract, the Idealistic restaurant corrected one problem after another following the directions of the ICAO officers. This was a clarification rather than a negotiation process, as it involved clarifying detailed requirements that rely on explanation and verification by inspectors or enforcement department officers.

During the clarification process, the Idealistic restaurant felt forced to break anti-corruption laws by engaging in bribery. In the process of applying for the fire license, the Idealistic restaurant heard about other restaurants' experiences, specifically that "many restaurants cannot satisfy requirements of Fire License, as it has extremely strict requirements; that is, all materials you use for decoration should be fireproofing."[33] The business owner was further scared after hearing about the fine imposed on another restaurant for not having this license. Consequently, the Idealistic restaurant felt it necessary to prepare *Hongbao* in an attempt to engage in bribery. The restaurant owner did not choose to bribe officials to overlook violations of fire license requirements and, in fact, over-complied by buying more fire extinguishers than required. The bribe was intended to secure the inspectors' cooperation.

The process of obtaining a catering service license clarifies this point. Friends suggested that the owner give inspectors *Hongbao*, but she felt reluctant to do so because she thought it immoral. Yet the Idealistic restaurant repeatedly corrected every problem inspectors pointed for four months without satisfying the inspectors. The owner thought, "Maybe because I did not give inspectors *Hongbao*, the inspectors came to check again and again."[34] Obtaining the license became a considerable problem, and beginning the period of trial operation added urgency. As a result, for inspectors to full acknowledge how the business could satisfy their requirements, the owner invited them for lunch and gave them gifts. Subsequently, the inspectors fully clarified the requirements, and she ensured that the restaurant complied. Again, she engaged in bribery not to evade the requirements but to gain the cooperation of the inspectors.

---

[33] Interview with the owner of the Idealistic restaurant on May 22, 2012.

[34] Interview with the owner of the Idealistic restaurant on May 22, 2012.

3.6   Daily Operation

The owner and her staff confronted many legal requirements in the daily operation of the Idealistic restaurant, some she clearly knew, some she partly knew, and some she did not know at all. In this part, compliance behaviors related to six daily operational requirements—meat quarantine certificates, dish disinfection, health certificates, *Fapiao* receipts, handwashing, and nail cutting—are described. Compared to the period of obtaining opening licenses, the interaction between the restaurant and inspectors decreased, but the interaction between the restaurant owner and workers increased in the development process of daily operational compliance behaviors. Furthermore, the restaurant culture and operation ideology are embodied by these compliance behaviors.

3.6.1   Pork and Chicken

The Idealistic restaurant sourced most food products directly from farmers, and organic pork and chicken were especially popular menu items. Although the restaurant advertised the slaughter of a pig fed traditionally, without manufactured feeds, according to article 26 of the Food Safety Law, it is forbidden to sell meat from animals that have not undergone quarantine. Usually, restaurants buy their meat from the market, and this meat has passed quarantine checks and has a quarantine certificate. Therefore, restaurants can obtain quarantine certificates directly from butchers. Yet what would the owner do, as they slaughter their own pigs?

Initially, the Idealistic restaurant slaughtered pigs in the traditional manner,[35] and using traditional food preparation methods was an important value for this restaurant. However, to do so, they needed to rise early in the morning, hire a butcher, boil a large pot of water, and help the butcher slaughter the pig. Later, they would buy a quarantine certificate from the butcher in the market to pretend their pork passed the quarantine check despite this not being the case. The owner believed their pork was much better than those sold in the market, despite not being checked, as the farmers feed the pigs natural, not manufactured food. Thus, they bought the counterfeit certificates not to cheat customers but to comply with the requirements of Food and Drug Administration Bureau (FDA) inspectors.

Later, the owner and her husband, who is also the co-owner of the Idealistic restaurant, thought it troublesome to slaughter pigs themselves, as it became difficult to negotiate time with the butcher, and obtaining the quarantine certificate was inconvenient. They decided to slaughter the pigs at a local slaughterhouse. Consequently, they simply needed to pay the slaughtering fee (30 CNY) and obtain the quarantine certificate (10 CNY) instead of paying the butcher and finding a quarantine certificate.

---

[35]Traditionally, villagers slaughter their pigs themselves or invite a butcher to help them with the slaughter at home.

On the surface, the owner did not comply with the legal norm and initially was dishonest, as she bought counterfeit quarantine certificates instead of sending her pigs to be checked, but later she followed official guidelines by having the pigs slaughtered in a slaughterhouse and obtaining genuine quarantine certificates. However, substantively the two methods do not differ in terms of food safety. According to the owner, the certificate does not mean the pork has been checked; it only means the pig was slaughtered in a certified slaughterhouse. When asked whether the pork had been checked in the slaughterhouse, she did not offer a direct answer. Instead, she claimed, "The slaughterhouse does not really do what they should do [check the pigs properly]. The quarantine check is just a fraud."

Her husband and her young brother expressed their scorn of quarantine certificates more explicitly when asked whether the pork had been checked in the slaughterhouse. Her husband said, "What is the certificate, you know? [They] just glance at the pig and give you a certificate." Her young brother added, "Even without a glance!" I followed the question with, "It is ridiculous. But you still want to get that quarantine certificate, don't you?" They simultaneously answered, "They will be checked, anyway." Her husband further elaborated on his deep suspicion about the quarantine check:

> I really doubt about those so called scientific tests. You see we slaughter pigs from long generations ago and there is no problems. But they just come out with such kind of quarantine check. What kind of use do it indeed have?[36]

Thus, the meat quarantine certificate may have been counterfeit, but the genuine certificate did not indicate the quality of their pork. Even so, the owner still obtains the certificate because "sometimes the inspector will check them." In other words, the Idealistic restaurant obtains these certificates only because the inspectors sometimes check them.

The restaurant's treatment of chicken exemplified this attitude. Although, according to the Food Safety Law, all meat should have undergone a quarantine check before selling it, the Idealistic restaurant did not have quarantine certificates for their chicken, even during the bird flu outbreak. The owner and her young brother (the chef) were asked separately whether they had quarantine check certificates for the chicken without implying any related rule. Both said they were unaware that quarantine certificate were required for chicken and that these certificates were required only for pork. In addition, the inspectors check only certificates for pork.[37]

Lacking a quarantine certificate does not mean that they paid no attention to meat safety per se. As the Idealistic restaurant emphasizes in its slogan, "to be careful of the food material," the restaurant follows the basic traditional principle of what is safe chicken, that is, live chicken, although this may not always be enough to overcome the complex contemporary food safety challenges such as bird flu. When her young brother was asked whether he knows how to prevent bird flu or how to process chicken, he answered no, but he discussed his understanding of it: "I think

---

[36]Interview with the owner's husband on May 22, 2013.

[37]Interview with the head chef of the Idealistic restaurant on April 17, 2013, and interview with the owner of the Idealistic restaurant on April 16, 2013.

bird flu maybe a matter about the dead chicken. We definitely do not cook the chicken if it is dead." He relayed an anecdote about dead chickens. Once, they transported four chickens from the village to the restaurant, which took more than two hours. Two of the four chickens in the bag, which had no holes for ventilation, had died upon arriving at the restaurant. Without hesitation, he threw them into the garbage can.[38]

3.6.2 Dishware Disinfection

Apart from food sourcing and handling, dishware disinfection is one of the most important and well-know requirements of food safety. According to article 27(5) of the Food Safety Law,[39] all dishes, cups, and containers that contain food eaten directly must be disinfected before use. On the operational level, restaurants are required to have a disinfection cabinet, clean cabinets to store the clean dishware, and records of the disinfecting log.[40] Inspectors check the first two requirements when a restaurant applies for a catering services license, and without this equipment, the catering services license will not be issued. However, this does not mean that this measure is strictly implemented to safeguard food safety in restaurants, as it focuses only on the appearance of such disinfection equipment without significant consideration of whether the capacity meets the volume of dishware in the restaurant. Many restaurants have only small disinfection cabinets that can hold hardly a quarter of their tableware. In addition, disinfection log records are supposed to be checked during inspections to ensure restaurants disinfect their tableware daily. However, news reports have exposed many restaurants that do not use their disinfection cabinets to disinfect tableware but only as dishware containers.[41] Many disinfection cabinets are never even turned on.

In the case of the Idealistic restaurant, when entering the restaurant, a stainless steel disinfecting cabinet measuring approximately 1.7 by 0.8 m was clearly visible upon entering the restaurant. It was large enough to accommodate most of the restaurant's tableware, including chopsticks, spoons, cups, plates, and bowls. It could reach temperatures of up to 120 °C, and it could be operated for 1–60 min. Every time the dishwasher completed washing the tableware, two servers would use a bamboo basket to carry all washed items to the cabinet, where they would place them inside one by one and turn on the machine for 15–40 min depending on the number of items. Once

---

[38] Later, the dishwasher picked them up, saying, "They did not die from disease. What a shame to throw them away! We can still eat them." She took them home and cooked them.

[39] http://www.gov.cn/flfg/2009-02/28/content_1246367.htm.

[40] Conclusions about operational requirements were drawn from interviews with six restaurant owners, who showed the same level of concern when talking about disinfecting dishes.

[41] This phenomenon is common in China. See http://food.china.com/hsjs/11101762/20111124/168 84538.html and http://www.chinanews.com/sh/2014/03-18/5961403.shtml.

the cycle was complete, the door would be opened to allow the items to cool before they were returned to two large plastic boxes for storage.

The disinfection operation was simply one of the servers' daily duties at the Idealistic restaurant. However, although they disinfected the dishware twice a day, they failed to complete the disinfection operation log every time as requested by inspectors. The owner was aware of this and stated, "We disinfect food wares every day but actually do not necessarily need to record every time."[42] She viewed the completion of these records as unnecessary, and this may have influenced the servers' attitudes. On August 5, 2013, the records had been completed only until July 15, 2013, and almost an entire month had been left blank. When the owner noticed the problem, she called over the lead server, Mei, who was responsible for this work to "come to fill in the records, otherwise we will get trouble if inspectors come to check." When asked why Mei did not fill in the records every day, the owner replied that "she probably dislikes being bothered with this thing." When asked whether she thought it necessary to complete the records every day, she sighed and said, "Alas, for people like us complying with the law so much… also it is not possible to be so perfect".

In addition to not filling in the records in time, two more flaws were found in their disinfection practice. The first relates to the required time for operating the disinfection cabinet. The servers did not know the correct disinfection times, as they had not received training. They simply chose the disinfection period based on their judgment of the amount of tableware, with some cycles as short as 15 min and others as long as 40 min. They used the dryness of the sanitized objects as a guide. If they chose 25 min the previous time, but found that some dishes were still wet, they would add 5 or 10 min for the same amount next time. Therefore, every server had her own standards and judgments.

Another flaw was that the big plates and bowls used to serve food to the entire table were not disinfected; only those for personal use were disinfected, such as chopsticks, spoons, small bowls, small plates, and cups. Servers' understanding of disinfection helps them to understand the reason for disinfecting the dishes. Once, when I was helping a server load the disinfection cabinet, she placed a wooden spoon used for fetching rice in the cabinet too. The server, Yan, stopped her, saying, "We don't need to put that in the cabinet." When I asked why, she answered, "It doesn't need to [go in]." When asked, "Then why do we disinfect other food wares?" she explained, "Because every customer uses chopsticks and small bowls to eat. These food wares touch customers' mouths directly, but the wooden spoon doesn't."[43] In their opinions, dishes are disinfected to prevent transmitting diseases from one customer to other customers. Hence, it is important to destroy the viruses from customers that may remain on the tableware they have used, but shared wares, such as plates, big bowls, and wooden spoons for fetching rice that do not touch customers' mouths have not been contaminated by customers and do not need to be disinfected.

---

[42]Interview with the owner of the Idealistic restaurant on May 28, 2013.
[43]Observation records from April 9, 2013.

3.6.3   Health Certificate

The display at the front entrance that contained the Idealistic restaurant's licenses also featured health certificates for the restaurant's workers. These cards show servers' and kitchen workers' photos, and the number of health certificates displayed varied from time to time, when the certificates of workers who had resigned were removed or when the certificates of new workers were added. These certificates are important measures for maintaining food safety in China. According to article 34 of the Food Safety Law, people who produce or sell food should undergo an annual health check and may work only after obtaining a health certificate. However, it is a common phenomenon in China that restaurant workers do not have their health certificates (Deng 2002). Moreover, according to news reports, in some regions, restaurant workers do not undergo health checks and hold counterfeit health certificates.[44]

At the Idealistic restaurant, workers did undergo health checks and obtain genuine health certificates. In the view of the owner, health certificates are important guarantees that their employees are healthy. When I casually spoke to the owner's husband, who is critical of the laws in China, about the recent strict enforcement of red crossing rules, the electronic motorcycle rule implemented several months prior, and the rating system for restaurants implemented a year earlier, he mentioned the health certificate system. When asked what he thought about the rules regarding health certificates, he answered, "It is good and should be a must condition. To working in catering industry, you have to make sure you don't have infectious diseases."[45]

However, not all workers at the Idealistic restaurant had health certificates, and not all workers obtained their health certificates before they began working there. A 66-year-old dishwasher did not have a health certificate while working at the Idealistic restaurant because, according to her, "[she's] very old already." She asked the head chef, who administered employees' health certificates, to overlook her lack of certificate due to her age, and the chef agreed. In addition, a kitchen worker who had been working at the Idealistic restaurant for less than a month had not undergone a health check and did not hold a health certificate, and a university student who worked at the Idealistic restaurant for three months did not obtain a health certificate.

Generally, the Idealistic restaurant would take its new employees to complete health checks and to obtain their health certificates, and workers remained at the restaurant for relatively long periods.

3.6.4   Handwashing

In restaurants, food is processed and served using the hands of the restaurants' workers. Thus, hand sanitation is an essential aspect of food safety. In "Operational Norms of Catering Services for Food Safety" issued by the National Food and

---

[44]http://diet.qx100.com/html/200607/3559794108327.shtml.
[45]Interview with the owner's husband on May 22, 2013.

Drug Administration Bureau in 2011, the importance of washing hands is explicitly stated.[46] It identifies eight conditions under which a worker should wash his or her hands. They are before processing food; after going to the toilet; after touching raw food materials; after touching polluted tools or equipment; after coughing, sneezing, and blowing one's nose; after dealing with animals or garbage; after touching one's ears, nose, hair, face, mouth, or other body parts; and after any activities that may pollute the hands. However, compared to obvious norms and requirements such as health certification and dishware disinfection, the washing of hands is a less visible requirement generally viewed as a personal hygiene norm. Few restaurants in China consider it a formal rule, including several upper-class establishments. None of the staff in the restaurants in which I conducted fieldwork could correctly indicate under which circumstances they should wash their hands. The owners, managers, and workers at the Idealistic restaurant were not aware that handwashing is regulated by legal norms.

Nevertheless, the Idealistic restaurant developed its own handwashing rules, specifically that workers must wash their hands after going to the toilet. Although this sounds like a basic rule a mother teaches her children, it highlights the Idealistic restaurant's focus on hand hygiene. Before implementing this rule, the owner observed that a kitchen worker did not wash his hands before entering the kitchen after going to the toilet. This angered her, as the thought washing one's hands after going to the toilet should be a basic norm and habit for everyone. She called the workers together and announced that every worker must wash his or her hands after going to the toilet.

The restaurant had five sinks: one in the entrance hall used by servers and customers; three are at the entrance to the kitchen, where all food materials and dishware were washed (one of which was removed later), and where kitchen workers washed their hands; and one outside the kitchen near the disposal area, where the garbage can, food waste bucket, and dirty table covers are placed. Workers usually washed their hands at the last sink after going to the toilet or disposing of garbage or waste and before entering the kitchen.

Except after going to the toilet, there were no specific regulations indicating when servers should wash their hands. While they may have washed their hands after clearing tables after customers leave, this did not occur every time, and they usually washed their hands only when they felt their hands were dirty or oily. For instance, Lian, a server, failed to wash her hands after clearing a table. On another occasion, she did not wash her hands, but she washed the cap of a teapot after clearing the table, and another time, although she did not wash her hands purposely, she washed the basin before making steamed bread buns. Nevertheless, she washed her hands immediately after tying her shoelace.

Servers usually washed their hands whenever they felt they needed to wash them depending on their personal norms. When I first began the participant observation at the Idealistic restaurant, I asked a server for details of what I should do to learn their norms of working. Once while helping Lian set tables for the coming dinner period,

---

[46]Refer to http://www.foodmate.net/law/shipin/173257.html.

I "suddenly realized" I had not washed my hands before fetching the clean dishware and asked, "Oh, I haven't washed my hands. Do I need to wash my hands?" Lian did not answer immediately, but after a minute she answered, "It is OK, I can set the table." I realized that she might have thought this was an excuse for not wanting to help with setting the tables, so I said, "It doesn't matter. I help you" and began setting the table without washing hands. Lian responded, "It doesn't matter whether you wash your hands or not." However, on a different occasion, when a drink spilled on my hand while I was helping Lian carry an order, Lian immediately asked me to wash hands. When asked why, Lian answered, "Such strong smell. It is not good if customers smell the alcohol from your hands." Nevertheless, different servers wash their hands differently. For example, although Lian did not wash her hands before making steamed bread buns, Yan did.

3.6.5   Keeping Nails Short

Keeping nails short is a norm identified in article 12 of "Operational Norms of Catering Services for Food Safety" issued by the National Food and Drug Administration Bureau in 2011.[47] It is a working norm generally known to all people working in restaurants, but it is not known as a legal requirement. This applied at the Idealistic restaurant, where most workers kept their nails short. According to the head chef, in the beginning some workers often forgot to cut their nails, and he simply reminded them to cut their nails without mentioning any punishment. However, he found that this did not work, as many workers still forgot to cut their nails short. He subsequently announced that those who had long nails would be fined 5 CNY per nail. After that, he seldom saw workers with long nails. The threat of sanctions was effective, and workers were reminded to cut their nails. When I asked Lian why she cut her nails so short, she answered, "Boss required, otherwise I will be fined."

However, it seems the effect of the threat of sanctions was limited. One day after that, I noticed Lian had long nails. When asked why she did not cut her nails this time, Lian answered, "I like to have relatively long nails." I asked, "Aren't you afraid of being caught by the boss?" Lian answered, "I will cut them short when they find out." When asked whether she was afraid of being find, Lian casually replied, "Then [I must be] fined."

---

[47]Refer to http://www.foodmate.net/law/shipin/173257.html.

3.6.6 "Fapiao" Receipts

Customers who eat at restaurants should receive *Fapiao*,[48] or tax, receipts. Restaurants can obtain their receipts either by buying a certain number of printed receipts from the taxation bureau in advance or by buying a permit to print a specific number of receipts from the taxation bureau. Article 20 of the *Fapiao* receipt Management Rule of the People's Republic of China[49] states that a "company or individual who sells products, provides services, and [engages in] other business activities should issue invoices to customers." It implies that restaurants should pay tax based on total turnover.

In practice, restaurants neither pay tax based on their total turnover nor issue *Fapiao* receipts to every customer. Restaurants pay tax based on their estimated turnover, which is calculated by the tax department and fixed for a certain period, usually at least a year. Moreover, in the view of restaurant owners, once a restaurant increases the estimated turnover amount, there is no way to decrease it. Consequently, restaurants often attempt to keep their estimated turnover as low as possible to pay as little tax as possible. Some restaurants do not issue *Fapiao* receipts to customers even if customers request them,[50] as this allows them to buy fewer *Fapiao* receipts and pay less tax.

Nevertheless, the Idealistic restaurant twice increased the number of *Fapiao* receipts they bought from the tax department; thus, they voluntarily pay more tax. In the first year, the Idealistic restaurant was estimated to pay 20,000 CNY per month in tax. However, in the second year, it took the initiative to increase the amount to 40,000 CNY per month when average turnover increased to 60,000 CNY, and in the third year, it again increased its payments to 60,000 CNY per month when the average turnover rose to around 90,000 CNY per month. the Idealistic restaurant kept raising the amount related to *Fapiao* receipts because it gave almost every customer a *Fapiao* receipt once requested to do so, and it did not issue counterfeit receipts. As the turnover increased, the restaurant increased its purchases of *Fapiao* receipts. It did not hide its increased turnover from the tax department.

Although the number of *Fapiao* receipts bought each month is relatively fixed, turnover often fluctuates. In some months, especially in winter when there are less customers, the restaurant had surplus *Fapiao* receipts, while in other months, especially in summer, it did not have enough *Fapiao* receipts, as requests for receipts increased. There has been an ongoing trend of China strengthening its finance management through regulating *Fapiao* receipts. For example, researchers must use *Fapiao* receipts to show their spending of research funds, and teachers and other public employees are required to hand in certain types of *Fapiao* receipts to claim certain rewards or payments. In addition, government officers need to use *Fapiao* receipts to show the spending of various public funds, and private companies need

---

[48] *Fapiao* is the Chinese term for a formal receipt bought from the tax department. It is a method of collecting tax.

[49] http://www.chinaacc.com/new/63/67/81/2005/12/dr65075413310321500219845-0.htm.

[50] See news reports, such as http://finance.china.cn/consume/xfjs/20120912/1014854.shtml.

to use *Fapiao* receipts to show their business spending and paying of tax. Thus, *Fapiao* receipts are important financial management instruments nationwide. As a result, people in these sectors collect *Fapiao* receipts as often as possible to claim reimbursements and rewards in future. Although a meal is seldom a business affair, customers may ask for *Fapiao* receipts to use them for other reimbursements or payment related to their projects or work.

Several methods are used to address the invoice shortage when it arises. The first is to provide customers with an informal receipt and ask them to return next month for the formal *Fapiao* receipt. Regular customers may agree to this, as was the case at the Idealistic restaurant. However, some customers forget to or simply do not return to fetch the *Fapiao* receipt. In some months, the Idealistic restaurant issued such informal receipts worth over 10,000 CNY. Although this is an effective means of dealing with short-term receipt shortages and surpluses and of dealing with receipt shortages, some restaurants use it to avoid issuing *Fapiao* receipts.[51] Hence, some customers became suspicious of the informal receipts and did not believe they would receive the formal invoices, so they refused informal receipts from the Idealistic restaurant.

The second method of dealing with receipt shortages involves borrowing *Fapiao* receipts from other restaurants. In some cases, the Idealistic restaurant borrowed *Fapiao* receipts from nearby restaurants if customers insisted on obtaining receipts and refused the informal receipts. Other restaurants borrowed receipts from the Idealistic restaurant in turn, and this is common practice in the restaurant industry.

A third alternative is offering discount to customers who claim *Fapiao* receipts but do not intend to use them for reimbursement. When the *Fapiao* receipts were going to run out at the end of a month, the servers would ask some customers who claimed *Fapiao* receipts whether they would accept discount in place of a receipt. Some customers were happy with this arrangement. Usually, if the bill exceeded 150 CNY, it would be reduced by 7 CNY. On bills between 100 and 150 CNY, 5 CNY would be discounted, but bills below 100 CNY usually would not be discounted. The discount calculation was not fixed, and it could increase or decrease a little, depending on the bill amount, the discount the customers requested, the difficulty of dealing with the customers, and even the mood of the server. Generally, the discount would not exceed the tax rate of 7.6%. Servers also did not ask every customer who claimed a *Fapiao* receipt. There was no uniform rule at the Idealistic restaurant about when to ask whether the customer would be willing to forgo a receipt. Servers would guess whether customers would use the *Fapiao* receipts for reimbursement, or they would ask when they felt like doing so.

The fourth technique for dealing with a *Fapiao* receipt shortage was to reuse invoice from other restaurants where the owners ate. Customers would accept these used invoices although they bore the stamp of a restaurant other than the Idealistic restaurant.

---

[51] News outlets have reported that some restaurant owners use this method to avoid giving customers invoices and to pay less tax. See http://qkzz.net/article/48ee7734-60b1-4243-bc77-50bb27f95e06.htm.

Some restaurants address the *Fapiao* receipt shortage by issuing counterfeit receipts. However, the owner refused to engage in this practice. An employee from a nearby shop who often came to the Idealistic restaurant mentioned the fake *Fapiao* receipts to her. She said she knew a street full of restaurants used them, and she knew the telephone number of the person who sold the counterfeit receipts. The fake *Fapiao* receipts are cheap, with 100,000 selling for only 500 CNY when the same number of authentic receipts would cost about 7500 CNY. Her husband considered the employee's suggestion, but she steadfastly refused. When I asked why, she answered, "We will be fined if it is discovered. As much as a couple of thousand." When asked whether the possibility of discovery is high, she answered, "I think it is high. Moreover, if customers know we use fake *Fapiao* receipts, we may lose them."[52]

3.6.7 Compliance as Interactive Process of Restaurant Ideology and Legal Requirements in Daily Operation Norms

The case study shows that the Idealistic restaurant did not fully comply with the six legal norms identified during daily operation. Specifically, the restaurant had quarantine certificates for its pork but not for its chicken, and it disinfected most, but not all, of its tableware. In addition, most workers had health certificates, but some did not, and although the restaurant voluntarily increased its tax contributions and refused to use counterfeit *Fapiao* receipts, its compliance with *Fapiao* receipt requirements remained flawed. Moreover, its internal rules related to washing hands did not completely align with the corresponding legal norms, and despite requiring that workers have short fingernails, workers did not strictly adhere to this rule.

The description of the compliance process highlights not only the intertwining of legal norms and organizational values but also the contests between the two. For example, the Idealistic restaurant initially wanted to slaughter pigs the traditional way to embody their idea of supporting small farmers and "using the closest way to the earth mother to make food."[53] However, using this traditional method meant it could not obtain the meat quarantine certificates required by food safety laws. Later, despite complying with regulations and having their pigs slaughtered at a certified facility, they did not recognize the legitimacy of the quarantine certificates they received, based on their experience.

As for dish disinfection, the belief that disinfection is extremely important for safeguarding customers' health is consistent with the disinfection legal norm. The Idealistic restaurant agreed with the aim of this legal norm and practiced it in its own way in terms of using organic cleaners and a high-quality heating disinfection cabinet. The restaurant's disinfection facilities exceeded the legal requirements and surpassed

---

[52]Interview with the owner of the Idealistic restaurant on May 29, 2013.

[53]This is one of the restaurant's slogans, or *"yong zui tu de fang fa zuo cai"* in Chinese.

the facilities of its peers. In addition, the daily task of dish disinfection was practiced well, and it had become a habit and part of everyday work. Nevertheless, the Idealistic restaurant felt some of the requirements, particularly completing the disinfection log, were mechanical and not required for effective disinfection. They viewed them as a waste of time and energy. Correspondingly, the requirement of completing a disinfection log was not strictly followed. The same interaction between legal requirements and restaurant values occurred in other daily operations. For example, despite believing in the importance of the legal requirement of health certificates, restaurant management has its own ideas of when the requirement is appropriate.

Subjectively, during the compliance process, conflict arose between restaurant values and requirements. The rationality of the aim, method, application conditions, and risks of every legal requirement was considered and measured against the values of the organization. The corresponding compliance behaviors reflect this process of conflict.

3.7   Discussion

3.7.1   Classifying Compliance Behaviors at the Idealistic Restaurant

This chapter has focused on describing the various compliance behaviors observed at the Idealistic restaurant, both those related to opening license requirements and those related to daily operation legal norms, by tracing back the process of how these behaviors emerged and developed. In this case, the process paints a complex compliance picture (summarized in Table 3.2). Various kinds of compliance introduced in Chap. 2 emerged in this case, and some nuanced forms of compliance appeared. In this section, these compliance behaviors are categorized as beyond compliance, partial compliance, attempted compliance, fraudulent compliance, skeptical compliance, conflictive compliance, and symbolic compliance.

Beyond-compliance behaviors exceed the legal requirements. In the case of the Idealistic restaurant, these behaviors include installing an environmental protection facility that exceeded legal requirements, buying more fire extinguishers than required, using environmentally friendly organic cleaner that leaves no chemical reside on dishes, and supplying organic good food that goes beyond the legal food safety regulations.

Several behaviors at the Idealistic restaurant can be classified as partial compliance. For instance, the restaurant had excellent dish disinfection facilities, and the tableware for personal service was disinfected daily to prevent the spread of diseases. This reflects genuine compliance that conforms to both the content and the spirit of the disinfection legal norm. However, the big plates used for table service were not disinfected, which violated legal requirements. Thus, the Idealistic restaurant

Table 3.2 Variations of compliance and noncompliance at the idealistic restaurant

Legal norms		Behaviors	Types of compliance
Opening Licenses	Environmental License	Followed application procedures	Compliance
		Installed environmental protection facility that exceeds the requirements	Beyond
		Obtained license	Compliance
	Catering Services License	Followed application procedures	Compliance
		Installed additional sinks	Compliance
		Obtained license	Compliance
		Removed one sink	Symbolic
	Business License	Followed application procedures	Compliance
		Obtained license	Compliance
	Fire License	Followed application procedures	Compliance
		Bought more fire extinguishers than required	Beyond
		Obtained license	Compliance
	Decoration License	Did not follow application procedure but was discovered by inspectors	Enforced
		Paid 1,000 CNY to inspectors privately as required to avoid formal procedure of sanctions or application	Creative
	Drainage License	Followed application procedures	Compliance
		Attempted various remedies when application stagnated	Attempted
		Used tap water mixture for test	Fraudulent
		Obtained license	Compliance
Daily Operations	Pork and Chicken	Bought organic pork	Beyond
		Bought counterfeit quarantine certificate	Conflictive

(continued)

Table 3.2 (continued)

Legal norms		Behaviors	Types of compliance
		Obtained genuine quarantine certificate but questioned the legitimacy of system	Skeptical
		Bought organic chicken	Beyond
		Did not have quarantine certificate for chicken	Noncompliance
		Used traditional methods to assess quality of chicken	Attempted
	Dish Disinfection	Used organic cleaner	Beyond
		Had high-quality disinfection cabinet	Compliance
		Disinfected dishware used for personal service but not dishware used for table service	Partial
		Falsified disinfection log	Fake
	Health Certificates	Most employees had real health certificates; some did not	Partial
		Employees underwent health checks before obtaining health certificates	Compliance
	Fapiao Receipts	Provided *Fapiao* receipts on request	Partial
		Reused used *Fapiao* receipts	Non-compliance
		Refuse to use counterfeit *Fapiao* receipts	Compliance
		Voluntarily paid more tax by increasing *Fapiao* receipt purchases	Compliance
	Washing Hands	Internal rule of washing hands before entering kitchen and using toilet	Partial
		Employees did not wash hands as legally required	Partial
	Cutting Fingernails	Internal rule that nails must be short	Attempted
		Most employees kept nails trimmed	Partial

partially complied with the disinfection legal requirements. Similarly, partial compliance applied to the health certificate system. Although most employees had obtained genuine health certificates after undergoing health checks, several employees, such as the elderly dishwasher, did not have health certificates. Furthermore, the Idealistic restaurant partially complied with norms related to washing hands and cutting nails. Despite implementing a rule regarding the washing of hands, the rule did not cover all conditions required by the legal norm, and workers did not wash their hands under all conditions required by the legal norm. Likewise, rules related to fingernail length were not implemented well, and some workers did not keep their nails trimmed at all times.

Although the failure to enforce the rule that workers must have short fingernails can be viewed as partial compliance from the perspective of the extent to which behaviors align with the law. However, from the perspective of the intention of the regulated, it can be classified as attempted compliance, as the Idealistic restaurant intended to comply with the letter and spirit of the law but did not achieve full compliance due to other factors, such as the incapability of management. Moreover, the disinfection behaviors reflected attempted compliance. The owner acknowledged the importance of safeguarding customers' health and invested in a quality disinfection cabinet, but the staff dismissed the serving platters as at low risk of influencing customers' health. This led to partial compliance with disinfection requirements.

Another example of attempted compliance is the restaurant's handling of chicken. The Idealistic restaurant bought organic chicken, which was perceived as safe, good food for customers. The simple, traditional method was used to select chicken to guarantee the safety of the meat, which aligns with the spirit of the meat quarantine certificate requirements. However, the restaurant neither obtained official quarantine certificates for its chicken nor complied with the letter of the quarantine certificate requirements. Thus, to maintain the food safety of chicken; the restaurant chose traditional methods over official ones. Finally, the process of obtaining the drainage license also can be categorized as attempted compliance, as the Idealistic restaurant insisted on obtaining the license despite official delays and advice to abandon its efforts.

During the application for the drainage license, the Idealistic restaurant attempted to comply but also engaged in fraudulent behavior; hence, part of the process can be categorized as fraudulent compliance. Fraudulent compliance occurs when fraudulent methods are used to achieve compliance. When the restaurant was finally able to proceed with the application procedure and send wastewater for assessment, it sent a sample containing tap water mixed with water in which vegetables had been washed.

Several compliance behaviors can be viewed as conflictive compliance, which refers to complying with one legal norm by violating another. For instance, to obtain a fire license, the Idealistic restaurant attempted bribery, and in an effort to supply good, safe food, it bought counterfeit quarantine certificates for its organic pork. Similarly, although the restaurant voluntarily increased its tax contributions and aimed to provide authentic *Fapiao* receipts, fluctuating customer numbers led to receipt shortage, which were addressed by reissuing used *Fapiao* receipt sometime. The restaurant thus violated legal requirements related to *Fapiao* receipts.

In some cases, the Idealistic restaurant chose not to engage in conflictive compliance behavior, and its behavior developed into skeptical compliance behavior. For example, it changed its pig slaughtering methods by having the animals processed at a certified facility. As a result, it fully complied with the quarantine certificate requirement, but the restaurant owners' experiences at the slaughterhouse left them dubious about the legitimacy of the quarantine certificate requirements.

Finally, symbolic or formalist compliance emerged at the Idealistic restaurant. During the catering services license inspection, the inspectors indicated that the restaurant needed three sinks in the kitchen instead of three. The restaurant installed a third sink, but it was removed not long after obtaining the license due to the limited space in the kitchen. The third sink was installed only as a symbol showing its commitment to the law, so when it obtained the license, the sink was removed along with its symbolic function.

The compliance behaviors described above exemplify the construction process from the perspective of the regulated, the Idealistic restaurant. Despite the complexity of those compliance behaviors, the characteristics of clarification and contesting are clearly illustrated in the opening license and daily operations process. The Idealistic restaurant had a strong intention to comply with the laws that it encountered, but it faced numerous challenges in clarifying the exactly operational requirements and in conflicts between legal requirements and its values. Consequently, various kinds of compliance emerged. Its compliance behaviors included full, beyond, creative, partial, attempted, conflicting, skeptical, symbolic or even fraudulent, and fake compliance. Nevertheless, the compliance behaviors at the Idealistic restaurant were oriented to a higher level of compliance, which shows its commitment to the law. Most of the time, its beliefs overlapped the spirit of the law and attempted to engage in positive behaviors that exceed legal expectations.

3.7.2 Characterizing the Subject of Compliance at the Idealistic Restaurant

The discussion raises two important questions: How can one understand the complex compliance behaviors that developed at the Idealistic restaurant? Why did the Idealistic restaurant engage in such complex behaviors? To study the Idealistic restaurant's compliance behaviors, it is necessary to turn to the five motivational postures Braithwaite (2003) proposed and the five management styles Kagan et al. (2003) identified.

The five motivational postures proposed by Braithwaite (2003) are commitment, capitulation, resistance, disengagement, and game playing.[54] These postures can be used to classify the actors' attitudes and interactions with regulators, which reflect the level of social distance the regulated place between themselves and the enforcement authorities. The first two postures, commitment and capitulation, are positive

---

[54]See Chap. 2 for a discussion of these motivational postures.

postures, while the remaining three, resistance, disengagement, and game playing, are negative and defiant. Commitment reflects a closer positive social distance than capitulation, and disengagement reflects a greater negative social distance than resistance. People who show resistance, although fighting regulations, remain within the regulatory system, while those who are disengaged place themselves outside the regulatory institution, cutting themselves off psychologically from the influence of the regulatory attempt. Game players remain within the sphere of the regulatory institution, but they use the letter of the law to circumvent the intention of the law (McBarnet 2002).

From the perspective of motivational postures, the Idealistic restaurant posture is clearly on of commitment. It believed most legal requirements were morally necessary, and it was inclined to obey them with good will. These include the regulations surrounding the environmental and fire licenses, dish disinfection, health certificates, and cutting fingernails. It actively over-complied with the requirements for the environmental license, acknowledged the importance of fire extinguishers by buying more than needed, and recognized the need to sanitize dishes by investing in a high-quality disinfection cabinet. It ensured that most of its workers underwent health checks and held valid health certificates, and it implemented its own rules regarding the trimming of fingernails, although inspectors do not monitor this requirement.

Moreover, the Idealistic restaurant displayed the posture of capitulation. Although it may not have felt legal norms were morally necessary, it still accepted the enforcement authorities as legitimate, and it remained willing to defer to its authority. This could be seen in the applications for decoration, catering service, and drainage licenses, and in the handling of the pork quarantine certificates and *Fapiao* receipts. Although the owners did not see the necessity of installing the third sink when applying for the catering services license, they installed the sink, and despite questioning the rationality of the drainage license, they were determined to obtain one. Additionally, they viewed the pork quarantine system as irrational, but still obtained certificates, and voluntarily paid more tax by applying for additional *Fapiao* receipts. See Table 3.3 for a summary of the restaurant's postures.

According to Braithwaite (2003), motivational postures of commitment and capitulation are inclined to forecast positive compliance behaviors and outcomes. However, although the Idealistic restaurant was inclined to comply with, or even surpass, the law, it still engaged in violation behaviors such as fraudulent and symbolic compliance. Brathwaite noted in her discussion of tax evasion and tax avoidance that motivational posture simply reflects attitudinal factors and that it cannot cover all reasons for noncompliance. However, her studies have not yet addressed this problem. The case of the Idealistic restaurant is a useful example for discussing violation behaviors in an organization that typically displays positive motivational postures.

The management style proposed by Kagan et al. (2003) refers to the combination of managerial attitudes and actions that mark the intensity and character of each management team's commitment to complying with regulatory responsibilities. It classifies the attitudes of compliance actors to legal requirements and

Table 3.3 Motivational postures at the idealistic restaurant

Motivational postures	Presentation	Compliance type
Commitment	Environmental license	Beyond
	Fire license	
	Dish disinfection	Beyond, partial, fake
	Health certificates	Partial
	Nail cutting	Attempted, partial
	Handwashing	Partial
	Business license	Full
	Chicken safety	Attempted
Capitulation	Pork quarantine certificate	Conflictive, skeptical
	Drainage license	Attempted, fraudulent
	Decoration license	Creative
	Catering services license	Full, symbolic/formalist
	Fapiao receipt	Conflictive

managerial commitment to regulatory requirements. Commitment includes managerial attitudes and actions. Kagan et al. (2003) five types of managers are laggards, reluctant compliers, committed compliers, strategists, and true believers.[55] The five types display increasingly greater commitment to compliance with and positive attitudes toward legal requirements, with laggards at the bottom and true believers at the top of the scale. Thus, a true believer is more committed to and more positive about legal requirements than a strategist, who is more committed to and more positive about legal requirements than a committed complier, and so forth.

Viewed from this perspective, the Idealistic restaurant generally can be classified as a true believer. It operated and made decisions based on the ethical and moral consideration of its responsibilities, such as food safety and environmental impact. Its decisions regarding the legal requirements that align with its values were not purely pragmatic but also principled, or "the right thing to do." Therefore, it engaged in many behaviors categorized as beyond compliance, such as providing not only safe food but good food, buying more fire extinguishing than required, installing quality environmental equipment that exceeded requirements, and using a natural detergent that is healthy and eco-friendly. Nevertheless, in some cases it partially complied with legal norms it considered "the right thing to do," such as dish disinfection, obtaining health certificates, handwashing, and nail cutting.

Furthermore, this apparent true believer engaged in negative compliance behaviors such as symbolic and fraudulent compliance, even in the same regulatory system in which it previously conducted beyond compliance behaviors. For example, it

---

[55] See Chap. 2 for a discussion of these management styles.

focused on maintaining food safety, yet engaged in symbolic compliance behaviors such as removing one sink after obtaining its catering services license. Similarly, it engaged in fraudulent and fake compliance behaviors, for example, by buying quarantine certificates and falsifying the disinfection log. Although it over complied when applying for its environmental license, it engaged in fraudulent compliance when applying for its drainage license, which is related to environmental protection. In addition, in some cases, to comply with one legal norm, it violated another, for example by buying falsified quarantine certificates and issuing used *Fapiao* receipts customers.

It seems this true believer was more inclined to comply with its own values, some of which aligned with legal norms but some of which differed from or even conflicted with the legal norms. This indicates that the organization operates within a semi-autonomous social field (Moore 1973) because it accepts some rules emanating from the larger world that surrounds it, while also generating rules and norms internally. For example, the Idealistic restaurant adhered to certain food safety guidelines, such as obtaining health certificates and sanitizing dishes, but it also had its own food safety values, such as feeding its pigs traditional, natural feeds. When legal norms coincided with its own beliefs, it was inclined to take action that produced beyond compliance, but when its beliefs differed from these norms, it engaged in partial or symbolic compliance. Moreover, when it did not agree with the legal requirements, it engaged in fake, conflictive, or skeptical compliance. Thus, although the Idealistic restaurant was compliance-oriented when it encountered the law, the "law" typically seemed to impede its compliance behaviors. This is analyzed in Part B.

Furthermore, the Idealistic restaurant shows characteristics of a committed complier. Despite facing numerous difficulties, it insisted on obtaining a drainage license. To obtain a legal license, it attempted various solutions, finally submitting a false water sample. The purpose of doing so was to show inspectors that it had complied with regulations, as inspectors might check the license. This is mirrored in the acquisition of counterfeit pork quarantine certificates shortly after opening.

References

Braithwaite, Valerie. 2003. Dancing with Tax Authorities: Motivational Postures and Non-compliant Actions. In *Taxing Democracy: Understanding Tax Avoidance and Evasion*, Valerie Braithwaite, ed., 15–39. Ashgate.

Deng, Aiyun. 2002. On Regulation and Management of Health Certificate for Food Related Workers. *Hubei Preventive Medicine* 13 (4): 40–41.

Huising, Ruthanne, and Susan S. Silbey. 2011. Governing the Gap: Forging Safe Science Through Relational Regulation. *Regulation and Governance* 5: 14–42.

Kagan, R.A., N. Gunningham, and D. Thornton. 2003. Explaining Corporate Environmental Performance: How Does Regulation Matter? *Law & Society Review* 37: 51–90. https://doi.org/10.1111/1540-5893.3701002.

Lange, B. 1999. Compliance Construction in the Context of Environmental Regulation. *Social & Legal Studies* 8 (4): 549–567.

McBarnet, Doreen. 2002. When Compliance is not the Solution but the Problem: From Changes in Law to Changes in Attitude. In *Taxing Democracy: Understanding Tax Avoidance and Evasion*, ed. Valerie Braithwaite, 229–244. Aldershot: Ashgate.

Moore, Sally Falk. 1973. Law and Social Change: The Semi-autonomous Social Field as an Appropriate Subject of Study. *Law & Society Review* 7 (4): 719–746.

Chapter 4
A Profit-Maximizing Restaurant

4.1 Introduction

This chapter focuses on the second extended case study on compliance processes, this time at the Profit-Maximizing restaurant. In this restaurant, I observed some compliance behaviors, for example, the business had the required opening licenses, as well as numerous violation behaviors such as using counterfeit *Fapiao* receipts and health certificates. Compliance and violation may coexist, even for the same legal norm, and at a static point, the organization may be in compliance, while at a different point it is in violation. For example, the Profit-Maximizing restaurant obtained an environmental license when it first opened, but instead of renewing it, the restaurant created a counterfeit license. Thus, compliance may change over time, and as the endogenous approach suggests, it is a learning process. Moreover, compliance is socially constructed, but at the Profit-Maximizing restaurant, instead of constructing compliance and learning to comply, the organization learns noncompliance, specifically evading legal requirements. A description of the compliance behaviors that take place at the Profit-Maximizing restaurant clarify the process observed in this case study.

As in Chap. 3, Chap. 4 begins with a description of the context and background of the restaurant, including its main characteristics, owner, and employees to create a picture to facilitate the understanding of the context of compliance behaviors and to highlight the restaurant leadership and employee components, which have a significant effect on compliance in the restaurant. A detailed overview of the various compliance behaviors, conducted by examining the procedures followed to obtain the opening licenses and to complete daily operations, follows.

Obtaining opening licenses is the first compliance behavior in which a restaurant engages. The learning process differed at the Profit-Maximizing restaurant and at the Idealistic restaurant. With opening licenses, compliance and noncompliance are clear: having the licenses means compliance, while not having the licenses means noncompliance. At this point, the Profit-Maximizing restaurant had obtained all the required licenses, which may be judged as compliance. However, as the process

Y. Wu, *Compliance Ethnography*, Understanding China,
https://doi.org/10.1007/978-981-16-2884-9_4

approach revealed, compliance was immensely complex at the Profit-Maximizing restaurant, with numerous kinds of compliance, including symbolic, fake, and fraudulent compliance, emerging. It was found that even clear-cut license compliance should be understood as a learning process. Applying for one license indicates the beginning of the compliance process, and the knowledge gained while applying for one license may further influence behaviors displayed when applying for other licenses.

Compliance with legal norms related to daily operations requires repeated daily action. This type of compliance cannot be assessed at a static point but relies on daily action, which implies that the process perspective is required to understand it. Furthermore, the process of compliance in terms of daily operations moves compliance down from the regulatory level to the organization level. If the owner and inspectors are involved in opening license compliance, restaurant employees are involved in compliance during daily operations.

The chapter ends with the characterization of the compliance behaviors described using the existing literature.

4.2   A Small but Profitable Restaurant

Before I became the boss of this restaurant, my salary as the chef was only 2,000 CNY. My former boss asked me to take over this restaurant and gave me one month for trial without charge. After one month, I got a 10,000 CNY net margin. So, I took over this restaurant.

—The owner of the Profit-Maximizing restaurant

The Profit-Maximizing restaurant was a small restaurant, much like the common small restaurants throughout China, situated in the middle of several similar establishments in a street near an old residential district and a flower and bird market. The restaurant sat between a noodle restaurant, a seafood restaurant, a barbecue restaurant, and a Han taste snack restaurant. There was nothing special about the Profit-Maximizing restaurant except that it served ethnic Dai food, and it was decorated in the common Dai style. It featured bamboo chairs and tables, and it had bamboo mats on the walls and floor. However, the décor was worn: the bamboo mats were dirty, and some bamboo chairs and tables were broken, with others having been replaced with wooden tables and chairs in the Han style. Some dry food materials, such as dry bread for a special desert, lay cluttered on a cabinet in a corner. The only room contained one round table and a large meat freezer. As in many businesses in China, a Buddha shrine sat above the cashier's counter as a blessing that brings good income for the business. On the counter, facing the restaurant, was a glass fish tank that contained several fish, lovingly tended by the owner. The fish tank was an important aspect of the restaurant's *Fengshui*, as fish and water are believed to bring fortune.

At only 80 square meters, 20 for the kitchen and 60 for customer seating, the Profit-Maximizing restaurant was small, with only 10 tables serving 50 customers.

However, when needed, several small, removable tables would be placed outside the restaurant, allowing service to another 20 customers. Despite its size, the restaurant was successful, and business was always good. In warm weather, the daily turnover reached up to 6000 CNY, dropping to 3000 CNY on quieter days. Monthly turnover was about 100,000 CNY, with a net monthly margin of around 30,000 CNY. The secret of its success was its owner, who had been operating the restaurant with cost saving as the key strategy. Reducing costs is demanding, and it requires physical strength for working hard and mental acuity that underlies all thought processes and restaurant affairs.

4.3 Meet the Owner

The owner's first cost saving strategy simply involved working hard. Like a spinning top, he was a flurry of activity almost every day from early morning to late night, stopping work around midnight. He was the most hardworking and busy person in the restaurant. He arranged everything, and everyone reported to him directly. He managed every detail in the restaurant, dealt with every problem that arose, and did any job necessary at the Profit-Maximizing restaurant, including washing dishes and cleaning the floor. To reduce costs, he paid with time and energy. While most restaurants obtain their food and ingredients—from oil to rice, and from meat to vegetables—through intermediaries, thus avoiding trips to the market, he initially insisted on sourcing his own stock to avoid paying intermediaries. This sometimes involved visiting wholesale markets far away for cheaper materials. Gradually, he became too busy to buy everything himself, so he sourced meat and vegetables from an intermediary, but he still insisted on buying oil and rice himself.[1]

Being hardworking is the most important trait for him, who owes ownership of this business to his diligence. He is of Dai ethnicity, was poor, and he grew up in a frontier prefecture. After graduating from junior high school, he began doing various forms of physical labor in his home prefecture, working as a laborer, garbage collector, barbecue worker, waiter, potato vender, and labor cart driver. His hands and feet were lacerated from collecting garbage, and he would work three jobs a day, sleeping only a few hours a night. He established a small fast-food restaurant, but he had to close it after only a month because it made no profit. He did many different jobs, but none with much success.

Things changed after he came to Kunming in 2003. He began to learn cooking in a restaurant. He observed the chef, bought a cookbook, and practiced by himself. Soon, he became a formal cook in a restaurant, cooking Dai food. He worked hard and never asked for a salary increase. He was the first to arrive, half an hour early, and the last to leave each day. Although he was a cook, he did everything he could in the restaurant, such as washing dishes and cleaning the floors. He worked for three

---

[1]Although price was one consideration, he suspected that the oil supplied by the intermediaries might be the gutter oil.

different employers before operating his own restaurant. Every employer liked him, and each increased his salary without prompting.

In 2008, after five years' hard work in restaurants, his luck changed. For personal reasons, the restaurant's previous owner decided to leave the industry, and wanted to pass the restaurant on to him, who was the head chef at that time. At first, he was not confident about taking over, and he preferred his safe, guaranteed salary of 2000 CNY per month. However, the former owner offered him a month to test his proposal, with the former owner carrying the cost of the experiment. He was responsible for cooking and management, and if the restaurant turned a profit that month, it would go to him. If the restaurant made a loss, he would not need to pay for it. With this considerable support, he ran the restaurant for one month, and the outcome surpassed his expectations—he made a profit of 10,000 CNY. This gave him the confidence he needed to take over the restaurant. The former owner offered him further support, selling the restaurant at 80,000 CNY and allowing him to pay off the 40,000 CNY shortfall. He achieved this in 10 months, and finally owned the restaurant himself.

Recruiting employees proved more difficult than acquiring the restaurant. At the outset, his large family supported him, and his brothers, sister-in-law, and other relatives became his first employees. To some degree, these employees helped him rather than worked for him. After a while, some of his relatives wanted to return home, so he had to recruit workers from outside the family. However, as was the case for the Idealistic restaurant, he had difficulty finding servers. He posted advertisements in front of the restaurant, asked acquaintance for introductions, and brought in young men and women from his or his wife's hometown. Sometimes, he employed students who had just graduated from junior high school or students on winter or summer vacation. The staff turnover rate was high at the Profit-Maximizing restaurant, with some workers leaving after several days, relatives working there temporarily while between jobs, and relatives working there for several months to learn how to cook before returning to their hometown to open their own restaurants.

His requirements for new recruits were low: they needed to be obedient and not make trouble. However, he refused to recruit two kinds of people—"those guys with dyed colorful hair" and "people from Z and H districts."[2] According to him, the young men with colorful dyed hair may be street hooligans, and they do not work well and often make trouble. Similarly, people from Z and H are inclined to fight with others, and many thieves come from those two places. During the observation period, three servers and four kitchen workers were employed at the Profit-Maximizing restaurant. Except for one kitchen worker who had been worked in this restaurant for two years, all the other workers were relatives of or somehow related to him. The three kitchen workers were his relatives, and two of the servers were their girlfriends. The other sever was the girlfriend of a former cook at the Profit-Maximizing restaurant who was friend with the owner.

---

[2]Interview with the owner of the Profit-Maximizing restaurant on August 21, 2013.

4.4 Learning to Dance with the Law

To run the restaurant was a great challenge. Besides working hard in the restaurant, the owner of the Profit-Maximizing restaurant had to deal with numerous outside affairs, that is, obtaining various opening licenses. Obtaining these licenses was the first legal norm with which the restaurant needed to comply. During the pilot study phase of this research, the Profit-Maximizing restaurant had obtained all the required opening licenses. Based on this static point, one may claim the Profit-Maximizing restaurant complied with regulations. However, when examining the process of its compliance behaviors taking place, specifically how it obtained and maintained these licenses, a more complex picture emerges.

Usually, applying for opening licenses costs a certain amount of money, as it involves buying new equipment, paying various administrative fees, and obtaining certificates. In the process of dealing with opening licenses and communicating with various people, the owner of the Profit-Maximizing restaurant gradually learned the rules in action behind these legal requirements, which are described in the sections that follow. This helped him save a great deal of money, of course, illegally.

The owner bought his restaurant directly from the former owner, and the change of ownership did not bring about other significant changes at the Profit-Maximizing restaurant, including in licenses. Initially, the owner did not think about licenses, but a visit from inspectors from the Industry and Commerce Bureau during which the inspectors found that ownership had changed brought the matter of licensing to the fore. The owner was required to obtain new licenses to run the restaurant. As explained in the previous case, a restaurant must obtain five to ten licenses,[3] with the business, environmental, catering services, taxation, and fire licenses being the most important. Obtaining the environmental, fire, and catering services licenses is a preconditions for obtaining a business license.[4] The process of obtaining each license is described in the subsections that follow.

4.4.1 Environmental License

The environmental license was the costliest for the Profit-Maximizing restaurant, who spent more than 4000 CNY of the total cost of just under 7000 CNY for all licenses

---

[3]These are business, environmental, catering services, tax registration, fire, drainage, liquor, decoration, tobacco, and cultural performance licenses. Every restaurant must have the first five, while the need for the remainder depends on the restaurant's situation. For example, if a restaurant wants to sell alcohol, it needs a liquor license. Although all restaurants must have a drainage license, it is not necessary to obtain this license before applying for a business license. Unless Drainage Department inspectors find out an establishment does not have a drainage license, having it or not will not influence the running of the restaurant. In practice, the Drainage Department seldom pays attention to small restaurants that use little water, so some restaurants remain unaware of the existence of this license.

[4]For more information about these licenses, please refer to Table 3.1.

on this license. When the owner took over the Profit-Maximizing restaurant, it did not have an environmental license. After he became the owner, he had to apply for this license, which is one of the prerequisites for a business license. As a requirement to be granted an environmental license, he had to install an oil filter in the sewerage system. He installed one himself at a cost of 300 CNY, but when the inspectors returned, they informed him that the oil filter was unsuitable and that he would have to have one fitted by a designated company for almost 1000 CNY. However, he had a different understanding of why he was asked to change the new oil filter. He said, "It is nothing related to the quality. It is about whether they [the inspectors] can get benefit [money] from it." According to him, the inspectors received kickbacks from the designated company if a restaurant contracted it to install its oil filter. In addition to the oil filter, he had to install a smoke purifier above the stove to purify the smoke the stove released. He installed one as required, but turned it on only during inspections. He remarked, "It [the smoke purifier] is just a decoration for me…It will not make a big difference, but is high powered and costs lots of electricity."[5]

4.4.2   Catering Services License

Next the owner of the Profit-Maximizing restaurant applied for the catering services license. After submitting the application form, FDA inspectors conducted an onsite inspection and asked him to replace the old stone kitchen table with a stainless steel one. He spent almost 200 CNY on a new stainless steel kitchen table, but instead of verifying whether he had made the change, the inspectors asked him to photograph this change and bring the photos to the license service window. The officers who attended to the paperwork at the license service window collected the photos and asked whether he made the change. He confirmed that he had, and the officers approved his application and issued his license. Later, He expressed his regret about buying a new table:

> If I had known they would not come to check on site, I would not buy the new table. I could just take photos in another restaurant where [they] had that kind of table. That is enough. People who came to the site and people who sit in the office to check your photos are not the same person. I only learned later that we did not really have to do such things.[6]

---

[5]Interview with the owner of the Profit-Maximizing restaurant on May 26, 2011. This behavior is similar to violation behaviors described in environmental compliance, for instance, illegal dumping (*Toupai*). See Benjamin van Rooij's *Regulating land and pollution in China*, Leiden University Press (2006), pp. 214–216.

[6]Interview with the owner of the Profit-Maximizing restaurant on May 25, 2011.

4.4.3 Fire License

The owner saved money when applying for the fire license. To obtain the fire license, he was required to have eight fire extinguishers, one fire exist sign, and one emergency light. Before he bought all equipment, however, his friends advised him that the inspectors would not conduct an onsite inspection and would only ask for photos and *Fapiao* receipts. This time, instead of buying all the equipment, He borrowed a fire exit sign and emergency light. He hung the sign and light at the restaurant and took photos of them, and he bought two fire extinguishers. With the two the former owner left, he had four fire extinguishers. He photographed the four extinguishers in different places to make it appear as though there were eight. In addition, he obtained *Fapiao* receipts for all the required equipment, and although they were authentic, he must have done so in an illegal manner,[7] as he did not buy all the items.

He brought the photos and *Fapiao* receipts to the administration office. After checking the photos showing the required equipment and the *Fapiao* receipt, and collecting the 300 CNY application fee (He did not know what this fee was for), the officers issued him fire license. As a result, he paid 540 CNY for the fire license, which would have been more expensive had he bought the required equipment.

4.4.4 Business License

In similar way, the owner saved money when obtaining a business license. To obtain a business license, He had to pay an annual fee, the amount of which depends on the number of employees he had, with one employee costing 120 CNY. Because he had nine employees, he should have paid 1080 CNY per year. However, he had an acquaintance working in the ICA, which is responsible for issuing business licenses. The acquaintance privately suggested him to report only three employees. He reported six employees, which was more than his acquaintance suggested but fewer than the real number. This saved him 360 CNY every year.

4.4.5 Taxation License

The owner used the same strategy to save on his taxation license. Obtaining this license troubled him for a while. Officially, he was required to report his monthly turnover to obtain a taxation license, and he would pay monthly tax at 7.6% of the turnover he reported. At that time, the Profit-Maximizing restaurant's monthly turnover was 70,000–80,000 CNY. If he reported the real turnover, he would be charged about 5000 CNY per month. He wanted to reduce costs and report a lower turnover, but he was unsure of the amount that would be acceptable for the tax

---

[7]Generally, people obtain these kinds of *Fapiao* receipts by bargaining with or paying the sellers.

office. The former owner reported a turnover of only 3000 CNY per month, but he thought this was because the former owner had bribed the tax officer. The former owner suggested that he give the tax officer *Hongbao* (a bribe), too, but he decided against this. He was not certain that the officer would accept the bribe,[8] and he viewed bribery as a crime for both the person giving and receiving the bribe. He explained, "I cannot harm other people. Furthermore, I cannot harm myself."[9] In addition, he had not clear opportunity to give *Hongbao*, as the tax officer was always accompanied by colleagues. He did not know the officer well and felt it was impossible to give *Hongbao* in the presence of the officer's coworkers. Consequently, he did not bribe the officer.

The turnover he reported was higher than that reported by the former owner, but lower than the real number. He reported 8000 CNY, which the officer approved without question. As a result, instead of paying 5000 CNY, he paid a little over 600 CNY per month in tax.

4.4.6 Opening License Renewal

Opening licenses need to be verified and renewed after one or three years. Verification and renewal take time and cost money. However, the owner found ways around it. He chose to deal with each license renewal differently. The business and catering services licenses are considered the most important legal documents, as they can be forced to close without them. Moreover, they are the most frequently checked licenses by ICA and FDA inspectors. For the two licenses, he followed the rules to renew them. He initiated the renewal of the catering services license every three years and the business license every year, as required, following the legal procedures. He prepared everything that was needed, but he did not worry about whether his restaurant would pass the renewal. He claimed that inspectors would overlook violations, and he would obtain approval:

> When applying annual verification, they [the inspectors] will come to the restaurant to check on site. But there is no big deal with that. They just come once and will not come again even they find out some places that are not qualified. I know that...[10]

When asked how he knew this, he replied,

> They are too busy with their other work. They [the inspectors] also hate to waste time [on this small restaurant]...I think it is common that they [the inspectors] will not be too strict

---

[8] According to Li Ling, to bribe someone involves many rules and codes, which purport to control the risk of exchange and reduce moral cost and moral dissonance. These rules and codes that reflect in the process of *Guanxi* practice are complex, personal, and need to be discreetly crafted into real bribe behavior. Reckless bribery may not only invite refusal but also brings risks of detection and punishment. For more information on bribery in the Chinese context, see Li (2011).

[9] Interview with the owner of the Profit-Maximizing restaurant on May 26th, 2011.

[10] Interview with the owner of the Profit-Maximizing restaurant on 5th September 2013.

with the small restaurant. The small restaurant does not make big problems. They are always strict with the places where big issues may happen, i.e., big ones, famous ones.[11]

In his perception, inspectors perform superficial checks. He pointed out that there was an open barbecue stove in the kitchen, which was supposed to be in a single room according to the law,[12] but inspectors never pointed this out.

Although the environmental license is a prerequisite of obtaining a business license when setting up a restaurant, which makes it seem important, it is not inspected as regularly as the catering services license. In his experience, the Department of the Environment never inspected the restaurant after the initial inspection when he first applied for the environmental license. Furthermore, he saw the environmental license as a means for the Department of the Environment to generate income: "Anyway, they [the regulator] will give me the renewed environment license once I give them money."[13] Thus, he diminished the legal status of the environmental license and denied the rationality of obtaining one.

As a result, he chose to create a counterfeit environmental license by buying a counterfeit official seal. He did not view this as risky, as there was a low possibility of being discovered by environmental bureau inspectors due to the irregularity of inspections. The FDA inspectors who often conducted site visits "[had] nothing to do with the environment bureau." Furthermore, he claimed he was not afraid of discovery, as he believed he could sue them for not doing their own work, such as failing to check and clean instruments[14] (the oil filter).

The liquor license was not viewed as important, as obtaining a license involves little regulation—restaurants simply register and pay a license fee. For this license, he dismissed the annual verification and waited for the relevant inspectors to conduct a site visit, saying, "If it is expired, I just need to pay some fines when the inspectors come and discover it."

---

[11] Ibid.

[12] The understanding of the owner of the Profit-Maximizing restaurant is inaccurate. According to article 16 of "Measures for the Supervision and Administration of Food Safety in Catering Services," cold dishes should be prepared in a single special room. It does not mention barbecue stoves. However, the Profit-Maximizing restaurant sold cold dishes but did not have a special preparation room. Inspectors never pointed this out, possibly because the Profit-Maximizing restaurant is prohibited from selling cold dishes in terms of its catering services license. Apparently, that the Profit-Maximizing restaurant violated it license by selling cold dishes was not discovered (or dismissed) by FDA inspectors.

[13] Interview with the owner of the Profit-Maximizing restaurant on 5th September 2013.

[14] When applying for environmental licenses, restaurants have to sign contracts with designated companies that are supposed to clean their equipment regularly, yet few restaurants receive this service.

4.4.7 Compliance Process as Learning Practice Rule in Opening Licenses

The Profit-Maximizing restaurant's opening license application and renewal processes indicates compliance and partial noncompliance. Initially, it obtained legal opening licenses, including its environmental, catering services, business, fire, and taxation licenses. When assessed at this static point, the Profit-Maximizing restaurant complied with those license rules. However, in terms of the procedures followed to obtain and maintain those licenses, the Profit-Maximizing restaurant obtained several licenses through noncompliance behaviors.[15] For example, although it obtained a fire license, it misrepresented the equipment it owned. Similarly, the number of employees was underreported when applying for the business license and its turnover was significantly underreported when applying for the taxation license.

How the Profit-Maximizing restaurant obtained those licenses illustrates the process of learning the practice rules related to opening licenses. When applying for the catering services license, the owner followed the inspectors' directions to replace the stone kitchen table with a stainless steel one, but through interaction with an FDA officer, he learned that the officer did not check the site to verify whether he implemented the changes, verifying it through photos instead. This experience taught him that he did not need to make the required changes. Later, when applying for the fire license, he heard from friends that Fire Department inspectors also did not conduct site visits but asked for photos and *Fapiao* receipts instead. Following his experience with the catering services license, he decided not to buy all the required equipment but to create stages photos and procure a falsified *Fapiao* receipt. As expected, his application was approved. He had now learned that there are oral and written requirements in addition to the verified requirements in action. The former requirements can be costly, but the latter can be complied with at much lower cost.

Consequently, he repeated the same behavior when applying for business and taxation licenses. Again, he was learning the practice rules in action. When his acquaintance working at ICA told him he could report fewer employees to ICA, he saw an opportunity to reduce costs. Yet he was unsure what number would not cause risk. He settled on reporting that he had six rather than nine employees, which seemed reasonable for a small restaurant. Practice rules in action might differ from one department to another. He learned this repeatedly when interacting with each department. He faced the same question regarding the most suitable turnover amount to report when applying for a taxation license. Because he did not have the same social connection with the tax officer as the previous owner of the restaurant, he was hesitant to submit too low a number. Eventually, he chose an amount lower than the turnover but higher than the previous owner's declared turnover—8000 CNY seemed reasonable, as it included an increase in turnover without costing too much in monthly tax payments. Therefore, through the overall process of applying for opening licenses,

---

[15]That the Profit-Maximizing restaurant committed fraud to obtain the licenses is not a crime according to the criminal law of China, but evading tax is.

he learned that official, written requirements, inspection requirements, and verified and acceptable requirements exist.

He learned two additional lessons during this process. The first was that the risk of bending the rules and saving costs as he did is manageable, as eventual sanctions for violating existing rules are negotiable:

> If you just do what they ask you, you will not earn money from this small business. To be honest will suffer losses. You must be tricky whenever needed. I do not *Fanfa* [break the law]. There is no big deal except some fines, and the fine will not be much. If he wants 2,000 CNY, it will be ok to just give them 1,000 CNY.

He learned this from his own experience and from that of the previous owner of the business. When ICA inspectors found that restaurant ownership had changed, the previous license was cancelled. He immediately applied for a new license, but he waited almost six months for it to be issued. During this period, his restaurant remained open, but according to the law, operating a restaurant without a business license is illegal. Therefore, ICA inspectors fined him 5000 CNY. He negotiated the value of the fine, telling the inspectors, "I have been doing my business well but you suddenly cancelled my license. How can you just ask me to close my business suddenly?" He proposed a fine of 1000 CNY, and the inspectors accepted. A nearby restaurant also received a 3000 CNY fine for the same reason, and that business owner negotiated for a 1500 CNY fine. The second lesson he learned is that relationships with officers (*Guanxi*) are crucial. Private and good relationships with officers not only make matters easier but also save costs, for example, through his friendship with the ICA officer and his former employer's relationship with the tax officer.

After learning these practical rules of the regulatory game, the Profit-Maximizing restaurant was more inclined to find ways to avoid costly and troublesome requirements, as shown during the license renewal process. This time obvious violations occurred. For example, the owner bought a counterfeit stamp to create an environmental license, and he intentionally did not renew his liquor license but waited for the fine. It is important to note that some compliance behaviors still occurred, as he followed the procedures for renewing the business and catering services licenses.

4.5 Daily Operation

After obtaining the restaurant's legal opening licenses, the owner of the Profit-Maximizing restaurant still faced numerous legal requirements related to daily operations, which involve the laws exemplified in the opening licenses. In this section, several daily operation requirements—dish disinfection, health certificates, *Fapiao* receipts, handwashing, and nail cutting—are discussed to examine the daily operation compliance behaviors. As was the case with the compliance behaviors for opening license, learning practical verification requirements was evident in these compliance processes at the Profit-Maximizing restaurant.

4.5.1 *Dishware Disinfection*

Dishware disinfection is one of the most important and well-known requirements of food safety, as is clear stated in food safety law. As shown in the case of the Idealistic restaurant, at least three elements reflect the legal requirements of dishware disinfection: the existence of a disinfection cabinet, daily disinfection, and maintaining a disinfection log.[16]

To meet the requirement to obtain a license, a glass-doored disinfection cabinet was installed at the Profit-Maximizing restaurant, which was similar to those in most small restaurants, measuring about 1.2 m tall and 0.4 m wide. This cabinet used ultraviolet rays to disinfect dishes. It was always full of cups, glasses, and teapots, and chopsticks and bowls used by the workers. The power was often off because it was not plugged in, and during my stay at the Profit-Maximizing restaurant, I never saw it plugged in.

There was no need for the Profit-Maximizing restaurant to disinfect chopsticks, bowls, cups, and small dishes used for personal service, as the restaurant used prepacked tableware that was supposed to be sterilized at the factory to serve customers. Thus, apparently the tableware the Profit-Maximizing restaurant used to serve customers met the legal disinfection requirements. Nevertheless, the owner did not truly believe that the tableware was properly disinfected and safe: "The packed tableware may be not clean. They may be just washed and packed without disinfection. Sometimes, you can find dirty things on it."[17] Packed tableware was used not for hygiene reasons but for convenience, to save costs, to derive income, and to build relationships.

Using prepacked tableware is convenient. Every day, the supplier would send several boxes of prepacked tableware to the Profit-Maximizing restaurant. When setting the tables, the servers placed the prepacked tableware on the table, with four or six place settings per table. This saved servers' time, as they did not need to set down bowls, cups, and small dishes one by one. When cleaning the table after customers finish eating, servers put the used tableware back in the boxes without washing or cleaning anything, and the supplier would collect the tableware the next day. Hence, using prepacked tableware is not only convenient but also is a cost-saving measure. Workers at the Profit-Maximizing restaurant did not need to wash all the tableware customers used but only the large dishes used for table service. Because tableware did not require washing, the Profit-Maximizing restaurant did not need to hire a dishwasher, thus saving employment costs. Moreover, breakages, which are common in restaurants, no longer cost the restaurant money, as the tableware factory absorbs minor breakages. What was even better was that the restaurant earned money by using prepacked tableware. It paid 0.7 CNY per set, but charged customers 1 CNY, earning a net profit of 0.3 CNY per set.

In addition to these apparent benefits, using prepacked tableware held a hidden advantage. According to the owner, the prepacked tableware factory could help him

---

[16]In some cases, inspectors use fast testing.

[17]Interview with the owner of the Profit-Maximizing restaurant on March 2, 2012.

deal with affairs related to the Sanitation Bureau. He bought prepacked tableware from this factory to establish a relationship with the factory owner. When he had minor problems with the Sanitation Bureau, the owner of the prepacked tableware factory would help him resolve them. For example, the owner helped him obtain a health certificate without undergoing a health check, which was supposed to be a precondition. If inspectors visit the Profit-Maximizing restaurant and identify minor problems related to sanitation, the owner of prepacked tableware factory can assist him.

How can the compliance behavior in Profit-Maximizing restaurant be defined in this case? The Profit-Maximizing restaurant was probably listed as compliant in government records regarding those prepacked dishes. The prepacked tableware it used was supposed to have been disinfected, and it is a legal market product that should satisfy all legal requirements. In contrast, the Profit-Maximizing restaurant may be classified as in violation in studies that operationalize compliance as attitude and policy goals. He obviously did not intend to obtain disinfected and safe tableware, as he claimed the prepacked tableware was neither disinfected nor clean. He did not care about dish disinfection and instead used prepacked tableware for convenience and saving cost. Furthermore, the Profit-Maximizing restaurant benefits financially from using it. Because the prepacked tableware was believed to be dirty and not disinfected, it violates the policy goal that restaurants should provide disinfected and clean tableware.

Although the Profit-Maximizing restaurant apparently complies with the legal norm of dish disinfection of tableware used for personal service by using prepacked items, prepacked tableware is not the only dishware used at the Profit-Maximizing restaurant. Other items include large plates, small seasoning plates, large soup-spoons, rice spoons, drinking glasses, and so forth. The Profit-Maximizing restaurant does not adequately disinfect that tableware. According to the owner, "[they are theo-retically] disinfected with disinfectant fluid, or by the disinfection cabinet, [but] we hardly use disinfectant fluid. I just put one bottle there and show it to the inspector when they come."[18] Disinfectant fluid is not used because using "it is troublesome. Someone must do this work and it costs lots of time. Inspectors do not check the dishes. Even if they check, there will not be problem because the dish is clean." Consequently, the Profit-Maximizing restaurant seldom disinfected its dishware.

Nevertheless, the Profit-Maximizing restaurant had disinfection logs, but unsur-prisingly, these written logs reflected no disinfection facts, acting as a Potemkin Village, which is "an impressive facade or show designed to hide an undesirable fact or condition."[19] The disinfection logs were fake records created to hide the fact that tableware was not disinfected. Again, according to government records, the Profit-Maximizing restaurant may have been considered in compliance with the law while the opposite applied.

---

[18]Interview with the owner of the Profit-Maximizing restaurant on March 2, 2012.

[19]Merriam-Webster Online Dictionary, https://www.merriam-webster.com/dictionary/Potemkin%20village.

4.5.2 Health Certificate

The health certificate system is another important measure implemented in China to safeguard food safety, as discussed in Chap. 3. Unlike the Idealistic restaurant displaying workers' health certificates on the wall where customers see them immediately after entering the main gate, the Profit-Maximizing restaurant made it difficult to customers to see its workers' health certificates. Several certificates were displayed behind the cashier's desk in deep shadow, and customers would have to stand on the cashier's side of the counter to read what is written on the small square cards. Fortunately, few customers were interested in the cards, and the invalidity of the cards was never exposed.

The health certificates were invalid for two reasons. First, although some certificates were indeed issued by officials, and bearing authentic stamps, fraudulent procedures were followed to obtain them. According to article 34 of the Food Safety Law, health certificates are issued only after the applicant undergoes a health check. He paid health check fees but did not send workers for health checks. With the assistance of the owner of the prepacked tableware factory, his workers obtained "legal" health certificates.[20] Second, some health certificates were simply counterfeit, as were the stamps they bore.[21] To save money, and for the sake of convenience, he would reuse the unexpired health certificates of employees who had resigned by replacing the original photos with photos of new employees. Although the cards are stamped across the photo, he circumvented this by adding a new stamp by carefully following the outline of the original stamp. Thus, genuine health certificates obtained using fraudulent procedures would become fully counterfeit.

His perception of the health certificate system reveals several reasons for using partially and fully fraudulent certificates: "Most of people are healthy, only small part will bring with virus. I know my workers. They are healthy." However, his personal views alone would not motivate him to risk creating counterfeit health certificates. His previous experience showed that the risk is small and dismissible. Every time the FDA inspectors visited the Profit-Maximizing restaurant to check health certificates, he observed whether they brought documents cross check the restaurant's certificates. If they had done so, he would have hidden the fake certificates and admitted that they did not have health certificates, as this would have created less of a problem than admitting the certificates had been falsified. If they did not bring the documents, he would simply show them the fake certificates. This proved an effective strategy, as

---

[20]This phenomenon also was discovered in another study on health certificates in China. For example, Zhang found that many people viewed health certificates as a revenue stream for the CDC, as they could obtain health certificates by paying a fee and without undergoing health checks. Refer to Zhang, Ningsheng, 1999, "Reasons and countermeasures of not having health certificate for food industry workers," *Anqing Medical*, 20.

[21]The falsification of health certificates is a common practice, and counterfeit health certificates are available for purchase. However, at the Profit-Maximizing restaurant, the owner produced the certificates himself after buying a fake stamp. For more information on the counterfeiting of health certificates, see Qiu (2007), Fang et al. (2008) and Wang et al. (2009).

the inspectors never carefully looked at the fake certificates or checked them against the application documents.

Therefore, compliance behavior related to health certificates at the Profit-Maximizing restaurant is complex. Although the organization partly complied with regulations by completing the correct paperwork and some workers held genuine health certificates issued by the Center of Disease Control (CDC), it did not comply with the substantial legal requirement of undergoing health checks. In some cases, partial compliance was absent, as the documents had been falsified. This makes it difficult to capture the characteristics of compliance behavior related to health certificates without first understanding the process that took place.

4.5.3 Fapiao *Receipts*

As shown in the case of the Idealistic restaurant, restaurants pay tax based on the number of *Fapiao* receipts they buy from the Taxation Bureau.[22] Because the number of receipts bought depends on estimated turnover, many small restaurants attempt to keep their estimated turnover as low as possible to pay as little tax as possible. This applied at the Profit-Maximizing restaurant. While the real monthly turnover was around 80,000 CNY, he reported only 8000 CNY, so he paid only about 600 CNY tax per month. Subsequently, the city published a new tax policy that stated *Fapiao* receipts under 15,000 CNY would be free of tax for small business. Thus, he has raised the estimated turnover to 15,000 CNY and *Fapiao* receipts to this value free of charge. During the observation period for this study, the Profit-Maximizing restaurant's monthly turnover had reached around 100,000 CNY, with 30,000 CNY in monthly profit. However, the reported turnover remained 15,000 CNY.

The Profit-Maximizing restaurant required *Fapiao* receipts for customers who needed formal receipts,[23] but it had a turnover of 100,000 CNY with only 15,000 CNY in receipts. Thus, the restaurant did not have enough receipts for its customers. He managed the significant gap between the demand for *Fapiao* receipts and the receipts available by using counterfeit receipts. When he bought 8000 CNY in real *Fapiao* receipts from the tax office, he had to buy fake *Fapiao* receipts[24] valued at about 35,000 CNY. When he received 15,000 CNY in genuine *Fapiao* receipts from

---

[22]For a comprehensive overview of the *Fapiao* receipt system, please see Chap. 3, Sect. 6.6, and Guan (2006).

[23]In most organizations, *Fapiao* receipts play an important role in the reimbursement of employees' business expenses, with these receipts providing evidence that employees indeed spent certain amounts on business affairs. Yet in some cases, businesses use *Fapiao* receipts to avoid tax by collecting receipts from their employees and claiming the amounts as operational costs to be deducted from tax. Some companies even require employees to submit *Fapiao* receipts to receive their salaries. (See Zhao (2011).) Similar things occur in the public sector, where workers use Fapiao receipts to claim business expenses. In addition, workers must submit *Fapiao* receipts to claim certain expenses.

[24]Counterfeit *Fapiao* receipts for restaurants are readily available. Although the owner of the Profit-Maximizing restaurant did not indicate how he bought fake receipts, he undoubtedly had the phone

the tax office, he bought counterfeit *Fapiao* receipts valued at about 40,000 CNY. Counterfeit *Fapiao* receipts are significantly cheaper, costing 1% of their face value. Real receipts cost about 7% of their face value.

Like the Idealistic restaurant, the Profit-Maximizing restaurant offered discounts to customers who claimed *Fapiao* receipts but did not intend to use them for reimbursement. However, discount was not used to reduce the use of *Fapiao* receipts as in the case of the Idealistic restaurant. At the Profit-Maximizing restaurant, discounts were offered only when customers requested them. In addition, it was cheaper to provide counterfeit receipts than to offer discount, as the counterfeit receipts cost only 1% of their face value, and discounts always exceeded this rate. The amount of discount offered depended on the value of the bill, but seldom exceeded 5% of the bill value.[25] For example, if a customer's bill came to 103 CNY, 3 CNY would be discounted, which translates to a discount of 2.9%. Similarly, a 124 CNY bill would be rounded down to 4 CNY, yielding a 3.2% discount. Thus, instead of using it to reduce the number of *Fapiao* receipts, discount was used to increase customer satisfaction and retain regular customers. As the owner noted, "[Even though I need to pay more,] I still give customers discount if customers ask for it...I'm doing business and do not care about such small money. They feel happy to get discount and they will come back again."[26]

At the Profit-Maximizing restaurant, counterfeit *Fapiao* receipts were used first, as the genuine receipts were useful and left for when they were really needed, such as for customers who submitted them for reimbursement, customers who could identify fake receipts, people who wanted to buy genuine receipts, and some *Guanxi* who needed genuine receipts. As discussed in the section on opening licenses, he gradually established *Guanxi* with some inspectors. One way to do this is to give inspectors genuine *Fapiao* receipts. For example, when FDA inspectors needed *Fapiao* receipts to claim rewards or reimbursements, they would visit the Profit-Maximizing restaurant, and he would provide them free of charge. Although this did not happen often, he was always prepared. In the first three years, inspectors came only twice and received genuine *Fapiao* receipts valued at about 3000 CNY. Moreover, some people who needed real *Fapiao* receipts to claim reimbursements would buy the receipts, and he would sell genuine receipts at 10% of the face value. When customers claimed *Fapiao* receipts, the cashier would judge whether it was likely that they needed genuine receipts to claim reimbursement. If the cashier felt this was the case, the customer would receive a genuine *Fapiao* receipt. If the cashier thought the customers simply

---

number of someone who sold fake receipts. When he needed more, he simply called, and the fake receipts were sent to the restaurant or a designated collection point. He may have obtained the number through friends or from someone selling counterfeit receipts door-to-door. As seen in the previous case, some is always offering these receipts.

[25] Generally, discount would not exceed 5% of the bill value except in extreme cases. For example, a customer asked that a 159 CNY bill be reduced to 150 CNY. The server initially did not agree, but the customers kept bargaining. This was a regular customer, and the server knew the person was difficult, so she agreed to the discount. In this case, it was 5.6% of the bill value.

[26] Interview with the owner of the Profit-Maximizing restaurant on March 2, 2012.

wanted the receipt for the scratch prize,[27] the customer would receive a counterfeit receipt. The cashier, Wang, could make these judgments because most customers at the Profit-Maximizing restaurant were regulars, and she knew most of them well. During the observation period, Wang shared details of regular customers' lives with me, pointing out rich customers, those who kept mistresses, and those who were stingy and difficult. Nevertheless, some customers who were not regulars but who required genuine receipts sometimes received counterfeit receipts in error.

The Profit-Maximizing restaurant clearly violates the *Fapiao* Management Measurement by using counterfeit *Fapiao* receipts. However, the owner did not view this as risky:

> I bought fake *Fapiao* receipt, not only me, the big restaurant bought more...They (enforcement departments on fake *Fapiao* receipt, such as police) will spy on fake *Fapiao* receipt, however, they will not come to restaurants. They just spy on those who sell fake *Fapiao* receipt.

Although the police focus on the counterfeiters rather than the restaurants using the counterfeit receipts, the Profit-Maximizing restaurant's customers realized that the restaurant provided counterfeit receipts. Yet this did not seem problematic or risky. One day, a customer asked for a *Fapiao* receipt and told the cashier, Wang, that the previous receipt he obtained from the Profit-Maximizing restaurant "could not be reimbursed." This was a subtle way of saying the *Fapiao* receipt was not genuine. Wang answered, "It should be able to be reimbursed. If you cannot use it, just come back and I will change it for you." The customer nodded and did not say anything. From that time, all *Fapiao* receipts Wang gave that customer were genuine. Thus, although customers realize that some of the *Fapiao* receipts were not genuine, they did not complain to the tax office or other enforcement departments, such as the police, so the risk of discovery by an enforcement department is low. Furthermore, the owner did not think it particularly risky even if a customer did complain an enforcement department. According to him,

> They [the tax office] know that we use fake *Fapiao* receipt. There are also someone will complain to them. But it is impossible that they come to blame us... unless the complains are quite a lot which goes to the police station, and some special campaign is taking place... Generally speaking, they do not come to blame us.

4.5.4 Washing Hands and Cutting Fingernails

As shown in the previous case, washing hands and keeping nails trimmed are behaviors specified in the FDA's (2001) "Operational Norms of Catering Services for Food Safety." On the walls of almost every restaurant in China hang paper signs about the

---

[27]To encourage customers to request *Fapiao* receipts and pressure restaurants to report their real turnover, the tax office in China issues *Fapiao* receipts that contain scratch prizes ranging from several CNY to several hundred CNY. Usually, customers claim their prizes from the restaurants from which the *Fapiao* receipts originated, and the restaurants are reimbursed by the tax office later.

norms restaurant workers should follow that clearly list washing hands and cutting fingernails often. While keeping fingernails trimmed short is often accepted practice in restaurants and a practice regularly checked during the daily meeting, few restaurants require their employees to wash their hands,[28] and rules related to handwashing generally are overlooked.[29]

At the Profit-Maximizing restaurant, the rules of washing hands and cutting nails were not observed. Workers viewed the length of their fingernails as a personal matter, and trimmer their nails according to their own preferences. The kitchen workers responsible for the barbecue and cutting boards had long nails, as did the servers, although theirs varied in length. The servers preferred long nails for aesthetic reasons, and often wore nail polish, while the kitchen workers considered long nails practical, as they prevented cuts and burns to the fingers. Only one kitchen worker, who was responsible for cold dishes and drinks, always cut his nails short, although he noted that he did so out of habit. The same attitude applied to washing hands, and workers also simply did what they wanted to and what they were accustomed to. For example, I observed a kitchen worker return to preparing food after smoking outside. He fetched a piece of pork from the freezer and placed it on the cutting board without washing his hands. However, before cutting the cucumber, he washed his hands. Later, he fetched beef from the freezer and used a cleaning cloth to clean the ice on the freezer's floor. He did not wash his hands before cutting the beef.

When asked whether the Profit-Maximizing restaurant had any rules about washing hands and cutting nails, the owner responded,

> It is not necessary for such small restaurant…I do not make any rules for workers. The restaurant is just open and keeps going on (*Kaizhe Zouzhe*). It will not make any trouble for not having a rule. There is no need to bother with rules…Customers do not pay attention to those small things. What customers care about is what kinds of dishes the restaurant has, and how the dishes taste. They can see that we are busy. We are busy and there is not time for such kind of service things. So it [such service things] becomes normal. I also tell them [the employees] do not leave the nails too long.[30]

---

[28] Not too surprising, the issue of washing hands is also overlooked in academic research papers about restaurants in China. In contrast, hand hygiene in restaurants has been studied extensively in quite a lot of papers in international academia. Some researchers directly observed the washing hand practices in restaurants. See Henderson et al. (2008), "Dirty hands in the restaurant kitchen: Fact or fiction?" and Green et al. (2006). Some researchers studied workers' perspectives on handwashing behaviors and factors related to the practices. See Pragle et al. (2007), and Green et al. (2007).

[29] In China, handwashing is more likely to be mentioned in slogans related to food safety (e.g., "Washing hands reduces disease") than in academic literature. However, in an epidemiological study of diarrhea caused by Norovirus, handwashing was found to be an important factor in the prevention of diarrhea (Zhong et al. 2014). In contrast, handwashing among medical personnel has received significant research attention. However, those studies on handwashing compliance focus mainly on investigating the status of handwashing behaviors among medical personnel and on interventions to improve handwashing compliance. The studies lack the perspective of compliance theory and scientific research methods. The influential factors related to handwashing identified in those studies are being busy with work (Wu et al. 2005), lack of attention (Peng et al. 2007), lack of washing facility (Xu 2015), poor management (Peng et al. 2007), and conformist mentality (Xu 2015).

[30] Interview with the owner of the Profit-Maximizing restaurant on August 21, 2013.

4.5.5 Learning Process in Daily Operation (Non)Compliance Behaviors

The description of the (non)compliance behaviors regarding dish disinfection, health certificates, *Fapiao* receipts, handwashing, and fingernail cutting clearly show the learning process responsible for their development. the Profit-Maximizing restaurant used prepacked tableware to appear to comply with the legal requirements of dish disinfection. Although he questioned whether the prepack items had been disinfected properly, he still used them for convenience, cost saving, and maintaining an important business relationship. Other tableware, such as serving plates, small seasoning plates, and large soup-spoons, were not disinfected. the Profit-Maximizing restaurant kept one bottle of disinfectant fluid, a disinfection cabinet, and a fake disinfection log to indicate that it satisfied disinfection requirements. From previous inspections, the owner learned that these are the three points inspectors check and that "generally speaking, inspectors did not check the dishes."[31]

Health certificates at the Profit-Maximizing restaurant were either genuine, but obtained using a fraudulent procedure, or counterfeit. However, the owner had learned that the risk of noncompliance was minor and dismissible. He carefully observed how FDA inspectors checked the health certificates and whether they compared them to archived documents to verify their authenticity, and he even prepared two different responses to the possible outcomes. Yet inspectors never carefully examined the health certificates, and they definitely did not perform any cross checking. As a result, he views his noncompliance as risk free.

Moreover, the Profit-Maximizing restaurant obviously violated the regulations related to *Fapiao* receipts by using counterfeit ones. To save money, the Profit-Maximizing restaurant underreported its turnover and bought few *Fapiao* receipts— far from enough to issue customers genuine receipts on request. Consequently, the owner used counterfeit *Fapiao* receipts to supplement the real ones. On the one hand, he learned to strategically use counterfeit *Fapiao* receipts to reduce the risk of discovery by customers, but on the other hand, he learned that customers' reactions to counterfeit receipts are mild and manageable, and thus will not cause a great deal of trouble. In addition, he learned that enforcement agencies focus on those selling counterfeit receipts rather than on those using them, which further reduced the perceived risk.

Although the Profit-Maximizing restaurant generally violated these three legal requirements, it showed some level of compliance in cases of perceived risk related to violation. However, the Profit-Maximizing restaurant dismissed the legal requirements related to nail cutting and handwashing. This, too, was the result of the owner's experience of working in small restaurants. Not having such requirements does not cause trouble, and customers do not pay attention to those requirements in small restaurants. It is also impossible for inspectors to inspect such things.

---

[31] Interview with the owner of the Profit-Maximizing restaurant on March 2, 2012.

From previous experience, others' experiences, customers' reactions, inspection procedures, and the reaction of enforcement departments, the Profit-Maximizing restaurant learned to avoid compliance with the daily operational requirements discussed.

4.6 Discussion

4.6.1 Classifying Compliance Behaviors at the Profit-Maximizing Restaurant

The case of the Profit-Maximizing restaurant shows how the business responded to various legal norms, such as opening licenses, renewing of licenses, health certificates, dish disinfection, *Fapiao* receipts, handwashing, and nail cutting. In contrast to the survey-based compliance literature that focuses on particular predefined instances of compliance, I traced back the development of compliance behaviors. As is evident, compliance in the Profit-Maximizing restaurant is complicated when one examines the process. For most legal norms it faced, the Profit-Maximizing restaurant showed some degree of compliance rather than total noncompliance, and this was more prevalent than compliance and noncompliance.

The Profit-Maximizing restaurant engaged in fraudulent compliance, which involves an attempt to comply, but the compliance behavior is reached through fraudulent procedures or via fraudulent behaviors in the process. For example, it attempted to comply with the legal requirements of a business license but underreported its number of employees. Similarly, it attempted to comply with the legal requirements of the tax license but underreported its turnover. For the fire license, it used staged photos to meet requirements, and for the health certificates, it did not follow the correct procedures related to health checks. Thus, when viewing compliance from a static point, the Profit-Maximizing restaurant seems to have complied, as it held business, fire, and tax licenses, and its employees had health certificates. However, if one traces back the process, the fraudulent aspects emerge, and these can be considered violations.

Furthermore, symbolic compliance[32] was evident. This refers to the situation where the regulated shows signs of attention to the legal requirements and some intention to comply, but the signs do not necessarily lead to substantial conformity (Edelman 1992). With symbolic compliance, the regulated complies with the letter of the legal norms but not with the spirit of the law. Usually, it involves substantial noncompliance. For example, the Profit-Maximizing restaurant installed a smoke purifier when applying for its environmental license, but the purifier was not used in daily operations to purify the cooking smoke. To show its compliance to dish disinfection requirements, the Profit-Maximizing restaurant installed a disinfection

---

[32] Also known as cosmetic compliance; see Krawiec (2003).

cabinet and bought disinfectant fluid to show inspectors that the restaurant complied with these requirements, but this equipment was not used in daily operations. The items acted as signs, but they did not lead to substantive disinfection behaviors. Similarly, using prepacked tableware was supposed to satisfy disinfection requirements, but it became a symbol of disinfection without necessarily linking to disinfection behavior. In addition, the Profit-Maximizing restaurant obtained a catering services license and followed the procedure to renew it, but the restaurant violated the conditions of the license by serving cold dishes. Therefore, this was compliance with the letter and not with the spirit of the law.

The behavior related to handwashing seemed to be noncompliance but in fact was symbolic compliance. Because inspectors cannot directly observe handwashing behaviors, inspectors measure this norm by determining whether establishments offer adequate handwashing facilities (Sun et al. 2014). Although workers did not wash their hands every time before working, the Profit-Maximizing restaurant had one handwashing basin in the kitchen in addition to three washing basins. As a result, handwashing in the Profit-Maximizing restaurant was also symbolic compliance.

Fake compliance also occurred at the Profit-Maximizing restaurant. For example, the falsified disinfection log acted as a Potemkin Village to disguise the reality that tableware was not being disinfected; thus, it hid noncompliance. Likewise, the falsified environmental license and health certificates were instances of fake compliance. The difference between fake compliance and symbolic compliance is that symbolic compliance may lead to full compliance but fake compliance does not.

The Profit-Maximizing restaurant's failure to renew the liquor license until sanctions are imposed is an example of forced compliance, which refers to situations in which the regulated comply immediately once only when facing threat of punishment. Once the threat of punishment is removed, the regulated return to a state of noncompliance until the threat reappears. The Profit-Maximizing restaurant did not initiate renewal of its liquor license and instead waited for the inspectors to visit and threaten punishment. If the inspectors and the threat appeared, the Profit-Maximizing restaurant would renew the license immediately, but only at that time. If the inspectors and the threat did not appear, the Profit-Maximizing restaurant would keep trading with an invalid license.

Finally, noncompliance—where the regulated complies with neither the spirit nor the letter of legal requirements and does not attempt to create a facade of compliance—occurred at the Profit-Maximizing restaurant. For example, restaurant workers did not follow the nail-cutting requirements but had long nails. The difference between noncompliance and forced compliance is the threat of punishment. While forced compliance can appear to be noncompliance in the period before the threat of punishment appears, the regulated engaging in noncompliance do not acknowledge the possibility of threat and do not prepare for compliance once the threat appears. Although the legal requirement is to keep fingernails short, it is almost impossible for inspectors to check whether workers cut their nails, and the Profit-Maximizing restaurant did not perceive any threat at this point. For a summary of the compliance behavior observed at the Profit-Maximizing restaurant, see Table 4.1.

Table 4.1 Variations of compliance and noncompliance at the Profit-Maximizing restaurant

Legal norms		Behaviors	Types of compliance
Opening licenses	Environmental license	Followed application procedure	Compliance
		Installed equipment as the license required	Compliance
		Obtained license	Compliance
		Installed smoke purifier but did not use it in daily operations	Symbolic
		Falsified renewed license	Fake
	Catering services license	Did not initiate application until inspectors identified problem	Enforced
		Bought stainless steel kitchen table	Compliance
		Obtained license	Compliance
		Followed renewal procedures	Compliance
		Use fraudulent health certificates to renew license	Fraudulent
		Obtained renewed license	Compliance
		Violated license condition be serving cold dishes	Noncompliance
Opening licenses	Business license	Followed application procedure	Compliance
		Underreported employees	Fraudulent
		Obtained license	Compliance
	Fire license	Followed application procedure	Compliance
		Falsified number of fire extinguishers, photos, and *Fapiao* receipts	Fraudulent
		Obtained license	Compliance
	Tax license	Followed application procedure	Compliance
		Underreported monthly turnover	Fraudulent
		Obtained license	Compliance
	Alcohol license	Obtained license	Compliance

(continued)

Table 4.1 (continued)

Legal norms		Behaviors	Types of compliance
		Did not renew the license but waited for inspector to find out	Forced
Daily operations	Dish disinfection	Used packed tableware	Skeptical
		Had disinfection cabinet but did not use it	Symbolic
		Had disinfectant fluid but did not use it	Symbolic
		Did not disinfect restaurant-owned tableware	Noncompliance
		Falsified disinfection log	Fake
	Health certificates	Initially, some employees had genuine health certificates	Compliance
		Employees did not undergo health check before receiving health certificates	Fraudulent
		Some employees had counterfeit health certificates	Fake
	Fapiao Receipt	Provided *Fapiao* receipts on request only	Partial
		Used counterfeit *Fapiao* receipts	Fake
		Gave some customers genuine *Fapiao* receipts	Compliance
	Washing Hands	Employees did not wash hands every time before working with or touching food; Have a washing basin as required	symbolic
	Cutting Fingernails	Employees had long nails	Noncompliance

From the view of the endogenous approach, compliance is socially constructed and defined through regulatory encounters. Hence, the compliance behaviors described exemplify the construction process from the perspective of the regulated. Both opening license administration and daily operations show the processes of how those behaviors came into being. The processes clearly involved a learning process regarding acceptable behaviors in practice. The owner of the Profit-Maximizing restaurant learned from the interaction with inspectors and enforcement officers that practical verification requirements exist alongside the legal requirements. He learned this from his own experience, his former employers' experiences, his acquaintances, and the reaction of customers what is acceptable and cost-cutting behaviors, and what risk can be ascribed to each behavior. Furthermore, he learned to manage the risks of each requirement.

In contrast to the Idealistic restaurant, the Profit-Maximizing restaurant engaged in processes oriented to the lowest level of compliance that would lead to not falling foul of regulatory departments. The Profit-Maximizing restaurant's compliance was generally profit-maximizing compliance, which sometimes resulted in symbolic compliance, sometimes led to fake and fraudulent compliance, and sometime led to forced compliance and noncompliance.

4.6.2   Characterizing the Subject of Compliance at the Profit-Maximizing Restaurant

To understand the complex compliance behaviors displayed at the Profit-Maximizing restaurant, I turned to the five motivational postures Braithwaite (2003) proposed and the five management styles Kagan et al. (2003) proposed. Braithwaite's (2003) five motivational postures are commitment, capitulation, resistance, disengagement, and game playing.[33] These postures categorize actors' attitudes toward and interactions with regulatory bodies, which reflects the level of social distance the regulated place between themselves and the enforcement authority. The first two postures, commitment and capitulation, are positive postures that indicate compliance, while the three remaining postures, resistance, disengagement, and game playing, are negative and defiant. Commitment reflects a closer positive social distance than capitulation, and disengagement reflects a greater negative social distance than resistance. People who show resistance, although fighting regulations, remain within the regulatory system, while those who are disengaged place themselves outside the regulatory institution, cutting themselves off psychologically from the influence of the regulatory attempt. Game players remain within the sphere of the regulatory institution, but they use the letter of the law to circumvent the intention of the law (McBarnet 2002).

From the perspective of motivational postures, the Profit-Maximizing restaurant had a posture of game playing. It was always working to find loopholes in legal requirements and to minimize cost to obtain legal status, as its fraudulent, symbolic, and fake compliance behaviors showed. For instance, it bought fewer fire extinguishers than required and staged photos after learning that the requirements would not be verified. It underreported its employee numbers when applying for a business license, and underreported its turnover and used counterfeit *Fapiao* receipts to reduce tax costs. He claimed, "If you just do what you are asked to, you do not earn money. To be honest will suffer losses. You have to be tricky whenever possible."

---

[33] See Chap. 2 for a comprehensive overview of motivational postures.

The compliance behavior of the Profit-Maximizing restaurant further indicates a posture of capitulation. It always cooperated with the enforcement departments and inspectors, at least apparently, and believed the enforcement inspectors to be cooperative in turn. When the inspectors pointed out something that needed to be corrected, the Profit-Maximizing restaurant always corrected it, even if symbolically, as evidenced by its symbolic compliance behaviors. For instance, when inspectors asked the Profit-Maximizing restaurant to install a smoke purifier, the owner installed one, even if it was never used. During the renewal of its catering services license, the Profit-Maximizing restaurant was required to label its freezers and cabinets to indicate what foods and products they contained, and despite the owner's skepticism regarding the practicality of this process, he complied with the instruction. However, the labels disappeared after several cleaning cycles. Moreover, the Profit-Maximizing restaurant attempted to maintain a good relationship with the enforcement officers, specifically the inspectors, and he built a level of mutual trust with the inspectors, as can be seen from the changes to the inspection procedures, which developed from close inspection using a flashlight to simply chatting outside like friends. Thus, the Profit-Maximizing restaurant and the inspectors respect each other and communication well, and their relationship is cooperative.

Nevertheless, a posture of disengagement arose at times, as indicated by fake and forced compliance behaviors. When the Profit-Maximizing restaurant needed to renew its environmental license, it did not engage with the relevant department, and chose to falsify the restaurant's certificate. The same applies to the liquor license renewal. In addition, the Profit-Maximizing restaurant distanced itself from the hygiene-related daily operations by claiming there is no need to enforce nail cutting and handwashing regulations in such a small restaurant.

Finally, a posture of resistance also emerged. When ICA inspectors wanted to fine the Profit-Maximizing restaurant 5,000 CNY, he complained that the fine was too heavy for the infraction and negotiated a lower amount. Further, fake compliance behaviors embody the resistance posture, although implicitly. When he falsified the environmental license without fear of being caught, and claimed he could sue the department for not doing its work (i.e., not checking and cleaning the equipment), he showed his dissatisfaction with and resistance toward the regulations related to the environmental license. For a brief summary of the motivational postures identified at the Profit-Maximizing restaurant, see Table 4.2.

As the table shows, different motivational postures exist in the Profit-Maximizing restaurant toward different regulatory systems, and they are expressed when facing the same regulatory requirements and the same types of compliance behaviors. The most significant interactions occurred within the FDA's regulatory system. Generally, the Profit-Maximizing restaurant had an attitude of capitulation toward FDA inspectors, doing what inspectors required, and finally building mutual trust with inspectors. The inspection later became conversations between friends, which differed considerably from the initial inspections. However, the game-playing posture also was evident and widespread in the interactions with the FDA regulatory system. After learning that the practical requirements inspectors verified differed from the legal requirements, the owner of Profit-Maximizing restaurant chose to "play" the system

Table 4.2 Motivational postures at the Profit-Maximizing restaurant

Motivational posture	Presentation	Compliance types
Game playing	Bought fewer fire extinguishers than required	Fraudulent
	Used staged photos	
	Underreported employees	
	Underreported turnover	
	Obtained health certificates without doing health checks	
	Kept disinfection fluid only for inspection	Symbolic
	Had disinfection cabinet but never used it	
	Provided genuine *Fapiao* receipts only to those who needed to claim expenses	Fake
Capitulation	Temporarily labeled containers despite the owner not seeing a reason to do so	Symbolic
	Installed smoke purifier despite the owner not seeing the need for one; did not use it	
Disengagement	Avoided environmental regulation system by not contacting Environmental Bureau and creating counterfeit renewed license	Fake
	Avoided alcohol regulatory system by not actively contacting Alcohol Management Bureau and waiting for inspectors to identify the violation	Enforced
	Believed there is no need to enforce nail cutting and handwashing requirements	Noncompliance
Resistance	Falsified renewed environmental license the owner claimed he could sue Environmental Department	Fake

by complying symbolically or fraudulently. He did not disinfect the dishes daily but simply kept a bottle of disinfection fluid in case inspectors came to check, and he had a disinfection cabinet but never switched it on. Similarly, he obtained health certificates without doing health checks and provided counterfeit health certificates during inspections once it realized the inspectors did not check carefully or perform cross checks.

Thus, the motivational postures of both capitulation and game playing exist in terms of the FDA regulatory system. The same types of compliance behaviors may also involve different motivational postures. In the case of the fake compliance behaviors of creating a counterfeit renewed environmental license, motivational postures of both resistance and disengagement can be found. By not contacting the environmental license enforcement department, the Profit-Maximizing restaurant removed itself from the regulatory system while simultaneously expressing it dissatisfaction with and resistance to this system by falsifying the license. In symbolic compliance behaviors, both capitulation and game playing can be found. On the one hand, symbolic compliance behaviors show the organization's intention of cooperating with the regulatory system, but on the other, the organization played games by complying only symbolically.

This combination of capitulation and game playing casts new light on motivational postures. Motivational postures offer a technique for classifying actors' attitudes and interactions with regulatory teams in the hope of illuminating the social distance between the regulated and regulatory authority. This concept was originally oriented toward social psychology and initially reflected the interaction between the regulated and the authority from which compliance is constructed. When Braithwaite et al. (1994) proposed the concept of motivational posture, with four postures at that time, the attitudinal dimension reflected in this concept involved mainly the attitudes of the regulated toward authority personnel, or interactions between authority personnel and the regulated. It did not indicate much about the attitude of the regulated toward legal norms per se. In a later paper on tax evasion and avoidance, Braithwaite (2003) added the posture of game playing, which focuses on the attitude of the regulated toward the law. As McBarnet noted, "Game playing is a particular kind of attitude to law: law is seen as something to be moulded to suit one's purposes rather than as something to be respected as defining the limits of acceptable activity" (as cited in Braithwaite 2003: 19).

The case of the Profit-Maximizing restaurant highlights that the attitudes of the regulated toward authority and the law could be separated from each other. The regulated can have a positive or cooperative attitude toward representatives of the authority and a negative attitude toward the law the authority is enforcing. If one were to classify this combination into one motivation posture, one might call it a "corrupting" posture. Corrupting reflects acceptance of the enforcement authority as a legitimate authority and an attempt of maintain a good relationship with the authority, not for compliance, but for finding loopholes in the law and minimizing the costs of complying with the law.

The management style proposed by Kagan et al. (2003) refers to the combination of managerial attitudes and actions that mark the intensity and character of each management team's commitment to complying with regulatory responsibilities. It classifies the attitudes of compliance actors to legal requirements and managerial commitment to regulatory requirements. Commitment includes managerial attitudes and actions. Kagan et al. (2003) five types of managers are laggards, reluctant compliers, committed compliers, strategists, and true believers.[34] The five types display increasingly greater commitment to compliance with and positive attitudes toward legal requirements, with laggards at the bottom and true believers at the top of the scale. Thus, a true believer is more committed to and more positive about legal requirements than a strategist, who is more committed to and more positive about legal requirements than a committed complier, and so forth.

From the perspective of management style, the Profit-Maximizing restaurant was part laggard and part strategist. It had a "negative attitude towards many regulatory requirements and [complied] only to avoid costly enforcement actions" (Kagan et al. 2003). It perceived most regulatory requirements negatively and considered them

---

[34] See Chap. 2 for a comprehensive overview of these management styles.

unnecessary, such as installing and using a smoke purifier for environment protection, buying enough fire extinguishers for fire prevention, and performing health checks, disinfecting dishware, and enforcing handwashing and nail cutting regulations for food safety. For example, in terms of the FDA requirements, the Profit-Maximizing restaurant complied symbolically or fraudulently with some regulatory requirements only to avoid costly enforcement actions. This is particularly evident from the violations related to the disinfecting of dishes.

However, the Profit-Maximizing restaurant was not fully a laggard. Unlike true laggards, the Profit-Maximizing restaurant worked to develop cooperative relationships with regulatory agencies, as discussed in an earlier part of this section. In addition, not all its compliance behaviors related to avoiding costly enforcement actions, and it initiated several compliance processes. For instance, it applied for catering services license renewal. Thus, it may have been, at least partly, a strategist at this point by linking the regulatory objectives to its business goals. As a matter of long-term "business sense," the Profit-Maximizing restaurant actively met the regulatory requirements with a margin of safety, such as at least operating legally. Additionally, the Profit-Maximizing restaurant resembles the strategist in its strategic and proactive relationships with regulators, that is, in seeking to build reliable and cooperative relationships with inspectors.

Understanding the phenomenon that an organization can have characteristics that matches the laggard and the strategist, which display different levels of managerial commitment to regulatory requirements, relies on understanding the concept of management style. Managerial attitudes and actions toward the regulatory authority are not differentiated by managers' attitudes and actions towards legal requirements but are combined into managerial commitment to the regulatory system. As shown above, the two can differ greatly and are not always in concert.

The Profit-Maximizing restaurant presents a complex picture of different compliance behaviors. Symbolic compliance, fraudulent compliance, fake compliance, forced compliance, and noncompliance all occurred at this small restaurant, leaving the observer wondering why the Profit-Maximizing restaurant engaged in those different types of compliance. This question cannot be fully answered using either the motivational posture or the managerial style approach. Different motivational postures underpin these compliance behaviors, and some motivational postures appear simultaneously, which requires explanation. The managerial styles identified suggest a successive engagement of commitment and attitude toward legal requirements; however, managerial styles at significantly different levels coexisted at the Profit-Maximizing restaurant in terms of the legal requirements from the same legal system, such as the FDA system. This requires further investigation.

As the case of the Profit-Maximizing restaurant shows, attitudes toward regulatory authorities can differ greatly from attitudes toward regulatory requirements, which can create a complex picture of compliance behaviors. Cooperation between the regulated and enforcement officers is always seen as a good sign for fostering compliance behavior in regulatory research. However, at the Profit-Maximizing restaurant, both cooperation and negative compliance behaviors, such as symbolic compliance, fraudulent compliance, fake compliance, forced compliance, and noncompliance, occurred. In this case, cooperation with enforcement officers did not seem to lead to improved compliance. This is linked to the type of enforcement officers brought into the restaurant, and it is discussed in Part B.

Kagan et al. (2003) claimed that laggards are usually apt to refuse access to social scientists, so it is difficult to study the compliance behaviors of laggards. In this way, the case of the Profit-Maximizing restaurant provides an interesting and valuable study of laggards.

References

Braithwaite, Valerie. 2003. Dancing with Tax Authorities: Motivational Postures and Non-Compliant Actions. In *Taxing democracy: Understanding tax avoidance and evasion*ed. ed. Valerie Braithwaite, 15–39. Ashgate.

Edelman, Lauren B. 1992. Legal Ambiguity and Symbolic Structures: Organizational Mediation of Civil Rights Law. *American Journal of Sociology* 97 (6): 1531–1576.

Fang, Jiancun, Dawei Xi, Xiaoyun Liu, and Xinxiu Liu. 2008. Analysis of a Case that Fake Health Certificate for Public Business Place Workers [*1 qi gonggong changsuo congye renyuan weizao jiankangzheng anli fenxi*]. *Preventive Medicine Tribune [yufang Yixue Luntan]* 14 (11): 1042.

Green, Laura R., Carol A. Selman, Vincent Radke, Danny Ripley, James C. Mack, David W. Reimann, Tammi Stigger, Michelle Motsinger, and Lisa Bushnell. 2006. Food Worker Handwashing Practices: An Observation Study. *Journal of Food Protection* 10(October 2006): 2320–2566.

Green, Vincent Radke, Ryan Mason, Lisa Bushnell, David W. Reimann, James C. Mack, Michelle D. Motsinger, Tammi Stigger, and Carol A. Selman. 2007. Factors Related to Food Worker Hand Hygiene Practices. *Journal of Food Protection* 3(March 2007): 535–804.

Guan, Qiang. 2006. Discussing Rationality of *Fapiao* Receipt Tax System from the Crime Cases of Fake *Fapiao* Receipts. *Accountant*, January 2006.

Henderson, A., M. Kitts, G. Challender, and S. Henderson. 2008. Dirty Hands in the Restaurant Kitchen: Fact or Fiction? In *CAUTHE 2008: Tourism and Hospitality Research, Training and Practice; Where the 'Bloody Hell' Are We?* eds. Scott Richardson, Liz Fredline, Anoop Patiar, and Megan Ternel, 269–272. Gold Coast, Queensland: Griffith University.

Kagan, R.A., N. Gunningham, and D. Thornton. 2003. Explaining Corporate Environmental Performance: How Does Regulation Matter? *Law & Society Review* 37: 51–90. https://doi.org/10.1111/1540-5893.3701002.

Krawiec, Kimberly D. 2003. Cosmetic Compliance and the Failure of Negotiated Governance. *Washington University Law Quarterly* 81: 487–544.

Li, Ling. 2011. Performing Bribery in China: Guanxi-Practice, Corruption with a Human Face. *Journal of Contemporary China* 20 (68): 1–20.

McBarnet, Doreen. 2002. When Compliance is not the Solution but the Problem: From Changes in Law to Changes in Attitude. In *Taxing Democracy: Understanding Tax Avoidance and Evasion*, ed. Valerie Braithwaite, 229–244. Aldershot: Ashgate.

Peng, Zhanxian, Xiaoyan Li, Yanfang Liu, Edi Wen, and Jinzhen Ou. 2007. Investigation of Handwashing Compliance and Perception among Medical Personnel [*Yihu renyuan xishou yicongxing yu renzhi qingkuang de diaocha*]" *Practical Preventive Medicine[Shiyong yufang yixue]*, 14(4): 128–130.

Pragle, Aimee S., Anna K. Harding, and James C. Mack. 2007. Food Workers' Perspectives on Handwashing Behaviors and Barriers in the Restaurant Environment. *Journal of Environmental Health* 69 (10): 27–32.

Qiu, Yingshi. 2007. Analysis of 6 Cases That Fake Health Certificate for Food Process Workers [6 qi weizao shipin congye renyuan jiankangzheng anli fenxi]. *Zhejiang Journal of Preventive Medicine [zhejiang Yufang Yixue]* 19 (6): 47.

Sun, Jing, Chaohui Ma, Ning Zhang, Na. Cui, Yanyan Liu, Li. Li, and Yadong Wang. 2014. Current Situation of Quantitative Grade Management on Food Safety in Catering Industries in Beijing [Beijing shi canyinye shipin anquan lianghua fenji guanli xiankuang fenxi]. *China Journal of Public Health [zhongguo Gonggong Weisheng]* 30 (5): 576–579.

Wang, Shitong, Xiangxia Wang, and Aiting Wang. 2009. Analysis of a Case That Fake Health Certificate and Training Certificate [*Yiqi weizao jiankangzheng he peixun hegezheng anli fenxi*]. *Henan Journal of Preventive Medicine [henan Yufang Yixue Zazhi]* 20 (2): 153–154.

Wu, Xinjuan, Lili Ma, and Zhaoxia Jia. 2005. Study on the Condition of Hand-Washing Compliance in Clinic Nurses and Influential Factors [Huli renyuan xishou yicongxing xianzhuang ji yingxiang yinsu yanjiu]. *Journal of Practical Nursing [zhongguo Shiyong Huli Zazhi]* 13 (7A): 11–13.

Xu, Xiaohong. 2015. To Improve the Compliance of Hand Hygiene of Medical Staff Intervention Measures [Tigao yiwu renyuan shou weisheng yicongxing de ganyu cuoshi]. *The Medical Forum [jiceng Yixue Luntan]* 19 (3): 11–12.

Zhao, Zu'an. 2011. Company pay Salary, Workers have to Submit Fapiao Receipt? *Employment and Safeguard*.

Zhong, Jianming, Kaijie Deng, Feng Pang, Jingbin Zhang, and Li. Cao. 2014. An Investigation of Cluster Outbreak of Gastroenteritis due to Norovirus Infection in a Primary School [Yiqi xiaoxue nuoru bingdu changweiyan juji yuqing de diaocha]. *China Tropical Medicine [zhongguo Redai Yixue]* 14 (6): 755–757.

Chapter 5
Compliance Pluralism

5.1 Introduction

So far, this book has been a tale of two restaurants, the Idealistic restaurant and the Profit-Maximizing restaurant. The Idealistic restaurant, which intended to provide healthy and environmental friendly food, was established and co-owned by a highly educated, idealistic, and morally concerned woman. It can generally be classified as a true believer, but also sometimes can be viewed as a committed complier. As such, it is not surprising that, at the Idealistic restaurant, commitment to compliance and capitulation to regulatory pressures were evident. In contrast, the Profit-Maximizing restaurant aimed to provide tasty and economic food at the lowest price while maximizing profits. The owner of the Profit-Maximizing restaurant had learned from experience, and he was pragmatic and unconcerned with morals. Thus, at the Profit-Maximizing restaurant, game playing was evident, but signs of capitulation, disengagement, and resistance emerged. Moreover, at times the Profit-Maximizing restaurant could be classified as a laggard, and at times a strategist.

Despite these core differences between the two restaurants, compliance and noncompliance occurred in both. Although the Profit-Maximizing restaurant clearly engaged in fraudulent and fake compliance behaviors, and in noncompliance behaviors, in certain instances, it was compliant. In addition, although the Idealistic restaurant was more compliant than the Profit-Maximizing restaurant, it also engaged in fraudulent, fake, and symbolic compliance behaviors.

In this chapter, I will move beyond these two restaurants and draw out broader implications from the compliance behavior variations found both for the methods of studying compliance and for what compliance is and entails. This is achieved by including three other restaurants and their compliance behaviors. To maintain the focus on the findings and implications of the main case studies, only selected examples from other restaurants are described (for other information see Appendix C).

Y. Wu, *Compliance Ethnography*, Understanding China,
https://doi.org/10.1007/978-981-16-2884-9_5

5.2 Compliance Pluralism

The techniques used to label compliance in the existing literature often capture only one aspect of compliance behavior towards a single rule at a specific static point. However, this book indicated that compliance is complex and fluid. Within one restaurant, different types of compliance may occur in relation to different legal norms, different behaviors may occur in relation to the same legal norm, and these behaviors may change over time. To capture these complexities and fluidities, I proposed the concept of compliance pluralism.

As discussed in Chap. 2, previous research has attempted to classify compliance in terms of various characteristics of compliance that surpass the dichotomy of compliance and noncompliance. Scholars have evaluated compliance and identified various kinds of compliance based on the extent of compliance, or the quality of compliance, or the incentives of the regulated to comply with the law. They have proposed various kinds of compliance, such as partial, deep, shallow, symbolic, beyond, creative, coincidental, and conflictive compliance. Those compliance labels capture different prominent dimension or characteristics of compliance, and they are implicitly based on an assumption that there is a given compliance situation that can be characterized with one of these labels. In other words, they see compliance as a static situation that can be characterized.

However, the descriptive analysis of compliance conducted in this book has shown that compliance is complex and fluid. First, varied types of compliance occurred in a single organization, in this case in a restaurant. In the Idealistic restaurant, twelve types of compliance were identified (see Table 3.2, Chap. 3), including compliance and noncompliance, beyond, partial, attempted, fake, conflictive, skeptical, fraudulent, creative, enforced and symbolic compliance. At the Profit-Maximizing restaurant, eight types of compliance were identified (see Table 4.1, Chap. 4), including compliance and noncompliance, and partial, symbolic, fake, fraudulent, enforced, and skeptical compliance. In the other three restaurants in which I studied fewer legal norms in less depth, at least two types of compliance coexisted in the same restaurant (see Appendix C).

Second, compliance with one legal norm included a cluster of behaviors, and within each restaurant, a multitude of legal norms applied. Therefore, when attempting to understand restaurants' compliance behavior, one must examine multiple behaviors for multiple legal norms. Consequently, in the restaurants studied, variation in compliance behavior existed overall in combinations of more or less compliance, and more or less substantive versus more or less formalistic and fraudulent compliance. Furthermore, multiple legal norms existed, each with multiple behaviors, which each evoked plural responses, even within one restaurant. For example, to comply with the legal norm of obtaining a catering services license, a restaurant not only needs to install the required equipment and satisfy the required environmental conditions but also needs to ensure that all employees have valid health certificates. To obtain health certificates, employees first need to undergo health examinations. However, both the Idealistic restaurant and the Profit-Maximizing restaurant fully complied with the first requirement but fraudulently, symbolically, or partially complied with the second. Compliance regarding dish disinfection is another good example. Many corresponding behaviors must be completed to comply with the disinfection norm: restaurants need to buy equipment or tools (disinfection cabinet, disinfectant), include all dishware (various spoons, bowls, dishes, chopsticks), sanitize dishware before every use, and complete the disinfection log every time.

Yet, as described in the Idealistic restaurant and the Profit-Maximizing restaurant cases, the restaurant might have completed one behavior or exceeded legal expectations, but then partially completed the second and falsified the third. For example, at the Idealistic restaurant, four kinds of compliance behaviors were identified related to disinfection norms—beyond, partial, full, and fake compliance. At the same restaurant, three kinds of compliance behavior were identified related to *Fapiao* receipts, namely noncompliance, partial compliance, and full compliance. Even more compliance types were identified regarding opening licenses. At the Profit-Maximizing restaurant, four kinds of compliance occurred in terms of disinfection norms: skeptical, symbolic, and fake compliance, and noncompliance. Similarly, three kinds of compliance behaviors were identified when observing the health certificate norm: full, fraudulent, and fake compliance. Likewise, the Profit-Maximizing restaurant displayed several types of compliance when obtaining its opening licenses.

Third, the types of compliance changed during the process of complying with the same aspect of the same legal norm. At the Profit-Maximizing restaurant, full compliance occurred when applying for the new environmental license (the required equipment was installed), but later, during daily operations, this became symbolic compliance (not turning on the equipment). A year later, when it was time to renew the environmental license, it evolved into fake compliance (falsifying the license using a counterfeit stamp). Initial full compliance regarding the liquor license developed into enforced compliance (it did not initiate license renewal but waited for sanctions instead). With the catering services license, enforced compliance changed to full compliance during the application process, but when renewing the license, this changed to fraudulent compliance. The types of compliance changed during the process of applying for and renewing every opening license, and for most daily operational legal requirements.

Even at the Idealistic restaurant, which was generally inclined toward compliance, types of compliance change during the process. When applying for the catering services license, full compliance changed to symbolic compliance (removed one sink) and partial compliance (not all workers had health certificates). When applying for the drainage license, compliance and attempted compliance evolved into fraudulent compliance (used tap water for the test).

At L restaurant, which is described fully in Appendix C, changes in compliance related to the same legal norm also emerged. The owner of L restaurant opened two restaurants one after the other. For the first restaurant, she followed the fire license requirements, bought the required number of fire extinguishers, and obtained her fire license. After the closure of the first restaurant, she opened the second restaurant where a previous restaurant had been. She rented the site and obtained the opening licenses from the previous restaurant, just like what the Profit-Maximizing restaurant did when the owner got the restaurant from previous owner. Legally, those licenses were invalid for the owner of L restaurant. She had to apply for her own opening licenses for her new restaurant, but she did not do so, and she failed to buy the fire-safety equipment required by licensing law. Therefore, L restaurant's behavior changed from full compliance to fake compliance in terms of the fire license.

These examples show that categorizing compliance behavior captures the characteristic of the behavior only at a static point but the behavior may change at another point. Thus, the classification methods described in the literature capture one aspect of response behavior in terms of one rule at one static point. Within one restaurant, the types of compliance may vary between legal norms, with different behaviors emerging for each, which might change over time, and compliance type may change in relation to the same norm as compliance behaviors develop. Hence, it is difficult to ascribe the regulated and their compliance behaviors to a single category. Even the nature of compliance related to the same legal norms differ. For example, at the Idealistic restaurant, both negative and positive compliance behaviors related to disinfection were identified. Consequently, how can one characterize the Idealistic restaurant's compliance with the disinfection legal norm? The same question arises when considering many other legal norms. Furthermore, how can one characterize the general compliance behavior of one restaurant? The descriptions used above create too much complexity to find a simple answer to these kinds of questions.

It is clear that compliance in one restaurant involves many rules, behaviors, and static points during the process of responding to legal norms. As a result, I argue that understanding compliance requires the concept of compliance pluralism, which refers to the presence of various compliance behaviors in a social sphere during the process of responding to legal requirements. This concept is based on the notion of legal pluralism proposed by Griffiths (1986) and Merry (1988). Through legal pluralism, the concept of law is expanded to include state law, customary law, and other social ordering or norms that regulate people's lives. It stimulates discussion of the interaction between customary law and state law, social ordering, and legal ordering. With the concept of compliance pluralism proposed in this book, it is possible to broaden the view when discussing compliance to shift the focus from a single compliance assessment at one static point to different types of compliance throughout the process and to the process of compliance developing from one form to another.

Compliance pluralism means compliance involves numerous rules. In practice, the regulated will always face several kinds of law and several enforcement departments, and they must learn and adapt to various regulatory systems. Compliance with one law may differ from, but is inevitably related to, compliance with another law. Moreover, different regulatory systems influence the regulated in specific ways and work together to shape the regulated actors' compliance behaviors by working on the subject cognitively, attitudinally, and ideologically.[1] In terms of compliance

---

[1] In *Law enforcement: The game between inspectors and inspectees*, Bruijn and coauthors (2007) discussed the effects of multiple laws on regulatees' compliance behavior. However, they examined

pluralism, scholars and regulators may want to involve multiple laws the regulated face, study compliance behaviors related to different laws in one organization and the interaction between them, and discuss how these compliance behaviors or regulatory interactions shape the subject of the regulated. With such analyses and discussion, the compliance behavior of the regulated can be better understood, and problems with compliance behavior may be anchored more easily.

In addition, compliance pluralism means compliance with one legal norm involves many concrete aspects or behaviors. Compliance is not abstract but always is related to corresponding behavior, and one legal norm usually regulates several substantial behaviors. In other words, to comply with one legal norm, the regulated should engage in several substantial behaviors. For instance, to comply with fire license legal norms, restaurants should have enough fire extinguishers, install fire exist signs and emergency lights, and ensure that the main door opens outward, in addition to several other behaviors. Restaurants engaging in one compliance behavior will not necessarily engage in another compliance behavior that forms part of the collection of compliance behaviors related to the same legal norm. Therefore, scholars and regulators must take care to explicitly identify the concrete behaviors the compliance involves and to be cautious of whether the compliance involves other aspects or behaviors when characterizing regulated actors' compliance with certain legal norms. This will enable scholars to comprehensively study different aspect of the same legal norm.

Furthermore, compliance pluralism means compliance may change during the compliance process. Compliance takes many forms at different points. All the restaurants studied obtained their opening licenses. Thus, if one were to evaluate compliance when checking their enforcement records, they all appear to comply with the legal norm of holding opening licenses and to be operating legally. Yet if one were to evaluate their compliance when checking adherence to the regulations set out in these licenses during daily operations, the results will differ, and tracing back the application processes for these licenses would further complicate matters. The compliance pluralism approach enables researchers to explicitly recognize the points at which they conduct their compliance assessments, to accept changes to compliance before and after that point, or to discuss the change that occur before and after, and to deeply study the motivation for or mechanism related to each change.

Finally, compliance pluralism originates from different understandings of what the law requires. This is not simply a matter of interpreting the legal rules, as endogenous scholars have argued but it encompasses pluralism of expectations about what compliance is. Pluralism means the assessment of compliance can differ from the perspectives of different actors. The regulated understand compliance differently to

---

the effects of multiple laws by focusing on the conflict between laws and the dilemmas brought about by this conflict. The authors argued that the regulatees would strategically share the dilemma with inspectors and largely force the inspectors to identify a trade-off between different laws. As a result, the regulatees may finally comply with reduced requirements. In the present study, it has been found that the existence of multiple laws has a greater influence on compliance behavior. The regulatees will learn and adapt to different regulatory systems, and during this process, various regulatory systems will work together in shaping the regulatees' compliance behavior.

the regulator. From the point of view of the regulated, they complied with the law, as they have done what inspectors asked them to do and have obtain legal licenses. Although they may be fined at times, they do not think they have violated the law. In their eyes, they always comply with the law. Instead, the regulator may judge whether the regulated comply with the law based on one static point and the records related to that static point, that is, during an inspection or when the regulated engages in a specific behavior. This finding resonates with Yapp and Fairman (2005) study of compliance with food safety legislation in small businesses. They found that SMEs believed they were compliant when they had carried out all work inspectors required, even if they were judged as noncompliant in terms of the formal compliance concept stipulated by regulatory agencies (Yapp and Fairman 2005).

Elffers et al. (1992) questioned why three ways of measuring compliance in a study on tax evasion yielded different results, and why there was a lack of association between the three kinds of results. They speculated that tax evasion behaviors may consist of at least three independent conceptual aspects, and that the three unrelated aspects are measured by the three measurement methods. This may be better understood by considering compliance pluralism. Compliance is not static but pluralistic, and it involves numerous behaviors related to the same legal norm, changes during the compliance process, and is assessed differently by different actors. The plural results obtained by using different measurement methods may have arisen simply because they reflected different aspects or different concrete behaviors of tax evasion, because they reflected different points of the changing behavior, or because they reflected different perspectives of different actors. In a word, the plural result simply reflected the pluralistic character of compliance. Because compliance involves a multitude of concrete behaviors or aspects, changes during the compliance process, and is understood differently from different points of view, different measurement methods produce dissimilar results. Every result is real at the measurement point and time point and from that point of view. However, each result addresses only one aspect of compliance during the compliance process.

Compliance pluralism shares some similarities with, yet differs from, "contextual compliance" proposed by Yan et al. (2015). They argued that farmers' compliance with regulations regarding pesticide use is highly contextual in terms of the deterrence perception and cost–benefit calculation. Both deterrence perception and cost–benefit calculation are situational and subjective depending on the type of legal norm, the type of regulated actors, the location and economic conditions at play, the availability of third-party enforcement actors, and the particular and varied subjective views, experiences, and conditions of each individual actor. Compliance pluralism is similar to contextual compliance in terms of its situational and subjective nature. However, there are also significant differences between the two. The conception of compliance pluralism is intended to capture the characteristics of the phenomenon of compliance, and it is drawn out from descriptions of compliance behaviors. Contextual compliance does not directly address compliance but describes the nature of deterrence perception and cost–benefit calculation, which are considered closely linked to compliance. Furthermore, the meaning of compliance pluralism is considerably broader than its situational and subjective nature. In compliance pluralism, the situational nature is broadened to include a diachronic perspective, as compliance behavior is fluid and changing. In addition, it considers the interaction between past and future compliance behaviors. Various compliance forms and behaviors existed in one restaurant during the process of responding to legal norms, and these behaviors were interrelated. Compliance that occurred previously and with one legal norm influenced compliance that occurred later and with other legal norms. Compliance pluralism reminds researchers attend to the contextual situation of compliance, the changing nature of compliance, and the interaction between different forms of compliance when studying compliance.

Compliance pluralism introduces a new kind of understanding of compliance. It allows researchers to place their compliance data from different sources in a certain position in the framework of compliance based on the relevant time point, the source of the data, the specific legal requirement it relates to, and the specific perspective of the actor. Then they can further discuss the interrelationship between various compliance data, the compliance change inclination, and the social relations and social constructions behind the variation. It challenges most existing compliance measurement methods which only reflect compliance data at a static time or very particular times, and suggests that compliance researchers should identify their compliance data explicitly in terms of the time point it presents, the specific aspect of one legal norm, and even the specific perspective of the actor who provided the data.

Furthermore, seen from the view of compliance pluralism, it may become quite difficult to avoid the compliance variation of the regulated actors in the regulatory system. Although this may seem somewhat pessimistic, as it seems impossible to promote genuine singular compliance from the regulated actors, despite the ever-present specter of variation, the regulated actors show a definite inclination toward compliance. As shown later in following Chapters, although both negative and positive compliance existed in all restaurants studied here, all restaurants generally showed three kinds of inclination or three kinds of actor characteristics— true believer, game player, and blind complier. Other types of actor may also exist. Different kinds of regulated actors generally showed different clusters of compliance behaviors, and within each cluster, variation existed to an extent.

5.3 Compliance Processes

In the cases studied, compliance behaviors occurred and developed through various processes. Instead of identifying steps in the process as was the case in Henson and Heasman (1998), Fairman and Yapp (2004), and Chemnitz (2012), I attempted to capture the characteristics of the processes through which compliance behaviors occurred, as this could serve as the first step in further discussing the general processes that take place during compliance.

From the description of compliance behaviors in the two core restaurants, it is clear that a clarifying process occurred during the applications for opening licenses.

Moreover, a contesting process took place during the development of compliance behaviors in daily operations at the Idealistic restaurant; at the Profit-Maximizing restaurant, a learning process emerged. The owner of the Idealistic restaurant experienced long process of clarifying the exact requirements with which she needed to comply. This process stems from the very nature of law, because, as numerous scholars have noted, the law is never clear enough. To transform the theory of law into substantial behavior, the regulator and the regulated must constantly interpret and clarify specific legal norms and make them operable. Endogenous researchers have devoted great effort to addressing this point in terms of how the law is negotiated and of how compliance is constructed to bridge the gap between the theoretical and practical application of the law (Lange 1999). However, as shown in Chap. 3, the clarifying process differs from the negotiation process, which supports the views held and advocated by endogenous theorists. The clarifying process did not involve mutual discussion between the regulator and the regulated about the legal norms and real-life practices. Information flowed unilaterally from the regulator to the regulated.

The clarifying process shares several similarities with learning processes, as described by Van Rooji (2013). During the clarifying and learning processes, the regulated not only learn the content of legal requirements and the required substantial operations but also learn how they are enforced and how their peers comply. However, differences exist. In the clarifying and learning processes described here, verification from the regulator has been included and found essential, while in Van Rooij's model, verification from the regulator is lacking or unclear.

The clarifying process cannot be fully captured by the compliance steps identified by Henson and Heasman (1998). Although it involves several of these steps, such as identifying the regulation, identifying the change, and implementing the change, it also involves other steps, such as verification by the regulator. From the description of the case studies, the clarifying process can be depicted as a recurring series of steps: identifying the regulation, responding to the regulation, verification of the regulation by the regulator, and further identifying the regulation. Hence, the clarifying process is similar to the learning process discovered at the Profit-Maximizing restaurant, where the process of developing compliance behaviors taking place is a learning process in terms of learning the practical verified requirements.

Practical verified requirements refer to the legal requirements most likely to be enforced by the regulator. In practice, inspectors focused on particular regulations and largely overlooked others. The compliance behavior processes that took place at the Idealistic restaurant also involved the process of learning the practical verified requirements. However, when the owner of the Profit-Maximizing restaurant learned that the regulator would not verify certain requirements, the compliance behaviors involved with those legal requirements would not take place, for example, the restaurant would not complete the disinfection log. The same clarifying process occurred at the Idealistic restaurant in terms of constantly clarifying the most "necessary" and specifically enforced requirements. In other words, the practical verified requirement was "the law" restaurants learned in this process, which might have differed from the law the regulator attempted to enforce. Thus, restaurants' legal knowledge is more complex than simple recognition of whether one requirement is law or of what is written in a law. During this process, restaurants further gained knowledge about how the laws were enforced, that is, whether compliance was verified, and about how other restaurants responded to those requirements, and it seems various aspects of knowledge integrated and produced a comprehensive legal knowledge, which can best be described as what the law is in their minds. This comprehensive legal knowledge, rather than the written legal norms, may be the starting points for compliance behaviors. Therefore, this concept is critical in explaining restaurants' compliance behaviors, and it is discussed in Chap. 6 when examining how laws arrived at restaurants.

Contesting is another characteristic of the process through which compliance behaviors related to daily operational norms took place at the Idealistic restaurant. Despite the Idealistic restaurant's intention to comply with the law, it had a strong inclination to employ traditional and ecofriendly food processing methods that poorly suited, or even conflicted with, the modern regulatory system. As a result, doing what they believed was good and healthy led to the violation of certain regulatory rules, such as those surrounding pork quarantine certificates. In some cases, the Idealistic restaurant did not view the legal requirements as proper and necessary, so the development of compliance behaviors was characterized by competition or conflict between organizational beliefs and legal norms. For example, legally, the Idealistic restaurant was obliged to complete the disinfection log every time after disinfecting dishes, but the owner considered this redundant and a burden rather than necessary for people like them who always voluntarily "comply with the [aim of the] law."[2] This belief outweighed the legal requirements, and the Idealistic restaurant developed fake compliance behaviors related to this legal requirement.

In this instance, the contesting process closely aligns with the negotiation process Van Rooij proposed in terms of interaction between the regulated actors' ideas and the legal norm. However, the natures of the two processes differ significantly. Negotiation takes place between the regulated and the regulator when the two interact, and during the negotiation process, the two parties discuss the application of the legal norms and link the legal norms to real practice. However, the contesting process does not necessarily involve the regulator, and it may occur between the regulated actors' perceptions or beliefs and the legal norms.

In other words, by describing compliance behavior, I noted that compliance behaviors take place through several kinds of process, such as the clarifying, learning, and contesting processes. Each process captures one main characteristic of the process through which some compliance behaviors take place. Describing these kinds of process is important, as it could reveal critical junctions and turning points that could contribute to further explaining compliance behaviors.

---

[2]The Idealistic restaurant used organic cleaner and a high-quality disinfection cabinet to sanitize dishes, which is beyond compliance in terms of other aspects of the disinfection norms.

5.4   Characterizing Compliance Subjects

The case studies have important implications for characterizing the subject of compliance behaviors. Compliance is a pluralistic process, and significant variation can occur even within the same organization. It involves multiple rules and behaviors, and a series of dynamic processes that change over time. Hence, the labeling of a subject with such complex behaviors is challenging. Labels such as "complier" and "violator" do not fit any restaurant as a whole, and even the more subtle characterizations proposed by Kagan et al. (2003) and Braithwaite (2003) have some problems in capturing the complexity.

In Chaps. 3 and 4, the two in-depth case studies were analyzed in terms of the typologies proposed by Kagan et al. (2003) and Braithwaite (2003), and it emerged that each restaurant showed a combination of different motivational postures and management styles. In terms of motivational postures, the Idealistic restaurant reflected a combination of commitment and capitulation, while the Profit-Maximizing restaurant showed a combination of game playing, capitulation, resistance, and disengagement. In terms of management styles, the Idealistic restaurant seemed to be a combination of true believer and committed complier, while the Profit-Maximizing restaurant was a combination of laggard and strategist. L restaurant's (see Appendix C) motivational posture also was a combination of game playing and capitulation, while its management style was a combination of laggard and strategist. W restaurant (see Appendix C) shows a motivational posture combination of game playing and capitulation, as well as a management style combination of laggard, reluctant complier, and strategist. Therefore, to capture the characteristic of compliance actors using the concepts of motivational posture and management style is neither adequate nor reliable.

Moreover, the analysis shows that the regulated actors' attitudes or beliefs regarding legal norms should be differentiated from those related to enforcement departments or inspectors, although they sometimes are closely interrelated. To differentiate between the two helps one to understand the combinations of various motivational postures and management styles. As introduced in Chap. 2, the concept of motivational postures is based on the regulated actors' beliefs regarding and attitudes toward legal norms and enforcement departments or inspectors. It does not differentiate the regulated actors' attitudes toward legal norms from those toward enforcement departments or inspectors. The same applies to the concept of management style. However, this research has shown that the regulated are always inclined to show a posture of capitulation when facing inspectors, while they may hold an extremely negative attitude toward the legal norms inspectors are supposed to enforce. If one considers their beliefs regarding and attitudes toward legal norms, it becomes apparent that have motivational postures of game playing, resistance, or disengagement. For instance, the owner of the Profit-Maximizing restaurant held a negative view of most legal norms. He saw opening licenses and health certificates as ways for regulators to collect money, and he saw dish disinfection as unnecessary and troublesome. However, when facing inspectors, he generally followed inspectors' instructions, showing an inclination to cooperate despite not agreeing with the requirements at heart.

The concepts of motivational posture and management style assume that the regulated have the same attitudes toward legal norms and enforcement departments or inspectors. That is, if the regulated consent to the legal norms, they will also show commitment when interacting with enforcement departments or inspectors, and vice versa. However, in practice, this does not always hold true. The regulated may disengage from legal norms if they do not agree with them, yet at the same time cooperate with enforcement departments or inspectors. Similarly, the regulated may even set aside legal norms without experiencing moral dilemmas, yet cooperate with enforcement departments or inspectors. Bearing in mind that the regulated may have different beliefs regarding and attitudes toward legal norms and enforcement departments or inspectors will help researchers to evaluate compliance actors.

This book suggests that the different beliefs regarding and postures toward legal norms and regulatory authority should be considered when classifying compliance actors. For example, the restaurants described in this book can be classified as three types, with the Idealistic restaurant falling into the first category, the Profit-Maximizing restaurant and H restaurant into the second, and L restaurant and W restaurant into the third. Restaurants in the first category take a positive moral view of legal norms, and their beliefs largely align with these norms. They attempt to comply with legal norms and cooperate with enforcement departments or inspectors as much as possible. Nevertheless, their positive view of legal norms and regulations might deteriorate if their attempts to comply are repeatedly obstructed in practice, if they are treated unfairly, or if they keep learning that others receive regulatory approval through dishonesty. This kind of restaurant can be called a true believer.

Restaurants in the second category are not morally concerned with legal norms, and most of their beliefs conflict with these norms. Alternatively, they see law as something to be molded to suit their purposes rather than as something that should be respected. They always attempt to find the loopholes in the law and play in the gray area of the law to minimize the costs of obeying the law. This kind of actor is similar to the game player, as the motivational posture of game playing implies. However, as this game player always cooperates with regulators, is willing to remain within the regulatory field, and follows the practical rules of the regulatory game, once the practical rules change, its compliance may be inclined to change correspondingly. Consequently, this type of restaurant can be called a game player.

In the third category, restaurants do not have significant or obvious moral considerations related to legal norms, but they show considerable cooperation with regulators and are inclined to follow the regulator's practical verified requirements. They sometimes comply with the law and sometimes violate the law due to differences between the law as it is written and its practical verified requirements. This kind of restaurant can be called a blind follower.

Based on the principle of differentiating between the beliefs and attitudes of the regulated regarding enforcement departments or inspectors and regarding legal norms, other types of compliance actors may emerge. For example, some restaurants may not be inclined to cooperate with, or may even resist, enforcement departments or inspectors, but share the beliefs underpinning the legal norms. This kind of restaurant can be called a challenger of the regulatory system. If a restaurant resists enforcement departments or inspectors while at the same time holding a negative moral view of legal norms, it can be called a resister of the regulatory system. No challengers or resisters were evident in my research, as every restaurant studied was inclined to cooperate with enforcement departments or inspectors. Furthermore, it may be difficult for restaurants to choose not to cooperate with or even to resist regulators, as most hope to remain within the regulatory system.

5.5   Conclusion

Compliance has been studied for decades, and a plethora of studies has been devoted to understanding and explaining compliance. Considering the existing body of research, one may wonder how an ethnographic approach, describing compliance behaviors, can benefit and contribute new knowledge to existing compliance research. In this first part of this book, I has described, through ethnographic case studies, various complex compliance behaviors and how they occurred and developed. It emerged that describing compliance behaviors is fruitful in itself in terms of showing the complexity and fluidity of compliance, which generally has been overlooked. This revealed important periods in producing compliance behaviors, such as the start-up phase, and enabled me to reexamine the typology of the subject developed in earlier studies.

The complexity and fluidity of compliance has painted a picture of pluralism. Multiple kinds of compliance coexisted in the same restaurant, and compliance with one legal norm included a cluster of various compliance behaviors. Further, types of compliance might change during the process, even in terms of the same aspects of the same legal norm. To capture this complexity and fluidity, I proposed the concept of compliance pluralism to better capture the nature of compliance and facilitate the study of compliance in future research. In addition, by describing compliance behaviors from the beginning business operation, the diachronic development of compliance was identified as meaningful in compliance study. In other words, how compliance behavior takes place in the start-up phase of business operations is important for forming its compliance habits and in the development of subsequent compliance behaviors.

Moreover, through tracing the compliance process, various processes with clear characteristics were identified that differed from those noted in the existing literature. From describing compliance behaviors and the subject, this book also highlighted several limitations of the existing typologies and showed that in characterizing the regulated, researchers should differentiate between the regulated actors' attitude toward or beliefs regarding legal norms and those related to enforcement departments or inspectors, although they sometimes are closely interrelated. This allowed the identification of three types of subject: true believers, game players, and blind followers.

Part II of this book aimed to explain the complex and fluid compliance behaviors discussed in Part I using compliance models and theories developed in Western literature. The explanations are conducted on three levels, namely the regulatory, organizational, and individual levels, as briefly mentioned in Chap. 1. Each level has its own foci of explanation, which are discussed in the section that follows.

In Chap. 6, the focus is on the regulatory level, particularly on how legal norms entered the restaurants studied. From the perspective of the regulated actors, the focus is on the comprehensive legal knowledge formation of the regulated actors. I attempts to explain their behaviors by discussing how the regulated actors perceived the laws, examining what knowledge the regulated actors had of the laws, and determining how their comprehensive legal knowledge related to their compliance behaviors.

Chapter 7 focuses on the organizational level. At this level, restaurants as units are broken down and viewed as groups of people, and the laws that arrive at the restaurants are transmitted to these groups. To influence these people's behaviors, the laws interact with the groups' organizational norms, which form part of the groups' concerns. Thus, how laws were transmitted through the restaurants, especially how organizational norms align or compete with legal norms in organizational management and socialization processes, is discussed.

In Chap. 8, the focus shifts to the individual level. The individual finally engages in compliance behaviors, so it is important to discuss the variables that influence behavior at the individual level. This is achieved in two ways: first, by examining actors' subjective explanations for their behaviors, and second, by analyzing the association between several key influential variables identified in compliance literature and actors' behaviors. Subjective explanations, in terms of how the regulated actors subjectively explain their compliance behaviors, offer opportunities for discovering new, previously unstudied explanatory variables, while the analysis of variable associations between existing explanatory variables at individual level and individual compliance behaviors allows me to relate this research to existing compliance literature. Some variables at individual level discussed in this chapter reflect the comprehensive legal knowledge and organizational norms discussed in Chaps. 6 and 7.

References

Braithwaite, Valerie. 2003. Dancing with Tax Authorities: Motivational Postures and Non-Compliant Actions. In *Taxing Democracy: Understanding Tax Avoidance and Evasion* ed Valerie Braithwaite, 15–39. Ashgate.

Bruijn, Hans, Ernst ten Heuvelhof, and Marieke Koopmans. 2007. *Law Enforcement: The Game between Inspectors and Inspectees*. Boca Raton, FL: Universal Publishers.

Chemnitz, C. 2012. The Impact of Food Safety and Quality Standards on Developing Countries Agricultural Producers and Exports (Doctoral dissertation, Humboldt-Universität zu Berlin, Landwirtschaftlich-Gärtnerische Fakultät).

Elffers, Henk, Henry S. J. Robben, and Dick J. Hessing. 1992. On Measuring Tax Evasion. *Journal of Economic Psychology* 13 (4): 545–567.

Fairman, R., and C. Yapp. 2004. Compliance with Food Safety Legislation in Small and Micro-Businesses: Enforcement as an External Motivator. *Journal of Environmental Health Research* 3: 44–52.

Griffiths, John. 1986. What is Legal Pluralism? *Journal of Legal Pluralism and Unofficial Law* 24: 1–55.

Henson, S., and M. Heasman. 1998. Food Safety Regulation and the Firm: Understanding the Compliance Process. *Food Policy* 23 (1): 9–23.

Kagan, R.A., N. Gunningham, and D. Thornton. 2003. Explaining Corporate Environmental Performance: How Does Regulation Matter? *Law & Society Review* 37: 51–90. https://doi.org/10.1111/1540-5893.3701002.

Lange, B. 1999. Compliance Construction in the Context of Environmental Regulation. *Social & Legal Studies* 8 (4): 549–567.

Merry, Sally Engle. 1988. Legal Pluralism. *Law & Society Review* 22 (5): 869–896.

Van Rooji, Benjamin. 2013. Compliance as Process: A Micro Approach to Regulatory Implementation. On file with the author.

Yan, Huiqi, Benjamin van Rooij, and Jeroen van der Heijden. 2015. Contextual Compliance: Situational and Subjective Cost-Benefit Decisions about Pesticides by Chinese Farmers. *Law & Policy* 37 (3): 240–263.

Yapp, C., and R. Fairman. 2005. Assessing Compliance with Food Safety Legislation in Small Businesses. *British Food Journal* 107 (3): 150–161.

Part II
Explaining Compliance Behaviors

Chapter 6
Metamorphosis of Legal Knowledge: How Did the Laws Arrive at the Restaurants?

6.1 Introduction

In this part of the book, I'm going to analyze factors influencing the variation in compliance behavior identified in Part A. This chapter focuses on the law itself. Compliance behaviors are responses to the "laws" perceived by the regulated actors. As the discussion in the preceding chapters has indicated that restaurants' knowledge and understanding of these laws may differ from the written laws regulators aim to enforce, it is important to consider restaurants' understanding of these "laws". In this chapter, I will examine this by discussing how restaurant owners and managers formed their legal knowledge and on the type of legal knowledge they had. In addition, how enforcement agents introduced law to the regulated during enforcement encountered and the transmission of law during these encountered are discussed.

Most of the existing compliance literature centers on variables related to deterrence theory, procedural justice, and enforcement (Thornton et al. 2005; Van der Heijden, 2009, 2016). Less attention has been paid to understanding the extent to which the law penetrates the regulated organization, and thus to understanding what actual knowledge of the law shapes the behavior. Some studies have measured the general level of knowledge about the law and have attempted to link compliance levels with "legal knowledge" or "legal awareness," hence seeing "legal knowledge" as part of the capacity to comply (Yan 2014; Winter and May 2001). While this capacity is of course important, the regulated actors' legal knowledge does not merely involve how completely the regulated actors recognize the law, and the relationship between legal knowledge and compliance behaviors cannot be captured through "capacity" or "precondition." Knowing a legal norm may not always be a necessary condition for compliance. As Kim (1999) noted, even in the United States, knowledge of the law, even among specialists and of basic norms, is limited.

Moreover, as endogenous researchers such as Hutter (1997) and Lange (1999) pointed out, legal norms are often not clear enough, and their content and meaning are often constructed through interactions between the regulator and the regulated. The regulated actors' legal knowledge, which is an outcome of these interactions, also does not constitute a static reflection of how much and how well they know the written laws, but a construct that needs to be explored and clarified. Specifically, it is important to determine the nature, extent, and content of the regulated actors' legal knowledge. From this it can be inferred that the norms ultimately guiding the behavior of the regulated may not be the same as the original legal norms the regulator aims to enforce.

Furthermore, the legal system in China is still quite young, and recognition of the law among the population is limited. Under such circumstances, one cannot assume that the regulated know the law. Thus, it is essential to examine anew what the regulated know about the law, how they form their legal knowledge, and how the law evolves from the written to the applied form. To this end, the legal knowledge formation process of the regulated, as well as the regulatory encounter, which is the most important moment for the development of legal knowledge, is examined.

Therefore, this chapter focuses on the transmission of legal norms to the restaurants at the regulatory level through a discussion of restaurants' legal knowledge formation. First, several questions about legal knowledge, including the definition, composition, the source of acquisition, and its influence on compliance, are answered. Subsequently, the (comprehensive) legal knowledge formed in the restaurants studied, especially the role enforcement encounters played in the (comprehensive) legal knowledge formation of restaurants, is examined. Finally, conclusions are drawn regarding the explanation of compliance through the discussion of legal knowledge formation, and implications are identified for further compliance and enforcement study.

6.2   The Process of Legal Knowledge Formation

There is a common but not explicitly discussed premise in legal discourse and compliance study that the regulated knows the law before complying with it, and legal knowledge is considered a prerequisite of compliance (Yan 2014; Winter and May 2001). However, as Kim (1999) and other researchers[1] have shown, lay people generally are ignorant of the law. Kim (1999) conducted a survey of workers in several U.S. states to examine their understanding of the default rule of employment at will. She found that workers did not understand the default presumption but erroneously believed that the law afforded them protection again discharge without a just cause. For six

---

[1] See, e.g., Robert C. Ellickson. 1994. *Order without Law: How Neighbors Settle Disputes*, 48–50. Harvard University Press; Stan L. Albrecht, and Miles Green. 1997. Cognitive Barriers to Equal Justice Before the Law. *Journal of Research in Crime and Delinquency*, 14: 206, 209; Robert C. Ellickson. Of Coase and Cattle: Dispute Resolution Among Neighbors in Shasta County. *Stanford Law Review*, 623: 668–670; Austin Sarat. Support for the Legal System: An Analysis of Knowledge, Attitudes, and Behavior. *American Politics Research* 3(1): 12–15. For general information, see Martha Williams, and Jay Hall. 1972. Knowledge of the Law in Texas: Socioeconomic and Ethnic Differences. *Law & Society Review*, 99; Note, Legal Knowledge of Michigan Citizens, *Michigan Law Review*, 1463 (1973).

diagnostic questions that stated four lawful and two unlawful discharge reasons, respondents could answer about only 40% of the questions correctly in Missouri and California, while respondents in New York fared worse, on average answering only 25.2% correctly. Moreover, not only was the error rate widely distributed in these states, but the error rate also had a systematic direction and distribution. In another words, workers' understanding was systematically erroneous in widely dispersed populations. Workers' understanding reflected the norm in the internal labor market, and workers did not differentiate between the norm and the law. The results of Kim's study underscore the importance of not assuming that the regulated know the law but examining regulated actors' understanding of the law. Consequently, when attempting to explain restaurants' complex compliance behaviors, the first step is to examine restaurants' legal knowledge.

To examine restaurants' legal knowledge, this book will explore the legal knowledge formation process instead of measuring the actors' legal knowledge. The definition of legal knowledge remains disputable, and the measurement of legal knowledge deserves a lengthy discussion that falls beyond the scope of this book. In addition, instead of measuring whether restaurants know the law and to what extent they can repeat the law correctly, knowing how restaurants developed what legal knowledge is more appropriate, as it allows the discovery of factors that influence their legal knowledge and help to promote legal knowledge acquisition. Studying the process through which restaurants developed their legal knowledge brings the focus to the term "legal knowledge," particularly its meaning and construction. Therefore, it allows space to discuss the definition of legal knowledge and promotes understanding of legal knowledge. To gauge whether the restaurants knew written legal norms, and to assess the extent of their knowledge, I drew on interview content. This enabled me to determine whether the law really existed in the restaurants studied. It was found that restaurants clearly lacked knowledge of written legal norms.

Before delving into the main discussion, several questions regarding legal knowledge require clarification.

6.2.1   Definition of Legal Knowledge

First, what does legal knowledge mean? In a narrow sense, it refers to only the recognition of written legal norms, that is, whether a behavior is lawful or unlawful according to the written legal norm. In a broader sense, it refers to one's knowledge about the law, including one's direct recognition of written legal norms and one's perceptions of what the law is, what is required by law, and what may or may not be done. This may involve other information about legal norms, such as one's subjective interpretation of legal norms, perception of legal norms, compliance experience related to legal norms, and so forth. This knowledge forms the regulated actors' real recognition of what the law is. As Kim (1999) found in her research, workers' understanding of what the law of employment at will is deviated systematically from the formal law and largely related to the informal norm in the labor market. Workers had "strong beliefs about what norms of fairness require of an employer in a given situation" to "conflate these obligations with those required under the law" (Kim 1999: 480).

In this book, the broader sense of legal knowledge was employed, referred to as "comprehensive legal knowledge" for the sake of disambiguation. In Winter and May's (2002) view, two kinds of information are related to legal norms. One is to provide "facts," which entails such things as descriptions of requirements, timelines for adherence to those requirements, and means for adhering to rules. The other involves communicating other information related to legal norms, which concerns "the extent to which others are complying with rules, the value or appropriateness of a given set of rules, the duty to follow rules, and the fairness with which rules are being applied" (Winter and May 2002: 118). Inspired by Winter and May's (2002) concept, I views comprehensive legal knowledge as consisting of two kinds of knowledge related to legal norms: doctrinal legal knowledge and legal practice knowledge. Doctrinal knowledge concerns the content of the written legal norm in terms of whether the regulated know the exact content of the articles of the written legal norms, for example, whether the written law prohibits a certain action. This is the definition of legal knowledge in the narrow sense. Legal practice knowledge refers to the subjective acknowledgement of the enforcement of legal norms and the behavior of others related to legal norms. This subjective knowledge provides two clusters of supporting information to understand the law. The first addresses the regulated actors' personal knowledge about enforcement, such as the fairness with which rules are being applied, inspectors and enforcers working methods, and the importance enforcers ascribe to specific legal norms. The second involves the regulated actors' personal knowledge about other regulated actors, such as how other regulated actors perceive legal norms, how they deal with the legal requirements, and how difficult they find satisfying the legal norms. The two clusters of knowledge together provide important legal practice knowledge for the regulated.

Winter and May argued that individuals who receive information might act as "cognitive misers" to evaluate the appropriateness of information sources (see Jones 2001: 101). Similarly, the regulated may process their knowledge about legal norms, modify it, and finally form their own comprehensive legal knowledge of what the law is. Therefore, doctrinal legal knowledge and legal practice knowledge influence each other, as discussed in Sect. 3.4 of this chapter.

6.2.2 Methods of Acquiring Legal Knowledge

The regulated obtain and form their legal knowledge in several ways. The first is by directly studying the written legal norms. Moreover, they are taught directly what laws are by regulators, legal education institutes, and law popularization departments. These practices directly expose the regulated to the written legal norms, allowing them to learn what the law allows and prohibits. This can be categorized as an explicit legal knowledge source, and knowledge acquired this way is mainly the doctrinal legal knowledge. The regulated, especially in small businesses, do not always learn the legal norms in this explicit manner, as revealed in several studies (Henson and Heasman 1998; Yapp and Fairman 2005; Winter and May 2002). If they do, they may also learn some other legal practice knowledge in subtle and unexpected ways at the same time. For instance, the Food Safety Regulatory Department requires a representative from every restaurant to attend a training class on food safety law, which seems to be an explicit method of acquiring doctrinal legal knowledge. However, as the owner of the Idealistic restaurant who attended such a training class reported, many restaurants did not attend these classes but would also obtain the completion certificate of training class after paying a prescribed fee. Their absence seemed to make no difference. As a result, the owner developed the understanding that many restaurants did not pay attention to learning the law related to them. This understanding was an unintended consequence or outcome of this explicit learning method, and it inevitably influenced her knowledge related to legal norms.

The second way to obtain legal knowledge is through informal sources such as friends and other people's experiences. These sources provide common practices related to rules and anecdotes that shape the regulated actors' understanding and knowledge of what the law is (Kim 1999). When knowledge is acquired in this manner, the regulated do not explicitly know what is written in the law but implicitly learn what the law seems to be, and what allowed and prohibited under the law. This can be categorized as an implicit source of legal knowledge.

Moreover, regulated actors can obtain legal knowledge through interaction with the regulators during the enforcement process. The regulated understand what is allowed and what is prohibited based on the regulator's interpretation, sanctions, suggestions, and so forth. Thus, the regulated do not directly learn what is written in the law but indirectly obtain knowledge of what is permitted and what is prohibited from the enforcement authority. This is a popular view in compliance research that follows the endogenous approach (Lange 1999; Hutter 1997). In this knowledge form, doctrinal legal knowledge and legal practice knowledge have already been combined to a certain extent.

To explore the legal knowledge formation process, the three methods of obtaining legal knowledge are examined in the context of the restaurants studies, specifically whether the organizations obtained knowledge in this way, how they obtained knowledge, and what they learned through each method. Additionally, how the doctrinal legal knowledge and legal practice knowledge restaurants obtained from the three learning methods interacted with each other and resulted in their comprehensive legal knowledge is examined. It emerges that the legal knowledge formation process also involves learning and contesting activities.

6.3 Legal Knowledge in Restaurants

6.3.1 Limited Doctrinal Legal Knowledge

When conducting the field research, I developed the impression that knowledge of legal norms was absent in the restaurants. During the study period, restaurant owners and workers hardly mentioned legal norms. It seemed that these norms had been removed from their daily lives. Only once did the owner's husband in the Idealistic restaurant mention the law and express his perceptions of law. During a conversation about public activities related to pollution, which was a popular topic at that time, he expressed his dissatisfaction of how laws were used in reality: "If the law benefit for the government, government will talk about the law. Otherwise, government won't mention the law…Laws are used by people. The question is how people use laws."[2]

When interviewing restaurant owners, I always asked what the person did to prepare for opening the restaurant, expecting indications that they studied the relevant laws and regulations. Usually, they spoke of choosing the site, decorating the restaurant, hiring employees, selecting food and ingredients, and so on, but hardly mentioned legal norms that were related to restaurant opening. I had to prompt them for information on legal norms, and did so by asking about the opening licenses required. Of all restaurants studied, only the Idealistic restaurant intentionally searched for legal requirements of the opening licenses required and visited the enforcement departments to apply for opening licenses. The other restaurants did not consider opening license until inspectors, usually from the FDA or ICA, conducted inspections of their restaurants while they were decorating (L restaurant, W restaurant, and H restaurant) or in the usual course of business (the Profit-Maximizing restaurant). When they spoke about applying for their opening licenses, none of them mentioned the law related to these opening licenses. Instead, they spoke about the exact requirements the inspectors asked for without mentioning any laws related to these requirements. Similarly, when discussing daily operational behaviors regulated by laws, restaurants seldom mentioned corresponding legal norms.

Generally, when asked directly whether a specific behavior is regulated by law, the interviewees were unable to answer clearly. For instance, when asked about health certificates, the owner of L restaurant said she had paid for some employees' health certificates at the first L restaurant, but asked employees to pay for their own certificates at the second restaurant. When asked whether the regulations stated that who should pay for the health certificate, she answered, "There is no definite regulation to regulate it.[3] However, I think one should logically pay for his or her

---

[2] Interview with the owner's husband on May 22, 2013.

[3] According to article 34 of the Food Safety Law and article 23 of Regulation on the Implementation of the Food Safety Law, the owners of the restaurant are responsible for establishing and implementing a system to manage employees' health and for moving workers with diseases that may adversely affect food safety to work positions that will not influence food safety. Thus, it seems to be the employees' responsibility to undergo health checks and obtain health certificates. Article 34 of the Food Safety Law states, "Food producers and traders shall establish and implement an

own health certificate." When asked how she knew this and whether she had read this in legal articles or heard it from someone, she replied, "I did not read any legal articles, nor hear anyone talk about this. I just do it in my own restaurant." Even the owner of the Idealistic restaurant, who was highly educated and used to search for information of opening licenses, did not know the exact legal norms related to health certificates. When asked whether she knew why all food services staff required health certificates, she answered, "I don't know. I just think they need have one." I prompted her for more information by asking whether she had seen a regulation that stated that everyone should have a certificate, she replied, "I just think it should be so."

Restaurants also may remain ignorant of legal norms related to regulations even after obtaining legal licenses or operating for a considerable time. For instance, the head chef at H restaurant, who was responsible for managing the kitchen workers, did not know the legal norms related to daily operations in the kitchen. He had learned restaurant management from the radio and online videos, and when asked whether he knew any legal norms related to cooking dishes, he answered, "There is not any legal norms related to that." Similarly, as seen in Chap. 3, the owner of the Idealistic restaurant knew nothing about the quarantine certificates required for chicken, and she was unaware of legal requirements regarding handwashing regulations, although she established internal rules about washing hands after going to the toilet and before entering the kitchen. The Profit-Maximizing restaurant was unaware of handwashing and nail cutting regulations and instead viewed these are "service" factors.

In conclusion, the restaurants studied lacked doctrinal legal knowledge. They were unaware of legal norms, despite dealing with the issues regulated by those norms. In other words, restaurants did not know the laws related to them. As the owner of the Profit-Maximizing restaurant, "There is no law [to open a restaurant]. I just do what they ask me to do. They ask me to apply opening license, I apply opening license. They ask me to pay tax, I pay tax."[4] Furthermore, they lack interest in finding out what exactly the law is. The owner of L restaurant did not know the tax rate for her restaurant although she had paid tax for two restaurants. She did not ask the inspectors about the tax rate because "it [was] only about several hundred CNY and [I did] not want to make such trouble." This supports Kim' argument that people have little knowledge about even basic legal norms. Furthermore, Kim showed that the workers' confusion about norms and law explained the systematic errors in people's misunderstanding of law. In her study, the internal norm of fairness in the labor market shaped workers' expectations of their legal rights. The answer given by the

---

employee health management system. Anyone who suffers from an infectious disease of digestive tract, such as dysentery, typhoid, or virus hepatitis, active tuberculosis, and purulent or weeping skin diseases that adversely affect food safety must not engage in work in direct contact with food for consumption. The personnel involved in food production and trading shall take a medical check-up each year, and can work only after they have obtained a health certificate." Article 23 of Regulation on the Implementation of the Food Safety Law reiterates this information and adds that "[t]he check-up items shall go in accordance with regulations made by the local province, autonomous region, or municipality directly under the central government.".

[4]Interview with the owner of the Profit-Maximizing restaurant on May 26, 2011.

owner of L restaurant clearly shows that apathy regarding what was regulated by legal norms partly explains her ignorance of law.

6.3.2 Abundant Legal Practice Knowledge

Though restaurants generally lacked doctrinal legal knowledge, they had significant legal practice knowledge related to the implementation of legal norms. As discussed in Sect. 2.1, legal practice knowledge includes two clusters of knowledge, namely personal knowledge about enforcement and personal knowledge about the behaviors of other regulated actors. Both formal and informal conversations with the owners of the two core restaurants revealed explicitly and implicitly knowledge of the two clusters of legal practice knowledge. For example, when questioned about the risk of using falsified information to renew the catering services license, the owner of the Profit-Maximizing restaurant answered,

> There is no risk. Inspectors in FDA is too busy to come to do inspection...I know they are very busy, not only because the number of inspectors is small, but also there are lots of affairs they have to take care of, food and drug. For small restaurants like mine, they are too busy to come to do inspect. They have to inspect on the drug, which is much more important. If they do not do inspection on drug well, they have to be responsible for problems that happen suddenly. Small restaurant usually do not have big problem. Big problems always happen in those big restaurants.[5]

Therefore, the legal practice knowledge about FDA enforcement the Profit-Maximizing restaurant obtained is "enforcers are too busy to care about small restaurants."

Table 6.1 contains a summary of the expressions of legal practice knowledge at the Idealistic restaurant and the Profit-Maximizing restaurant. Examples were plentiful, but it is important to bear in mind that legal practice knowledge may interact with doctrinal legal knowledge, and it is changeable. The table shows only the state at the points at which they were stated implicitly or explicitly.

6.3.3 Sources of Legal Knowledge in Restaurants

Restaurants obtain doctrinal legal knowledge and legal practice knowledge in three ways, through explicit study, implicit processes, and the enforcement process, as discussed in Sect. 2.2. When the owner of the Idealistic restaurant explained how she began the restaurant, she mentioned an official source of the explicit study of legal norms. Every restaurant is required to participate in official training organized by the FDA when it applies for its opening licenses. The course, "Training of Food Safety in Catering Service Industry," aims to promote restaurants' knowledge of

---

[5]Interview with the owner of the Profit-Maximizing restaurant on September 5, 2013.

Table 6.1 Clusters of legal practice knowledge at the idealistic restaurant and the Profit-Maximizing restaurant

The Idealistic Restaurant		
Opening licenses	KOE[a]	Some enforcers were pleasant and communicated well Some enforcers purposely created difficulties for people who did not bribe them or did not know them Sometimes, enforcers were too inflexible on some requirements. Some inspectors were simply bandits
	KOR[b]	Some restaurants bribed enforcers to obtain licenses easily
Health certificates	KOE	Inspectors were not particularly strict or thorough Inspectors were satisfied once several certificate were displayed
	KOR	Most restaurants should have health certificates for their employees
Dish disinfection	KOE	Enforcers must inspect equipment and records, but it is impossible to know whether restaurants disinfect dishware
	KOR	Many restaurants do not disinfect dishware
Fapiao receipts	KOE	Using counterfeit receipts carries a heavy fine
	KOR	Some restaurants use fake receipts; some do not
The Profit-Maximizing Restaurant		
Opening licenses	KOE	Generally, inspectors were kind and gentle Enforcers did not really care about legal requirements and instead cared about whether they could benefit from them. Enforcers were too busy to care about small restaurants Enforcers in the office did not verify materials restaurants submitted
	KOR	Some restaurants could obtain opening licenses without satisfying requirements if they knew enforcers
Health certificates	KOE	Enforcers do not check carefully but simply glance at them Inspectors were satisfied once several certificate were displayed
	KOR	Most restaurant had health certificates, but they may be counterfeit
Dish disinfection	KOE	Enforcers rarely checked the dishware Enforcers were contented if they could see the disinfection cabinet and disinfection fluid

(continued)

Table 6.1 (continued)

	KOR	Most small and medium sized restaurants used packed dishware that might not have been disinfected
Fapiao receipts	KOE	Tax officers knew the restaurant used counterfeit receipts but did not really care
		Even if someone complained to the tax office, tax officers rarely fined restaurants, unless a special campaign was underway
		If a person knew tax officers in the district and bribed them, they would allow one to pay less tax
		Tax officers knew restaurants under-reported their turnover
	KOR	Many restaurants use counterfeit *Fapiao* receipt, and using them is an open secret

[a]Knowledge of enforcement; [b]Knowledge of other restaurants' behavior

food safety–related laws. Since 2012, the local FDA has strengthened food safety training among restaurants, and it requires them to attend annual training. However, it seems restaurant owners do not value this training. According to the owner of the Profit-Maximizing restaurant, "The training is not real training. They just collect money. It is just a show without substantial action." He did not attend the training but sent a worker. The owner's husband of the Idealistic restaurant, expressed a similar perception of the training: "It trains several hundred people at the same time. Teachers just ask you to underline some sentences that will be tested later. The test is open book exam. The training is just running in a form." Despite his negative view of the training, he attended the training once and gained some knowledge from it. When asked whether he would like to participate in such training again, he answered, "I think we need to learn this knowledge related to restaurants. We do not know the knowledge. If we know, we may do it well so as to avoid problems when being inspected." He further pointed out that he learned during the training that the Idealistic restaurant was not licensed to serve cold dishes. The trainer emphasized this point and even announced that there would be a special inspection to regulate the sale of cold dishes. I asked him what he was going to do then. He said he would discuss it with the head chef. However, as I observed during my stay, the Idealistic restaurant still serve cold dishes. In conclusion, the effects of this official method of explicitly learning the content of legal norms are limited, and restaurants had negative perceptions of the training.

When restaurants pay for the training when applying for their catering services licenses, they receive a collection of legal norms related to the restaurant. Thus, self-study of these norms is another method of explicitly studying the legal norms. However, this seldom happens. Of those interviewed, the owner of the Idealistic restaurant was the most likely to read these norms, as she was highly educated and actively searched for information about legal norms when opening the restaurant.

However, she explained that she tried to read the documentation when she received it, but she gave up after several pages because it was too boring and she had many things to deal with while running the restaurant.

In addition, restaurants can search for legal norms via the Internet or various other ways to explicitly study the content of legal norms. Yet the reality is that restaurants seldom do this, and even if they do, the results are disappointing. The owner of the Idealistic restaurant looked for information online and visited the district service center to ask for information about what she needed to do when she was preparing to apply for opening licenses. Nevertheless, she still encountered numerous obstacles during the license application process, as discussed in Chap. 3. It took seven visits to the ICA office to clarify the legal requirements for a business license, and it took four months to find out what was required to obtain a catering services license. Other restaurants did not actively search for information about opening licenses and legal norms, and some reported that they had known nothing about opening licenses until inspectors visited their restaurants. The owner of L restaurant had no specialist skills or knowledge when she opened her restaurant, so when asked what she did to prepare, she answered,

> First is to learn how to cook, second is to choose the site and do decoration. I knew nothing about the license at that time. It is during the process of decoration that the inspectors from ICA came to my restaurant and informed me to apply for license.

Compared to the explicit learning method, the implicit method is significantly more common in restaurants. Aside from the owner of L restaurant, all the restaurant owners had some restaurant related experience. Thus, from experience they obtained some level of both doctrinal and legal practice knowledge about opening a restaurant. For example, the owner of the Idealistic restaurant learned from the NGO's restaurant in another province where she had been employed that restaurants need to get various opening licenses and that dishware disinfection is required. Moreover, while employed at the NGO's restaurant, she developed legal practice knowledge about the difficulty of obtaining a fire license and the severity of sanctions for not having this license. Similarly, before opening his own restaurant, the owner of the Profit-Maximizing restaurant obtained considerable legal practice knowledge from the previous owner, specifically that restaurants with private relationships with inspectors or enforcers can escape some requirements and thus save costs.

Additionally, they learned from friends with restaurant knowledge or experience. For example, before contacting the Fire Department inspectors, the owner of the Idealistic restaurant heard from her friends about the enforcement actions of this department in her province and about other restaurants' experiences of dealing with it. This information included knowledge of fire license requirements—specifically that the requirements are difficult to satisfy—and that she should attempt to bribe the inspector. When the owner of the Profit-Maximizing restaurant prepared his fire license application, he heard from friends that the enforcement by the Fire Department was slack and that the requirements would not be verified on site. The owner of W restaurant learned from friends who were opening a restaurant that restaurants need to apply for various opening licenses and that it is necessary to have fire extinguishers in the restaurant.

Interaction with enforcement departments and inspectors, the third learning method, is the most important way for restaurants to learn doctrinal legal knowledge and legal practice knowledge. Based on data from the five restaurants, the first contact with enforcement departments occurs after the restaurant site is confirmed and rented. If restaurant owners have previously obtained some knowledge about applying for opening license from implicit sources, they[6] (in this case only the Idealistic restaurant) may initiate contact with the opening license departments. Subsequently, the Bureau will send inspectors to perform an onsite inspection and inform the regulated. For some restaurants (the other four restaurants in this study), inspectors typically initiate contact with the restaurant when the restaurant is being decorated. While information obtained implicitly is always fragmented and inconsistent, and sometimes even contradictory, the knowledge gained through the enforcement process is reliable.

Whether restaurants obtain explicit doctrinal knowledge of the law from interaction with inspectors and regulators is questionable. If so, the doctrinal legal knowledge restaurants actually receive is extremely limited. For example, at the Idealistic restaurant, during an annual inspection, the inspectors told the head chef to replace the red plastic vegetable containers (for storing vegetables after washing but before cooking) with white ones because "it is not allowed to use colorful containers. Only white [can be used]." No law was mentioned. The same scenario played out at the Profit-Maximizing restaurant, where inspectors told the owner that he was not allowed to place colorful plastic bags in the refrigerator without stating the exact content of the relevant legal norm. In these cases, the restaurant owners learned what inspectors required, not what the law required.

In contrast, during the enforcement process restaurants obtain considerable legal practice knowledge, typically from observing inspectors' behaviors, communicating with inspectors, and responding to inspectors' requirements. For example, the owner of the Profit-Maximizing restaurant would observe how inspectors checked health certificated every time. From his observations, he learned that the inspectors simply glanced at the health certificates and did not check them carefully or verify their authenticity. As a result, he obtained legal practice knowledge that is the enforcement of health certificate norms is slack. In terms of communication with inspectors, the owner of L restaurant used to recall one communication occasion. When conducting on-site inspection, the inspector rejected her environmental license application by stating that the location of her restaurant was so close to a river that it is prohibited to open restaurants. She questioned this decision by pointing out another restaurant that was located even closer to the river. The inspector could not explain but stating that it is not him who approved that restaurant. This answer implicitly showed other

---

[6]Although some restaurants know they must apply for opening licenses, they still do not initiate contact with the enforcers but wait for the inspectors to visit. This applied to H restaurant, W restaurant.

ways to gain the license despite of the location restriction. Consequently, the owner of L restaurant obtained this legal practice knowledge from the inspector's answer. Another example is from the Profit-Maximizing restaurant. Inspectors asked the Profit-Maximizing restaurant to replace the stone kitchen table with a stainless steel to meet the requirements for a catering services license, and the owner complied. Nevertheless, when he later reported the change to the enforcement department, he learned that the department did not verify changes on site and required only photographic proof.

In summary, restaurants generally did not obtain doctrinal knowledge of the content of legal norm by themselves, nor did the official training program provide this knowledge effectively, nor did they obtain this information during the enforcement process. Instead, restaurants obtained abundant legal practice knowledge through the official training program, enforcement process, friends, and other informal sources.

6.3.4 Comprehensive Legal Knowledge

The legal practice knowledge restaurants obtained influences their doctrinal legal knowledge, the combination of the two forms the comprehensive legal knowledge that direct their compliance behavior. Comprehensive legal knowledge shows how people understand what the law is and reflects their understanding of law better than simple doctrinal legal knowledge does. For example, when the inspector responded to the owner of L restaurant that "It was not me who approved that restaurant", the owner of L restaurant was inspired to search for other legal practice knowledge. In this case, she looked to informal sources for an interpretation, and learned from an acquaintance that enforcement differed if the acquaintance helped the restaurant owners to deal with inspectors. The distance between river and restaurant, which initially had been seen as a compulsory condition, was demonstrated to be inessential. Thus, doctrinal legal knowledge obtained from the inspectors was challenged by the legal practice knowledge that enforcement could be flexible. As a result, the doctrinal legal knowledge was shaken, and the regulated actors' comprehensive legal knowledge about the environmental license became that the distance between restaurants and the river is not a necessary legal requirement for obtaining an environmental license. The comprehensive legal knowledge conflicted with the doctrinal legal knowledge.

In other words, restaurants' legal knowledge of what the law is developed not only through learning the content of legal norms but resulted from both doctrinal legal knowledge and legal practice knowledge. What restaurants knew about the content of legal norms was verified by legal practice knowledge related to enforcement and other regulated actors' behaviors. Therefore, restaurants' comprehensive legal knowledge equates to practical verified requirements. When restaurants learned the legal norms, they added their own interpretations to these norms. Legal practice knowledge related to legal norms was used to verify that doctrinal legal knowledge, in terms of whether the information is correct, whether it is compulsory. Verification in practice is inevitable in the legal knowledge formation process, and is supported by one's legal practice knowledge. Albert Einstein said, "Knowledge is experience. Everything else is just information". So the regulated need to verify the information of legal norms in practice and to form their comprehensive legal knowledge.

Doctrinal legal knowledge may also influence legal practice knowledge. Legal practice knowledge is subjective knowledge about enforcement and others' compliance behavior that is obtained through personal experience. Legal practice knowledge and doctrinal legal knowledge may differ in terms of what "the law" is. As shown above, one way the regulated actors deal with the difference is to modify or dismiss their doctrinal legal knowledge so as to match what they learn from experience, that is, their legal practice knowledge. However, these actors also can deal with the difference by trusting their doctrinal legal knowledge and insisting that it is correct, and modifying or dismissing their legal practice knowledge. As the theory of cognitive dissonance (Festinger 1962) and information processing discussed by Winter and May (2002) show, a consistently strong set of messages from credible sources will convince people to accept new information that does not fit perceived notions. Thus, when the regulated actors constantly learn the same doctrinal legal knowledge from credible sources, they are likely to reevaluate the difference between this doctrinal legal knowledge and legal practice knowledge, see the limitations or inappropriateness of their previous legal practice knowledge, choose to trust and believe the doctrinal legal knowledge, and modify or dismiss their legal practice knowledge. In this way, the regulated actors deal with the difference between doctrinal legal knowledge and legal practice knowledge and form their comprehensive legal knowledge. Although this is theoretically possible, it did not occur in these cases studied in this book, possibly due to the generally limited presence of doctrinal legal knowledge in restaurants.

6.4 Effects of Enforcement Encounters

Enforcement encounters are important moments when the law is transmitted to the regulated organization. As discussed previously, interaction with inspectors or regulatory departments is an important source of legal knowledge. Because enforcement is usually the central topic of improving compliance, the enforcement encounter was further examined from the perspective of the regulated to identify its contribution to the comprehensive legal knowledge of restaurants in terms of what kind of laws the regulated have received during the enforcement process and the influence of this kind of law on restaurants' compliance behavior. This examination showed that the enforcement encounter in reality does not bring in the written law it is supposed to; instead, it introduces a different law, which teaches restaurants that the legal norm is the secondary factor to be complied with, while the enforcer is the primary compliance objective. This significantly undermines the legitimacy of the written law and contributes to the complexity of compliance.

Enforcement encounters occurred during the opening license application and routine inspection processes. The regulators, usually inspectors, visit restaurants to perform inspections. During these inspections, the regulated actors inevitably observe how the inspectors work, what they focus on, and what they always dismiss. If the inspector discovers no violations, the inspection ends, leaving the regulated with new legal practice knowledge about enforcement. This legal practice knowledge is stored or used as evidence to verify or reinforce the regulated actors' previous legal knowledge. If some violations are discovered, the inspector may inform the regulated actor and ask the regulated actor to correct the violation. In this case, more interaction and communication takes place between the regulator and the regulated, and brings about an opportunity of improving or changing the regulated actors' original legal knowledge. For this to happen, the regulated actor and the regulator need to discuss the specific legal norm bilaterally in theory and reality, attempt to link the legal norms to practice, and find an appropriate "law in practice," as Lange (1999) showed in the waste management research. The finally "law in practice" that results from the negotiation between the regulator and the regulated actors is also the constructed compliance.

However, in these cases studied in this book, the interaction and communication between inspectors and restaurants were not bilateral and typically set aside the legal norms instead of addressing them. In such interaction and communication, the meaning of the legal norms and their potential adaptation in practice are not be discussed. In some cases, despite restaurant owners' misgivings, they were less likely to speak out and negotiate with inspectors. For instance, when applying for its fire license, the owner of the Profit-Maximizing restaurant was required to install a lighted exit sign by inspectors from the Fire Department. In his view, the dining section of the restaurant was not large enough to warrant this, and the two exits were so big and obvious that the exit sign was not necessary for direction. Yet he did not express his views or negotiate with the inspectors. He simply indicated that he would fulfil these requirements. Consequently, drawing on his legal practice knowledge that enforcers would probably not verify these requirements, he chose to fraudulently respond to the requirements without changing his behavior. To prove he had implemented the changes, he borrowed an exit sign from a friend, photographed it, and showed the photos to the Fire Department as required. As he thought, the Fire Department did not verify the photos but approved his application and accepted the photos as evidence that the Profit-Maximizing restaurant satisfied the requirements. This experience not only further verified his previous legal practice knowledge that enforcers would not always verify what they required but also eroded the newly formed doctrinal legal knowledge. The law introduced during the encounter with the enforcement officers differed from what it was supposed to be, and what the law required was considered unnecessary by the regulated.

When the owner of the Idealistic restaurant expressed her views of specific legal requirements and attempted to negotiate with inspectors, she failed and later learned that negotiation is unnecessary. She described an attempted negotiation with FDA inspectors during the catering services license application. While inspectors noted that the kitchen should have three sinks for washing dishes, one for washing with cleanser, one for rinsing, and one for disinfection, she attempted to convince the inspectors that the existing two were adequate, as the restaurant used tea seed powder to wash dishes and disinfected dishes in the disinfection cabinet. She also pointed out that the kitchen was too small to install so many sinks. Nevertheless, the inspectors insisted that at least three sinks were required. Finally, she installed another sink to pass the inspection and obtained the License, but she removed it soon after. Ironically, when the inspectors performed the annual check a year later, they did not mention the missing sink.

In this case, the attempted negotiation was proven unnecessary. There was no benefit to linking legal norms to practice, and the owner of the Idealistic restaurant never accepted the legal norm—and she soon stopped practicing it. In other words, the specific doctrinal legal norm regarding the required number of sinks was not successfully introduced to the Idealistic restaurant. In contrast, the Idealistic restaurant obtained unexpected legal practice knowledge that after passing the initial inspection and obtaining the opening licenses, some requirements met to obtain the licenses, that is, having the specified number of sinks, are not included in the focus of daily operations. Similarly, the head chef at the Idealistic restaurant claimed that "it is OK once there are several health certificates hanging there"[7] and allowed some workers to forgo obtaining health certificates. As a result, the comprehensive legal knowledge the Idealistic restaurant formed after such interactions reversed the doctrinal legal knowledge that inspectors attempted to introduce.

We can also recall what happened when the owner of L restaurant questioned a legal requirement that was informed of by environmental inspectors. This opportunity to introduce the law to L restaurant also ultimately led to the introduction of a different law. That is, it is more important to comply with the regulator than with the legal norm. According to the legal norm regarding the distance between the restaurant and river highlighted by the inspectors, L restaurant would not be issued with an environmental license. Yet the owner of L restaurant finally obtained the environmental license, not by addressing the legal norm but by dealing with the enforcer by approaching an acquaintance of an acquaintance in the Environmental Department. In this case, the legal requirement regarding the distance was set aside, and the owner of L restaurant obtained the legal practice knowledge that some legal norms may be set aside if one has an acquaintance in that enforcement department. This legal practice knowledge inevitably eroded the newly formed doctrinal legal knowledge of environmental distance. In light of this legal practice knowledge, it is unsurprising that when the owner of L restaurant opened the second L restaurant, she did not apply for an opening license but invited the relevant inspectors to dinner. Thus, she addressed the inspectors instead of dealing with the legal norms.

This legal practice knowledge is related to a wider and more common legal practice knowledge that lingers in China's legal environment, namely the culture of *Guanxi*, or acquaintances (Bian 1994; Gold 1985; Guthrie 1998; Kipnis 1997; Li 2011; Potter 2002; Walder 1986; Wang 2004; Yan 1996; Yang 1994, 2002). People believe that relationships with acquaintances play a significant role in law enforcement. If the

---

[7]Interview with the head chef of the Idealistic restaurant on August 11, 2013.

regulated have acquaintances in regulatory departments or know inspectors, they are treated differently. The restaurants studied here learned this legal practice knowledge from their experiences of enforcement encounters. Initially, when the owner of the Profit-Maximizing restaurant first took over the restaurant, inspectors visited the restaurant often to check its sanitation. Every time, they used a small flashlight to look around carefully, and they even looked at the bottom of the freezer and small corners that would easily be missed while cleaning. The owner of the Profit-Maximizing restaurant was fined for some minor violations several times. However, later, after he established a relationship with the inspectors by showing respect and cooperation and offering them certain benefits (specifically, providing free *Fapiao* receipts),[8] the inspectors no longer used a flashlight to check the restaurant. In fact, they no longer went inside to perform inspections. When they visited, he would say hello to them, and they would chat for a while outside the kitchen and smoke a cigarette together. The inspectors would count this as an inspection, and the Profit-Maximizing restaurant was of course seldom fined.

The owner of the Idealistic restaurant had a painful experience in this regard. To apply for the fire license, the restaurant needed a certificate showing the history of the house it was renting. Because the house was more than 40 years old and originally had belonged to a factory but later changed ownership several times, it was difficult to obtain complete information. She spent two weeks and showed five other certificates to obtain the information from the House Administration Center. What worsened matters was that when the officer at the Fire Department viewed the certificate of the house issued by the House Administration Center, she was informed that a single piece of information about the building of the house was missing. Consequently, she had to return to the House Administration Center to ask for another certificate. If she had followed the formal procedure, she would have had to find the formal certificate showing exactly when the house had been built, which would have meant another round of searching. She was surprised to meet a classmate who happened to work in that House Administration Center. The classmate assured her that resolving the problem would be easy. Her classmate simply wrote the date provided by her on the certificate, although it was not accurate, and stamped it. Finally, with the help of her classmate, she obtained the certificate, which satisfied the Fire Department. She concluded, "I really experience the difference this time. If you have acquaintance, it is so easy to get the stamp. If you do not have acquaintance, you just be tortured to die."

This legal practice knowledge about acquaintances also existed at H restaurant and L restaurant. The owner of H restaurant said,

> If you know the inspectors and have a good relationship with them like acquaintance, they will point out problems for you to correct. If you do not know them or do not have a good relationship with them like a stranger, they may just issue ticket for you to pay. It is common. People treat acquaintance and strangers differently.

The owner of L restaurant noted,

---

[8]Interview with the owner of the Profit-Maximizing restaurant on May 26, 2011. Inspectors have to use *Fapiao* receipts in their own offices to claim certain payments and refunds.

If you know the regulator just like acquaintance, they will teach you how to do (to satisfy legal requirements) and issue the license to you soon. If you do not know them just like a stranger, you may need to go a dozen times for a simple things for which an acquaintance may just need to go once or twice. There is a big difference between stranger and acquaintance to apply opening license.[9]

This explains to a certain extent why restaurants were always inclined to cooperate with inspectors. On the one hand, inspectors or regulators were seen as more important than the legal norms they enforce; on the other hand, cooperating with inspectors might have helped them to form acquaintances in the regulatory system that would greatly benefit the restaurants.

Consequently, when responding to the legal norms inspectors enforce, restaurants first and generally were inclined to immediately do what inspectors requested of them. For instance, the owner of the Profit-Maximizing restaurant immediately labeled the freezers and cabinets as inspectors required, the owner of L restaurant created a disinfection log as soon as required, and the Idealistic restaurant replaced the red plastic boxes with white ones immediately when asked to do so. The owner of W restaurant decided to hand over money instead of applying for an opening license as soon as he was required to do so. Thus, the restaurants would satisfy inspectors' requirements on requests and engage in symbolic compliance, at least with those legal norms enforcers emphasized.

In other words, when enforcers requested and emphasized certain requirements, the behavior itself would be perceived as plural subjective deterrence—the risk perception where restaurants believed they would experience sanctions externally from enforcement authority or another private sources if they did not satisfy the legal requirements—by the restaurants. Plural subjective deterrence as one of the critical variables influencing compliance behaviors and mediating comprehensive legal knowledge and compliance behaviors will be discussed in Chap. 8.

Furthermore, whether restaurants engaged in behavior that aligned with legal norms substantially, symbolically, fraudulently, or partially largely depended on the restaurant's comprehensive legal knowledge of those specific legal norms. That is, it depended on whether the requirement was viewed as compulsory and likely to be verified, whether noncompliance would bring sanctions, whether the sanctions were significant, and whether others complied, and so forth. In addition, compliance would be influenced by other factors and variables discussed in subsequent chapters. As to the legal norms inspectors largely overlooked, such as handwashing and fingernail trimming, compliance would not be as common unless the restaurant's beliefs aligned with them.

Moreover, the compliance behaviors in which restaurants engaged initially changed when their comprehensive legal knowledge changed in the process of legal knowledge formation. For instance, previous genuine compliance could change to symbolic compliance if newly formed doctrinal legal knowledge was shaken by the legal practice knowledge that inspectors did not verify the requirement.

---

[9]Interview with the owner of L restaurant on May 10, 2012.

6.5 Conclusion

In this chapter, the legal knowledge formation of the regulated was discussed. A broader view of the definition of legal knowledge was taken, which means one's knowledge about what the law is. The focus was on the legal knowledge formation process, and on how restaurants' comprehensive legal knowledge was formulated and what their comprehensive legal knowledge was. It was found that restaurants had limited doctrinal legal knowledge but plenty of other legal practice knowledge related to the enforcement and peers' compliance behaviors. The two kinds of knowledge interacted and formed restaurants' comprehensive knowledge of what the law is. Additionally, the comprehensive legal knowledge of restaurants is subjective and practical.

Enforcement encounters provide important moments for introducing laws to the regulated. However, the enforcement encounters observed here did not bring the written law into restaurants. Instead, it brought, as revealed by the regulated actors' comprehensive legal knowledge, a different kind of law. In this law, some legal requirements were not viewed as compulsory in the real situation as they seemed when the regulated first encountered them. Similarly, some legal requirements could be dismissed because they were never verified. Bribing enforcers was seen as an easy and common way to obtain opening licenses. Enforcers would receive benefits from enforcing laws instead of caring about the aim of the law. Further, once restaurants passed the initial inspections and obtained their opening licenses, some requirements that were previously emphasized would be overlooked in daily operation. In addition, personal relationships and acquaintances were viewed as more important than legal norms, and complying with the enforcer was more important than complying with the written legal norms.

Restaurants generally would comply with the legal norms inspectors emphasized, such as obtaining opening licenses, at least formally. Therefore, all restaurants except W restaurant, had the required opening licenses. Yet restaurants actually complied with inspectors' enforced requirements and not the legal norms per se. Their aim was largely to satisfy inspectors rather than the legal norm. Due to the variations in restaurants' comprehensive legal knowledge and contestation with their beliefs, restaurants would engage in behaviors that conformed to the legal norm substantially, symbolically, fraudulently, or partially. Hence, there were variations in the compliance behaviors of the Idealistic restaurant and the Profit-Maximizing restaurant. Moreover, restaurants' comprehensive legal knowledge is changeable, as both doctrinal legal knowledge and legal practice knowledge are changeable. As a result, the compliance behaviors situated in the context of the restaurants' comprehensive legal knowledge are also changeable.

These findings support Kim's (1999) argument that the legal knowledge of the regulated may systematically diverge from the written law supposed to be passed on to the regulated. Thus, the regulated may have a different law in mind when researchers attempt to explain their compliance behaviors. This is problematic, as the regulated may not view the law researchers use to evaluate the regulated actors' compliance as the law. Compliance researchers must consider the comprehensive legal knowledge of the regulated, especially legal practice knowledge and its influence on doctrinal legal knowledge. Doctrinal legal knowledge plays an insignificant, sometimes ambiguous, role in shaping compliance behavior. Furthermore, instead of measuring whether the regulated actors know what is lawful or unlawful as what Kim did, I looked deeper into the formation of the comprehensive legal knowledge of the regulated actors to reveal a more vivid picture of legal knowledge and provide a possible avenue to explore the constructs of legal knowledge in greater detail.

This discussion of legal knowledge formation also moves matters one step forward from discussing the knowledge of rules as the awareness of rules. In their study on compliance motivations, Winter and May (2001) operationalized knowledge of rules as the regulatee's awareness of rules and found that it plays a critical role in compliance. Awareness of rules refers to the degree to which the regulated know about requirements and the means of adhering to them. Nevertheless, awareness of rules is only one aspect of the knowledge of rules. It cannot reflect the regulated actors' legal knowledge. In this book, the composition of legal knowledge is discussed, and I attempts to show what the regulated actors' legal knowledge (comprehensive legal knowledge) is. It was found that the regulated might know doctrinal legal knowledge in terms of what is required, but that their doctrinal legal knowledge was influenced by legal practice knowledge. As a result, comprehensive legal knowledge may finally differ from the doctrinal legal knowledge they obtain at the beginning.

In many endogenous research studies of compliance, it has been argued that the meaning of legal rules used in regulatory practice is often not predefined but is socially constructed through bargaining between the regulators and the regulated (Noble, 1981: 179; Winter, 1985; Lange, 1999). Yet the question of how legal rules become transformed and understood by the regulated is not explored in depth. This chapter focused on this very question and explored how legal norms enter restaurants and examined the formation of comprehensive legal knowledge of the regulated. It verified from the perspective of the regulated that knowledge of legal rules is not objective and as clear as we think it to be, but is socially constructed and verified constantly. Consequently, understanding what comprehensive legal knowledge that the regulated actors have will facilitate understanding and predicting of compliance behaviors, as it reveals the real "law" the regulated actors understand. In other words, variations in comprehensive legal knowledge reflect the very beginning of variations in final compliance behaviors. What the regulated actors refer to when making decision of compliance is not the objective legal norm but their comprehensive legal knowledge. Therefore, comprehensive legal knowledge as the first step in moving from legal norms to compliance, should receive more attention in future compliance studies. The discussion of comprehensive legal knowledge may also interest endogenous researchers in terms of studying the nature of law.

Finally, seen from the angle of the receptor of comprehensive legal knowledge, it can also be a consideration at individual level, when the regulated is an individual rather than an organization. Each regulated individual has his or her own comprehensive legal knowledge. Moreover, the discussion of comprehensive legal knowledge formation is appropriate for the individual level. In fact, every worker in a restaurant has his or her own comprehensive legal knowledge. However, workers' comprehensive legal knowledge is not discussed in this book, as other mainstream variables with direct and singular effects on compliance were used to explain workers' compliance behaviors, and some variables, such as plural subjective deterrence and descriptive norms, reflect parts of workers' comprehensive legal knowledge.

References

Bian, Yanjie. 1994. *Guanxi* and the Allocation of Urban Jobs in China. *China Quarterly* 140: 971–999.

Festinger, Leon. 1962. *A Theory of Cognitive Dissonance*. Stanford, CA: Stanford University Press.

Gold, Thomas. 1985. After Comradeship: Personal Relationships in China since the Cultural Revolution. *China Quarterly* 104: 657–675.

Guthrie, Douglas. 1998. The Declining Significance of *Guanxi* in China's Economic Transition. *China Quarterly* 154: 255–282.

Henson, S., and M. Heasman. 1998. Food Safety Regulation and the Firm: Understanding the Compliance Process. *Food Policy* 23 (1): 9–23.

Hutter, Bridget M. 1997. *Compliance: Regulation and Environment*. Oxford: Clarendon Press.

Jones, Bryan D. 2001. *Politics and the Architecture of Choice: Bounded Rationality and Governance*. Chicago: University of Chicago Press.

Kim, Pauline T. 1999. Norms, Learning, and Law: Exploring the Influences on Workers' Legal Knowledge. *University of Illinois Law Review* 2: 447–516.

Kipnis, Andrew B. 1997. *Producing Guanxi*. Durham, NC: Duke University Press.

Lange, B. 1999. Compliance Construction in the Context of Environmental Regulation. *Social & Legal Studies* 8 (4): 549–567.

Li, Ling. 2011. Performing Bribery in China: Guanxi-Practice, Corruption with a Human Face. *Journal of Contemporary China* 20 (68): 1–20.

Noble, D. 1981. From Rules to Discretion: The Housing Corporation. In *Discretion and Welfare*, ed. M. Adler and S. Asquith, 171–184. London: Heinemann Educational Books.

Potter, Pitman B. 2002. Guanxi and the PRC Legal System: From Contradiction to Complementarity. In *Social Connections in China: Institutions, Culture, and the Changing Nature of Guanxi*, eds Thomas Gold, Doug Guthrie, and David Wank, 178–196. Cambridge University Press.

Thornton, Dorothy, Neil Gunningham, and Robert A. Kagan. 2005. General Deterrence and Corporate Environmental Behavior. *Law & Policy* 27 (2): 262–288.

Van der Heijden, Jeroen. 2009. *Building Regulatory Enforcement Regimes: Comparative Analysis of Private Sector Involvement in the Enforcement of Public Building Regulation*. Delft University of Technology (Doctoral Dissertation).

Van der Heijden, Jeroen. 2016. The Long, But Promising, Road from Deterrence to Networked Enforcement. In S. Drake and M. Smith (Eds), *New Directions in Effective Enforcement of EU Law* eds S. Drake and M. Smith, 77–104. Cheltenham: Edward Elgar.

Walder, Andrew G. 1986. *Communist Neo-Traditionalism: Work and Authority in Chinese Industry*. Berkeley, CA: University of California Press.

Wang, Yuqiong. 2004. A Relational Analysis of Arable Land Protection and Governmental Powers [Gengdi Baohu Yu Zhengfu Zhineng De Xiangguanxing Fenxi]. *Problems of Agricultural Economy [Nongye Jingji Wenti]* 4: 57–61.

Winter, G. 1985. Bartering Rationality in Regulation. *Law and Society Review* 19: 219–246.

Winter, Soren C., and Peter J. May. 2001. Motivation for Compliance with Environmental Regulations. *Journal of Policy Analysis and Management* 20 (4): 675–698.

Winter, Soren C., and Peter J. May. 2002. Information, Interests, and Environmental Regulation. *Journal of Comparative Policy Analysis* 4 (2): 115–142.

Yan, Yunxiang. 1996. *The Flow of Gifts: Reciprocity and Social Networks in a Chinese Village.* Palo Alto, CA: Stanford University Press.

Yan, Huiqi. 2014. *Why Chinese Farmers Obey the Law: Pesticide Compliance in Hunan Province, China.* Amsterdam University (Doctoral Dissertation).

Yang, Mayfair. 1994. *Gifts, Favors, and Banquets: The Art of Social Relationships in China.* Ithaca, NY: Cornell University Press.

Yang, Mayfair. 2002. The Resilience of *Guanxi* and Its New Development: A Critique of Some New *Guanxi* Scholarship. *China Quarterly* 170: 459–476.

Yapp, C., and R. Fairman. 2005. Assessing Compliance with Food Safety Legislation in Small Businesses. *British Food Journal* 107 (3): 150–161.

Chapter 7
Toxic Culture: How Did Organizational Norms Mediate the Transition of Laws?

7.1 Introduction

Compliance behavior in the restaurants occurred within the organizational setting, where owners, managers, and workers interact, and where organizational norms are formed and compete with legal norms to produce the behavior the law set out to regulate. An organization comprises an employer and employees, or the owner or top managers and workers. In the restaurants studied, certain legal norms concerned only the owners or top managers, and corresponding compliance behaviors could be fulfilled or decided only by the owners or top managers. For instance, when applying for environmental licenses, only restaurant owners' decisions and compliance behaviors mattered. If the restaurant owner decided to apply for the license, prepare the required documents, and install the required equipment, the owner would complete compliance with this legal norm by him or herself. Nevertheless, several legal norms concern the behaviors of all restaurant employees, and complying with these involves the behaviors of all employees. For example, if the restaurant wanted to comply with the legal norm of health certificates, all employees in the restaurant had to undergo health checks and obtain their own health certificates. Only restaurant owners' compliance decisions were not enough—compliance required the management of employees to ensure all employees engaged in the compliance behavior required. In this case, compliance stemmed from within the organization. Hence, it is not simply a matter of how regulatory authorities interact with restaurant owners or top managers or how and what the owners or top management knows about the law, but rather how legal norms enter each level of the restaurant, and how employees' behaviors are managed to ensure compliance with the law.

To discuss the transmission of law within restaurants, the organizational culture that maintains the function and operation of restaurants should be considered. According to the theory of semi-autonomous field proposed by Sally Falk Moore (1973), organizations are social fields with their own rules and norms that can both resist and shape outside rules and thus affect behaviors inside organization. In other words, when legal norms attempt to enter restaurants to regulate employees' behavior,

Y. Wu, *Compliance Ethnography*, Understanding China,
https://doi.org/10.1007/978-981-16-2884-9_7

they are mediated and transformed by internal rules and norms. These organizational norms may well be in line with legal rules and consequently help to promote legal compliance, but they may also oppose and compete with the law and form an obstacle. Similarly, Heimer (1999) showed that legal norms (which she called institutions) compete with other norms stemming from either the professional field or the familial field.

In the cases studied, the law may also compete with restaurant norms when seeking to regulate the behavior of restaurateurs, servers, and cooks. Therefore, organizational norms are vital, as they can both transform external legal rules and compete with them in shaping organizational behavior at all levels in the restaurants. Therefore, to explain compliance behavior, it is necessary to discuss how laws are transmitted in restaurants, how legal norms interact with organizational norms, and what the outcome of their interaction is. It follows the same logic described in Chap. 6 to explain compliance behavior by examining the final "legal norms" with which people in restaurants are concerned. In this chapter, however, the focus is on the organizational level, and the discussion centers on the interaction between organizational norms and legal norms, or on how the organizational norm complicate the transmission of legal norms into organizations.

Hence, in this chapter, the meaning of organizational norms in restaurants, in terms of what they are, how they are formed, and how they compete and interact with legal norms in shaping compliance behaviors, is discussed. Organizational norms are types of social norms, and social norms have long been a focus in explaining compliance. To this end, the existing literature on organizational norms, social norms, and compliance is reviewed to clarify the meaning of organizational norms in this context. Subsequently, where organizational norms come from and how they arise, what compliance behaviors resulted from which organizational norms, and how organizational norms interact with or complicate legal norms are discussed. Through these discussions, organizational factors (Huisman 2016), along with organizational norms that contribute to various restaurant compliance behaviors, are identified, and the implications for improving organizational compliance are highlighted.

7.2 Organizational Norms and Compliance

7.2.1 Organizational and Social Norms

An organizational norm is an explicit or implicit rule of behavior or a typical and an acceptable behavior in an organization (Russell & Russell 1992).[1] It is one subset of

---

[1] In many organizational studies, the term "organizational norm" is ambiguous. Some view organizational norms simply as a part of organizational culture (Russell & Russell 1992), while others view it as situated between the cultural and sociostructural systems of the organization, mediating and reflecting elements of both systems and providing behavioral guidance to individual actors (Allaire and Firsirotu 1984).

social norms. Nevertheless, social norms are not well defined in the literature, and exactly what they are seems unclear. As Scott (2000: 1607) argued,

[T]he academic debate currently suffers from conceptual pluralism and terminological disarray. Indeed, we lack even a basic consensus on the proper definition of a social norm. This tower of Babel quality is, in part, a reflection of the complexity of the social phenomena that we are seeking to understand.

Hechter and Opp (2001: xiii) noted that "as there is no common definition of social norms, there can be little agreement about how to measure them... Much less clear, however, are the conditions responsible for their emergence."

Among the various definitions of social norms, Cialdini and Trost (1998: 152) defined social norms as "rules and standards that are understood by members of a group and that guide and/or constrain social behavior without the force of law." Furthermore, they identified four categories of influences encompassed in this definition: general societal expectations of behavior (injunctive norms), standards that develop out of observation of others' behavior (descriptive norms), expectations of valued others for one's own behavior (subjective norms), and one's own expectations for proper behavior or ethical beliefs (personal norms). This definition and these categories were applied here. However, the social norms discussed in this chapter are the injunctive and descriptive norms within the organization, and the subjective and personal norms have been excluded because they function at the individual level, while the two included norms function at the organizational level (Ehrhart and Naumann 2004).

Furthermore, besides injunctive and descriptive norms, managerial norms exist in organizations. These norms are created by top management and used to manage employees. In other words, the managerial norms form the "law" in the restaurant that regulates employees' behaviors. However, managerial norms are not included in the definition of social norms proposed by Cialdini and Trost (1998) unless they have transformed into injunctive or descriptive norms, which occurs on occasion. In this chapter, how managerial norms, injunctive norms, and descriptive norms interact and relate to legal norms is examined. An injunctive norm is the perception of what most people think others should do in a given situation (Bobek et al. 2013; Cialdini et al. 1990). It reflects the moral rules of the group and specifies what should and should not be done, and it reflects the moral rules of the organization that were invented to regulate the behaviors of its members. A descriptive norm is what one perceives other people to do in a given situation (Bobek et al. 2013; Cialdini et al. 1990). It describes what is typical or normal. The two norms can seem identical and can easily be confused because what is approved (injunctive norm) may be what is typically done (descriptive norm). Nevertheless, often, what is typically done is not what is morally seen as what ought to be done. Furthermore, the two are conceptually and motivationally distinct (Cialdini et al. 1990). Therefore, it is meaningful to discuss the two norms in the restaurant context to reveal both the "ought to" norms and the "most done" norms. Both norms influence employees' behavior in different ways.

7.2.2   How Social Norms Influence Compliance

Social norms, including injunctive and descriptive norms, have significant influence on legal compliance. In regulatory literature, how social norms influence legal compliance has been discussed in several ways. Although many researchers did not explicitly use Cialdini and Trost's definition of social norms, the social norms they discussed fall into the category of injunctive norms as "the moral rules of the group that specifies what should be done and should not be done." Thus, the mechanisms they discovered of how social norms influence compliance are applicable in this discussion.

In terms of descriptive norms, Cialdini (2007) argued that descriptive norms mobilize people into compliance via social information, and they direct behaviors forcefully, sometimes even unconsciously. He introduced several studies which have revealed the effects of descriptive norms on compliance. In one study, it was found that the belief of "others were conserving" rather than any other reasons people reported that correlated highly (twice) with reported energy saving efforts. People usually ignore or severely underestimate the effects of descriptive norms on their behavior. Descriptive norms send the message, "If a lot of people are doing this, it's probably a wise thing to do," which serves to initiate norm-congruent behavior. Moreover, descriptive norms may have both positive and negative effects on legal compliance. If the message sent by a descriptive norm aligns with the law, people may be mobilized to engage in compliance behavior. Conversely, if the message sent by a descriptive norm normalizes unwanted behaviors that violate the law, the unwanted behaviors are institutionalized, and people tend to engage in the unwanted behaviors.

Injunctive norms mobilize people into compliance via social evaluation (Cialdini 2007). People care about the evaluations of others, especially friends and family, and are inclined to do what they think they are expected to do. Expectations regarding what most others approve or disapprove of are quite influential (Larimer and Neigbors 2003; Van Empelen et al. 2001). Injunctive norms can also direct action by promising informal sanctions (mostly in the form of interpersonal approval or disapproval) for what is deemed by others to be morally relevant behavior. Reputation is one of the most important informal sanction mechanisms. In the socioeconomic model proposed by Sutinen and Kuperan (1999), social norms affect compliance by influencing actors' social reputation. Individuals who violate social norms suffer from the loss of social reputation among peers.

Injunctive norms can mobilize organizations in similar ways. Gunningham et al. (2004) found that social license granted by local communities motivated paper pulp firms to go beyond compliance in environmental protection. The social license is based on the degree to which a corporation and its activities meet the expectations of local communities. The firms were forced to meet the expectations of local communities and obtain social license to improve their reputations, which held long-term benefits to the business; to avoid costly legal enforcement mechanisms that local

communities may employ by initiating suits; or to avoid tighter new legal requirements that might result from local communities' unmet demands. Van Erp (2008)
further discussed the reputational sanctioning derived from social norms in compliance, and the strategy of naming and shaming in public and private regulation. Reputation is considered a form of capital that is even more important than a company's
financial capital. In contrast to Van Erp and other researchers who view social norms
as internalized and violations of social norms as a source of individual guilt, Posner
(1998, 2000) viewed social norms from the perspective of utility of attracting partners for cooperative relationships in society. He argued that people who comply with
social norms send a signal to potential cooperative partners that they are good and
reliable partners.

Social norms further influence compliance through identification. According to
self-categorization theory, people comply with the social norms if they identify themselves as part of the group to which the social norms are attributed (Wenzel 2004;
Gino et al. 2009). If the identification is strong, social norms will have a strong influence through their internalization as personal norms. If the identification is weak, the
influence will be weak. Individuals are more noncompliant the more noncompliant
their peer groups are, and more compliant the more compliant their peer groups are
(Geerken and Gove, 1975; Vogel 1974; Witte and Woodbury 1985). This could also
infer that individuals in a group where social norms deviate from the law are more
likely to violate the law.

Although researchers have different explanations for how social norms influence
legal compliance, such discussions have a common base; that is, there is a division
of social norms, including social norms that align with legal norms and social norms
that do not. As Alm et al. (1999) have shown, the social norms that tend toward
noncompliance are differentiated from the social norms that advocate compliance.
They observed that when the social norm tended toward noncompliance, the legal
compliance dropped to almost zero. Therefore, when examining how social norms
influence legal compliance, the interaction between social norms and legal norms
must first be discussed. The transmission of legal norms into organizations is mediated and influenced by the social norms existing in organizations. In the section that
follows, how social norms mediate the transmission of legal norms is discussed.

7.2.3 Competition Between and Activation of Organizational and Legal Norms

A restaurant is a semiautonomous social field that generates its own rules internally
but is also vulnerable to rules and decisions emanating from the world surrounding it
(Moore 1973). It has means to induce and coerce compliance internally, but it is also
affected and invaded by the larger social matrix in which it exists. The law enforced
by the state is only one of many factors that affect people's behaviors in a semiautonomous social field. When legal norms enter and impinge on the semiautonomous

social field, they encounter the internal rules, and they inevitably are challenged by the internal norms. In restaurants where managerial norms, descriptive social norms, and injunctive norms exist to guide behaviors, legal norms that are enforced externally interact with these managerial and social norms before influencing restaurant behaviors. They interact with each other in two significant ways, through competition and activation.

Competition is especially likely to occur when an organizational norm and a legal norm related to the same behavior differ but coexist. Heimer (1999) studied the competition between legal, medical, and familial institutions in infant intensive care units and found that the legal institutions gain influence by working through internal organizational processes. The influence of law varies with whether legal actors have learned how to present them when medical decisions are to be made, transform legal issues into organizational problems, introduce choice points that require action, and alter the possibility space of eligible solutions. The competition among the three institutions helps to explain why some laws have more influence than others do. In Heimer's research, the competition occurred during the decision-making process and manifested itself in four stages: participating in decision making, defining problems, proposing solutions, and insisting that decisions be made at specific times.

Moore (1973) researched Tanzania's attempts to legislate egalitarianism in an attempt to abolish chiefships and increase the power of representative legislative bodies and councils. However, the legislation did not and could not completely abolish the informal position of advantage enjoyed by some ruling families, because the ruling families were better educated than the rest of the population, and they became the new elite in the new government administration positions. Thus, the local literacy structure competed with the law related to egalitarianism, and the aims of the law could not be fully realized. Similarly, legal norms face competition from existing organizational norms in the process of transmitting legal norms into restaurants and influencing employees. All managerial norms, descriptive norms, and injunctive norms may compete with legal norms. As the outcome of such competition, legal norms may be resisted or reshaped, or they may successfully gain full or partial influence.

Activation is the second type of interaction between norms. Vandenbergh (2003) discussed the activation effect between social norms and the law and law enforcement. He used the term "norm activation" to show that the law and law enforcement may "trigger" existing norms to influence compliance decision making. For example, "researchers found that individuals who were aware of the human health impacts of burning and accepted responsibility for it were less likely to burn yard waste than others." In other words, the social norm of health awareness activated by the law and law enforcement helped to promote the compliance with the legal norm, that is, not burning yard waste. In addition, existing norms that align with legal norms promote compliance with the legal norms. Tyran and Feld (2006) showed that mild laws or lawmaking imposed exogenously with limited deterrence activates cooperation norms. These cooperation norms (including commitment and conditional cooperation) promote compliance with the mild law.

The studies of Vandenbergh (2003) and Tyran and Feld (2006) were conducted from the perspective of law making and law enforcement and examined how law making and law enforcement activate social norms that improve compliance with the law. Yet the activation between law and social norms can also be reversed. That is, organizational norms may activate knowledge of the law or what the legal norm aims to regulate, especially the organizational norm and legal norm align and the legal norm is absent in the organization. This is significant in this study because restaurants had limited doctrinal legal knowledge, and enforcement encounter did not significantly introduce explicit knowledge of the written law into restaurants.

7.2.4 The Formation of Organizational Norms

Organizational norms compete with or activate legal norms, and legal norms are transmitted from outside the organization, as discussed in the previous chapter, while organizational norms emerge internally within the organization. This section addresses the formation of organizational norms, including managerial, injunctive, and descriptive norms.

Without differentiating between injunctive and descriptive norms, Feldman (1984) discussed the development of group norms. He argued that most norms develop in one or more of four ways. First, norms may be formed via explicit statements by supervisors or coworkers. Explicit statements by the leader may also reveal the leader's preferences for a way of analyzing problems or doing certain work to increase the predictability of group members' behavior. Specific role expectations of certain individual group members and norms that cater to supervisor preferences may be established to help group members avoid embarrassing interpersonal interactions. Norms set explicitly by the leader and frequently emphasized often express the central values of the group. Second, norms may develop during critical events in the groups' history, when boundaries of behavior are noticed or a conscious decision toward certain behavior is concluded. Consequently, corresponding norms are established. Third, the first behavior pattern that emerges in a group often sets group expectations and becomes a group norm. Norms make life routine and predicable. Fourth, some group norms emerge simply because individual members bring them with them from other work groups in other organizations. This is called carry-over behaviors from past situations. Feldman's work largely explains the formation of managerial norms and highlights the four ways in which other organizational norms may emerge, but he did not differentiate between descriptive and injunctive norms. Due to their relevance to this study, descriptive and injunctive norms require further examination.

Descriptive norms derive from what other people do in a given situation. Few studies have addressed their formation in the organizational context. Aarts and Dijksterhuis (2003) noted that at some point, descriptive social norms could be so embedded that they are simply signaled by a certain environment. For instance, remaining silent in the library is an embedded descriptive social norm, and the environment of the library alone reminds one of that descriptive norm. In other words, certain environments may help to form certain descriptive norm. Nevertheless, several other factors contribute to the formation of descriptive norms, but to identify them, it is important to understand why descriptive norms develop.

According to Cialdini and Trost (1998), descriptive norms develop to achieve the goal of effective action. When people find themselves in a new or ambiguous situation without knowing exactly what appropriate behaviors are, they tend to rely on "social reality" to decide their behavior (Festinger 1954). Watching others' behavior provides information about such social reality in terms of what is "normal" in that novel or ambiguous situation (Gilbert 1995; Stiff and Mongeau 2016). In this way, a descriptive norm is formed in the perception of the observers, and the observers tend to imitate what they observe and conform to the descriptive norm. Hence, a descriptive norm is formed in the process of people imitating what other people do in certain situations. Therefore, it is important to bear in mind that people tend to imitate others in ambiguous situations and that descriptive norms may develop on these occasions.

However, people will not follow other people randomly. Researchers have found that people are most likely to follow those they view as similar to them (Festinger 1954) or those who successfully model effective behavior (Cialdini and Trost 1998). As noted by Allison (1992: 284), "imitation may be ubiquitous but it is not indiscriminate." Furthermore, the influence of other people's observable behavior on people's behavior may be reduced, and descriptive norms do not function in certain situations. For example, their functioning depends on whether the descriptive norm is activated and salient in that environment (Cialdini et al. 1990; Gino et al. 2009). If it is salient and activated, people are more likely to be influenced. If not, people are less likely to be influenced. For instance, people who saw someone litter subsequently littered more than those who did not see anyone litter if the environment was clean, but this effect was reversed when the environment was dirty. This occurred because the descriptive norm of not littering was not salient in the dirty environment. In addition, Gino et al. (2009) revealed that dishonesty behaviors conducted by in-group members had a significant influence on the extent of dishonesty, while dishonesty behaviors by out-group members reduced the participants' likelihood of acting dishonestly themselves.

Consequently, to study descriptive norm formation in restaurants, I investigated the model employees chose to follow and examined how the model was established and what factors influenced employees to choose and follow the model. The relevant socialization processes, specifically the management process, provided an excellent opportunity to study the questions surrounding the formation of descriptive norms, and they are discussed in subsequent sections.

Injunctive norms specify what should be done and are therefore the moral rules of the organization. Many researchers study organization or group norms without differentiating the types of norms as Cialdini and Trost (1998) did, but most of the organizational norms studied are injunctive norms. For example, Feldman (1984) defined group norms as "informal rules that groups adopt to regulate and regularize group members' behavior." Informal rules also are injunctive norms, as they regulate

group members' behaviors by specifying what group members should do. Therefore, when discussing the formation of injunctive norms, researches about general
organizational and group norms were discussed.

Why do injunctive norm develop? Cialdini and Trost (1998) argued that they
develop to build and maintain social relationship, and Shaw (1981) contended that
norms formed are only with respect to behaviors that have some significance for the
group. Feldman (1984) answered this question by differentiating task maintenance
duties and social maintenance duties. According to Feldman, organizational norms
develop, first, to facilitate the survival of the organization; second, to increase the
predictability of group members' behaviors; third, to avoid embarrassing interpersonal problems; and fourth, to express the central values of the organization and
clarify the distinction of the organization's identity. Moreover, Allaire and Firsirotu
(1984) established the position of organizational norms in a conceptual framework
of organizational culture. According to Allaire and Firsirotu, injunctive norms have
a further function, that is, to mediate the cultural and sociostructural systems of an
organization, shape organizational members' behavior, and effectively achieve the
goal of the organization (Allaire and Firsirotu 1984).

Following Allaire and Firsirotu's model, organizational (injunctive) norms can
be seen as reflecting both the cultural system and the sociostructural system of the
organization, and as mediating the interaction between the two systems. Furthermore, individual actors in an organization with their particular endowments, experience, and personality also are contributors to and molders of organizational norms
by influencing the organizational culture. As a result, the organizational injunctive norms that specify the moral behaviors in an organization are influenced by
three elements—organizational culture, organizational sociostructure, and individual
actors. Characteristics of individual actors include their particular skills, experience,
and personalities. In terms of organizational culture, the cultural system in an organization "embodies the organization's expressive and affective dimensions in a system
of shared and meaningful symbols manifested in myths, ideology, and values and
in multiple cultural artifacts" (Allaire and Firsirotu 1984: 213). In simple terms,
organizational culture consists of several components, including myths, ideology,
and values. The organizational sociostructure is composed of the interworkings of
formal structures, strategies, policies and management processes, and all ancillary
components of an organization's reality and functioning (formal goals and objectives,
authority and power structure, control mechanisms, reward and motivation, process
of recruitment, selection and education, sundry management processes). (Ibid.)

Therefore, to study the formation of injunctive norms, all three elements—
culture, sociostructure, and individual actors—should be considered. Cialdini and
Trost (1998) argued that the other three constructs of social norms, namely descriptive norms, subjective norms, and personal norms also influence injunctive norms.
Subjective norms and personal norms can be incorporated into the element of individual actors, because the two norms can be seen as what individual actors bring
with them as "particular endowments," "experience," or "carry-over behaviors from
past situations."

In response to the literature, the formation of organizational injunctive norms was studied by considering three factors, namely the organizational cultural system, the sociostructural system, and the individual actor.

7.2.5 Organizational Socialization and Management Processes

The formation of organizational norms can be studied by examining organizational socialization processes and, specifically, management processes. Organizational socialization is the process by which a new member of an organization learns the value systems, norms, and required behavior patterns of the organization he or she is entering (Schein 1988). Socialization occurs continuously throughout one's career within an organization in terms of boundary passages (Van Maanen and Schein 1978). During organizational socialization, the organization influences individual members, while individual members also influence the organization, although the two kinds of influence peak at different points in time. Organizational norms are both the context and product of organizational socialization. Hence, during the process of organizational socialization, the new member is not only influenced and shaped by existing norms but also brings challenges to the existing norm system (Van Maanen and Schein 1978) and shapes the organizational norms.

Furthermore, both organizational and legal norms aim to provide guidance for members' behavior, and this guidance occurs through organizational socialization. Organizational socialization is the very process through which organizational members are taught how to behave properly in the organization and taught what behaviors are organizationally expected, permitted, or disallowed. All norms functioning in organizations enter into this process to teach and influence organizational members. During this process, some norms may compete with other norms that point to different accepted and expected behaviors, or some norms may be activated by other norms and have a more significant influence on organizational members. Therefore, the process of organizational socialization is the most important process for the interaction between organizational and legal norms. Consequently, studying the process of organizational socialization provides space to discuss the formation of organizational norms and, simultaneously, the interaction between organizational and legal norms.

Organizational socialization can be studied from several perspectives. Van Maanen and Schein (1978) studied the development of organizational socialization by discussing the tactics involved in organizational socialization, which refers to the ways in which individuals are socialized from one role to another. These tactics may be consciously designed or used unconsciously or by accident. Nonetheless, they are all related to the management of the organization. Van Maanen (1978) identified six major tactical dimensions for organizational socialization. They are collective versus individual socialization processes, formal versus informal socialization processes, sequential vs. random steps in the socialization process, fixed versus variable social-ization processes, serial versus disjunctive socialization processes, and investiture vs. divestiture socialization processes. Van Maanen and Schein (1978) further claimed that there is seemingly no logical or conclusive end to a list of organizational social-ization tactics. The six tactical dimensions are used as a framework to describe organizational socialization processes and to study the outcome of socialization in terms of recruits' responses as custodians, content innovators, and role innovators.

This book was not intent to study the outcome of organizational socialization but to examine how organizational norms develop and compete with or activate legal norms in the process of organizational socialization. Thus, describing the socializa-tion process in management rather than capturing the characteristics of the socializa-tion processes was more relevant. Although Van Maanen and Schein (1978) did not directly describe the steps of the socialization process in the management context, their description of the six tactics revealed corresponding management activities in the socialization process. For example, collective and individual tactics, formal and informal tactics, and investiture and divestiture tactics occur mainly in the training stage. Sequential and random tactics, fixed and variable tactics, and serial and disjunc-tive tactics are not restricted to training periods but extend to evaluation and rewarding activities.

A review of the literature on organizational socialization further highlighted management activities on which organizational socialization discussions focused. For example, orientation and training in organizational socialization has been a key focus of several studies (Wanous and Reichers 2000; Scott et al. 2008). In addition to these widely researched management activities, three other management activi-ties involving employees, that is, hiring, monitoring, and problem resolution, were included in this book. The entire management chain—hiring and training, moni-toring, evaluating and rewarding, resolving problems—provides opportunities for workers to learn the required norms while influencing organizational norms. During the discussion of these management activities and of organizational socialization, the six tactical dimensions were considered to identify factors contributing to the formation of organizational norms and to the interaction between organizational and legal norms.

7.3 Socialization and Management Processes in Restaurants

Organizational norms, especially injunctive and descriptive norms, are developed in the process of organizational socialization, specifically during the management process. The organizational founder and manager introduce managerial norms that reflect the founder's and managers' personal norms, the organizational culture they intend to nurture, and the sociostructure of the organization. However, these managerial norms may be challenged by the members of the organization and modified throughout the entire management chain and socialization process, including during recruiting, training, monitoring, evaluating and rewarding, and resolving problem. During this process, some may develop into injunctive and descriptive norms shared by organizational members. Meanwhile, critical events may occur during the management process, and consequently, new managerial norms may form and then go through the same process. Injunctive and descriptive norms may also emerge during the formation of the organization, and set organizational expectations and become managerial norms. Some descriptive norms may form gradually in the process of newcomers imitating old members' behaviors. Finally, both injunctive and descriptive norms become important elements for management.

In this section, the socialization and management processes in restaurants, including hiring, training, monitoring, evaluation and rewarding, and problem resolution, are examined, especially in the two core restaurant cases.

7.3.1 Hiring

Recruiting new workers has been a significant challenge for most restaurants in recent years.[2] Restaurants require a large staff, but finding workers is difficult for several reasons. First, because of the low social status and poor reputation attached to restaurants jobs, job seekers tend to see restaurant work as a last resort. Traditionally, servers' jobs are seen as work that involves serving those of higher social standing and those who are better off than the servers, and people who work as servers may feel inferior. Second, salaries in restaurants, except those of head chefs, are relatively low, while working hours are long. Restaurant workers usually work from 9:00 a.m. to 2 p.m., take a 2.5-h break, usually at the restaurant, and work until 9 p.m. or later. In some restaurants, instead of working split shifts, workers work early and late shifts. Nevertheless, with both shift schemes, workers usually work more than nine hours a day, with one day off per week. In busy restaurants, workers may work for several months without a day off. As a head chef, who had worked his way up from the lowliest position in the restaurant, remarked, "Once doing restaurant work, you have little time for yourself and limited space for knowing outwards world. So, the world for workers is relative narrow and closed."[3] This contributes not only to a lack of

---

[2]Difficulty finding servers and restaurant workers is a common phenomenon, despite China's large migrant population, which reached 236 million in 2012. Migrants often fill these jobs. This phenomenon has social and economic causes, including low salaries and constraint of the household system. This kind of labor shortage is not a gross shortage of labor but a structural shortage. This "labor shortage" in the catering industry has been discussed by numerous researchers, including Zhao and Ran, who analyzed the phenomenon and reported their findings in "Reasons and suggestions to the 'labor shortage' in Catering industry," Economic Research, 2011 (31).

[3]Interview with FW, male, 34, on February 16, 2014.

labor but also to the high staff turnover in the restaurant industry. Third, restaurant work is considered unchallenging, with little room for personal development.

For these three reasons, young people shy away from restaurant work and prefer other work such as sales, office jobs, or factory work, which are seen as more sophisticated, with greater opportunity for personal development and more free time. Not only is recruitment difficult, but also it is difficult to retain workers, and high staff turnover is a persistent problem in the catering industry.[4] The high turnover rate is caused by similar reasons: few restaurant workers do the work by choice, and they feel no attachment to their jobs.

The Idealistic restaurant and the Profit-Maximizing restaurant also faced these challenges related to recruitment and staff turnover. The owners of both restaurants expressed their frustration about hiring and retaining workers. When asked about their requirements of hiring new workers, they often replied "almost no requirements," "do not have chance to select workers," and "it is difficult to get workers." In addition, the turnover rate was high. From October of 2011 when the Idealistic restaurant opened to February of 2014, the worker turnover rate was as high as 54.54%,[5] which means 54.54% of the total employees left. It was impossible to calculate this rate for the Profit-Maximizing restaurant, as even the owner can not count all the workers that left, but anecdotal evidence suggests that it was very high. During the study period, in 2013, the owner of the Profit-Maximizing restaurant contacted me to request help, as an emergency had arisen—all three his servers had resigned at the same time. He asked for my assistant working as server in his restaurant the next day because no one else was available.

These recruitment and staff turnover challenges had a significant and direct effect on restaurants' norms. Restaurants owners generally reduced employment criteria. For example, the Profit-Maximizing restaurant only refused boys with dyed hair and people from certain counties because he thought they were troublemakers and difficult to manage. The Idealistic restaurant had only one requirement—that candidates were healthy and not suffering from any major diseases. Other qualities, such as workers' knowledge and education, whether they agreed with the restaurant's culture or ideology, reasons of applying, and whether they intended to stay long, were not considered. Although S restaurant was a sophisticated, luxury establishment, it hired workers who had just completed school and had no cooking or restaurant experience. None of the restaurant owners in the study mentioned having a health certificate as an employment criterion.

---

[4] According to Yafeng Huang and Jianyu Xie's "Investigation of the mobility of restaurant workers" (2011), the normal staff turnover rate should be between 6 and 20%, but this rate exceeds 40% in the restaurant industry.

[5] Staff turnover rate can be calculated in several ways. One popular method, the total resignation rate, is calculated using as follows: total resignation rate in a certain period = number of employees who resigned in that period/number of employees employed in that period. Refer to Donghua Liu and Meiling Cai, "Calculation methods for the employee resignation rate," *Foreign Investment in China*, (2013). The rate of 54.54% was calculated using the formula number of employees who resigned from when the Idealistic restaurant opened until the measurement point/number of employees employed in that period.

Despite the low requirements for new workers, it was still difficult for owners to find new workers. Owners had to rely on their social networks to recruit workers, and they turned to relatives, friends, neighbors, and previous employees to find staff.[6] This is a common phenomenon in the catering industry, and many restaurant workers are hired this way, especially in small restaurants. Usually, most employees in a restaurant are related in some way. For instance, at the Idealistic restaurant in 2013, all eight employees had prior relationships, whether as neighbors, friends, or relatives. Hua, a server, was the young sister in law of the owner. Lian, a server, came from the same village as Hua. Han, a server, was a friend of Lian, while Yan, a server, was the daughter of the dishwasher. Xing and Xian, kitchen workers, were relatives of the owner, and two other kitchen workers were friends of Xing. At the Profit-Maximizing restaurant, two kitchen workers were relatives of the owner; Wang and Mei, both servers, were the kitchen workers' girlfriends, and Lu, a server, was the girlfriend of a former kitchen worker. Although using social networks helped the owners to find workers, it also prevented them from managing employees strictly and affected the formation of certain organizational norms. This point will be discussed in detail in the next section when describing organizational norms in restaurants.

In summary, the challenges related to staff recruitment and retention affect organizational norms and management, as owners and managers are reluctant to manage employees strictly. This point is further examined in the section on managerial norms in the two core restaurants.

7.3.2 Training

In large restaurants, formal training programs may be established for newcomers. For instance, at S restaurant, which had 120 employees and where I interviewed 12 workers but did not gain full access for onsite participant observation, new employees attended a training program before officially starting work. Smaller restaurants, in contrast, do not offer formal training for new workers, and most restaurants consider serving work too simple to require formal training. However, despite the perceived simplicity of the work, newcomers still need to become familiar with the work they are supposed to do. In smaller restaurants, this occurs through informal training that involves shadowing an experienced employee who does the same work to learn what to do and how to do it. As such, this can be viewed as mentoring rather than as training. During the mentoring period, the newcomer imitates the mentor's behavior and learns restaurant norms from the mentor. Thus, the mentor plays an important role in socializing the newcomer and transmitting organizational norms.

---

[6]Although many platforms provide opportunities to find workers, such as online advertisements, onsite advertisements, and the formal labor market, social networks, or *Guanxi* networks, still have an important function in finding employment or staff in China. To learn more about the role of social networks in occupational processes, refer to Yanjie Bian, "Chinese social stratification and social mobility," Annual Review of Sociology, 2002 (28): 91–116.

All small restaurants in this study trained newcomers informally and individually using the method of mentoring. While conducting participant observation at the Profit-Maximizing restaurant, the Idealistic restaurant, and H restaurant, I experienced the processes newcomers would experience. I was assigned to a server or told to shadow a server to learn the job. During mentoring, I was taught how to clean tables and floors, where to stand, what to do when customers arrive, and how to set tables. None of the mentor servers systematically trained me on acceptable and unacceptable behaviors. Instead, they usually explained the working procedures in a simple manner, for example, by saying,

> Clean the floor when you come and place the tableware on tables before customers come. When customers come, you should ask how many people there are with them and guide them to the table. After that, you need to get menus and hot tea. Then you stand here or there. If customers call the waitress, you go ask what they want. After customers leave, you collect tableware [and take it to the] kitchen, and clean the table. That is all.

The mentor servers neither received payment for training newcomers nor knew exactly what and how to teach newcomers. Usually, I simply observed how they acted on various occasions and imitated them, as is common practice.

At H restaurant, newcomers received even fewer instructions and simply observed and imitated the mentors' behavior. Yu, a server at H restaurant, experienced a similar type of mentoring:

> My mentor did not teach me. She did not like to talk to me. I just follow her and imitate. At the first day, I saw she added tea for customers during the meal and I imitated. However, I saw she just put teapot on the table and customers would add by themselves the next day. Later, I also imitated to just put teapot on the table.[7]

Consequently, it is easy to learn norms that have been routinized in the work procedure, such as how to greet to customers and how to set and clear tables, but difficult to learn norms that are not routinized in daily practice, such as washing hands and cutting nails.

The mentoring process created an ambiguous environment for socialization within which descriptive norms are easily formed and transmitted. Furthermore, the descriptive norms related to what has been done gradually evolved into injunctive norms related to what ought to be done. In this way, employees learned these injunctive norms without clearly understanding the injunctive norms. As H restaurant, kitchen workers were using a large tablecloth to dry the chopsticks. I asked one of them why they were doing this, and he answered, "They are wet if we do not dry them." When asked who instructed him to perform this task, he responded, "I do not know. My mentor worker taught me to do it when I just came in."[8] The tablecloth was dirty, as it had not been changed for some time; thus, drying chopsticks and other dishes in this manner violated the legal norm of tableware disinfection. In this instance, the kitchen worker learned the descriptive norm of drying dishware with a tablecloth and accepted the injunctive norm of "chopsticks should be dried" or "wet chopsticks are

---

[7]Interview with HY, female, 17, on September 9, 2012.
[8]Interview with HN, male, 17, on August 21, 2012.

not acceptable." Yet he did not know where the injunctive norm came from or why he had to adhere to the norm.

The same situation existed at the Idealistic restaurant. Descriptive norms were learned directly, while injunctive norms were learned indirectly, as mentor servers only showed newcomers how to perform tasks and did not explain why they needed to be performed in a certain manner (or at all). For example, when I imitated the mentor server's behavior by placing washed dishware into the disinfection cabinet, including small bowls, small plates, chopsticks, and spoons, the mentor server did not tell me which items to include and which items to exclude. I loaded all the items into the cabinet, but the server removed the spoon for serving rice and said there is no need to disinfect the rice spoons. She did not intend to explain why the rice spoons do not need disinfection, and when I asked for clarification, the server explained only that "customers hold the chopsticks and small bowls, and their mouths will touch these tableware, but they do not eat directly with rice spoons." Later, when the server set the timer on the disinfection cabinet, I asked for guidance on the length of the cycle, but the server responded that she did not know either and guessed. I learned that the server's mentor had not taught the server correct disinfection times; consequently, every newcomer saw that the mentor server set a particular time for the disinfection cabinet and imitated that behavior without knowing the exact operational standards. Although the new servers did not know anything about disinfection or have experience of disinfection, they soon learned at the Idealistic restaurant to disinfect certain dishware and leave out others, just as the kitchen worker at H restaurant learned to dry chopsticks with a dirty tablecloth.

Managerial norms were less visible in the mentoring process. Although the owner of the Idealistic restaurant had established rules about handwashing, I learned nothing about this rule during mentoring period, and my mentor never instructed me to wash hands. The mentor server sometimes washed her hands after clearing tables or before preparing steamed buns, but not always, and I could not deduce by observation when I needed to wash my hands. Furthermore, no other employees mentioned handwashing on any occasion. It was not mentioned during employee meetings, and the owner and head chef did not mention it. I was informed of the handwashing rule only after asking about it. Some servers did not like to ask questions, and thus they simply never learned about this rule. For example, Han never learned the rule despite having started work a month before me.

Since newcomers might not learn these norms, they would bring or develop their own norms about these behaviors. As a result, deviant descriptive norms developed among the workers. Workers washed their hands whenever they felt their hands were dirty, or whenever they felt they needed to, So different servers had different handwashing behaviors. Moreover, the server who mentored me did not mention fingernail length requirements until I asked her why she had such short nails and she pointed out that the owner required this and would fine her if she violated the norm. From the mentoring process, I learned that managerial rules do not have a lasting influence on employees' behaviors unless they are socialized into injunctive rules or become routine in the form of descriptive norms.

In addition to individual mentoring, group training took place at the Idealistic restaurant but not at the Profit-Maximizing restaurant. The group training focused on the ideology of health and ecology, and the owners of the Idealistic restaurant went to great lengths to educate employees by organizing employees to watch movies, read books, and discuss ideas related to healthy food, organic agriculture, and the dangers of chemical fertilizers and pesticides. Yet, other more practical topics, such as restaurant rules, food safety instructions, cooking skills, food processing skills,[9] and communication skills, were not addressed. When I told the owners' husband that servers did not know the appropriate length of disinfection cycles and asked whether they had organized any training about disinfection, he simply answered, "They should have known it," and went on to claim that they had attempted to organize some training but that employees had not enjoyed it, so they had stopped. The training they organized was similar to studying activities offered by an NGO, where people with the same interests gather to watch movies, read books, and discuss their thoughts about those movies and books. However, the employees did not enjoy these activities and remained silent throughout study sessions. The owner's husband asked employees' opinions about the study activities, such as whether they wanted to proceed, and if yes, how they can add interest, but they remained silent. As a result, he stopped the weekly training, or more precisely, study activities. When asked whether compulsory work-related training should be provided, he replied that there was nothing complex about servers' work. Later, I asked for employees' opinion on the training sessions. Ms. Mei, the head server, said most of the movies they watched during the training sessions were in English, and the Chinese subtitles were difficult to follow. She always felt sleepy when watching those movies. She said she preferred to learn substantial skills related to her work, such as how to introduce herself to customers, serve customers, and answer customers' questions, during training sessions.[10]

Compared to at the Idealistic restaurant where some managerial norms existed, especially regarding handwashing and nail cutting, at the Profit-Maximizing restaurant I learned hardly any managerial norms. An interview with the owner of the Profit-Maximizing restaurant indicated that there were no managerial rules except being diligent and not playing with mobile phones during working hours. Nevertheless, during the mentoring process, I observed the descriptive norm that whenever there was no work at hand, workers would watch films on their phones. Thus, the only managerial norm the owner set for employees did not change into a descriptive norm.

Injunctive norms at the Profit-Maximizing restaurant were also vague, and employees could not clearly distinguish them. In one instance, a server overlooked the norms related to the division of labor and made an error when dealing with

---

[9]Because the Idealistic restaurant was a small restaurant, servers needed to perform a variety of tasks, such as serving customers, disinfecting dishes, making steamed bread, making fruit tea, and cooking rice. Sometime, if help was needed in the kitchen, they would do simple kitchen work, such as cutting, chopping, and slicing food.

[10]Interview with Mei on May 24, 2013.

formal receipts. Usually, only the cashier is responsible for billing and providing formal receipts to customers. However, because this was not clearly stated as a rule or norm, servers who preferred to draw up bills would do so.[11] A former server especially enjoyed the task of drawing up bills. One day, when drawing up a bill for some customers, who asked her for additional formal receipts, she gave them as many as they requested and charged them 2 CNY for all receipts. Later, the owner's mother, who had been sitting at the cashier's desk but did not know the procedures related to formal receipts, felt something was amiss, so she asked Wang, the server responsible for billing, what extra formal receipts cost. Wang indicated that it was considerably more than 2 CNY. The server who had made the error was Wang's older sister, and Wang learned only after this incident that her sister did not know the selling price of formal receipts despite having worked in another restaurant for a year and at the Profit-Maximizing restaurant for some time.

7.3.3 Monitoring

Monitoring is an important stage for transmitting existing organizational norms and developing new norms. By this stage, newcomers have become formal workers whose behaviors are monitored, supervised, and corrected. However, monitoring was slack at the Idealistic restaurant and absent at the Profit-Maximizing restaurant. During an informal interview with Yan and Han, servers at the Idealistic restaurant, I asked whether the head chef, who was responsible for employee management, checked their nails. Yan said,

> The head chef said one day on the meeting, 'Look at your nail which is long and black. You are not allowed to have long nails. If I find anyone has long nails, you pay five yuan [CNY] for each long nail. After that, we were all scared and cut nails short.[12]

Yet the servers further indicated that the head chef would check employees' nails only occasionally, and during my stay in the restaurant, I did not observe such occasions.

Monitoring requires human resources and willingness, both of which were in short supply at both the core restaurants studied. Monitoring behavior is time consuming, as it involves observing workers and correcting their behaviors when necessary or reporting them to the manager or owner. At the Profit-Maximizing restaurant, the owner took charge of everything. There was no head server or kitchen supervisor because, according to him, there was no need for a monitoring or midlevel management position because the restaurant was small and no one was suitable. He contended, "No one except me can manage waitresses. There are only several waitresses, and they come to restaurant around the same time. No one is qualified to

---

[11] Wang, who was responsible for billing, complained that some servers always performed this task themselves.

[12] Interview with Yan and Han on April 12, 2013.

manage others and no one will be convinced to other's management." Furthermore, some workers were his relatives, and an external manager would not have been able to manage them as they would listen only to him, or, according to him, they did not even listen to him. Consequently, he managed all restaurant affairs and employees while also working as head chef. He was simply too busy to monitor workers' behaviors. He did not even have time to hold employee meetings to discuss problems but briefly spoke to workers during mealtimes instead. Without monitoring, it was impossible to enforce managerial norms, and it was difficult to change these norms into injunctive or descriptive norms. Similarly, the injunctive and descriptive norms that aligned with managerial norms were not reinforced, and those that conflicted with managerial norms were not correct in time. As a result, norms were unclear.

At the Idealistic restaurant, although several persons were supposed to monitor workers' behaviors, monitoring tended to be ineffective. The employees considered the owner, her husband, and her young brother (also the headchef) as the owners of the business, and the restaurant had a head server to manage the servers and a kitchen supervisor to manager the kitchen workers. However, the owner did not manage workers directly but was responsible for work related to the food suppliers, communication with inspectors, and interaction with customers. Her husband was supposed to manage employees, but he was reluctant to do so[13] and employees seemed reluctant to listen to him.[14] Therefore, the head chef was responsible for the daily management of employees. Although the management of the kitchen workers and servers had been delegated to the kitchen supervisor and head server, the two lacked the ability, time, and willingness to manage others. For instance, the head server was diligent and always doing regular serving work. She was more set on being the first to serve dishes or clean the tables than on organizing servers or managing their work. Furthermore, as noted in the section on hiring practices, most workers at the restaurant were related or socially connected. One of the servers originally helped the head server get the job at the Idealistic restaurant, so the head server was reluctant to truly "manage" this server and seriously monitor her behavior. She was equally reluctant to manage other servers who had been at the restaurant longer than she had. Consequently, the head server did not function well as a midlevel manager

---

[13]The owner's husband argued that the head chef managed the employees. One day, Yan, a server, broke a small spoon, and the owner's husband saw this. I quietly asked the owner's husband whether Yan would be penalized, and the owner's husband answered, "I don't know. You have to ask the head chef.".

[14]On several occasions, the owner's husband asked workers to do something, but the workers refused. When the owner's husband asked Yan, a server, to take out some yeast when Shi, another server, added yeast to the water while preparing steamed buns because he thought Shi added too much, Shi answered, "I cannot take out any now. I just leave some when add to the flour." She went on to mix the water and yeast. the owner's husband asked how she would know how much should be left when she added the yeast water to the flour, and Shi replied, "It is also not possible to know how much yeast I should take out when you asked me to do so. What should I do if I take out too much?" The owner's husband did not say anything and left. Later, Yan, who had witnessed the exchange, poured all the yeast water into the flour. When I commented on this, Yan answered, "Who cares!".

in monitoring servers' behaviors. Thus, at the Idealistic restaurant, managerial norms were not enforced in a regular manner.

In addition, neither restaurant was willing to monitor its employees' behavior for compliance with management norms related to personal hygiene even if it had the management capacity. There are several reasons for this. First, the owners generally did not take such behaviors seriously and focused instead on whether the workers did their work and made the restaurant operate smoothly. The managerial norms related to nail length and handwashing were not their focus, and that employees did not comply with those norms would not cause significant problems. Second, the owners preferred to rely on the employees to manage themselves, especially at the Idealistic restaurant. When I asked who was responsible for monitoring when workers washed their hands, the owner stated, "No one. I rely on them to monitor themselves after we making the rule for them." Hence, the handwashing and nail cutting rules were established but not monitored, and whether employees complied with them relied on the employees themselves.

Then what did the two restaurants monitor? At the Idealistic restaurant, it was food sanitation and work efficiency, while at the Profit-Maximizing restaurant it was only diligence. As elaborated on in Sect. 3.5, at the Idealistic restaurant, when foreign matter was found in food, the head chef would call employee meetings and restate the importance of food sanitation. Work efficiency included to responding customers quickly, serving dishes quickly, and finishing work without mistakes. Mistakes that occur would be written in a notebook every day, and read and discussed at the regular employee meetings.

At the Profit-Maximizing restaurant, the owner monitored employees covertly. He observed how each employee worked and remembered it, as is discussed in Sect. 3.4. He seldom spoke to employees about their work, even when problems emerged, such as foreign matter in the food. During the observation period for this study, the owner only once communicated with an employee about her work. He asked Ms. Wang why the genuine formal receipts were being used so fast, and Ms. Wang responded that many customers asked for formal receipts and that she had to issue genuine receipts because those customers needed real ones. The owner said nothing further. Later, Ms. Wang stated that she felt aggrieved about that. She thought the owner had blamed her for the number of receipts used. She complained, "What does the owner mean? I did not put formal receipts into my pocket. Customers require the real one for reimbursement. How can I give them the fake one?" Therefore, at the Profit-Maximizing restaurant, on the one hand, the owner did not monitor employees' behavior strictly, but on the other hand, employees feared the owner and were sensitive about criticism.

This kind of monitoring negatively affected the practice of managerial norms at the Profit-Maximizing restaurant, and managerial norms were often challenged. For instance, the owner introduced a uniform for all employees and bought each employee two T-shirts for work. Yet this requirement was abandoned after several days because someone did not like the T-shirts and stopped wearing them, and then others began to imitate this behavior. The owner told them that if they did not want to wear the T-shirts they should return them to him, meaning that they should wear their

T-shirts, but some workers returned their T-shirts. The owner did not say anything to them but did not ask others to return their shirts. Finally, all workers stopped wearing the uniform. A similar situation occurred regarding health certificate. Even if the owner required employees to undergo health checks and obtain health certificates, some employees would not do as he instructed.

7.3.4 Evaluating and Rewarding

Evaluating employees' work, rewarding good performance, and penalizing poor performance play a significant role in motivating workers to carry out the required behaviors and in correcting undesired behaviors. At the Profit-Maximizing restaurant, the only standard for evaluating workers was whether workers were diligent. the owner of the Profit-Maximizing restaurant would pay bonuses to workers he observed to be diligent and hardworking, but he would not disclose who receive bonuses or tell the staff how much the bonuses were. In other words, at the Profit-Maximizing restaurant, evaluation and rewards took place in secret. This hindered the formation of an explicit managerial norm and an explicit injunctive norm regarding this trait. Inexplicitly, all workers who had worked at the Profit-Maximizing restaurant for a time knew the owner's preferences and requirements of them to a certain extent. As one worker said, "I feel the owner want us to do work every minute." Yet these managerial and injunctive norms were not confirmed or reinforced explicitly with overt evaluation and praise; thus, they did not develop into a descriptive norm.

In contrast, by learning the apparent descriptive norm that everyone plays with his or her mobile phone whenever there is time, employees show the opposite inclination, as occurred when the owner of the Profit-Maximizing restaurant attempted to introduce a uniform. Thus, the description norms employees learned from others had a more significant influence on their behavior than managerial or injunctive norms did. Sometimes, the owner would become angry with employees because of their behavior, and he would threaten to dock their salaries, but those employees knew it was an idle threat and did not take him seriously. According to a kitchen worker,

> The owner said he will deduct our money. However, he is just not that kind of person. He does not really deduct money but just scare us. He just feels angry about some of our behaviors and says some angry words. We know that. He is the owner. We have to give him the face. We will follow when he asks us to do something.[15]

Hence, the managerial norms established by the owner were difficult to change into injunctive and descriptive norms at the Profit-Maximizing restaurant during the evaluation and reward process. Instead, employees developed their own descriptive norms, and those descriptive norms were reinforced due to the dysfunctional evaluation and reward system.

At the Idealistic restaurant, employees who engaged in unwanted behaviors were penalized using a system of penalty points. Each mistake and misbehavior would be

---

[15]Interview with NY, male, 30, on September 2, 2013.

recorded and would be ascribed a certain score. Every month, these scores would be added, and a corresponding monetary amount would be deducted from the 100 CNY bonuses employees received each month in addition to their salaries. Employees would be told how much money had been subtracted for which transgressions when the head chef handed them their salaries. Misbehaviors included tardiness, breaking tableware, and forgetting to turn off the liquefied gas; having long nails and not washing hands were also included initially, but these two norms were not monitored, and the servers knew the head chef did not deduct money from their bonuses for these transgressions. Yan, a server, noted, "He just scares us. Generally speaking, he does not deduct our money [for long nails]."[16]

In fact, the Idealistic restaurant evaluated employees' work by observing whether they finished their work without causing trouble, that is, whether they were diligent. The rule of cutting nails would not be mentioned unless food quality problems emerged. For instance, it was reemphasized when a ring appeared in a dish. The rule of handwashing was hardly mentioned since it was introduced, because no obvious problems related to food quality would emerge due to handwashing. Consequently, these two managerial norms were not reinforced during the evaluation and reward process at the Idealistic restaurant. Although they became injunctive norms to a certain extent, they were ineffective. The disinfection and health certificate norms were simply ignored in the evaluation process.

7.3.5   Problem Resolution

During organizational operations, problems inevitably arise, and no organization can prevent this from happening. When problems arise, organizations must resolve them. These problem resolution processes are critical occasions for reinforcing existing organizational norms or developing new organizational norms. Existing organizational norms are presented through several key aspects of the resolution process. Evaluation of the problem is the first aspect, and it includes deciding whether the problem is normal or abnormal, whether it needs to be addressed specifically, and whether it has a significant influence on the business. The evaluation reveals the organizational norms, which in turn reflect which values will be reinforced. The second aspect is how the problem is dealt with and resolved, specifically, whether anyone or anything is directly responsible for the problem. The third aspect is what influence this problem will have on future management. This is closely related to the first aspect of evaluating the problem, because if a problem is evaluated as critical and having a significant influence, the organization may take further measures to avoid reoccurrence. If a problem is evaluated as a normal problem with an insignificant influence, the organization may not put any efforts into preventing the problem from reoccurring.

---

[16]Interview with TY, female, 18, on April 16, 2013.

In restaurants, customer complaints about dishes are a common problem. For instance, customers may find foreign matter in their food, and they may complain to the server or owner, ask for a refund, ask for a new serving or dish, or even refuse to pay the bill. The restaurants studied ascribed contrasting importance to these problems. At the Idealistic restaurant, if a customer found any foreign matter in a dish, the dish would be returned to the kitchen and refunded. Moreover, the dish would be taken to an employee meeting, where the head chef would show it to all employees and attempt to find the source of the contaminant. In addition, new rules might have been developed to reduce the likelihood of this problem reoccurring, and behaviors not directly related to this problem might have been regulated further.

For example, customers found a ring in their dish one day. The head chef considered this a serious abnormal event that had a significant negative effect on the customers. He held an employee meeting and announced the penalty system described in Sect. 3.4. Penalties would apply not only for wearing accessories when forbidden to do so but also would set the standards for punishing other transgressions, such as having long nails, being late for work, forgetting to perform tasks, and so on. According to the head chef, the ring incident was a critical event that forced him to change his management style. Previously, he had been hesitant to fine employees and instead simply asked them to deal with problems that arose. However, he found that simple reminders were useless, as the same problems emerged repeatedly. Sometimes, customers would find hair or insects in dishes. Nevertheless, when the ring incident occurred, he decided to become stricter. Thus, he created the system of penalizing misbehavior, such as fining employees 5 CNY per minute for being late and 5 CNY for every long nail. The head chef's reaction to this event is similar to broken windows policing (Kelling and Coles 1997) that attempt to address every small infraction. Yet as discussed in the previous section, although the penalty rule as a managerial norm reminded employees of rules, it did not contribute much to compliance with the handwashing and nail cutting norms.

In contrast, the owner of the Profit-Maximizing restaurant considered foreign matter in dishes normal and unavoidable. Foreign bodies that appeared in dishes include hair, insects, flies, and even cockroaches. Every time customers found foreign matter in dishes and required the dishes to be changed, the servers would simply take the dishes back to the kitchen and report it to the owner casually by stating, "There's [something] in it and the customers asked to change it." Usually the owner would hastily and unhappily glance at the dish without a word. The restaurant would not charge customers for that dish. Sometimes, if the dish had not been eaten, the server would pick out the hair in the dish and serve it to another customer. When the cockroach was found, the customers were not charged for their entire meal, but no other action was taken. The owner said, "It is normal for the hair falling out. You do not find hair in dishes everyday but just once or twice in several months. Not just hair, there may be cockroach sometimes."[17] From the owner's reaction, it is clear how norms of cleanness of dishes were overlooked. It is also understandable

---

[17]Interview with the owner of the Profit-Maximizing restaurant on August 21, 2013.

that norms related to cutting nails and washing hands were unlikely to exist at the Profit-Maximizing restaurant.

7.4   Organizational Norms in Restaurants and Compliance Behaviors

Close examination of daily management activities revealed the existing organizational norms in restaurants that are related to various compliance behaviors. To discuss the relationship between organizational norms and legal norms, and to determine how organizational norms mediate the transmission of legal norms in restaurants, the organizational norms that relate directly or indirectly to the four legal norms, that is, health certificates, dish disinfection, handwashing and cutting nails, are discussed in this section. The organizational norms discussed here include managerial norms, injunctive norms, and descriptive norms.

7.4.1   Organizational Norms at the Idealistic Restaurant

7.4.1.1   Norms of Healthy Food

Providing healthy food is an overarching and the most prominent norm at the Idealistic restaurant. This managerial norm originally was introduced by the owners. As shown in Chap. 3, the Idealistic restaurant was established based on the concepts of organic food and community support agriculture. After the restaurant opened, the owners and the head chef attempted to pass the ideology of organic and healthy food to their employees through group training sessions on the negative effects of chemical fertilizers and pesticides; the damage to people's health, the earth, and the environment and soil changes caused by modern farming methods; organic food production; and so forth. According to the owner, they wanted to train employees on the ideology of the restaurant, not only to improve their knowledge about organic food so as to do their work well but also to pass this ideology on to them as a part of their life experience. When talking about the ideology of the Idealistic restaurant, the head chef said, "I hope our workers stay in this restaurant and have the belief of being healthy. They feel healthy first and then let customers feel healthy. We should believe in what we are doing."[18]

Furthermore, the owners and the head chef typically recognized the health risks that accompanied workers' violation of norms. When discussing these violations, they would focus on educating workers and promoting their health consciousness. For example, when Hua, a server and the head chef's wife and the owner's sister-in-law, opened a large pack of napkins and failed to double seal the napkins to prevent

---

[18]Interview with the head chef of the Idealistic restaurant on May 24, 2013.

contaminating, the owner explained that this was inappropriate, as it increased the risk of rodent contamination and the risk of passing infectious diseases to customers.

Moreover, this norm is evident from the Idealistic restaurant's reaction when customers complain of foreign matter in the food. According to Yan, a server, she once served a bowl of chicken soup to a customer. Before she took the dish to the table, she saw a small, dead fly floating in the soup. She scooped it out without thinking and served the soup to customers. Later, when the head chef heard of this, he did not praise her; instead, he later announced in a meeting that servers were not allowed to remove flies from dishes and serve the dishes to customers. The server should report it to the head chef, and the kitchen should prepare a new dish for the customers.

Their ongoing efforts influenced employees both consciously and unconsciously, and the norm of health and providing healthy food has become injunctive at the Idealistic restaurant. I heard employees mentioning "health" often when discussing their work during interviews and observation.

However, this norm may not effectively change into a descriptive norm among employees, as can be seen from several employees' personal perceptions and experiences. Yan, the server who scooped the fly out of the chicken soup, said, "It is normal [to find flies in dishes at home]."[19] She further related that she once found a fly in her food at a rice noodle restaurant. She did not complain. She returned a second time and found another fly. Again, she did not complain. When she returned a third time, she found a third fly. I asked Yan why she kept returning, and she simply stated that after the last time, she would never go to that restaurant again. However, it was obvious that she did not think that foreign matter in one's food is a big problem. When asked what she thought about head chef's requirement to always provide customers with a newly prepared dish after finding a foreign object, she replied, "I don't know what to say. This is the owner's matter. I just do what he asks."[20]

The norm of healthy food at the Idealistic restaurant aligns with the aims of food safety laws that regulate restaurant behaviors. As a result, employees at the Idealistic restaurant generally mentioned the benefit of health more often than employees in other restaurants did when asked about their perceptions of legal norms related to food safety, that is, health certificates, disinfection, handwashing, and nail cutting.

7.4.1.2 Norms of Handwashing

The Idealistic restaurant established a managerial norm on the behavior of handwashing: All workers must wash their hands after going to the toilet and before entering the kitchen. This managerial norm transformed into an injunctive norm accepted by all employees. Furthermore, a descriptive norm concerning handwashing developed: Workers should wash their hands after going to the toilet and whenever they feel their hands are dirty.

---

[19]Interview with Yan on April 12, 2013.
[20]Ibid.

When the Idealistic restaurant first opened, the handwashing norm did not exist. It came into being after the owner saw a kitchen worker return to the kitchen after going to the toilet and begin working without washing his hands. She was disgusted with this behavior, as in her view, washing one's hand after using the toilet should be a common habit everyone engages in spontaneously. Consequently, she called an employee meeting, discussed this event, and later announced the managerial norm that everyone should wash his or her hands after using the toilet. Later, the head chef added that workers should wash their hands before entering the kitchen. He even made a sign that read, "Want to go inside? Wash your hands!" and hanged it on the wall outside the kitchen.

After interviews with the staff at the Idealistic restaurant, it became apparent that this managerial norm had transformed into an injunctive norm, although in a modified form. When asked when they are supposed to wash their hands, all servers except Ms. Han, replied that they should do so after using the toilet; all kitchen workers, except a new worker, replied that they should wash their hands before entering the kitchen. Therefore, servers and kitchen workers emphasized the different parts of this managerial norm that are most relevant to them. Servers entered the kitchen often to place dirty dishware in the washing basin, but they returned to the dining area quickly, so there seems no need for them to wash their hands before entering the kitchen, and to do so every time would be impossible. For kitchen workers, the owner cared about whether they washed their hands before working in the kitchen.

Based on the observations and interviews, all servers washed their hands after using the restroom, while most kitchen workers washed their hands before entering the kitchen and after taking a break outside or using the toilet. However, if kitchen workers simply went outside to fetch something, such as eggs, rice, or a mixer, they would not wash their hands before returning to the kitchen. Servers who entered kitchen to fetch something or put used tableware in the washing basin also did not wash their hands. Thus, the injunctive norm they mentioned transformed into a slightly modified descriptive norm.

In addition, employees washed their hands at other times that the managerial norm did not identify, but these times differed from one employee to the next. The server who mentored me did not wash her hands before fetching bowls from the disinfection cabinet, but washed her hands after lacing up her shoes. She sometimes washed her hands after clearing a table, but not every time, and she washed the basin but not her hands before kneading dough. In contrast, another server would wash her hands before kneading dough although she also washed the basin. Based on observation, workers had their own standards that governed when else they washed their hands. That is, they washed their hand when they felt they were dirty, but employees had different notions of dirty hands. Consequently, no other descriptive norms existed about when they should wash their hands.

Although the Idealistic restaurant developed managerial, injunctive, and descriptive norms about handwashing, these norms did not fully align with the legal requirements, the law requires washing hands on far more occasions. These include before processing food, after using the toilet, after touching raw foodstuff, after touching contaminated equipment and tools, after coughing, sneezing, or blowing one's nose, after dealing with animals or waste, after touching any part of the body, and after performing activities that may contaminate the hands.[21]

7.4.1.3   Norms of Cutting Nails

The Idealistic restaurant had a managerial norm that required workers to keep their nails short, which was in place since the restaurant opened. Every employee was asked to keep his or her nails short when joining the team. In practice, monitoring was slack, and no complement penalty rule had been instated until a customer found a ring in his or her food. After establishing the penalty rule, employees were quite scared, and they kept their nails short and refrained from wearing any body accessories for a time. Yet things soon returned to the way they had been before. A few of the servers left their nails long again. One day, I chatted to Lian, a server, while she did stitching work and noticed that her nails were at least a centimeter long and neatly manicured. I jokingly asked Lian whether she was afraid of being fined, and Lian casually answered, "Just let them fine me." Over the following days, I focused on whether the head server, Mei, or the head chef would discover Lian's long nails and react to them. However, none of them paid any attention, and Lian was not reprimanded. It seemed that the head chef and owners did not address these matters again. Furthermore, some servers claimed that the owner was unlikely to deduct money from their bonuses for these types of transgressions.

Thus, while the managerial norm of nail cutting had transformed into an injunctive norm of everyone knowing they were not supposed to have long nails, not all servers kept their nails short. Nevertheless, from what I observed, no kitchen workers had long nails. Therefore, keeping nails short had become a descriptive norm among kitchen workers. The head chef may be the key for the difference between servers and kitchen workers regarding the nail cutting norm. Because he worked in the kitchen every day, he may have paid more attention to kitchen workers' nails and reminded them to cut their nails short when he saw anyone with long nails. Consequently, it is easy for kitchen workers to form the descriptive norm of keeping nails short. In contrast, no one paid attention to servers' nails and kept reminding them of the norm. I experienced this firsthand, as my mentor never checked my nails and reminded me to keep my nails short.

7.4.1.4   Norms of Disinfection

The Idealistic restaurant had managerial, injunctive, and descriptive norms concerning disinfection, but all of them deviated from the legal norm of disinfection to a certain extent. The three kinds of norms were the same in terms of what should be disinfected and what was disinfected. That is, dishware used for personal service should have been and was disinfected after every wash to prevent the spread

---

[21] These are stated in article 12 of "Food Safety Operation Norm in Catering Service Industry.".

of disease, while other large plates, bowls, and rice spoons customers used that did not touch their mouths did not require disinfection and were not disinfected.

All servers knew to disinfect dishware in the disinfection cabinet and understood that this was done to prevent spreading infectious diseases from one customer to others. Disinfection received so much attention because a friend of the owner contracted hepatitis B. They suspected the disease had been transmitted via a pair of chopsticks he had used in a small restaurant that might not have been disinfected properly. Hepatitis B was rife in that area. This scared her, and since then, she valued disinfection. She bought a high-quality disinfection cabinet for her own restaurant and required servers to disinfect the tableware every time after washing. The most important purpose of disinfection was to prevent spreading infectious diseases.

This norm had been operationalized as part of the regular work servers needed to do every day. At the end of every meal service, two servers would carry a large box full of all kinds of dishware that had just been washed, such as, chopsticks, spoons, and cups, to the hall where the disinfection cabinet had been placed. They would pack the cabinet and set the timer for heating and disinfection. After the cycle was completed, one server would open the cabinet and allow the dishware to cool, which usually took more than half an hour. When the dishware was touchable, a server would unpack the cabinet and place the items on the tables or in another large box called the cleaning cupboard.

However, the injunctive norm about tableware disinfection did not include all tableware, as the tableware used for table service was not disinfected. Although this was never discussed, the Idealistic restaurant practiced this norm daily. When I asked a server why other big plates and bowls were not disinfected, she answered, "No one thinks of disinfecting the big ones. They will dry by themselves…I feel the small ones are more important…".[22]

7.4.1.5 Norm of Self-responsibility

Though various rules regulated employees' behavior at the Idealistic restaurant, there was a norm that self-responsibility and self-awareness were considered more important than rules. Workers were expected to self-regulate instead of the restaurant regulating their behaviors. Whenever problems arose due to employee misbehavior, the head chef and the owners would emphasize that it was because employees did not focus on their work or did not do their work carefully. I participated in the Idealistic restaurant's employee meetings. During these meetings, all problems that had arisen in the past several days would be discussed by the head chef, such as calculating a bill incorrectly, forgetting to add dishes customers ordered later to the bill, serving customers oily dishes, and finding hair in food. The most frequent comment from the head chef was that problems arose because staff did not pay attention to their work. He would ask, "If you take care of your work, how can you make those problems?" When I discussed creating operational rules, regulating operational processes, and

---

[22]Interview with Yan on August 9, 2013.

training workers with the owner's husband and her young brother, both expressed the view that although operational processes and rules are important, they may not be useful, as serving work is very simple and anyone can do it well if he or she pays attention. After this discussion, the owner's husband talked to the workers during the next employee meeting, saying, "Yesterday, Wu asked me if I trained you how to do your work or not. I just think that everyone may have his or her own preference on doing work…" At the end of that meeting, the owner's husband asked the head server, Mei, to look for a training video other restaurants used to train servers. Mei replied that she had searched for these videos several times but did not find anything that was interesting and suitable. The head chef immediately responded, "Then we can sit down and discuss how it is not fit for us. If you can think more than them and do better than them, that will be great." Mei, who had just completed junior school, looked down and pouted, and said nothing more.

The owner and head chef clearly relied on the employees themselves to think about how to improve the work processes but provided little instruction and control. This norm was shaped partly by the sociostructure of the Idealistic restaurant. As shown in Sect. 3.3, the Idealistic restaurant lacked the human resources and capability to often monitor employees' behavior. Consequently, relying on employees to self-regulate was a better choice for them. Besides, this norm reflects the owners' personal ideology and preference, as shown by the owners' personal experience of working for an NGO. They hoped employees would develop a level of moral responsibility toward the Idealistic restaurant, support the restaurant, and grow with the restaurant. They did not want to control employees strictly and believed that if workers wanted to do their work well, they would. They felt that they needed to provide various kinds of benefits to attract employees, such as creating a warm and "human" working environment, providing social security programs for employees, and showing that workers would be allowed to become shareholders of the Idealistic restaurant once the restaurant matured.

However, the workers, who tended to be less educated and very young, did not value the social security program and were not attracted to the future the Idealistic restaurant proposed. For instance, the Idealistic restaurant helped employees buy five kinds of social insurance. This is extremely rare even for large restaurants, and almost impossible for such a small restaurant. To do this, the Idealistic restaurant paid less than 600 CNY for each worker, and workers paid more than 100 CNY for themselves. Seven workers agreed to buy insurance in the beginning, but later, workers gradually withdrew. In the end, only one still bought insurance. They thought paying 100 CNY for social insurance was too high compared to their low salaries, which were about 1500–1900 CNY.

7.4.1.6 Norm of Health Certificates

At the Idealistic restaurant, there was a managerial norm, an injunctive norm, and a descriptive norm related to health certificates. The managerial norm was not explicitly announced, but according to the owners and head chef, they required every worker to obtain a health certificate to prevent the spread of infectious diseases. The injunctive norm indicated that a health certificate was required to ensure there were no infectious diseases in the restaurant. All employees mentioned this when I asked them about health certificates. Nevertheless, the descriptive norm was that workers who would like to work at the restaurant for a relatively long time would obtain health certificates, and those who intended their employment to be short term, did not need to do so. Xing, a kitchen worker, said,

> That I got health certificate means I plan to stay here for a long time…even if restaurants do not pay for the health certificate, I will also get if restaurant requires because if I want to learn something here, I have to stay long.[23]

The head chef expressed a similar view: "If workers want to leave, they will not apply the health certificate. If they would like to stay long, they will get their health certificate. Getting health certificate is individual affairs."

I observed who obtained health certificates and who did not. Among the full-time workers, an elderly female dishwasher did not obtain a health certificate during her short stay (about four months) at the Idealistic restaurant. One student interns, who was American and worked at the Idealistic restaurant for three months during his stay in China, did not have a health certificate. Another Chinese student intern worked at the restaurant for the entire summer holiday before she went to another university did not get her health certificate. Two experienced workers from the mother restaurant who came to help at the Idealistic restaurant for three months did not have health certificates.

I asked the head chef why the dishwasher did not have a health certificate. He explained,

> She said she will leave soon. She has over 60 years old, but is healthy. She never gets ill during her stay in restaurant. Furthermore, she is Yi people, an ethnic group. To draw blood for her is a taboo. She also tries to save cost for us. I can feel. She said, "I'm so healthy. Don't be afraid that I will make any trouble. You do not need to waste money on me."

Therefore, workers without health certificates were permitted to remain at the Idealistic restaurant for a relatively short time based on this descriptive norm.

Compared to the legal norm of health certificates, none of the corresponding managerial, injunctive, and descriptive norms fully reflected the legal norm. According to the law, all restaurant workers must obtain health certificates before they begin working. Very few of the employees had health certificates before starting work at the Idealistic restaurant. Instead, they usually obtained them after several days, or sometimes, after one or two months, once the head chef had time to take them for a medical examination. This was partly due to the difficulty of hiring employees and the high employee turnover rate. Having a health certificate was not a precondition of or requirement for employment. Furthermore, the Idealistic restaurant allowed new employees some time to become familiar with the restaurant and to decide whether they would like to work there in the long term. Thus, employees were allowed to obtain health certificates much later than legally required.

---

[23] Interview with TX, male, on May 29, 2013.

This norm was also partly shaped by the managerial structure and the busy schedule of the head chef. The head chef was solely responsible for taking employees to apply for health certificates, but he was extremely busy with various tasks, including working in the kitchen, preparing ingredients, fixing broken tools, developing new dishes, and so forth. He once told me, "I'm too busy to find time to take them to [get health certificate]."[24]

7.4.2 Organizational Norms at the Profit-Maximizing Restaurant

7.4.2.1 Norm of Tasty Food and Food Sanitation

In contrast to that at the Idealistic restaurant, the overarching norm related to food at the Profit-Maximizing restaurant was that "customers care about what [there is] to eat and how the dish tastes in our restaurant, others are not big deal."[25] Others refer to washing hands, cutting nails, dish disinfection, health certificates, and foreign matter in food. There were no rules about handwashing or nail cutting at the Profit-Maximizing restaurant because, according to the owner,

> It won't make any trouble for not having a rule. There is no need to bother with rules…Customers don't pay attention to those small things. What customers care about is what kinds of dishes the restaurant has, and how the dishes taste."[26]

The drive to provide tasty food was so overwhelming that food sanitation became the last thing to consider, or more precisely, not something to consider. This is evident from the restaurant's reaction to food contamination. When customers found hair or other foreign objects in their food and required that the restaurant replace the dish, the server would return the food to the kitchen and report the issue to the owner. Usually, the owner would glance at the dish unhappily but without comment. The customers would be refunded for that dish, and the server would remove the contaminant and serve the food to another customer if the food had not been touched by previous customers. The owner felt, "It is normal for the hair dropping. The hair does not fall down in dishes every day. It usually happens once in several months. Not only hair, there also may be cockroach." The food at the Profit-Maximizing restaurant indeed contained cockroaches at times. Wang, a server, explained that a customer once found a cockroach in his steamed stinky tofu. The customer was refunded for his meal. He returned several days later and ordered the same meal, but this time he instructed the server, "Don't let cockroach go inside again this time. Be hygienic. OK?" According to Wang, the customer liked stinky tofu, and "our stinky tofu is

---

[24]Interview with the head chef of the Idealistic restaurant on August 11, 2013.
[25]Interview with the owner of the Profit-Maximizing restaurant on September 5, 2013.
[26]Ibid.

very delicious. So he likes to eat in our restaurant."[27] Thus, it seems not only the owner and employees but also the customers did not care about food contamination.

As introduced earlier, managerial and injunctive norms are established with certain aims, either building and maintaining social relationships (Cialdini and Trost 1998), or regulating behaviors that have some significance for the group (Shaw 1981). In other words, managerial and injunctive norms are developed to address something that may become a problem if is not regulated. Hence, when the owner and customers of the Profit-Maximizing restaurant perceived foreign matter in food as normal and inevitable, they ignored the food sanitation. There is obviously no need to develop managerial and injunctive norms to regulate it. Consequently, the managerial and injunctive norm of food sanitation in the Profit-Maximizing restaurant were negative. The descriptive norm was "do not care about food sanitation."

7.4.2.2 Norms of Cutting Nails, Handwashing, and Disinfection

There was no managerial norm related to cutting nails, washing hands, and disinfection at the Profit-Maximizing restaurant. Cutting nails was considered a service activity the restaurant could ignore. The owner even felt the staff should be permitted to have long nails: "I ask them not to paint nails, but do not say anything about long nails. Young girls want to be beautiful. It is not good to ask them to cut nails short."[28] Most employees also considered it unnecessary to cut their nails short if their nails were clean, and some kept their nails long. During observations at the Profit-Maximizing restaurant, I saw at least two kitchen workers and two servers having long nails. Therefore, the general injunctive norm and descriptive norm regarding nails at the Profit-Maximizing restaurant accept long nails. However, surprisingly, servers may be pressured by their peers to cut their nails if their nails are too long. According to one of the servers, a former had long nails, and her thumbnails were especially long. The former server was too embarrassed to serve dishes to customers, so she asked the other servers to serve for her. Later, the other servers asked her to cut her nails short, and she complied. I asked why the former server was asked to trim her nails, and the server replied, "Because we feel it is not good. She is a server. The long nails may go into the soup or dishes. If customers see the long nails in their soup or dishes, they may ask to refund it."[29]

There was no common injunctive norm regarding handwashing at the Profit-Maximizing restaurant. Employees washed their hands based on their own personal preferences and norms. For instance, a kitchen work did not wash his hands after playing with his mobile phone and before fetching a clean eggplant, but he washed his hands before cutting the eggplant on the cutting board. Later, he opened a freezer, fetched some meat, wiped the freezer with a cloth, and then processed the meat on the cutting board without washing his hands. Both the owner and employees felt

---

[27]Interview with Wang, on August 20, 2013.

[28]Interview with the owner of the Profit-Maximizing restaurant on August 21, 2013.

[29]Interview with Wang, on August 20, 2013.

handwashing was a personal habit, and they could not explain exactly when they would wash their hands. For instance, a kitchen worker noted that he would wash hands when he felt uncomfortable, and sometime after playing with his mobile phone and before starting work in the kitchen, but not every time.

As discussed in Chap. 4, the Profit-Maximizing restaurant served customers with prepacked dishware. Other tableware owned by the restaurant and used for table service, such as large serving plates and small plates for sauces, were not disinfected. The general injunctive norm related to the restaurant-owned dishware was that it did not need to be disinfected, as the owner claimed, "I think we have washed the dishware clean."[30]

7.4.2.3 Norms of Diligence and Cost Savings

The owner did not pay attention to regulating employees' behavior concerning hand-washing, cutting nails, or even dish sanitation, focusing instead on diligence and cost savings. His only requirement of employees was diligence, and his employees confirmed this: "I feel the owner want us to do work every minute."[31] However, this managerial norm did not change into an injunctive norm or a descriptive norm. As the owner himself claimed, "The only requirement I have is that they do their work. However, you have seen these days, they only do work when I come here, if I do not come, they just sit here and watch cellphone."[32]

Another requirement, which the owner did not mention, was cost savings, according to his employees. When asked whether the owner would reprimand the staff for any behaviors, a server replied,

> Almost nothing. Only that when we wash hands under the running faucet with strong water flow, the owner will ask us to turn down the water flow. If there are no customers, we will turn off the light right away. Otherwise, the owner will blame us. He is quite economical."[33]

7.4.2.4 Norms of Health Certificates

During the observation period at the Profit-Maximizing restaurant, it became apparent that neither the owner nor the employees took health certificates seriously. These certificates were considered as useless except for inspections. When asked about the use of health certificates and the risk of not having them, a server answered, "[the use is that] I can show to the person who comes to do inspection."[34] The owner said, "Get health certificate if they [inspectors] come to check. If they do not check, do not need to bother with it."[35] The practical use for inspection was valued more than the

---

[30] Interview with the owner of the Profit-Maximizing restaurant on September 5, 2013.

[31] Interview with NL, female, 18, August 20, 2013.

[32] Interview with the owner of the Profit-Maximizing restaurant on September 5, 2013.

[33] Interview with NL, female, 18, August 20, 2013.

[34] Interview with NY, male, 24, on September 2, 2013.

[35] Interview with the owner of the Profit-Maximizing restaurant on May 26, 2013.

meaningful significance for food safety. On one hand, this was because the owner wanted to save on every cost; on the other, this was because he had a perception that most employees he knew were healthy.

Due to the owner's careless attitude toward health certificates, employees generally did not feel it was their responsibility to obtain health certificates but relied on the owner to obtain certificates for them. They shared a descriptive norm that the restaurant, not them, faced risk related to not having health certificates and benefitted from having these certificates. If the restaurant owner asked employees to submit health certificates, the employees obtain them. Otherwise, employees did not need to. After attending an FDA food safety course, Yang, a kitchen worker, understood the purpose of health certificates: "[The health certificate system is to prevent the spread of] infectious disease. Those who get infectious disease are not allowed to enter the kitchen."[36] Nevertheless, he also felt that if the owner asked him to submit a health certificate and paid for it, he would apply for one; otherwise, he would not, because, "After all, it doesn't matter for myself. I'm OK for either having or not having…It is the restaurant who gets caught if there are no health certificates."[37]

7.4.3 Organizational Norms and Compliance Behaviors

The organizational norms, including managerial, injunctive, and descriptive norms, at both the Idealistic restaurant and the Profit-Maximizing restaurant were closely related to compliance behavior (see Table 7.1). At the Idealistic restaurant, the norm of healthy food was the basic managerial and injunctive norm, so most behaviors concerning the four daily operational legal norms studied in this book were positively oriented through, for example, partial, beyond, genuine, and attempted compliance. To realize its health ideology, the Idealistic restaurant developed various managerial norms, including washing hands, cutting nails, and checking for foreign matter in food. However, another significant norm existed, that is, "self-responsibility and self-awareness are more important than rules and work process design for doing work well." This norm reduced the motivation to monitor employees' behavior and weakened the execution of the managerial norms.

For instance, the Idealistic restaurant attempted to comply with the managerial norm of cutting nails, but engaged in only partial and attempted compliance. The specific norms in the Idealistic restaurant that concerned handwashing, disinfection, and health certificates differed from the legal norms, and these differences produced variations in compliance behaviors. For example, a norm of washing hands "after using the toilet and before entering the kitchen" was established, but it only partially aligned with the regulations of the legal norm related to handwashing. Consequently, although employees practiced this norm consistently, the Idealistic restaurant only partially complied with the legal norm. A similar situation arose regarding dish

---

[36]Interview with NY, male, 24, on September 2, 2013.
[37]Ibid.

Table 7.1 Organizational norms and compliance behaviors

Restaurant	Organizational norms	Compliance behaviors
The Idealistic restaurant	Healthy food (managerial norm, injunctive norm, descriptive norm)	N/A
	Handwashing [employees should wash their hands after using the toilet and before entering the kitchen.] (managerial norm, injunctive norm)	Partial
	Handwashing [Workers wash their hands at the two time points and whenever they feel their hands are dirty.] (descriptive norm)	
	Cutting nails [Employees are not allowed to have long nails.] (managerial norm, injunctive norm)	Attempted, partial
	Disinfection [dishware used for personal service should be disinfected to prevent the spread of infectious diseases.] (managerial norm, injunctive norm, descriptive norm)	Partial, full, beyond, fake
	Disinfection [big plates and bowls used for table service do not need to be disinfected.] (descriptive norm)	Partial, full, beyond, fake
	Self-responsibility and self-awareness [responsibility for own actions is more important than rules and work processes designed for doing work well.] (managerial norm, injunctive norm, descriptive norm)	N/A
	Health certificates [Health certificates are needed to ensure there is no infectious disease in restaurant.] (managerial norm, injunctive norm)	Partial, full
	Health certificates [only longer-term workers should obtain health certificates.] (descriptive norm)	

(continued)

Table 7.1 (continued)

Restaurant	Organizational norms	Compliance behaviors
The Profit-Maximizing restaurant	Tasty food and food safety [the taste of the dishes are the most important.] (managerial norm, injunctive norm and descriptive norm)	N/A
	Cutting nails [long nails are acceptable.] (injunctive norm, descriptive norm)	Noncompliance
	Handwashing [handwashing is based on personal preference and habit.] (descriptive norm)	Noncompliance
	Disinfection [we do not need to disinfect dishware.] (injunctive norm, descriptive norm)	Skeptical, symbolic, fake, noncompliance
	Diligence and saving costs [those who are diligent and economical are good workers.] (managerial norm, injunctive norm)	N/A
	Health certificates [health certificates are not much use except for passing inspections.] (injunctive norm)	Fake, fraudulent
	Health certificates [it is the restaurant's, not the employees', responsibility to obtain health certificates.] (descriptive norm)	

disinfection, with only some of the dishware being disinfected. In terms of health certificates, another descriptive norm existed: "Workers who would like to stay at the restaurant for a relatively long time should obtain health certificates. If they do not intend to stay long, they can work without health certificates." This descriptive norm provided room to escape the managerial norm of health certificates, resulting in partial compliance with the related legal norm.

At the Profit-Maximizing restaurant, the most prominent injunctive norm, "The taste of dishes are more important than anything else," reduced the necessity of the four daily operations legal norms. Noncompliance with these legal norms was permitted under this organizational norm. Furthermore, cost savings was emphasized as a managerial and injunctive norm at the Profit-Maximizing restaurant, so the owner did not spend money on compliance. As a result, most compliance behaviors at the Profit-Maximizing restaurant were negative and included skeptical, symbolic, fake, and fraudulent compliance, as well as noncompliance. Regarding the substantial legal norm of health certificates, another descriptive norm existed: "Employees will obtain health certificates only if the owner asks them to do so, because the restaurant is exposed to risk by not having these certificates, and it, not the employees, benefits from having health certificates." This descriptive norm reduced the moral pressure on employees of having health certificates and placed it on the owner alone. When this is combined with the norm of cost savings, which he valued very much, the result is obvious—he avoids whatever costs he can avoid.

7.5 Interaction Between Legal Norms and Organizational Norms

Both legal norms and organizational norms guide restaurants' behavior. Legal norms are transmitted from outside, while organizational norms are produced internally. Legal norms influence restaurant employees' behaviors through the mediation of organizational norms. The mediation of organizational norms or the interaction between legal norms and organizational norms involves activation and competition. In this section, how activation and competition occur in restaurants is examined.

7.5.1 Activation

Theoretically, organizational norms may activate legal norms and legal norms may activate organizational norms. Several scholars have studied how legal norms activate existing social norms and enhance legal compliance (Vandenbergh 2003). However, in this book, it was found that the activation of legal norms by organizational norms was more prominent, because restaurants had little doctrinal knowledge of legal norms as discussed in Chap. 6.

Organizational norms activate legal norms by activating the required behaviors without referring to the corresponding legal norms and by activating the development of knowledge of legal norms. The first activation method was prevalent, but the second was rare, although it does exist in theory. For instance, organizational norms might exist that require employees to review regulations related to their work or norms that require training employees on up-to-date regulations. These norms activate legal norms and facilitate the transmission of legal norms in an organization by motivating members of the organization to develop knowledge of the legal norms.

The first kind of activation, that is, activating the required behaviors without referring to the corresponding legal norms, is discussed in this section. The Idealistic restaurant had specific norms related to handwashing, cutting nails, disinfection, and health certificates. Although these norms did not fully align with the corresponding legal norms, they promoted some behaviors required by legal norms. Thus, employees may comply with legal norms to certain extent without knowing the relevant legal norms.

Even the owners and head chef who established these norms did not know the related legal norms. They simply viewed the handwashing and nail cutting norms as necessary to safeguard food sanitation, which they considered basic principles everyone should follow. Even dish disinfection, which is clearly regulated by food safety law, the Idealistic restaurant considers as a restaurant industry regulation rather than a law. However, the norm it developed about disinfection, that "dishware used for personal service should be disinfected to prevent the spread of infectious diseases," partially activated the desired behaviors. Similarly, the norm of healthy food aligned with food safety law and activated employees' behaviors that comply with food safety law.

This activation also was evident at S restaurant, which emphasized disinfecting glasses with disinfection fluid. The norm of cleanness activated compliance with the disinfection norm. Because it was an upper-class restaurant, customers had high expectations about the cleanliness and appearance of dishware. According to servers at S restaurant, some customers would carefully inspect the dishware before using it, and they would ask for replacement items if they found so much as a fingerprint on it. Glasses are easily stained by beverages, and washing them with disinfection fluid leaves them clean and shiny. Therefore, at S restaurant, disinfecting glasses was emphasized repeatedly, and it became a routine task for servers. When servers discussed the norm of disinfection, cleaning glasses was a significant aspect of the task. However, as discussed in the next section, while the norm of cleanness activated the legal norm of disinfection to a certain extent, it also competed with the legal norm of disinfection once it had been overemphasized.

7.5.2 Competition

Competition occurs when organizational norms support behaviors that differ from those required by legal norms. Legal norms, which are transmitted from outside and enforced outside the restaurant, aim to keep the social order of restaurant operation, and safeguard the public good and the interests of others. They may be infringed upon by restaurants' improper or selfish behaviors to maximize profit. However, organizational norms serve the maintenance and survival of an organization. Although organizational norms and legal norms may be congruent sometimes, they inevitably frequently differ. Several kinds of competition between norms exist.[38]

Some organizational norms may compete with legal norms by making legal requirements seem unreasonable. At the Profit-Maximizing restaurant, the norm of tasty food was set above the importance of other behaviors that are actually regulated by legal norms, including health certificates, handwashing, and cutting nails. The behaviors required by those legal norms were shaped by this organizational norm as a "service thing" that is unnecessary in such a small restaurant.

Furthermore, organizational norms may compete with legal norms by rationalizing the low possibility of meeting the legal requirements. This was especially prevalent

---

[38]From the criminological perspective, organizational norms also enable normalization of organizational involvement in criminal activities (Van Baar and Huisman 2012).

in restaurants with high staff turnover rates. Due to staff retention problems, the Idealistic restaurant developed two significant norms related to health certificates: "Workers do not need health certificates during their probation periods," and "Short-term workers can work without health certificates." These norms allowed the Idealistic restaurant to rationalize the low possibility of obtaining health certificates for all employees. In this way, the organizational norms competed with the legal norms and impeded compliance with legal norms.

Organizational norms may also compete with legal norms by reducing the responsibility of achieving the goals of legal norms. At the Profit-Maximizing restaurant, although many employees knew they required health certificates to work in a restaurant, they generally shared a norm that the owner was responsible for obtaining health certificates for them, as they do not benefit from having these certificates and have lost nothing by not having them. This norm reduced their responsibility to comply with the health certificate norm and shifted the responsibility to only the owner.

Some organizational norms may impede the enforcement of legal norms. At the Idealistic restaurant, emphasizing self-responsibility and self-awareness while scoring the enforcement of rules impeded the practices related to legal norms among employees. Although the Idealistic restaurant established rules concerning hand-washing and cutting nails that activated compliance with legal norms, it did not take adequate responsibility for monitoring and enforcing the rules, but largely relying on employees to comply with these rules. Consequently, it created the possibility for employees to escape the rules. Although the owners of the Idealistic restaurant attempted to nurture employees' health consciousness by educating them about the ideology of health, the training was on a level employees found difficult to understand and relate to their own lives. Likewise, they attempted to promote the self-awareness and self-responsibility of employees by asking employees to think about how to do their work well, but provided little assistance for finding the answers. As a result, although the Idealistic restaurant intended to establish rules that align with legal norms, its organizational norms prevented it from achieving the purpose of these rules and hindered the internal enforcement of legal norms.

Moreover, certain organizational norms that activate legal norms may also create competition if they are overemphasized. For instance, cleaning dishware and glasses was a key point at S restaurant. It emphasized washing glasses with disinfection fluid to clean them, and cleanness became much more important than safety, which is the overall aim of the disinfection legal norm. Consequently, disinfection fluid residue became a critical problem at S restaurant and a new food safety problem. H, a server, explained that glasses that had been soaked in disinfection fluid had to be rinsed twice in clean water according to the standard procedure on which they were trained. However, glasses usually were rinsed only once due to time constraints and a shortage of basins. Besides, they might have cleaned glasses and dishware again with cloths soaked in disinfection fluid before using them to serve customers. Some servers even believed that dishware smelling of disinfection fluid was superior to items with a neutral odor.

Furthermore, the organization norm of efficiency may compete with legal norms of food safety. The norm of efficiency is a focus in many restaurants, but focusing on efficiency tends to eclipse the legal norm of food safety. This also occurs in large, upper-class restaurants. Although S restaurant provided group training for employees, it did not provide special training on food safety. According to several workers at S restaurant, the focus was on speed, taste, and customer feedback. Food safety was not a key point. Servers were trained on how to serve customers and deal with complaints, but not on the legal norms related to their work.

7.6   Conclusion

This chapter focused on organizational norms, the interaction between organizational norms and legal norms, and the influence of such interaction on regulated behavior. In contrast to the previous chapter, which showed how the comprehensive legal knowledge of restaurants shaped compliance behaviors, this chapter showed how organizational norms activated or competed with legal norms and influenced compliance, and how compliance behaviors originated from organizational norms when the related legal norms never actually entered the restaurants (e.g., handwashing). In other words, in addition to legal norms, organizational norms, including managerial, injunctive, and descriptive norms, may provide reference for compliance behaviors.

Organizational norms are formed, and at the same time shape employees' behaviors, during the process of socialization, more specifically in this case during the management process. Through the discussion of organizational socialization processes and management processes, factors involved in the formation of different organizational norms and in mediating the function of legal norms, were discovered. For instance, the overarching ideology of the organization, or the owner's or founder's ideology, sets the basic tone for compliance with legal norms. Restaurants with ideologies that aligned with the purpose of legal norms or supported the legal norms were inclined to comply with legal norms. In contrast, restaurants with ideologies that scorned the purpose of legal norms or competed with legal norms had more difficulty complying with legal norms.

The resources and ability available for internal monitoring are influential factors that mediate the internal enforcement of legal norms. High employee turnover rate is an important factor, as it complicates each stage of socialization and management, and it may alter organizational norms. High employee turnover actually reflects the uncertainty of the receptor of organizational and legal norms, and efforts and resources are allocated to educate and motivate receptors to conform to norms. However, if the receptor may move outside the norm system soon, how can the efforts and resources be invested to educate and motivate them, and to what extent are the receptors willing to comply with these norms?

Moreover, customers, as the most direct and immediate evaluation institution of restaurants, play a significant role in the formation of organizational norms and the function of legal norms. Customers are the existing fundamentals of restaurants, and customers' norms are important indicators of restaurants' norms. Customers with norms that align with and support legal norms pressure restaurants to develop corresponding organizational norms and thus contribute to compliance with legal norms. Alternatively, they encourage restaurants to remain noncompliant.

This research provides richer insights into the interaction between social and legal norms and into how social and legal norms work together to influence compliance by moving beyond Alm et al.'s (1999) dichotomy between social norms that tend toward noncompliance and social norms that advocate compliance. Additional dimensions of social norms related to compliance have emerged in this study. Some organizational norms reduced the reasonability of legal norms, and then compliance dropped to almost zero, while some organizational norms rationalized the low possibility of meeting the legal requirements, and then compliance was partially realized. Further, some organizational norms reduced the responsibility of safeguarding the goals of legal norms, and then the realization of compliance relied on the one given such responsibility, and some organizational norms impeded the enforcement of legal norms, and compliance was not complete and steady but alternating from compliance to noncompliance. These research findings echo and enrich existing research on how social norms affect compliance.

It is known that social norms contribute to compliance by using social influence or social sanctions in terms of manipulating reputation, and shame, social identity. This research shows another way in which social norms contribute to compliance—through interaction with the law and law enforcement. Researchers have shown how law and law enforcement influence social norms and then promote or reduce compliance (Vandenbergh 2003; Shapiro and Rabinowitz 2000). Shapiro and Rabinowitz (2000), in their research on voluntary compliance, showed that workers' compensation laws create a belief that a substantial number of workplace accidents are inevitable. When considered in conjunction with the fact that workers and employers share the cost of accidents, which suggests that workers and employers are jointly responsible for these costs, it reduces employers' responsibility to provide a safe workplace. Thus, the compliance motivation of employers may be weakened by the mixed message society sends about who is responsible for protecting workers. Vandenbergh (2003) highlighted the complex relationships between enforcement, social norms, and compliance. From the perspective of the regulated, this research shows that existing social norms may also impede or activate the law and law enforcement. Consequently, to improve the efficiency of law enforcement, the existing social norms and the interaction between social norms, legal norms, and law enforcement should be further researched.

Moreover, this research suggests a more significant connection between managerial, injunctive, and descriptive norms. While managerial norms certainly influence injunctive norms, they do not necessarily turn into injunctive norms. As revealed in the discussion of the training process, managerial norms play a minor role in mentoring. During training, newcomers may learn a little about the managerial norm, whereas in other parts of the socialization process (e.g., monitoring, evaluation and rewarding), the managerial norm may not be referred to or enforced well.

Descriptive norms may directly reflect managerial and injunctive norms if these norms are routinized behaviors. By learning the routinized behavior during the socialization process, newcomers repeat the norm. As a result, the managerial and injunctive norms evolve into a descriptive norm. This managerial and injunctive norm is complied with until new elements enter the organization and challenge this norm.

In some cases, managerial, injunctive, and descriptive norms related to the same behaviors are different. Managerial and injunctive norms function through evaluation, and factors related to social evaluation, such as resources and willingness to enforce the managerial and injunctive norms, may hinder compliance with injunctive norms and leave loopholes for noncompliance. In this way, managerial and injunctive norms do not become descriptive norms, and some new descriptive norms may develop.

Injunctive norms may develop from descriptive norms. As discussed, training in the restaurants studied—an important stage in the socialization process—was mainly individual with mentoring. During this process, neither managerial nor injunctive norms were made clear to newcomers. Instead, newcomers imitated their mentors and formed corresponding descriptive norms. Descriptive norms provide social information to newcomers about what is appropriate and adaptive in a particular setting, and they are further confirmed if no other managerial or injunctive norms compete with them. Consequently, the content of descriptive norms often is considered injunctive norms. The descriptive and injunctive norms of disinfection at the Idealistic restaurant are an excellent example of this. This echoes scholars' argument that descriptive norms directly influence injunctive norms because what is typical done shapes what is perceived as what ought to be done (Bobek et al. 2013; Cialdini et al. 1990).

From another perspective, descriptive norms are formed in the process of interaction between individuals in the organization, the sociostructure of the organization, and organizational managerial and injunctive norms. For instance, at the Idealistic restaurant, the descriptive norm about health certificates developed during the interaction between several factors, such as high employee turnover rate, a shortage of human resources, and the Idealistic restaurant's injunctive norm of obtaining health certificates and perception of health certificate enforcement. That is, descriptive norms here are norms the organization developed after combining various factors in the process of socialization and management. It relates to practical verified behaviors that share similarities with practical verified requirements, as discussed in Chap. 6. In this way, descriptive norms are actually an institution that combined those factors and the very institution that mediates the transmission and function of legal norms in restaurants.

In this book, it was found that descriptive norms are linked more closely to final compliance. Similarly, Cialdini et al. (1990) found that compliance with corresponding injunctive norms is enhanced by introducing descriptive norms, which seems to suggest that descriptive norms are more powerful than injunctive norms. However, Cialdini et al. (1990) cautioned against jumping to this conclusion, arguing that the differential focusing of attention on descriptive or injunctive norms is the key. The findings of this research provide further evidence that supports this view by revealing the formation processes of the two norms.

First, descriptive norms formed easily when other managerial and injunctive norms in that setting were unclear or not emphasized, for example, during the mentoring process. Second, descriptive norms may be produced in the process of interaction and competition between individuals in the organization, the sociostructure of the organization, and other organizational norms, including managerial and injunctive norms. In the first condition, descriptive norms have a more significant influence on compliance than injunctive norms do, as even the injunctive norms may develop from descriptive norms. In the second condition, the descriptive norm reveals more adaptive behaviors for the setting than the existing injunctive norms do. However, more research about the relationship between injunctive norms, descriptive norms, and compliance is required. Although this research has addressed this to some degree by examining the formation process, more evidence and specific research are needed.

Finally, this research highlights a different way to study the influence of social norms on compliance. Instead of measuring social norms in terms of the extent to which they value compliance, I deeply examine how and what social norms, here organizational norms, formed. This approach allowed additional dimensions of organizational norms related to compliance to emerge, and provided possibilities to manipulate organizational norms so as to influence compliance with legal norms.

References

Aarts, Henk, and Ap. Dijksterhuis. 2003. The Silence of the Library: Environment, Situational Norm, and Social Behavior. *Journal of Personality and Social Psychology* 84 (1): 18–28.

Allaire, Yvan, and Mihaela E. Firsirotu. 1984. Theories of Organizational Culture. *Organization Studies* 5 (3): 193–226.

Allison, P.D. 1992. The Cultural Evolution of Beneficent Norms. *Social Forces* 71: 279–301.

Alm, James, Gary H. McClelland, and William D. Schulze. 1999. Changing the Social Norm of Tax Compliance by Voting. *KYKLOS*, 52 (Fasc. 2): 141–171.

Bian, Yanjie. 2002. Chinese Social Stratification and Social Mobility. *Annual Review of Sociology* 28: 91–116.

Bobek, Donna D., Amy M. Hageman, and Charles F. Kelliher. 2013. Analyzing the Role of Social Norms in Tax Compliance Behavior. *Journal of Business Ethics* 115: 451–468.

Cialdini, Robert B. 2007. Descriptive Social Norms as Underappreciated Sources of Social Control. *Psychometrika* 72 (2): 263–268.

Cialdini, Robert B., and Melanie R. Trost. 1998. Social Influence: Social Norms, Conformity, and Compliance. *Handbook of Social Psychology, 98 Edition*, 151–192.

Cialdini, Robert B., R. R. Reno, and C. A. Kallgren. 1990. A Focus Theory of Normative Conduct: Recycling the Concept of Norms to reduce Littering in Public Places. *Journal of Personality and Social Psychology* 58: 1015–1026.

Ehrhart, Mark G., and Stefanie E. Naumann. 2004. Organizational Citizenship Behavior in Work Groups: A Group Norms Approach. *Journal of Applied Psychology* 89 (6): 960–974.

Feldman, Daniel Charles. 1984. The Development and Enforcement of Group Norms. *The Academy of Management Review* 9 (1): 47–53.

Festinger, Leon. 1954. A Theory of Social Comparison Processes. *Human Relations* 7: 117–140.

Geerken, M.R., and W.R. Gove. 1975. Deterrence: Some Theoretical Considerations. *Law and Society Review* 9: 497–514.

Gilbert, D.T. 1995. Attribution and Interpersonal Perception. In *Advanced Social Psychology*, ed. A. Tesser, 99–147. New York: McGraw-Hill.

Gino, Francesca, Shahar Ayal, and Dan Ariely. 2009. Contagion and Differentiation in Unethical Behavior the Effect of One Bad Apple on the Barrel. *Psychological Science* 20 (3): 393–398.

Gunningham, Neil, Robert A. Kagan, and Dorothy Thornton. 2004. Social License and Environmental Protection: Why Businesses Go Beyond Compliance. *Law & Social Inquiry* 29 (2): 307–341.

Hechter, Michael, and Karl-Dieter. Opp. 2001. Introduction. In *Michael Hechter and Karl-Dieter Opp*, ed. Social Norms, xi–xx. New York: Russell Sage Foundation.

Heimer, Carol A. 1999. Competing Institutions: Law, Medicine, and Family in Neonatal Intensive Care. *Law & Society Review* 33 (1): 17–66.

Huang, Yafeng, and Jianyu Xie. 2011. Investigation of the Mobility of Restaurant Workers [*Can ting yuan gong liu dong xing diao cha*]. *Operation and Management* [Jing Ying Yu Guan Li] 5: 39–41.

Huisman, Wim. 2016. Criminogenic Organizational Properties and Dynamics. In *The Oxford Handbook of White-Collar Crime*, ed. Shanna R. Van Slyke, Michael L. Benson, and Francis T. Cullen, 435–462. New York: Oxford University Press.

Kelling, George L., and Catherine M. Coles. 1997. *Fixing Broken Windows: Restoring Order and Reducing Crime in Our Communities*. New York: Simon & Schuster.

Larimer, M.E., and C. Neigbors. 2003. Normative Misperception and the Impact of Descriptive and Injunctive Norms on College Student Gambling. *Psychology of Addictive Behavior* 17: 235–243.

Liu, Donghua, and Meiling Cai. 2013. Calculation Methods for the Employee Resignation Rate [*Yuan gong li zhi lv de ji suan fang fa*]. *China Investment* [Zhong Guo Wai Zi] (January 2013), 281: 274.

Moore, Sally Falk. 1973. Law and Social Change: The Semi-Autonomous Social Field as an Appropriate Subject of Study. *Law & Society Review* 7 (4): 719–746.

Posner, Eric A. 1998. Symbols, Signals, and Social Norms in Politics and the Law. *The Journal of Legal Studies* 27 (S2): 765–797.

Posner, Eric A. 2000. Law and Social Norms: The Case of Tax Compliance. *Virginia Law Review* 86 (8): 1781–1819.

Russell, Robert D., and Craig J. Russell. 1992. An Examination of the Effects of Organizational Norms, Organizational Structure, and Environmental Uncertainty on Entrepreneurial Strategy. *Journal of Management* 18(4):639–656.

Schein, Edgar H. 1988. Organizational Socialization and the Profession of Management. *Sloan Management Review* 30 (1): 53–65.

Scott, Robert E. 2000. The Limits of Behavioral Theories of Law and Social Norms. *Virginia Law Review* 86 (8): 1603–1647.

Scott, Elaine S., Martha Keehner Engelke, and Melvin Swanson. 2008. New Graduate Nurse Transitioning: Necessary or Nice? *Applied Nursing Research* 21: 75–83.

Shapiro, Sidney A., and Randy Rabinowitz. 2000. Voluntary Regulatory Compliance in Theory and Practice: The Case of OSHA. *Administrative Law Review* 52 (1): 97–155.

Shaw, M. 1981. *Group Dynamics*, 3rd ed. New York: Harper.

Stiff, James. B., and Paul A. Mongeau. 2016. *Persuasive Communication*. New York: The Guilford Press.

Sutinen, J. G., and K. Kuperan. 1999. A Socio-Economic Theory of Regulatory Compliance. *International Journal of Social Economics* 26 (1/2/3): 174–193.

Tyran, Jean-Robert., and Lars P. Feld. 2006. Achieving Compliance when Legal Sanctions are Non-deterrent. *Scandinavian Journal of Economics* 108 (1): 135–156.

Vandenbergh, M. 2003. Beyond Elegance: A Testable Typology of Social Norms in Corporate Environmental Compliance. *Stanford Environmental Law Journal* 22: 55–144.

Van Baar, Annika, and Wim Huisman. 2012. The Oven Builders of the Holocaust: A Case Study of Corporate Complicity in International Crimes. *British Journal of Criminology* 52 (6): 1033–1050.

Van Empelen, P., H.P. Schaalma, G. Kok, and M.R.J. Jansen. 2001. Predicting Condom Use with Casual and Steady Partners among Drug Users. *Health Education Research: Theory and Practice* 16: 293–305.

Van Erp, Judith. 2008. Reputational Sanctions in Private and Public Regulation. *Erasmus Law Review* 1 (5): 143–161.

Van Maanen, John. 1978. "People Processing: Strategies of Organizational Socialization." *Organizational Dynamics* 7 (1): 19–36.

Van Maanen, John., and Edgar H. Schein. 1978. Toward a Theory of Organizational Socialization. *Annual Review of Research in Organizational Behavior* 1: 1–89.

Vogel, Joachim. 1974. Taxation and Public Opinion in Sweden: An Interpretation of Recent Survey Data. *National Tax Journal* 499–513.

Wanous, John P, and Arnon E. Reichers. 2000. New Employee Orientation Programs. *Human Resource Management Review* 10(4): 435–451.

Wenzel, Michael. 2004. Social Identification as a Determinant of Concerns About Individual-, Group-, and Inclusive-Level Justice. *Social Psychology Quarterly* 67 (1): 70–87.

Witte, Ann, and Woodbury, Diane. 1985. The Effect of Tax Laws and Tax Administration on Tax Compliance: The Case of the US Individual Income Tax. *National Tax Journal* 1–13.

Chapter 8
The Individuals: How Did Individuals Make Compliance Decision?

8.1 Introduction

Chapter 6 highlighted the complex and changing compliance behaviors situated in the varied and changeable comprehensive legal knowledge of restaurants, while Chap. 7 showed that organizational norms further complicate the legal norms in restaurants by both activation and competition, and as a result, produce variations in compliance behaviors. In this chapter focuses on the individuals who finally engage in these compliance behaviors, specifically on their reasons for engaging in compliance or noncompliance behaviors and on explaining their behaviors in light of variables at the individual level. To examine these aspects, variables suggested in the existing literature as key individual compliance variables—plural subjective deterrence, personal norms, descriptive norms, perceived obligation to obey the law, recognition of legal requirements and practical constraints—are employed. To a certain extent, some of these variables, such as plural subjective deterrence and descriptive norms, reflect what was discussed in Chaps. 6 and 7. Plural subjective deterrence reflects part of an individual's comprehensive legal knowledge and part of the outcome of the interaction between legal norms and organizational norms in terms of the subjective perception of risk or deterrence individuals face if they violate certain (legal) norms. Descriptive norms reflect aspects of legal practice knowledge and of organizational norms in terms of what others do. Thus, these variables are used to show that the three levels, namely the regulatory, organizational, and individual levels, are not completely independent but can be integrated to some degree.

Field data gathered through in-depth dialogue interviews with 35 restaurant workers and owners are used to support the argument. A database was established containing the interview data. Several legally required behaviors were discussed with each interviewee, and because the analysis in this chapter focuses on using variables to explain behaviors and not on explaining people, each behavior is treated as a case. Hence, if one interviewee discussed three kinds of requirements during the interview, three cases of required behaviors were added to the database. In total, 108 behaviors were used as cases for analysis. This database-building technique allowed

© The Author(s), under exclusive license to Springer Nature Singapore Pte Ltd. 2021
Y. Wu, *Compliance Ethnography*, Understanding China,
https://doi.org/10.1007/978-981-16-2884-9_8

me to focus on behavior explanation. Data collected for the discussion at individual level may be biased compared to that collected from the general restaurant working population, and the data used here is not viewed as representative of the general population.

Compliance behavior is explained, first, by describing and analyzing interviewees' subjective explanations for their behaviors to avoid restricting the explanations to the chosen variables and allow other variables at individual level to emerge and, second, by explaining their behaviors in terms of the selected variables through variable association analysis. Comparing variable association analysis with individuals' subjective explanations was used to highlight the differences in behavior explanation between the methods used. For instance, the analysis showed that descriptive social norms were obviously associated with compliance behaviors in these restaurants based on objective variable association analysis. However, in individuals' subjective explanations, it is rarely mentioned when explaining noncompliance behaviors. Therefore, objective variable association analysis suggests that descriptive social norms are an important factor in explaining individuals' compliance behaviors, while in individuals' explanations descriptive norms are almost invisible.

Compliance behaviors are complex and changing, as shown in Part A of this book. To analyze individual compliance variables, the compliance behaviors identified had to be simplified and coded in a dichotomy. This certainly introduced a level of deviation from the real-world situation and became a limitation for such analysis of the variables.

This chapter begins with an overview of the literature related to the variables discussed in this chapter to clarify the definition of each variable and to explain how the variables were operationalized and coded. This provides a basis for situating the variables in my theoretical framework to reveal the complete framework that combines all three levels. Subsequently, the data collection method is discussed to explain the guidelines followed during dialogue interviews with individuals to collect data on the compliance variables and to show how the dependent variable, compliance behavior, was measured and coded. To analyze the influence of the individual compliance variables on compliance behavior, the dependent variable was coded with a dichotomy in terms of compliance and violation.

Next, the findings of the analysis of the individual data are discussed in terms of how individuals subjectively explained their compliance and violation behaviors, how individuals perceived each variable, and whether each variable was statistically associated with compliance behavior in the variable association analysis. In addition, the findings of the variable association analysis are compared with the subjective explanations to highlight potential differences. Finally, conclusions are drawn regarding the overall individual analysis, and the limitations of this kind of variable association analysis at individual level are addressed.

8.2 Compliance Variables in Theory

A rich body of literature from multiple disciplines, including economics, anthropology, psychology, criminology, political science, and sociology of law, has discussed the question of why people obey the law, and researchers have proposed numerous approaches and factors that explain individual compliance. These approaches are briefly reviewed in this section before introducing and discussing each variable selected for the analysis.

Two conventional approaches emerged from among the approaches identified in compliance literature. The first is the amoral rational choice approach, or the instrumental approach (Tyler 1990). From this approach, people are seen as amoral calculators, pursuing their self-interest and making decisions by calculating the costs and benefits of compliance and violation. They comply with rules that are more beneficial than costly (Kagan and Scholz 1984). Deterrence is most often studied using this approach, as the fear of punishment may raise the costs of violation and keep people from breaking the law (Nagin and Blumstein 1978), and cost–benefit calculation also is studied using this approach. The second is the normative approach, or the social model, in terms of which regulated actors obey the law due to motivation from their internal morality (Tyler 1990; Lee 2008) and from social norms (Van Rooij and Van Geelder 2012; Cialdini 2007; Cialdini et al. 2006; Cialdini and Goldstein 2004; Kahan 1997; Keizer et al. 2008, 2011). Several variables are studied within this approach, such as personal norms, perceived obligation to obey the law, descriptive social norms, and injunctive social norms.

The two approaches are not necessarily mutually exclusive and are interrelated in certain ways. Several researchers have attempted to integrate the two approaches and broaden deterrence theory to incorporate both amoral rational motivations and social norm motivations, or "intrinsic and extrinsic motivations" (Sutinen and Kuperan 1999). Vandenbergh (2003) presented a conceptual framework that adds norms to a rational choice approach in corporate environmental compliance.

In addition to these two traditions, another influential model is used to explain compliance, namely the three personas of regulated actors proposed by Kagan and Scholz (1984). The three personas of noncompliers—amoral calculators, political citizens, and incompetent entities—reveal three variables that explain compliance or violation. While the first two personas and corresponding variables align with the traditional approaches, that is, cost–benefit calculation and legal legitimacy, the third reveals another variable not included in the traditional approaches, namely capacity. In terms of capacity, people may not comply with the law due to their incapacity to do so although they may be inclined to. "Violation of law thus derives from not being able to comply instead of not being willing to" (Huisman 2001: 234). The variable of capacity adds a new dimension to examining compliance and violation; instead of focusing on only motivations, restrictions are included.

From these approaches and models that explain compliance and violation, several key variables were derived and used to analyze restaurant compliance behaviors at individual level—plural subjective deterrence, perceived obligation to obey the law, personal norms, descriptive social norms, and capacity.[1]

8.2.1   Plural Subjective Deterrence

Deterrence has been the most significant and popular theory in explaining compliance since the 1960s. Conventional deterrence theory focuses on state-imposed legal sanctions in the form of physical and material deprivations (i.e., fines and incarceration; Becker 1968). The likelihood (certainty) of legal sanctions and the magnitude (severity) of legal sanctions are at its core. Based on the assumption that actors are rational, the theory proposes that actors are inclined to comply with the law if the certainty of legal sanctions and the severity of legal sanctions are high. Moreover, in most studies, the certainty of sanctions has been proven to have a greater deterrent effect than the severity of sanctions (see Grasmick and Bryjak 1980; Klepper and Nagin 1989a, b). Traditional deterrence theory developed and expanded significantly by incorporating perspectives that are more complex and responding to challenges. One challenge was that researchers found sources of compliance other than the threat of legal sanctions, that is, norms, as shown in previous sections. To cope with this challenge, researchers with firm beliefs that actors always make rational decisions attempted to extend the deterrence theory. For instance, Grasmick and Bursik (1990) broadened the deterrence model by including deterrence from other sources, such as self-imposed punishment from internalized norms (shame) and socially imposed punishment from significant others (embarrassment).

Another challenge arose from empirical studies that showed both the certainty and severity of deterrence are subjective and not directly related to actual objective deterrence. Deterrence must be studied as a risk perception in the eyes of the regulated actors (Burby and Paterson 1993; Gray and Scholz 1991). As a result, the subjective perceptions of the risks and rewards of committing a crime received increasing attention in deterrence and compliance studies. As Decker et al. (1993: 135) claimed, "There can be no direct relationship between sanctions and criminal action; the two must be linked through the intervening variable of subjective perceptions of the

---

[1] Injunctive social norms were not included at individual level due to two considerations. First, many researchers have found that injunctive social norms only indirectly influence compliance, and the influence of injunctive norms was partially mediated by the effect of personal norms (Wenzel 2004; Bobek et al. 2013). According to Schwartz (1977), individuals internalize societal values (injunctive norms) and develop their personal standards of acceptable behavior (personal norms). Individuals may initially follow injunctive social norms to avoid social stigma, but over time, may continue to follow them for internal reasons, and the injunctive social norms become their personal norms. While injunctive social norms may also indirectly influence individuals' decision making regarding compliance via social evaluation, personal norms contribute to individuals' compliance more directly through self-imposed feeling of shame or guilt (Bobek et a. 2013; Grasmick and Bursik 1990). Second, the injunctive norms that are not internalized as personal norms usually contribute to compliance through social reputation, which is captured by plural subjective deterrence. Consequently, injunctive norms were excluded for the sake of brevity.

risks and rewards of committing a crime." Many scholars have turned their attention to the regulated entities' perceived deterrence, which focuses on what individuals subjectively believe they are at risk of when conducting certain behavior, instead of objective deterrence, which focuses on the likelihood (certainty) of legal sanctions and the magnitude (severity) of legal sanctions enforcement exerts (cf. Grasmick and Bryjak 1980; Grasmick and Green 1980; Greenberg 1981; Decker et al. 1993; Klepper and Nagin 1989a, 1989b; Nagin and Paternoster 1991; Paternoster et al. 1982; Paternoster 1987; Thornton et al. 2005; Van Rooij 2013a). Van Rooij (2013a) examined Chinese lawyers' subjective deterrence by asking about their perceived general risk, the possibility of detection, and the severity of sanctions.

Furthermore, scholars have broadened the understanding of sources of deterrence. While the traditional deterrence theory focuses only on deterrence originating from the state, scholars have increasingly identified the influence of and deterrence caused by so-called "third-party regulators" (Gunningham et al. 1998; Nielsen and Parker 2008; Hutter 2011; Van Rooij 2016). For instance, Nielsen and Parker (2008), in their study of Austrian businesses' compliance activities, found that the perceived risk from a range of third parties, including customers, shareholders, employees, and business partners, influences the compliance behaviors of businesses. Hutter (2011) explicitly examined nonstate actors that play a deterrence role in the food retail and hospitality sectors, which include consumers, the media, insurance companies, lawyers, and NGOs. Van Rooij (2016) found that Chinese lawyers perceived strong subjective deterrence largely from clients and only indirectly from state enforcement agencies.

This research follows the approach of "subjective deterrence," and more specifically "plural subjective deterrence," proposed by Van Rooij (2016). In this context, "plural subjective deterrence" involves multiple external sources of deterrence, including state and nonstate sources. Deterrence from other sources, such as self-imposed punishment from internalized norms, which is also involved in some extended deterrence model (see Grasmick and Bursik 1990), is not included here. Plural subjective deterrence brings the deterrence aspect of comprehensive legal knowledge discussed in Chap. 6 and the outcome of the interaction between organizational and legal norms discussed in Chap. 7 to the individual level to integrate the three levels.

Van Rooij (2016) understood deterrence broadly as risk and not only narrowly as the perception of detection probability and sanction severity. He claimed that the consideration of the "risk" of engaging in certain behaviors reflects the nature of deterrence for that behavior and provides a space for discovering and discussing rich and vivid sources of deterrence. In this study, this method has been employed, and deterrence has been operationalized as "troubles," which refers to whether the individual actors will be subject to sanctions externally from a state enforcement authority or other nonstate sources when they do not satisfy certain legal requirements. The meaning of "trouble" is similar to that of "risk" used by Van Rooij; however, it was more applicable in the context of restaurants and easier for employees and owners to understand.

The data on subjective deterrence was drawn from in-depth qualitative interview dialogues with both restaurant workers and owners. I asked interviewees whether they would "get into trouble" if they failed to complete certain actions, and did not mention that the behavior is regulated by legal norms. As indicated by the pilot study and shown in Chap. 6, doctrinal legal knowledge was rather limited among restaurants. Most interviewees might not have known that the behaviors mentioned to them are regulated by laws. This was done to reveal their considerations in real-life situations when engaging in certain behaviors and to avoid answers originating from their general fear of law in the abstract. If their answers indicated that they would definitely get into trouble, that the trouble would be significant, or that the likelihood of trouble was high, they were coded as having subjective deterrence. If their answers showed that there would be no trouble or that trouble would be negligible, they were coded as not having subjective deterrence.

8.2.2   Personal Norms

Personal norms refer to one's own expectations for proper behavior or one's ethical beliefs (Bobek et al. 2013). They are usually outcomes of individuals' previous social history and are always developing or changing. On one hand, they may be modified and change during the formation processes of comprehensive legal knowledge and organizational norms; on the other hand, personal norms are important in forming individual comprehensive legal knowledge, as different personal norms or beliefs influence how people evaluate doctrinal legal knowledge and how they choose and respond to legal practice knowledge. As described in part A, contestation occurs between the regulated actors' beliefs and legal norms. Personal norms as one kind of belief also influence individual comprehensive legal knowledge.

In the existing literature, personal norms were found to directly influence tax compliance decisions (Bobek et al. 2013; Wenzel 2004). Moreover, by testing two different versions of Ajzen's (1991) theory of planned behavior, Hanno and Violette (1996) and Bobek and Hatfield (2003) found that moral obligation (personal norms) influenced compliance decisions. The findings of Blanthorne and Kaplan (2008) suggest that individual ethical beliefs (personal norms) are particularly important, and subjective norms directly influence personal norms, which in turn affect compliance behavior. Wenzel (2004) measured personal norms with three items that show the moral concerns of certain compliance or violation behaviors. For instance, "Do you think you should honestly declare cash earnings on your tax return?" "Do you think it is acceptable to overstate tax deductions on your tax return?" (reverse coded), and "Do you think working for cash-in-hand payments without paying tax is a trivial offence?" (reverse coded). Bobek et al. (2013) and Bobek et al. (2011) further differentiated personal norms in general from personal norms related to specific compliance decisions and developed six items to measure personal norms. For instance, "I think I should honestly report cash earnings on my tax return" and "I think it is acceptable to overstate tax deductions on my tax return" are general items for personal norms related to tax compliance. "You would definitely think it was not okay (i.e., morally right) to deduct the additional $2,000" and "Would you feel justified in taking the additional $2,000 deduction" are specific items for personal norms related to tax compliance. Those measurements concern the moral evaluation of certain compliance behavior in terms of whether certain actions are right or wrong.

In this book, interviewees were asked about their personal perceptions of the requirements studied using questions such as "What do you think about health certificates in your personal view?" Their personal perceptions reflected moral consideration of those requirements in terms of reasonability or necessity, and in terms of whether they were morally right or wrong. If they definitely agreed with the requirements or had a positive attitude toward them, their answers were coded as positive. In contrast, if they pointed out that the regulation was unnecessary or impossible to achieve, or that it was acceptable to act contrary to the regulation, their answers were coded as negative.

8.2.3 Descriptive Social Norms

The variable of descriptive social norm originated from psychological study (Cialdini et al. 1990; Cialdini and Trost 1998; Cialdini 2007). In terms of this norm, people are more likely to obey the law if they believe others comply with it, with "others" referring not to significant people such as their friends or families but to general members of society. However, in this study, "others" is more likely to refer to peers in restaurants because the compliance behaviors considered are restaurant related. Descriptive social norms motivate people to comply by providing social information on what most others do in practice and evidence of likely effective and adaptive action (Bobek et al. 2003; Cialdini et al. 1990; Cialdini 2001). As Cialdini et al. (1990: 1015) stated, "If everyone is doing it, it must be a sensible thing to do."

It has been demonstrated in several studies that descriptive social norms are significantly related to compliance (Bobek et al. 2003; Scholz and Lubell 1998; Tyran and Feld 2002). In this book, the existing descriptive norms at organizational level, which refer to what most people do in restaurants, were examined and found to play a significant role in forming comprehensive legal knowledge and organizational norms (see Chaps. 6 and 7). In this section, interviewees' individual perceptions of social descriptive norms, and how that shapes their own decisions in compliance behavior, is investigated. To collect data on individuals' descriptive norms, I asked individuals about their perceptions by referencing to their peer groups working in restaurants, specifically, how they thought other people working in restaurants would behave. If they believed their peers complied with the legal requirements, the answer was coded as positive descriptive social norm. If not, it was coded as negative descriptive social norm.

8.2.4 Perceived Obligation to Obey the Law

Perceived obligation to obey the law (POOL) means people obey the law out of a sense of duty regardless of circumstances (Tyler 1990). It is also known as normative commitment (Burby and Paterson 1993), moral or ideological compliance (Levi 1988; McGraw and Scholz 1991), commitment based on civic duty (Scholz and Pinney 1995; Scholz and Lubell 1998), norm of law compliance (Vanderbergh 2003), systematic legitimacy (Van Rooij et al. 2014), and normative duty to obey (Winter and May 2001; May 2005). Although the terms differ, the core of this motivation remains the same, and the term "perceived obligation to obey the law" (POOL) is used in the book. POOL means people obey the law simply because it is the law, and they comply with the law out of a sense of duty developed through socialization. People with higher POOL are more likely to comply with legal rules, not out of a sense of fear, amoral calculation of cost and benefit, or because they agree with the aims and content of these rules, and not because they think most others comply with the rules or most others value compliance, but out of a sense of duty.

Winter and May (2001) found in the Danish context that normative duty to comply is as influential as calculated motivation in bringing about compliance. Tyler discovered a negative link between POOL and general criminal behavior, such that the more one perceived there to be an obligation to obey the law, the less likely one is to violate the law (Tyler 2006). Moreover, POOL stems from multiple source. Winter and May (2001) viewed it as based on the internalized general moral values of the regulated, comprised of their sense of civic duty to obey laws and general ideological values. Some scholars in the field of psychology found that how people view POOL is related to their different personality traits (Fine et al. 2016). Tyler (1997) considered it to be influenced by one's perception of legitimacy of legal authority and the fairness of lawmaking, the judiciary, and enforcement in society. According to Tyler (1997), POOL is stronger when one believes that the lawmaking, judicial, and enforcement institutions operate in a procedurally fair manner. In this way, the POOL is related to another commonly mentioned motivation, procedural justice (Tyler 1990; Leventhal 1980; Paternoster et al. 1997). Hence, if people believe they are treated fairly by legal institutions, the law is considered legitimate and to be abided by (Burby and Paterson 1993). Fairness is not so much the result of whether the legal institutions support the position of the regulated, but rather whether the procedure they used was fair (Braithwaite 2003; Tyler 1990, 1997, 2006). In this study, procedural justice is not discussed as an independent variable. Instead, the focus is on POOL due to the belief that procedural justice contributes to compliance by increasing or decreasing POOL (Tyler 1997).

Tyler measured POOL using six items formulated from three aspects: (1) measuring POOL regardless of the morality or content of the rules, (2) measuring POOL whether there are justifications for noncompliance, and (3) measuring the general importance of obedience and authority. Van Rooij et al. argued that the core of POOL concerns the perception people have that one should follow the law regardless of circumstances (Van Rooij et al., forthcoming). Furthermore, they defined five different circumstances, namely capacity, amoral calculation, social norms, personal norms, and procedural justice. Following Tyler's and Van Rooij's approach, Yan (2014) operationalized POOL as the regulated actors' general views on the obligation to obey the law regardless of three preconditions, and measured peasants' POOL through dialogue interviews. Yan asked peasants if they agree with the statement of POOL under the three preconditions, that is, people should obey the law (1) even if it is a bad law, (2) even if it is not enforced, (3) or even when the costs of obeying it are high. The first precondition represents the content of the law, the second the enforcement environment, and the third the cost of compliance. The approach followed in this study is similar to Yan's approach. The statement used was that people should obey the law (1) even if they think the law is not reasonable or they do not agree with the law, (2) even if it is not enforced and no one will inspect whether they comply with the law, (3) or even if complying with the law has high costs. The responses to this statement were divided into three categories: agree, disagree, and not sure.

8.2.5 Capacity

While previous variables address the intention of the regulated to comply and are motivations for compliance, capacity is a variable that may facilitate the translation of the intention into action or restrain the regulated from translating the intention into action (Kagan and Scholz 1984; Winter and May 2001; Vandenbergh 2003). In other words, people may disobey the law because they lack the capacity to comply with it, identified as incompetence by Kagan and Scholz (1984).

Capacity is a general yet multifaceted concept that encompasses the information, materials, resources, knowledge, and skills that may restrain people from taking action. According to Vandenbergh (2003: 77), "a lack of financial or technological resources may limit the ability to comply, even where there is an intent to do so. Moreover, the complexity of legal requirements may constitute another barrier to actual compliance." In addition, materials needed for engaging in certain behavior and human resources that facilitate the realization of compliance form part of capacity, and knowledge of rules is considered an aspect of capacity for compliance, or a prerequisite to compliance (Winter and May 2001, 2002; Spence 2001). According to Winter and May (2001), people should know or be aware of a regulation, clearly understand the requirements of the regulation, and understand the means for complying with the regulation before they taking the action of compliance.

As the variable of capacity involves many aspects, it is not possible to identify every aspect of capacity. Furthermore, different compliance behaviors may be constrained by different aspects of capacity. Some resource or capacity may significantly constrain one compliance behavior, but it may not be a precondition for conducting another compliance behavior. Therefore, in this study, the variables related to capacity were divided into two parts, namely recognition of legal requirements and practical constraints. The first involves the recognition of the existence of a relevant legal norm, which was captured by asking whether the individual knew that a certain requirement is a legal requirement. If so, he or she was aware of this specific regulation and clearly understood the requirements of the regulation. This is the basic capacity or prerequisite according to Winter and May (2001), and it was coded positive. Answers to the contrary were coded negative. The second part involves the practical constraints of compliance behaviors, including financial resources, human resources, time, and material facilities. Different compliance behaviors may be constrained by different practical constraints. Hence, interviewees were asked about their perceptions of different constraints related to different compliance behaviors. If individuals identified practical constraints for taking specific compliance action, it was recorded as negative. If not, answers were recorded as positive.

These explanations of why people obey the law provided an inventory, but not a comprehensive list, for analyzing individual's behaviors (Table 8.1).

Table 8.1 Variables at individual level

Variables	Reason for influence on compliance	Interview questions
Plural subjective deterrence	May comply with legal norms if deterred by possible sanction	Will you get into trouble if you do not have/do…?
POOL	Obey the law out of a sense of duty derived from socialization	Do you agree with the statement that people should obey the law (1) even if they think the law is not reasonable or they do not agree with the law, (2) even if the law is not enforced and no one will inspect whether they comply with the law, (3) or even if compliance is costly?
Descriptive social norms	More likely to obey the law if they believe others comply with it	Do you think most workers/restaurants have/do…?
Personal norms	More likely to comply with the law if that is also what they believe they ought to do	How do you think about…from your personal perspective?
Recognition of legal requirements	Knowledge or awareness of a regulation is required before compliance occurs	Do you think…is a law? Do you know that it is a law? How do you know?
Practical constraints	May restrain people from translating compliance intention into action	What do you think about to getting/doing…? What do you think about the cost? (Some answers were elicited spontaneously during interviews without asking direct questions.)

8.3 Dialogue Interview Method

In-depth, qualitative dialogue interviews were employed to learn interviewees' perceptions of each variable discussed in this chapter. As Van Rooij et al. (2014) claimed when he used this method to study lawyers' compliance, the dialogue interview enables me to develop a kind of trust with interviewees to obtain reliable answers to sensitive questions and allows for the richness of data necessary to understand the perspectives of the interviewees in the most open and truthful way. Some dialogue interviews were not completed in a single session but through numerous short conversations, but most were completed in a single session lasting one to two hours. Thirty-five interviewees were selected from four restaurants: Thirteen from the Idealistic restaurant, fourteen from S restaurant, seven from the Profit-Maximizing restaurant, and one from L restaurant.

The pool of interviewees included both employees and employers, and they were all treated independent individuals when asked to describe their decisions based on their thought processes. Some may argue that employers have vastly different influences and positions related to compliance behaviors than employees, so the patterns of employer decision making and compliance behavior may differ from those of employees. This may be true, and it requires further study to identify the differences between individuals in different positions in terms of compliance decision making and actions. In this book, however, due to the limited number of employers available, this difference was not analyzed (Table 8.2).

Dialogue interviews were conducted in a natural, relaxed, and safe atmosphere to acquire reliable information. In the restaurants that participated in the long-term observation, all 18 employees and both owners were selected for dialogue interviews. Interviews with the 20 interviewees took place after the participant observation in their restaurants for a long time, so they knew me well. Some interviews were conducted in the restaurant during breaks while only the interviewee was on duty, while others took place outside the restaurant where no other people from that restaurant were present.

The other 15 interviewees were from two other restaurants where onsite participant observation had not been conducted, namely S restaurant and L restaurant. For L restaurant, only the owner has been included, and I conducted three dialogue interviews with her on three different occasions, with one taking place in her restaurant. Several parts of the three interviews overlapped, which allowed for the verification of

Table 8.2 Number of interviewees and behaviors identified

Restaurants	Interviewees	Behaviors
The idealistic restaurant	13	35
The profit-maximizing restaurant	7	27
S restaurant	14	43
L restaurant	1	3
Total	35	108

answers. The 14 interviewees from S restaurant, selected based on their gender and work positions, included servers, bar staff, dining room attendants, dishwashers, and midlevel managers who managed the employees were interviewed. Consequently, this study does not claim to be representative of restaurant employees and owners in China. For the interviews with staff from S restaurant, I introduced myself at the beginning of each interview and casually conversed with interviewees to build rapport and create a relaxed atmosphere. A basic dialogue frame was employed to facilitate the flow of the dialogue and to avoid offending the interviewees. Although it was not strictly followed, the dialogue interviews did not offend interviewees and revealed reliable data, as rich information emerged and interviewees readily shared information about illegal behaviors.

The basic dialogue frame involved asking interviewees about their work experience and current jobs before addressing the topics under study. First, I asked interviewees about the kinds of jobs they had done, their reasons for leaving, and why they chose to work in a restaurant. Some interviewees would talk a lot about their work experience, their emotions while doing those jobs, and significant events or interesting points related to those jobs. Next, I returned to the topic of their current jobs by asking how they came to work in this restaurant. After this, conversation usually flowed naturally about the work they did in the current restaurant or the requirements in place for workers in the current restaurant.

During this phase, the topic of health certificates usually arose, which allowed me to ask how they obtained their certificates and to ask questions about their reasons for obtaining them, the practical constraints of doing so, their personal perceptions of health certificates, the trouble they would experience if they did not obtain certificates, and the relevant descriptive norm. If interviewees had counterfeit health certificates, it would be revealed during this process. In addition, if they indicated that they did not have health certificates, they would be asked to explain why not. Often, interviewees would mention pertinent information about heath certificates without being prompted to do so.

Subsequently, the conversation would move to other requirements for their work, either cutting fingernails, washing hands, or disinfection. Again, they would be asked why they do or do not perform certain actions, and the question structure related to health certificates described above would be repeated, although with substitutions made to match the topic. After discussing all behaviors that applied in their work (the inclusion and exclusion of variables occurred based on applicability),[2] I would ask about their perceptions of POOL. Because this question appeared somewhat abrupt and disconnected from the foregoing conversation, I would engage in casual and informal conversation to smooth the transition. Examples of topics include their perception of the relationship between their work and laws, for example, salaries, and conversation about TV programs that address legal phenomena or cases. The topic would be chosen depending on my assessment of whether the conversation would flow.

---

[2]For instance, some restaurant workers did not perform tasks related to disinfection, so they were not asked about this topic.

After spending some time on the transitional topics, I would indicate that I would like to know their perceptions of some general statements about law. I usually said, "there are different opinions of laws. I would like to know whether you agree with this statement about laws. The statement is that people should obey the law (1) even if they think the law is not reasonable or they do not agree with the law, (2) even if it is not enforced and no one will inspect whether they comply, (3) or even if compliance is costly." Some interviewees responded by simply stating that they agree or disagree, while others explained their reasons for their answers. Once they provided their general opinions, I would repeat the three preconditions one by one and ask for their opinions of each of them. At the end, I would ask whether the interviewees thought those behaviors we discussed were law.

8.4 Measurement of Compliance Behaviors

As shown in Part A of this book, data related to compliance behaviors were collected using various methods, including through participant observation, interviews, and reviewing materials and documents at sites, which allowed crosschecking and safeguarded the reliability of the data. Interviewees' compliance behavior first was recorded through participant observation and onsite documents or materials, and it included determining whether they had health certificates and long nails, whether they washed their hands as required, whether they disinfected dishware, whether they had opening licenses, and whether they used counterfeit *Fapiao* receipts. Additional details about these behaviors emerged through the interviews.

For instance, I determined whether restaurant owners had the various opening licenses by examining the documents displayed in restaurants, and then owners described the application processes during interviews, which revealed additional information about whether they had satisfied all licensing requirements. In addition, the requirement of nail cutting was easier to observe during interviews. In some cases, interviewees reported their behaviors related to each requirement, and then I would verify their answers by checking the onsite documents, for example, health certificates and opening licenses, or by comparing them to other interviewees' answers. Answer comparison was particularly useful at S restaurant, where no participant observation took place but 14 workers and managers were interviewed. Thus, data collection was somewhat limited at S restaurant, as some reported behaviors, such as handwashing and disinfection, could not be verified with observable data. As discussed in Part A, compliance behaviors are highly complex and include many dimensions that surpass the dichotomy of compliance or noncompliance.

In this chapter, to explore the influence of various variables on compliance, these complex compliance behaviors were coded into the simple dichotomy of compliance and violation. All behaviors were systematically coded based on the strict distinction drawn between compliance and violation. Behaviors coded as compliance include those that not only comply superficial, for instance, having an official certificate, but also completely satisfy all requirements for that certificate. Those who had valid

Table 8.3 Frequency of compliance behaviors

	Frequency	Percentage
Violation	56	51.9
Compliance	52	48.1
Total	108	100.0

certificates but did not satisfy all requirements were coded as violation. For instance, some interviewees had official health certificate, but they had not undergone health checks before obtain their certificates. These behaviors were coded as violations. Similarly, if restaurants had opening licenses but fraudulently complied with the requirements to obtain the certificates, the behavior was coded as violation. In other words, what was coded as compliance was full, genuine and beyond compliance. All other compliance, including fraudulent, fake, symbolic, partial, conflictive, and attempted compliance, were coded as violations.

Based on dichotomy coding, 52 behaviors, or 48.1%, were coded as compliance, while 57 behaviors, or 51.9%, were violations (Table 8.3).

8.5   Subjective Explanations of Compliance Behavior

This section addresses interviewees' subjective explanations to examine how the regulated explain their compliance behaviors and the extent to which interviewees mentioned the influential variables identified previously. As noted in Sect. 8.4 about the method employed during the dialogue interviews, I asked interviewees directly why they did or did not engage in specific behaviors immediately after interviewees indicated that they did or did not engage in certain compliance behavior. For instance, when interviewees explained how they came to work in the restaurant and what they needed to do, they might mention that they went to undergo a health check and to obtain a health certificate. The follow-up question would be, "Why did you obtain a health certificate," or if they did not mention obtaining this certificate, the question would be, "Did you obtain a health certificate?" If not, they would be asked, "Why did you not obtain a health certificate?".

8.5.1   For Compliance Behaviors

The most common explanation for compliance behavior was that the restaurant required it or that the restaurant was strict on the requirement. Some interviewees mentioned potential trouble or sanctions for noncompliance from the restaurant, with being fired being the most severe sanction. For example, "If I do not have a health certificate, I cannot work in this restaurant".[3] "I get health certificate because I plan to stay here long. I will get, even if I pay for myself, because I want to stay here long and learn knowledge. People have to get health certificate if he want to stay in this restaurant".[4] The next most serious sanction was being fined, for example, "The boss asks to cut nails short, otherwise, we will be fined. One long nails 5 or 10 CNY".[5] "The restaurant is strict on disinfection. If you do not disinfect dishware, you will be fined".[6] Some did not mention any specific sanctions but simply indicated that noncompliance would be detected at the restaurant. For instance, "Manager will check every day. Workers in restaurant are forbidden to have long nails".[7]

Others did not mention sanctions or detection, but emphasized that it was a rule or expected behavior in their restaurants: "The boss asked me to get health certificate. Even if I have to pay it by myself, once the boss requires, I will get".[8] "It is something that you must do as waitress in this restaurant. It is the routinized work for waitress".[9] "It is the restaurant rule. Workers in this restaurant cannot have long nails".[10]

The second most common explanation was that the government required it or that there was strict government enforcement. However, none of the interviewees mentioned the potential trouble or sanctions noncompliance would cause: "Inspectors are strict on disinfection. Inspectors have come to check for three times since I come [five months]".[11] "Restaurants have to have all legal licenses that government requires. Never thought about to escape the license".[12]

The above two explanations fall under the variable of plural subjective deterrence, described in Sect. 8.2.1, as they relate to some form of risk interviewees perceived related to violating these norms. Thus, 80.8% of responses indicating positive compliance behaviors (n = 42) explained this compliance by referring to deterrence subjectively perceived from either restaurants or a regulatory system.

The third explanation was that interviewees cared about food safety (personal norm) and that it would facilitate their work (operational benefit). Seven respondents (13.5%) ascribed their behavior to food safety. For instance, one server explained that dishware was disinfected "for food safety".[13] Six respondents (11.5%) ascribed the positive compliance behaviors to being beneficial for their work. For instance,

---

[3]Interview with SD on October 29, 2013.

[4]Interview with TX on May 29, 2013.

[5]Interview with TY on May 23, 2013.

[6]Interview with SD on November 6, 2013.

[7]Interview with SL on November 2, 2013.

[8]Interview with TS on May 29, 2013.

[9]Interview with SH on October 20, 2013.

[10]Interview with SM on November 6, 2013.

[11]Interview with SHH on October 9, 2013.

[12]Interview with TF on April 16, 2013.

[13]Interview with SJ on December 12, 2013.

> My work is to grab food materials with my hands. If I have long nails, [food] may go [under] my nails, and that make me uncomfortable. So I will cut my nails once I feel it is long. If I do not do this work, I may have long thumbs and long little fingers.[14]

Furthermore, the two explanations were always mentioned simultaneously (n = 4): "First, it is for safety and sanitation. All dishware in this restaurant are disinfected with disinfection fluid. Second, glasses will be much clean after disinfection".[15] "We must disinfect glasses. Bacteria will be killed by disinfection fluid and some stains that are not easily removed will be removed easily with disinfection fluid. Glasses will become shining after disinfected".[16]

Being beneficial for work may also combine with plural subjective deterrence (n = 1). For example, a server from S restaurant explained that he disinfected dishware because "disinfection fluid can remove the stain easily. It is the restaurant rule. I just follow the rule of washing glasses".[17]

In some cases, respondents referred to all three of these variables, namely being beneficial for work, plural subjective deterrence, and personal norms, when explaining why they complied with the relevant rules. For instance, a server from S restaurant explained why she disinfected dishware by stating that "it is good for health. And dishware looks clean. It is also an aspect that government regulates in catering industry".[18]

The final two explanations were personal habit or routinized behavior (n = 2) and knowledge of restaurant rules (n = 1). One respondent ascribed his handwashing behavior to his personal habits: "We have two washing basins around. It has become a habit, whenever I want to touch something [ingredients for making juice] here, I will wash my hands under the faucet first".[19] A server from S restaurant explained her disinfection behavior with, "It is something that you must do as waitress in this restaurant. It is the routinized work for waitress."[20] In this case, personal habit and routinized behavior can be seen as one kind of positive personal norm that means engaging certain behaviors is simply considered normal and the right thing to do without question. Another server from the same restaurant explained that he obtained a health certificate because he initially learned that this was a requirement when he decided to work in a restaurant: "I want to work in restaurant and know workers in restaurant should have health certificate. So I get health certificate by myself before I came to this restaurant".[21]

Individuals may explain one behavior by referring to several factors, so the total percentage of positive compliance behaviors does not equal 100.

---

[14] Interview with NY on September 2, 2013.

[15] Interview with SB on November 1, 2013.

[16] Interview with SJ on November 1, 2013.

[17] Interview with SM on November 6, 2013.

[18] Interview with SY on October 20, 2013.

[19] Interview with SB on November 1, 2013.

[20] Interview with SH on October 20, 2013.

[21] Interview with SJ on October 12, 2013.

Factors	Responses	Positive compliance behaviors (%)[a]
Positive plural subjective deterrence	42	80.8
Positive personal norm	9	17.3
Beneficial for work (operational benefit)	6	11.5
Recognition of legal requirements	1	1.9

Table 8.4 Factors identified in the subjective explanation of positive compliance behaviors

Notes Number of positive compliance behaviors = 52
[a]The denominator is the number of positive compliance behaviors (i.e. 52)

8.5.2 For Violation Behaviors

The most common subjective explanation for violation behaviors was that the restaurant did not require the behavior or did not enforce it strictly. In addition to no requirements in restaurants, some claimed they did not know the requirement. For instance, "I do not know. The boss never talks about that [cutting nails]".[22] However, some respondents clearly knew the requirements but attributed violation behaviors to restaurants' lack of enforcement: "The boss is not strict on [cutting nails]".[23] Some explanations showed that the individual placed the responsibility completely on the shoulders of the restaurant: "If the boss asked me to get and pay for it, I will get [health certificate]. Otherwise, I will not".[24]

The second common explanation was slack government enforcement. Often, this was mentioned in combination with other explanations of practical constraints, such as cost and incapability. Some viewed lax enforcement as less possibility of detection and less significant sanctions:

I [restaurant owner] used to use fake *Fapiao* receipts. The real *Fapiao* receipts is not enough to use.[25] No one has reported to government bureau that I used fake *Fapiao* receipts. Even if someone reports, I may just be fined 200 yuan [CNY]. That is much less than what I thought will be. I thought restaurants may be fined several thousand.[26]

Some referred to lax enforcement and to the effort required to comply:

---

[22]Interview with ND on September 22, 2013.

[23]Interview with NM on September 16, 2013.

[24]Interview with NW on September 4, 2013.

[25]To pay less tax, restaurants usually underreport their turnover. Because they are evidence of paying tax in China, formal receipts received from the tax office are linked to reported turnover. Thus, restaurants claiming lower turnover receive fewer formal receipts than they would need if every customer were to ask for a formal receipt. Therefore, this individual claiming that the genuine receipts were not enough implied that she had underreported the restaurant's turnover to evade tax and save on tax payments.

[26]Interview with LB on May 10, 2012.

I have written the disinfection log at the beginning. But I stop when I found they did not come to check. I just disinfect dishware once a week but not every day. It is troublesome. I put them in disinfection cabinet. However, according to the rule, the plastic container cannot be put in disinfection cabinet.[27]

Several respondents provided complex explanations combining low possibility of detection, negative personal norms related to the requirement, and incapacity of engaging in the required behaviors:

Workers will get health certificate if inspectors come to check. If they do not come to check, you do not need to get health certificate. You can use other restaurants' health certificates. The inspectors won't come to verify. Most people are healthy. Only very small part of people bring with the virus. I asked employees to get health certificate, but they did not. In fact, I hope they can do health check. It benefit to both of us.[28]

The above two explanations can be categorized as negative plural subjective deterrence, with 57.1% responses (n = 32) referring to this variable.

The third common explanation involved negative personal norms related to the required behaviors, with 25% of responses (n = 14) falling into this category. Some interviewees linked requirements with the scale of the restaurant: "There is no need for such requirement [cutting nails]. We are just small restaurants".[29] Several claimed that the requirements were not necessary considering some special personal situation such as age, health condition, and length of employment. For instance, "I'm old and I'm healthy. Furthermore, I won't stay long in the restaurant. There is no need to spend money for me [on a health certificate]".[30] Respondents further considered certain secondary requirements unnecessary for realizing the aim of the main requirement. For instance, completing a disinfection log is a secondary requirement of the main requirement of disinfection:

We use so good cleanser and surely will do the disinfection the best. We have to make sure the bacteria on tableware will be killed completely. We disinfect dishware every day, and it is not necessary to have records every time. However, inspectors just want to check the disinfection records.[31]

Moreover, respondents denied the necessity for such requirements: "I did not disinfect the big plate because I think we have washed them clean".[32]

Some respondents combined negative personal norms with cost savings. For instance,

"If you just do whatever they asked, you cannot make money from this business. You have to be tricky whenever needed. I will pay for the fine if the inspectors come to check. If they do not come, I will not renew [the liquor license]. There is nothing special. You just pay the administration fee every year and you have rights to sell alcohol.[33]

---

[27]Interview with LB on May 10, 2012.

[28]Interview with NM on September 5, 2013.

[29]Interview with NM on August 21, 2013.

[30]Interview with TD on May 23, 2013.

[31]Interview with TF on May 28, 2013.

[32]Interview with NM on September 5, 2013.

[33]Interview with NM on September 5, 2013.

The next popular explanation was practical constraints, as indicated by 19.6% of responses (n = 11). Practical constraints included being too busy, not having time, and not being willing to spend money. For example, "We wear white gloves so we do not need to wash hands. It is not possible to wash hands often during work time. Do not have time".[34] Some specific constraints also were mentioned. For instance, a kitchen worker from the Idealistic restaurant claimed he did not obtain a health certificate because he did not have a Chinese ID card, which is a precondition for applying for a health certificate:

> I have not got my citizen identity card, without which I am not able to get health certificate. My citizen ID card was lost and I haven't got the new one. After I get my new ID card, I will go to get health certificate because we need to know our health condition.[35]

The remaining explanations were ignorance of the requirement (7.1%, n = 4), not being responsible for the requirement (7.1%, n = 4), and the requirement being a latent rule in the catering industry (descriptive norm; 3.6%, n = 2). Each of these was mentioned by fewer than five respondents. Two respondents who stated that they were unaware of the requirements stated, "I don't know health certificate. I just came to this restaurant for less than two months",[36] and "I did not hear that chicken need [chicken quarantine] certificate".[37] Some claimed that it was not their responsibility to take care of those behaviors. For instance,

> It is the boss's responsibility to have health certificate and it is the boss who will be fined for not having health certificate. For me, I can work in restaurant without health certificate.[38]

> I have one, but as you know, it is fake. My photo is pasted on this health certificate, but it is not my certificate. If the boss take me to get and pay for it, I will get. He just said he would take us to sometime, but later he did not.[39]

Some ascribed their behavior to a negative descriptive norm: "I heard other restaurants just use the pipe [tap] water. So I send the pipe water instead of the real water in drainpipe [when applying for a drainage license]".[40]

In some cases, individuals ascribed their violation behaviors to a combination of multiple factors, such as negative plural subjective deterrence combined with positive practical constraints, negative personal norms, negative descriptive norms, and not being responsible for the behavior. In addition, negative personal norms were combined with positive practical constraints and not being responsible for the behavior, and negative descriptive norms were combined with practical constraints. For example,

> Inspectors just want to get benefit from these [environmental] licenses. I feel the instruments they ask me to install do not have much use, and it consumes too much electricity. There

---

[34]Interview with SH on October 9, 2013.

[35]Interview with TL on September 26, 2013.

[36]Interview with NL on August 20, 2013.

[37]Interview with TF on April 16, 2013.

[38]Interview with NY on September 2, 2013.

[39]Interview with NL on September 11, 2013.

[40]Interview with TF on April 17, 2013.

Table 8.5 Factors identified in the subjective explanation of violation behaviors

	Responses	Violation behaviors (%)
Negative plural subjective deterrence	32	57.1
Negative personal norm	14	25.0
Positive practical constraints	11	19.6
Negative descriptive norm	2	3.6
Not responsible	4	7.1
Do not know the requirements	4	7.1

Notes Number of violation behaviors = 56

Individuals may explain one behavior by referring to several factors, so the percentage of violation behaviors does not equal 100%

is no problem that some restaurants got environment license before and do not have the instruments they requires. If inspectors come to check and I will renew the license, if they do not come, I will not renew it. Inspectors usually do not come here. We are just small restaurants. If you just do whatever they asked, you cannot make money from this business. You have to tricky whenever needed. I do not violate the law. I will accept the fine if they want to fine. The fine will not be too much. If they ask for two thousand, it is OK that you give them one thousand.[41]

In this explanation, influential variables, including negative descriptive norms, negative personal norms, negative plural subjective deterrence, and practical constraints (cost) emerged (Table 8.5).

8.5.3   Operational Benefit and not Being Responsible

Most of the subjective explanations provided by interviewees matched the six variables introduced in Sect. 8.2, except the explanations of not being responsible for compliance and the behavior being beneficial for work. The latter is a type of operational benefit. Usually, it is not considered as an independent variable for compliance, but always addressed in cost–benefit calculation. In several cost–benefit studies of compliance, instead of focusing on the eventual costs of violating the law, scholars analyzed the immediate operational costs and benefits of both violation and compliance as they occur within everyday practices, and some found that positive perceptions of operational costs and benefits explained compliant behavior well (Yan et al. 2015).

---

[41] Interview with NM on September 5, 2013.

This chapter does not address cost–benefit calculation for two reasons. First, some behaviors obviously arise out of consideration of cost–benefit calculation, so the calculation seems irrelevant. Second, it was impossible to ask interviewees to calculate the costs and benefits of their behaviors, as most costs and benefits of compliance behaviors discussed here do not fall in the same category and cannot be compared or calculated. For instance, the costs of health certificates mentioned were mainly money and time, but the benefits of having health certificates (knowing one's health condition, being eligible for continued employment, not needing to hide during inspections, and being able to apply for a catering services license) cannot be captured in terms of money and time. Similarly, the identified costs of handwashing related mainly to time, but the benefits mentioned were feeling good and promoting good sanitation. These factors fall into different categories and cannot be calculated.

The same situation of not being able to calculate the costs and benefits of compliance was also found in other compliance studies. Yan (2014) discussed three kinds of compliance behaviors in pesticide use. She showed that while she could calculate the operational costs and benefits of two compliance behaviors—the use of specific types of pesticides and the time interval between spraying pesticides and selling vegetable—in terms of price and effectiveness, or cost and profit, she could not do that with the third compliance behavior, that is, disposal of pesticide containers, as "there is no direct and obvious operational costs and benefits calculation concerning disposal" (Yan 2014: 65).

Although only four respondents explicitly ascribed violations to their perception of not being responsible for the behaviors discussed, it reveals an important factor for violation that requires closer examination. It is reminiscent of the motivational posture of disengagement proposed by Braithwaite et al. (1994). Disengagement means the regulated actors have a negative posture toward the regulatory goal and regulatory community. They are not interested in playing the regulatory game or in improving or resisting the enforcement system. Instead, their main objectives are to avoid regulation and keep themselves hidden from view. So, the regulated actors who viewed themselves as not responsible were disengaged from those legal requirements. They never situated themselves inside the regulatory system, not necessarily intentionally as the disengagement posture implies, but simply because they did not realize they are objectives of the regulatory system. For those people, their compliance relies largely on the function of an intermediary that connects them to those requirements, that is, the restaurant. This is largely the result of how restaurant-related laws, that is, food safety law, are enforced in China—enforcement agencies consider the restaurant the least significant unit of enforcement and focus on restaurant owners instead of involving all workers in the catering industry.

Subjective explanation of irresponsibility should be seen as different from the technique of neutralization in criminology. From the perspective of neutralization in criminology (Sykes and Matza 1957; Minor 1981; Klockars 1974; Piquero et al. 2005), the explanation of not being responsible may be seen as denial of responsibility. The denial of responsibility means the violator defines himself as lacking responsibility for his deviant actions to protect his own image that may be damaged by his deviant actions. Strictly speaking, techniques of neutralization may not apply here, because the noncompliance behaviors discussed here are neither adjudicated as legal violations nor understood by the regulated actors as violating the laws, as shown by the majority of the regulated actors not knowing their behaviors are regulated by laws.

In this context, the subjective explanation of not being responsible should be viewed as their personal perception of the responsibility toward the behaviors discussed here instead of as a technique of neutralization. The theory of the technique of neutralization focuses on how deviant actors justify their deviant behaviors, which are obviously wrong in the dominant normative system to which they are also committed. By learning these techniques rather than by learning moral imperatives, values, or attitudes standing in direct contradiction to those of the dominant society, the juvenile becomes delinquent. In another words, by using the technique of neutralization, the juvenile persuades and convinces himself or herself to engage in deviant behaviors. However, this does not apply here. There is no strong contradiction between violation behaviors and the dominant normative system, as many required behaviors have not become injunctive norms for the regulated actors. Moreover, from another perspective, those techniques of neutralization also reveal the deviant actors' perception of the behavior itself in terms of who is responsible for the behavior, whether it is necessary, the value of the behavior, and so forth. In this book, the focus was on identifying the various factors that contribute to compliance during the compliance process. Respondents' perception of responsibility and relevant personal norms can be seen as part of these factors.

8.6   Interviewees' Understanding and Perceptions of Each Variable

This section contains a description of how interviewees perceived and understood the variables used to analyze their association with (non)compliance behavior. These variables are plural subjective deterrence, perceived obligation to obey the law, personal norms, descriptive norms, and capacity (recognition of the law and practical constraints).

8.6.1   Plural Subjective Deterrence

As shown in Table 8.6, 38% of respondents reported negative plural subjective deterrence for their behaviors, while 62% reported positive deterrence.

The respondents who mentioned negative deterrence can be divided into two groups based on their identification of the source of deterrence.

The first group identified a source of deterrence but perceived the deterrence was negligible. The perception of negative deterrence may have originated from

Table 8.6 Frequency of plural subjective deterrence		Frequency	Percentage
	Negative	41	38.0
	Positive	67	62.0
	Total	108	100.0

the perception of negligible detection possibility. They knew government enforcement of those behaviors took place and that they could face sanctions in case of noncompliance. Yet the likelihood of noncompliance being discovered was negligible, because they believed government inspectors did not care about that behavior, that is, "inspectors never asked about disinfection".[42] Alternatively, they may have believed inspectors check only the equipment, which is one of preconditions for the behavior, instead of the behavior itself: "[For disinfection,] inspectors just look at disinfection cabinet and disinfection fluid. They do not check if you have disinfected dishware or not".[43] Finally, they may have noted that they could disguise noncompliance to prevent possible detection: "Sometime they may come to check dishware. However, they will inform you in advance, and I can prepare for that".[44]

It may have originated from the perception of negligible sanctions. Some people perceived the possibility of detection but believed they would not be sanctioned even if their noncompliance behaviors were detected. For example, "It doesn't matter. Once the inspectors come, I will pay the money and get the new [liquor license certificate".[45] "We will be fined if the boss found out we do not wash our hands. However, I know he just scares us; he won't really fine us".[46] In addition, negative deterrence may have derived from a perception of differentiated enforcement. Some respondents knew there was general government enforcement for those behaviors, but they believed enforcement differed between themselves and another group of regulated actors based on business scale or age. They believed enforcers were not strict on them and they would not be caught. For instance, "Inspectors will check that in big restaurants, but is not strict on small restaurants. There is no risk for us".[47] Additionally,

Manager checks and workers having long nails will be fined. However, old workers have not been fined [the interviewee was an elderly woman]. The one who have long nails just be blamed and asked to cut short immediately. Once they find, they will ask me to cut it. However, the young waitresses and waters will be fined if the manager ask you to cut but you do not follow".[48]

---

[42] Interview with NL on September 11, 2013.

[43] Interview with LB on May 10, 2012.

[44] Interview with NM on September 5, 2013.

[45] Ibid.

[46] Interview with TY on May 23, 2013.

[47] Interview with NM on September 16, 2013.

[48] Interview with SD on November 6, 2013.

It may have originated from the perception of irrelevance. Some respondents believed they were not the targets of enforcement and sanctions. Thus, despite there being enforcement and sanctions, they were not influenced:

> Inspectors will come to check. They do not come to check often. The risk is low. They do not verify all workers health certificate. Once you have several health certificate, it will be OK. Restaurants will get lots of troubles if they find someone do not have health certificate. But there is not trouble for individual.[49]

Similarly, "Restaurant may be caught and fined. There is no influence for me. Without health certificate, I can also work in restaurant",[50] and, "There should be some troubles for restaurants, but the troubles won't be big. People without health certificate also can work in restaurants".[51]

The second group of responders denied there was any source of deterrence for the behaviors discussed, so they had a negative perception of plural subjective deterrence. Some reported a lack of enforcement from government inspectors: "Inspectors in environmental protection bureau do not inspect. Other inspectors from FDA won't find out even though you use fake environment license".[52] Further, several reported that the restaurants had no corresponding requirements and that customers did not care: "There is no trouble. The boss does not require us to cut nails. Customers do not care about such things".[53] Others held a general view that there was no source of "trouble." Respondents TP.9.8.2013 and NY.2.9.2013 indicated no sanctions were related to nail cutting, while NM.16.9.2013 reported no sanctions were related to handwashing and disinfection, and SH.9.10.2013, SJ.4.11.2013, SL.2.11.2013, SB.1.11.2013, SD.29.10.2013, and SZ.28.10.2013 reported no sanctions were related to handwashing. Likewise, respondents claimed, "I do not know. No one come to check my health certificate",[54] and, "I did not hear that whether we will be fined if we do not disinfect dishware".[55]

Respondents who perceived positive deterrence for noncompliance behaviors identified, first, multiple sources of deterrence, that is, government inspectors, restaurant managers or owners, and customers, with most identifying inspectors, managers, and owners. Several did not perceive difficulties arising from government enforcers but perceived difficulties only from customers and the restaurant: "There is no trouble from enforcement department. However, if customers get disease after eating our food, I will have trouble and be fined [for not washing my hands]."[56] "I cannot work in this restaurant [without a health certificate]. I don't know whether inspectors will find out if there is anyone who do not have health certificate".[57]

---

[49]Interview with TY on May 23, 2013.

[50]Interview with NL on September 11, 2013.

[51]Interview with TF on April 13, 2013.

[52]Interview with NM on September 5, 2013.

[53]Interview with NM on September 16, 2013.

[54]Interview with NL on August 20, 2013.

[55]Interview with TY on May 23, 2013.

[56]Interview with TF on May 28, 2013.

[57]Interview with TL on May 23, 2012.

Second, respondents reported varying likelihoods of detection. Some viewed it as high, and referred to frequent monitoring, for example, "The manager monitors all the time. Once you forget to disinfect, you will be found out and be fined".[58] Others referred to the certainty of detection, specifically through careful checks: "Government inspectors will come to check. They will check carefully".[59] "Manager will check [cutting nails]. Risk is high".[60] Others still viewed the detection possibility as low, which may have originated from infrequent monitoring. For instance, restaurant managers or owners might not have checked their compliance behavior often: "The boss will check, and one will be fined if is found to have long nails. The boss just check occasionally".[61] "Manager may check [cutting nails], but seldom".[62] In addition, respondents perceived different detection potential for different components of one behavior. For instance, several preconditions should be satisfied to obtain opening licenses, and while respondents perceived a high possibility of regulators checking the status of their licensing, they perceived a low possibility of enforcers checking whether they have satisfied those preconditions. For instance, "You have to get the license; however, inspectors do not verify the requirement on site. You can play some tricks on the requirements".[63]

Third, respondents reported the potential for sanction, with some perceiving a high likelihood of punishment: "Once you forget to disinfect, you will be found out [by the manager] and be fined".[64] "If the boss saw we do not wash [or hands] after smoking, we will be fined. Someone was fined".[65] In contrast, some respondents reported a low likelihood of sanctions: "No one has been fined for long nails".[66] "If the manager or boss find that you do not disinfect, you may be fined".[67]

Furthermore, the source of deterrence might have influenced sanction certainty. For instance, one respondent claimed, in terms of counterfeit *Fapiao* receipts, if customers complain only to the tax department and tax department was the only source of deterrence, he would not face sanctions, because "they [tax department] know we use fake formal receipts. However, they won't come to fine us".[68] Yet if customers complained to the police about counterfeit receipts, he might face sanctions. In addition, sanction certainty from the same deterrence source might have differed at different times. For instance, the likelihood of sanctions related to counterfeit formal receipts increased during special campaigns about counterfeit receipts,

---

[58]Interview with SD on November 6, 2013.

[59]Interview with SL on November 2, 2013.

[60]Interview with SJ on October 12, 2013.

[61]Interview with TF on April 13, 2013.

[62]Interview with TS on May 29, 2013.

[63]Interview with NM on May 26, 2011.

[64]Interview with SD on November 6, 2013.

[65]Interview with TX on May 29, 2013.

[66]Interview with TF on April 13, 2013.

[67]Interview with TC on August 19, 2013.

[68]Interview with NM on May 26, 2011.

Table 8.7 Frequency of perceived obligation to obey the law

	Frequency	Percentage
Negative	24	72.7
Positive	9	27.3
Total	33	100

but there would be no trouble at other times.[69] Similarly, they might have been sanctioned for noncompliance with disinfection regulations during specific inspections targeting disinfection, but they would have no trouble at other times. Moreover, higher-ranking enforcers might have caused difficulties about regulations that were overlooked during everyday inspections.

Fourth, respondents reported varying severity of sanctions. Respondents reported minor sanctions related to counterfeit *Fapiao* receipts and disinfection practices: "People may complain to the tax bureau [about counterfeit receipts], and restaurant may be fined. But the fine is not high. It is just about several hundred. I thought it would be several thousand".[70] "The head or manager will find and point out. Workers who do not disinfect for several times will be asked to entertain other workers in a meeting. Usually we are not really fined because they understand that our salary is low".[71] Others reported severe sanction: "If customers get disease from the tableware, how can you be responsible for that?" [disinfection].[72] The most severe sanction may have been exclusion from the restaurant, with numerous respondents indicating that they viewed health certificates as a type of work permit without which they cannot work in certain restaurants.[73]

8.6.2   Perceived Obligation to Obey the Law

POOL was the only variable counted based on respondents rather than in relation to each of the behaviors studied, because it addresses respondents' general perceptions of all compliance behaviors. Thirty-three people answered the question related to perceived obligation to obey the law,[74] with 24 (72.7%) indicating a negative attitude (see Table 8.7). Thus, they did not agree to comply with the law regardless of what the law is, whether it is enforced or not, and whatever the cost.

These 24 respondents raised several significant reasons for disagreeing with the POOL statement. The most common reason mentioned related to the nature of the

---

[69] Ibid.

[70] Interview with LB on May 10, 2012.

[71] Interview with SJ on November 1, 2013.

[72] Interview with SH on October 9, 2013.

[73] For instance responses of NW.4.9.2013, SD.6.11.2013, SH.20.10.2013, SJU.3.11.2013, SJA.1.11.2013, SZ.28.10.2013, and SL.4.11.2013.

[74] The rest of two people were not asked due to time limits and emergency departure.

law. Eight respondents claimed they would not comply with an unreasonable law. For instance, "It is OK to comply with the right law, but if the law is not right, I will not comply with it",[75] and "If the law is perceived as not reasonable, we cannot comply blindly".[76] One respondents indicated that she "may not always agree, because the law may not be justice".[77]

The second reason for disagreeing with the statement related to the second precondition, that is, enforcement. Seven respondents indicated that they might not or would not comply if there were a lack of enforcement: "So I may not obey or may obey if there is no one to enforce the law".[78] One respondent mentioned the behavior of others: "If there is no enforcement or there is no one to inspect on it, people will not do it".[79] Another respondent explained that he would not comply if there is no enforcement and the consequences of his actions were insignificant:

> "If there is no enforcement, I may not comply if what I do does not have much harm. What I have done is just small things and may not harm to others. The big restaurants will have bigger harm. Even though what I have done is essentially the same [violation] as that of big restaurants, it won't harm much to society. So I still dare to do it.[80]

The third reason for disagreement focused on the third precondition, that is, the cost of compliance. Six respondents indicated that they would not comply if the cost were too high. One indicated that he would not comply at all, "There is no need to comply with the law that costs too much. I will surely not comply with it".[81] Another mentioned partial compliance that aligns with the resources available: "If it cost too much, I will do what I can and leave other aside".[82] One participant claimed "profit is the core for people's behaviors".[83] A respondent even mentioned the cost–benefit calculation: "If compliance with the law is expensive, I will see how much benefit I will get. If what I get is less than what I pay, it is not [cost efficient] to comply with".[84]

The fourth reason, which was offered without prompting from the interviewer, was descriptive social norms. Two respondents indicated that they would comply only if the majority complied: "We have to obey, at least conceptually. However, in practice, I'm not sure. If majority of people do not comply, I will not comply. Minority should keep pace with majority".[85] "I do not fully agree. But if others comply, I will comply".[86]

---

[75] Interview with NM on September 16, 2013.

[76] Interview with SB on November 1, 2013.

[77] Interview with SHA on October 20, 2013.

[78] Interview with SD on November 6, 2013.

[79] Interview with SJ on November 1, 2013.

[80] Interview with NM on May 26, 2013.

[81] Interview with NM on September 16, 2013.

[82] Interview with ND on September 22, 2013.

[83] Interview with SH on October 9, 2013.

[84] Interview with NM on September 5, 2013.

[85] Interview with SM on November 6, 2013.

[86] Interview with SJ on November 3, 2013.

The fifth reason, raised by a more educated respondent, related to the politics of law. The respondent said, "I do not agree. It is impossible for people in China, because law is not a natural rule and you have to obey it. It is a tool for the party to govern people".[87]

Although some respondents raised a single reason for disagreeing with the POOL statement, others combined two or three. Several respondents claimed that they would not comply with the law if they did not agree with it or felt it was unreasonable, or if they felt the cost was too high.[88] Another participant indicated that he would not comply if the law was unethical and if there was no enforcement.[89]

Furthermore, several respondents had complex attitudes toward the variable. Some claimed to respect the law or legislative authority, but at the same time indicated that they would not comply with the law. For example, one respondent stated, "[the law] has been made from upper level leader, you have to obey," but also "I may not obey or may obey if there is no one to enforce the law. If I have capacity, I will obey. If I do not have, I may not obey".[90] Similarly, a respondent initially stated, "We have to comply with it before it is modified even though we do not agree with the law, since we are just citizen." However, the person followed up with.

> If there is no enforcement, I may not comply if what I do does not have much harm. What I have done is just small things and may not harm to others. The big restaurants will have bigger harm. Even though what I have done is essentially the same (violation) as that of big restaurants, it won't harm much to society. So I still dare to do it. However, if I know that I may be fined a lot of money or put in jail, I will not do it. If compliance with the law is expensive, I will see how much benefit I will get. If what I get is less than what I pay, it is not cost-efficient to comply with.[91]

Nine interviewees indicated a positive attitude, agreeing with the statement that once there is a law people should comply with it, regardless of the three preconditions. The most common reasons supplied included believing that everything the law regulates is reasonable and necessary and that no enforcement is impossible. Responses included, "Agree. It is just like the coin having two sides. What the law regulate is surely necessary once it has become a law. We have to obey",[92] and "Agree. There is no unreasonable law. It is not possible there is no enforcement".[93] One agreed, and she mentioned her illiteracy and consequent lack of knowledge about the law:

> I agree. We just ordinary people, do not know much about law. They ask to do something, I will do something. If you object, you have to have reasons. I know nothing. So, once they have regulation, I just obey.[94]

---

[87] Interview with TF on April 16, 2013.

[88] See response of TX.28.9.2013, TF.25.9.2013, and NM.16.9.2013.

[89] Interview with NL on September 11, 2013.

[90] Interview with SD on November 6, 2013.

[91] Interview with NM on September 5, 2013.

[92] Interview with SJ on October 12, 2013.

[93] Interview with TN on April 16, 2013.

[94] Interview with LB on May 10, 2012.

These reasons indicate that respondents' bases for agreement were not solid or strong and could be easily shaken. Agreement based on such reasons actually differs from Tyler's concept of "perceived obligation to obey the law" or "legitimacy" (Tyler 1990). Perceived obligation to obey the law rests on a presumption that citizens view the legal authority with which they are dealing having a legitimate right to dictate their behavior, and a conception of the obligation to obey any commands an authority issues. The supposition that the law is reasonable and enforced adds preconditions for such obligation. The claim of illiteracy is also a precondition. One may infer that once the illiterate person becomes literate and can argue against the law, the person's perception of "perceived obligation to obey" will change.

Only one response aligned with Tyler's argument of POOL (Tyler 1990): "Agree. Once the law is made, people should comply with it".[95] Another response revealed a perception that aligned with "normative duty to obey" proposed by Winter and May (2001) and May (2005), as the respondent noted that although she might not accept the law emotionally, she would comply with the law in action, and that failure to comply would leave her feeling despondent:

> I agree. I prefer to comply with the law in action even though I may not agree with the law. If I do not comply, I will feel sad. Even I should pay much, I will comply because those rules benefit in the long run. I live in this society, and should comply with rules for this society and think in a long run. I know there must someone absolutely will not comply, however, that is their value, not mine.[96]

8.6.3 Descriptive Social Norms

For the descriptive social norms variable, more categories than binary responses were revealed. Four kinds of responses emerged for how the regulated perceived descriptive norms related to the behaviors discussed. The first, "negative," describes 25 responses (23.1%) and refers to the actions the regulated saw most others perform to avoid compliance with the behaviors discussed. The second, "unsure," describes 18 responses (16.7%) and includes responses such as, "Some do, some do not," "I do not know," and "I do not care about that." The third, "positive," describes 47 responses (43.5%) and refers to the action the regulated saw others taking to engage in the behaviors discussed. The fourth, "positive self but negative others," which accounts for 18 responses (16.7%), refers to the responses that indicated that workers in the respondents' restaurants performed the action, but workers in other restaurants might not, and that the respondents themselves performed the action but did not know whether others did. For example, "Every worker in this restaurant washing glasses and dishware will use disinfection fluid. However, not all restaurants disinfect tableware".[97]

---

[95] Interview with SJ on November 4, 2013.

[96] Interview with TP on August 9, 2013.

[97] Interview with SJ on October 12, 2013.

Table 8.8 Frequency of descriptive norms

	Frequency	Percentage
Negative	25	23.1
Unsure	18	16.7
Positive	47	43.5
Positive self but negative others	18	16.7
Total	108	100.0

The fourth kind of response resonates with the research conducted by Gino et al. (2009) and Wenzel (2005) that showed that people clearly differentiate between "what our group does" and "what other groups do" when forming descriptive norms. For instance, interviewees from restaurants that tended to comply with the behaviors discussed were more inclined to claim such differentiation, particularly in relation to health certificates and disinfection. Many interviewees from S restaurant and the Idealistic restaurant understood that workers in large restaurants have health certificates or disinfect dishware, while the same conditions often were not met in small restaurants.[98]

Moreover, it emerged that the descriptive norms the regulated highlighted were delicate and nuanced. The regulated not only saw what others did but also how others did it. Compliance with a legal requirement involves many small behaviors. For instance, one of requirements for complying with the legal requirement of a fire license is to buy enough fire extinguishers. When asked what they thought other restaurants did when applying for their fire licenses, the owner of the Profit-Maximizing restaurant and the owner of L restaurant both indicated that other restaurants should have fire licenses, although they might not have the required number of fire extinguishers.[99] The same view applied to other opening licenses: "Most restaurants have business license but may make trick on the requirements".[100] "Other restaurants just send the fake water to do examination. Some restaurants just give *Hongbao* and get the [drainage] license".[101] In addition, regarding health certificates, one interviewee answered, "Every restaurant will have health certificate. The question is whether it is real or fake".[102]

---

[98] Although the Idealistic restaurant was classified as a small restaurant in this study, the restaurant's employees may not have shared this view. For example, one server argued that it was a medium restaurant.

[99] Interview with LB on May 10, 2013, and interview with NM on May 26, 2011.

[100] Interview with NM on May 26, 2011.

[101] Interview with TF on April 17, 2013.

[102] Interview with NL on September 11, 2013.

Table 8.9 Frequency of personal norms

	Frequency	Percentage
Negative	37	34.3
Positive some while negative some	14	13.0
Positive	57	52.8
Total	108	100.0

8.6.4 Personal Norms

Of the 108 responses, 57 responses (about 52.8%) indicated positive personal norms related to the behavior discussed, 37 responses (about 34.3%) indicated negative personal norms, and 14 responses (about 13%) view the behaviors as positive in some aspects but negative in others (Table 8.9).

Some with positive personal norms mentioned the benefit that aligned with the aims of those legal norms, such as preventing transmission of disease and ensuring food safety. For example, "It [disinfection] is necessary. Lots of people use the same tableware. We do not know who have infectious disease".[103] "We should cut nails short in order to safeguard sanitation and health".[104] "It [health certificate] is important for working in restaurant, to make sure that you do not have infectious diseases".[105] "Having health certificate is responsible for the safety of others. If you are not healthy or have infectious disease, you may transmit to other people".[106]

Some positive responses focused on the usefulness of these behaviors, including the benefits in certain work and the usefulness to themselves or the restaurant, and their contribution to decreasing customer complaints. Reasons mentioned included protecting the reputation of the restaurant, increasing customer satisfaction, personal convenience, passing inspections, and increasing employability: "I think it [health certificate] is important. If customers get sick after eating at the restaurant, it will harm the reputation of the restaurant".[107] "It [disinfection] is necessary. Customers will feel clean and good".[108] "It is not convenient to have long nails [cutting nails]".[109] "If I will stay long in restaurant, I think I should get one. So you can show to the one who come to check".[110] "People have disease will not be able to work in restaurant [health certificate]".[111]

Some positive responses noted that performing the behavior was a good habit or personal preference, mainly in reference to washing hands and cutting nails: "I

---

[103]Interview with SD on November 6, 2013.

[104]Interview with SDD on October 29, 2013.

[105]Interview with SH on October 20, 2013.

[106]Interview with SJ on November 3, 2013.

[107]Interview with SJ on November 1, 2013.

[108]Interview with SH on October 9, 2013.

[109]Interview with SJ on October 12, 2013.

[110]Interview with NL on August 20, 2013.

[111]Interview with SD on November 6, 2013.

think it is not a good habit to have long nails".[112] "I do not like long nails".[113] "It becomes a habit. I wash my hands before processing the food and after touching somewhere".[114]

Few responses addressed the necessity of the rule or behavior for or in the restaurant: "It [health certificate] is necessary. It is the rule for the whole catering industry".[115] "Workers in restaurant cannot have long nails. This is the basic norm in catering industry. Since you have chosen to work in restaurants, you have to respect the basic norm of this industry".[116]

Of fourteen responses that views behaviors positive in some aspects but negative in others, some perceived the reasonability of or moral necessity for aspects of particular behaviors but at the same time, showed negative perceptions of other aspects of the behavior. For example, some felt the required behavior was generally necessary, yet accepted exceptions for not satisfying the requirement, such as postponing compliance and excluding individuals with certain characteristics:

> Health certificate is a certificate that restaurants require. If someone has disease, he/she cannot stay in restaurant anymore, especially the kitchen. However, people also can work in restaurant without health certificate because they know they are healthy. If they have serious disease, they surely know and will accept treatment. Whether it is a must condition depends on the boss. When to get health certificate is not sure. It is better to get immediately when you start work in restaurant. But it is OK that you get after a period because you may not be adaptable for the work environment and resign soon.[117]

Several respondents agreed with the aims of the required behaviors but had negative attitudes toward the secondary requirements related to these behaviors, such as renewing health certificates annually, completing a disinfection log, and having a specific number of basins. For instance,

> It is necessary to get health certificate to demonstrate that I'm healthy. I think the rule of health certificate is reasonable because restaurant workers have to be healthy when you cook and serve for customers. However, I don't think it is necessary to renew the certificate every year. I know my body. If I really get disease, I won't do this work in restaurant.[118]

Similarly, "Disinfection is very important to prevent disease transmission, but the disinfection log is unnecessary",[119] and "I think I should get all required licenses. However, some regulation is too rigid and not flexible. I think some [washing basins] are not necessary [to obtain a catering services license]".[120]

---

[112]Interview with SZ on October 28, 2013.

[113]Interview with SH on October 20, 2013, and Interview with NY on September 2, 2013.

[114]Interview with SB on November 1, 2013.

[115]Interview with SJ on October 12, 2013.

[116]Interview with SL on November 2, 2013.

[117]Interview with TY on May 23, 2013.

[118]Interview with TL on May 23, 2012.

[119]Interview with TF on April 16, 2013.

[120]Interview with TF on April 16, 2013.

Other respondents were positive about the value of the required behaviors, but suspected that the behaviors were simply a formality that could not realize the aims they serve:

> Workers in restaurant must have health certificate. Sanitation is the most important thing for catering industry. How can you provide sanitation to customers if you do not satisfy the sanitation requirements? However, I feel health certificate is just a kind of form now. You do not have feedback about your health condition. It may be just a form to cope with the inspections.[121]

or:

> I think it is important. If customers get sick after eating at the restaurant, it will harm the reputation of the restaurant. However, it cannot fully reflect people's health condition since the items it checks is limited.[122]

The remaining 37 responses with negative personal norms toward the behaviors discussed indicated perceptions falling under several categories. Some denied the possible positive influence of those behaviors. For instance, disinfection was seen as unnecessary, as "dishware is usually washed clean".[123] Likewise, disinfection of serving plate was viewed as unnecessary because this type of dishware is not exposed to customers' mouths.[124] Long nails were acceptable because "they are clean".[125] Some respondents misunderstood the value of the behaviors, for example, by viewing trimmed nails as a service requirements that was unnecessary in small restaurants,[126] Some denied the moral value of those behaviors: "[liquor and environmental licenses are] just about money",[127] "fake formal receipts is much cheaper",[128] or "[washing hands] is troublesome".[129] Several interviewees denied the usefulness of the behavior. For example, in relation to health certificates, they stated, "I feel there is no use for health certificate sometime",[130] and it "is just a boring form," as "they do not really check for you seriously. I guess they never test the blood they draw from us. You just pay the fee and they give you the certificate".[131] Some were negative because they thought it impossible to perform those behaviors, such as disinfection[132] and handwashing.[133] Finally, some had a negative view of the behavior because they felt

---

[121]Interview with SH on October 9, 2013.

[122]Interview with SJ on November 1, 2013.

[123]Interview with NL on September 11, 2013.

[124]Interview with NM on September 16, 2013 and Interview with TY on May 23, 2013.

[125]Interview with NM on September 16, 2013.

[126]Interview with NM on August 21, 2013.

[127]Interview with NM on September 5, 2013.

[128]Interview with NM on May 26, 2011.

[129]Interview with SL on November 4, 2013.

[130]Interview with TX on May 29, 2013.

[131]Interview with SB on November 1, 2013.

[132]Interview with LB on May 10, 2012.

[133]Interview with SH on October 9, 2013.

Table 8.10 Frequency of recognition of legal requirements in trichotomy

	Frequency	Percentage
Negative	84	77.8
Guess positive	19	17.6
Positive	5	4.6
Total	108	100.0

it was none of their business and it did not apply to them, as people were permitted to work in restaurants without health certificates.[134]

8.6.5   Capacity

8.6.5.1   Recognition of Legal Requirements

Questioning interviewees about the recognition of legal requirements was somewhat challenging, as interviewees were likely to provide biased answers or to guess the correct answer. Consequently, this topic was addressed toward the end of interviews, once interviewees were somewhat familiar with the topic of law following the discussion of POOL. I employed additional probing questions to verify the information collected, specifically asking whether interviewees were certain the behavior discussed was a law and how they learned about it. A surprising number of interviewees indicated that they did not know whether behaviors were laws and that behaviors were not law, that they should not be laws, or that they thought they were not laws. Only five responses indicate that the interviewees clearly knew that the behaviors discussed were regulated by law, while 84 responses denied they were legal norms, and 19 showed that interviewees thought the behaviors might or should be regulated by laws but were uncertain.

When interviewees guessed that a behavior was a law but were uncertain, several responses related to descriptive norms. For example, regarding health certificates, interviewees said the behavior is probably regulated by law "since all workers in catering industry should have health certificate"[135] and "since so many restaurant have such requirement".[136] Another reason was related to perceived government regulation, that is, "because it is regulated by FDA",[137] and "because [obtaining opening licenses and using formal receipts is] something people have to do".[138]

---

[134]Interview with NY on September 2, 2013, and interview with NM on September 16, 2013.

[135]Interview with SH on October 9, 2013.

[136]Interview with SD on October 29, 2013.

[137]Interview with SY on October 30, 2013.

[138]Interview with NM on May 26, 2011.

Table 8.11 Frequency of recognition of legal requirements in dichotomy

	Frequency	Percentage
Negative	103	95.4
Positive	5	4.6
Total	108	100.0

Because the responses of "guess positive" show that respondents did not know the legal norms, they were combined with "negative" to indicate a lack of explicit legal knowledge of the written legal norms (see Table 8.11).

Only five of 108 responses showed that the interviewees knew the law regulates particular behaviors. Therefore, the majority of interviewees were unaware that the law regulated their work and that their behaviors were subject to various legal norms. Thus, ignorance of the law was a common phenomenon among restaurant workers and owners.

Moreover, several interviewees displayed an interesting understanding about what violation of the law is. For instance, the owner of the Profit-Maximizing restaurant understood his noncompliance with the requirements discussed as a different kind of violation. He argued,

> I do not violate the law (*Fanfa*,[139] 犯法). I understand the law as something that if you violate, you may be put in jail, or they will fine you and you cannot take discount. What I have done may be called *Weifa* (违法) at most, and I can bargain about the amount of fine…*Fanfa* must be criminal case and the one who violate will be imprisoned, while *Weifa* is to pay fine and the one who violate will not be imprisoned.[140]

Because he indicated that he understood that disinfection is regulated by a law, he was asked to explain how he understood disinfection after clarifying his perception of the difference between *Fanfa* and *Weifa*. He replied, "If we have to comply with the law, there should be someone to monitor us."[141] From this, it appears he closely associated different violations with different kinds of enforcement. What he called *Fanfa* in his perception was linked with severe and inflexible sanctions and rigorous monitoring. If the sanction can be negotiated and the monitoring is slack, he understood violations as *Weifa*, which he understood as not violating the law.

A waitress in the Profit-Maximizing restaurant did not differentiate *Weifa* from *Fanfa*, but she understood *Weifa* differently:

---

[139]The words "*Fanfa*" and "*Weifa*" are used interchangeably in China, with definitions varying from one person to the next due to the nuanced and ambiguous nature of the words. This has caused confusion not only for laypersons but also for law students and professionals. Some claim that they are the same, and that "*Weifa*" is the formal term and "*Fanfa*" is the informal term. Some claim that "*Fanfa*" refers to the violation of criminal law, while "*Weifa*" includes all kinds of violation of law. Others believe the reverse is true and that "*Fanfa*" includes "*Weifa*" and crime. Some argue that "*Fanfa*" refers to crime especially, while "*Weifa*" refers to less significant behaviors.

[140]Interview with the owner of the Profit-Maximizing restaurant on September 5, 2013.

[141]Ibid.

Even though you do not do what the law asks, you do not violate the law (*Weifa*) if no one enforce it and do inspection on it... You will violate the law (*Weifa*) if you harm someone or something. Once you do not injure others, you do not violate the law.[142]

Thus, "injuring someone" was an important factor in her understanding of violating the law, as was monitoring. Her response to whether she viewed having a health certificate as law further revealed this understanding: "I do not know in fact. However I think it may belong to a law, because if it is not a law, the FDA does not need to do inspection on it."[143] Another waitress in the Profit-Maximizing restaurant shared a similar perception that injuring someone is an important indicator when considering whether one's behavior is violation of law. She claimed, "There is no relation between my work and the law, because I do not *Fanfa*."[144] She provided two examples of what *Fanfa* referred to—fighting and drug trafficking.

Overall, the results show that interviewees were generally ignorant of the law.

8.6.5.2   Practical Constraints

Practical constraints include time, money, preference, or fear that impede people from engaging in certain behavior. If interviewees named perceived constraints, the response was coded as positive. Otherwise, they were coded as negative. For instance, when talking about opening licenses, the owner of the Profit-Maximizing restaurant often claimed that compliance with regulations affected the profitability of the business, which indicated that money was an important consideration and constraint to him. Therefore, this answer was coded as a positive response in terms of practical constraints. One interviewee stated that she hated to undergo the health check because she was afraid having blood drawn. Consequently, the practical constraint for her is fear, and her response was coded as positive.

The results show that 71 responses (65.7%) denied the existence of practical constraints preventing the behaviors discussed, while 37 responses (34.3%) indicated some practical constraints. Practical constraints they identified included "cost money"[145] (opening licenses, formal receipts), "troublesome" (disinfection,[146] washing hands[147]), "do not have time"[148] (health certificate), against personal preference, that is, "I like long nails"[149] (nail cutting), and fear, that is, "I hate to draw blood"[150] (health certificate).

---

[142] Interview with Wang on September 4, 2013.

[143] Ibid.

[144] Interview with Mei on September 5, 2013.

[145] See interview with NM on September 5, 2013, and interview with LB on May 10, 2012.

[146] Ibid.

[147] See interview with SH on October 9, 2013, and interview with SL on November 4, 2013.

[148] See interview with TF on April 16, 2013.

[149] See interview with NW on September 4 2013, interview with SJA on November 1, 2013, interview with SD on November 6 2013, and interview with NL on September 11, 2013.

[150] Interview with TH on April 13 2013.

Table 8.12 Frequency of practical constraints		Frequency	Percentage
	Negative	71	65.7
	Positive	37	34.3
	Total	108	100.0

8.7 Association Analysis of Compliance Behaviors and Influential Variables

This section explores the association between the variables discussed in the previous sections of this chapter and compliance behaviors (see Table 8.13). The results show that personal norms, plural subjective deterrence and descriptive norms are positively associated with compliance behavior, and the variable of practical constraints has weak and negative association with compliance.

As for personal norms, most responses related to negative personal norms indicated violation behaviors (86.5%, n = 32). Responses that stated positive personal norms were accompanied with a higher percentage of compliance behaviors (66.7%, n = 38). In addition, 64.3% of responses (n = 9) that indicated neither overwhelmingly negative nor overwhelmingly positive personal norms (or a combination of

Table 8.13 Cross Tabulation of Compliance Behaviors and Variables

		Compliance behaviors (percentage within variables)	
		Violation	Compliance
Personal norms	Negative	32 (86.5%)	5 (13.5%)
	Negative some while positive some	5 (35.7%)	9 (64.3%)
	Positive	19 (33.3%)	38 (66.7%)
Descriptive norms	Negative	25 (100.0%)	0 (0.0%)
	Not sure	13 (72.2%)	5 (27.8%)
	Positive	16 (34.0%)	31 (66.0%)
	Positive us while negative others	2 (11.1%)	16 (88.9%)
Plural subjective deterrence	Negative	33 (80.5%)	8 (19.5%)
	Positive	23 (34.3%)	44 (65.7%)
POOL	Negative	38 (52.1%)	35 (47.9%)
	Positive	17 (56.7%)	13 (43.3%)
Practical constraints	Negative	35 (49.3%)	36 (50.7%)
	Positive	21 (56.8%)	16 (43.2%)
Recognition of legal requirements	Negative	52 (50.5%)	51 (49.5%)
	Positive	4 (80.0%)	1 (20.0%)

negative and postive norms) showed compliance behaviors. The data indicates an associative trend where the more positive personal norms are displayed, the more compliance behaviors are revealed by the responses.

An obvious association between plural subjective deterrence and compliance behaviors exists. The majority of responses with negative plural subjective deterrence indicated violation behaviors (80.5%, n = 33), while the majority of responses with positive plural subjective deterrence indicated compliance behaviors (65.7%, n = 44).

Association between descriptive norms and compliance behavior is also apparent. Descriptive norms were divided into four categories that show an ordinal order, with "positive self but negative others" being more positive than "positive," "positive" being more positive than "not sure," and so on. All responses (100%, n = 25) stating negative descriptive norms indicate violation behaviors, and the majority of responses stating descriptive norms as "not sure" also indicate violation behaviors (72.2%, n = 13). The majority of responses stating positive descriptive norms indicate compliance behaviors (66.0%, n = 31), while a higher percentage of responses stating descriptive norms with higher levels of "positive self but negative others" indicate a higher percentage of compliance behaviors (88.9%, n = 16).

There seems to be a negative association between practical constraints and compliance behaviors that aligns with the theoretical prediction. Nevertheless, the association looks weak. Slightly more than half of responses (50.7%, n = 36) stating negative practical constraints indicate compliance behaviors, while 56.8% (n = 21) stating positive practical constraints indicate violation behavior. Fewer, but still a considerable number of responses stating negative practical constraints also indicate violation behaviors (49.3%, n = 35), and fewer, but still a large percentage of responses stating positive practical constraints indicate compliance behavior (43.2%, n = 16).

It seems that the variable of POOL has no association with compliance behaviors. Over half of responses stating negative POOL (52.1%, n = 38) indicate violation behaviors, while slightly more responses stating positive POOL (56.7%, n = 17) also indicate violation behaviors. Association between recognition of whether it is a law and compliance behavior also does not seem to exist. The majority of responses with positive recognition of whether it is a law (80%, n = 4) indicate violation behaviors, while more than half of responses stating negative recognition (50.5%, n = 52) also indicate violation behaviors.

Consequently, personal norms, descriptive norms, and plural subjective deterrence are positively associated with compliance behaviors, as the theories proposed. The practical constraints variable has a weak negative association with compliance behavior. However, POOL and recognition of legal requirements do not show such association with compliance. For POOL, it may be understood that the precondition of POOL does not exist here, as the majority of interviewees did not know the behaviors discussed are regulated by laws (95.4%, n = 103). It is impossible for people to engage in compliance behaviors out of their perceived obligation to obey the law when they do not actually know what is required is a law. For the variable of recognition of legal requirements, it seems most individuals did not recognize that they are laws. Only 4.6% of responses (n = 5) were positive in recognition, but the compliance rate was as high as 48.1%. That implies people may engage in compliance behavior although they do not know it is legally regulated. Therefore, in practice, knowing the law may be not a precondition of compliance as some scholars have argued (Kim 1999). Nevertheless, because the sample is not representative, statistical testing of these associations is not applicable, so these association trends are simply trends that require further testing in larger representative samples using formal statistical methods.

8.8 Comparison Between Subjective Self-Explanation and Variable Association Analysis

In this section, interviewees' subjective explanations for their behaviors are compared to the findings of the variable association analysis of the five pre-established variables and compliance behaviors to highlight the differences between the two methods of explanation.

Both analyses showed that plural subjective deterrence played a role in compliance behavior. This is clear from the variable association analysis and from interviewees' explanations of their behavior. The subjective self-explanation revealed that although some individuals ascribed their compliance behaviors to government regulation or strict government enforcement, none of them spontaneously mentioned potential sanctions from government enforcement. Similarly, when considering individuals' perceptions of the variable of plural subjective deterrence, among those who identified positive deterrence from government enforcement, only a few mentioned the possibility and certainty of sanctions from the government, and only one provided the possible sanction amount (counterfeit formal receipts[151]). Many others reported detection possibility without mentioning sanctions. Thus, it seems individuals may perceive positive subjective deterrence and engage in compliance behaviors based on such positive subjective deterrence when they simply acknowledge the possibility of deterrence. This finding resonates with Van Rooij's finding of a high perception of risk related to violating the law existing among lawyers, even when lawyers had vague notions not just of what sanctions could be expected but also of the probability of discovery (Van Rooij 2016). It seems subjective deterrence cannot be understood merely by studying detection probability and sanction severity. What accounts for the subjective deterrence in the perceptions of the regulated individuals and the variable of plural subjective deterrence needs to be further studied.

For other variables, less convergence occurred between the variable association analysis and the subjective self-explanations of the behavior. For example, the findings for personal norms and perceived descriptive norms differ. In the association analyses, respondents' compliance behavior is clearly linked to these two types of norms, while in the subjective explanation of their behavior only a few respondents mention these norms. Furthermore, the descriptive norm has an obvious

---

[151] See interview with LB on May 10 2012.

association with compliance behaviors in the variable association analysis, but in the self-explanations, it is rarely mentioned to explain violation behaviors. Only two violation behaviors were subjectively ascribed to negative descriptive norms, and none of the compliance behaviors was subjectively related to positive descriptive norms. This could be because descriptive norms influence people's behaviors mainly unconsciously, as Cialdini (2007) argued. Therefore, interviewees could not consciously ascribe their behaviors to descriptive norms. However, the association analysis showed that descriptive norms is a strong influential variable for compliance behaviors and that it deserves more attention in compliance research.

Another difference between the two analyses is that the subjective explanation analysis revealed two additional variables, namely not being responsible and operational benefits.

8.9   Conclusion

It is the individual that finally engages in compliance behaviors. In this chapter, the focus was on the individual level. Individual compliance behaviors were discussed in light of influential variables identified in the literature, with some being influenced by the regulatory and organizational levels. In addition, individuals were asked to provide their subjective self-explanations of their behaviors. The results show descriptive norms, personal norms, and plural subjective deterrence are the variables most associated with compliance behaviors. Individuals' recognition of the legal requirements in terms of whether they knew it is law was extremely limited and did not show association with compliance behaviors. This resonates with Yan's research on Chinese pesticide compliance (Yan 2014), specifically that the capacity of knowing the law is not necessarily a condition for compliance in China, and as shown more generally in studies in other contexts (Kim 1999). Additionally, the variable of practical constraints seems negatively and weakly associated with compliance behaviors.

Most individuals had a negative attitude toward the variable of POOL, and it is not associated with compliance behaviors. This implies that POOL may be not a suitable variable for explaining compliance behaviors in this context. First, as shown by the variable of recognition of the law, most individuals did not know that the required behaviors are regulated by laws. Hence, whether or not they engaged in the required behaviors was not a matter of law for them, and POOL is not suitable for explaining compliance behaviors here. Second, the majority of individuals provided negative responses related to POOL, which means they generally lacked of a sense of normative duty to obey the law. The variable of POOL cannot differentiate the regulated actors efficiently, so it may not be able to explain their behaviors.

In addition to the variables identified in the literature, perception of not being responsible appeared as a notable variable influencing compliance behaviors. It appeared not only in the general subjective explanation of violation but also as a kind of negative personal norm. In other words, the sense of not being responsible reflects the perception of disengagement with the required behaviors or the regulatory system. Individuals who had such perception did not situate themselves in the regulatory system and did not see that they had any relationship with those required behaviors. It explains violation behaviors where several factors with contradictive influences appear at the same time.

For instance, it seems the waitress Lu from the Profit-Maximizing restaurant explained her violation behavior of not cutting nails by referring to negative deterrence. She said, "The boss is not strict on such thing," and "Small restaurants do not pay attention to such things." It seems as though negative deterrence is the reason for her violation behavior. However, she at the same time revealed positive personal norms toward short nails, saying, "One will look clean if having short nails," and "Customers will feel uncomfortable if they see waitresses having long nails." Moreover, she indicated that she also knew that having short nails was a requirement in restaurants, that is, "Everyone working in restaurants knows that generally speaking they are not allowed to have long nails. It is written in the rules which hangs on the wall." She also indicated that she would cut her nails short if she went to a job interview with a big restaurant. It seems that positive personal norms and positive recognition of legal requirements, and maybe also positive deterrence from the regulator, did not motivate her into compliance. Because negative deterrence from restaurant, positive personal norms, and positive recognition of legal requirements, and maybe also positive deterrence from the regulator, exist at the same time, her behavior becomes difficult to explain. Nevertheless, it can be explained by referring to the variable of not being responsible—Lu thought she was not the one who was responsible for the legal requirement of cutting nails. From her perspective, restaurant owners are the ones who are responsible for complying with the requirement. If restaurant owners want to comply with the requirements, they will ask employees to cut their nails and enforce this. At that time, she will comply. Otherwise, it is not her business to consider that requirement, never mind to comply with it. Not being responsible combined with negative deterrence from the restaurant resulted in her violation behavior. The same situation also existed regarding requirements of health certificates and disinfection. This finding suggests that not being responsible as a factor influencing compliance requires additional discussion.

Despite the findings discussed above, several important points should be reiterated. As noted in Part A of this book and in the section on coding compliance behavior in this chapter, real compliance behaviors are simplified and integrated to fit the dichotomy of compliance and violation. What is coded as compliance or violation actually encompasses a series of substantial behaviors. Usually, not all of the subset behaviors are compliance or violation. Instead, what is common is that some of them are compliance, while some are violation. The strictest classification was followed here, and the series of behaviors was coded as violation once one subset behavior was violation. If other researchers do not follow this method to collect data but rely on government data or self-reporting based on one time point or one aspect of behavior, the compliance data they collect will differ and will show a higher level of compliance. As a result, the findings from this kind of analysis may be more inclined to reveal reasons for violation, as many compliance factors are overlooked.

Moreover, I does not claim that the data used here was representative of the general population, as one may easily find that restaurants, as well as individuals, were purposefully selected. Yet although the findings of the variable analysis in this book cannot be generalized to a larger population and needs to be examined in subsequent studies based on representative samples, the method used to define and operationalize variables can be used in future research, as they closely align with their function in compliance behavior.

References

Ajzen, I. 1991. The Theory of Planned Behavior. *Organizational Behavior and Human Decision Processes* 55: 179–211.

Becker, Gary S. 1968. Crime and Punishment, an Economic Approach. *Journal of Political Economy* 76: 169–217.

Blanthorne, C., and S. Kaplan. 2008. An Egocentric Model of the Relations among the Opportunity to Underreport, Social Norms, Ethical Beliefs, and Underreporting Behavior. *Accounting, Organizations and Society* 33 (7/8): 684–703.

Bobek, Donna D., and R. Hatfield. 2003. An Investigation of the Theory of Planned Behavior and the Role of Moral Obligation in Tax Compliance. *Behavioral Research in Accounting* 15: 13–38.

Bobek, Donna D., Amy M. Hageman, and Charles F. Kelliher. 2011. The Social Norms of Tax Compliance: Scale Development, Social Desirability and Presentation Effects. *Advances in Accounting Behavioral Research* 15: 37–66.

Bobek, Donna D., Amy M. Hageman, and Charles F. Kelliher. 2013. Analyzing the Role of Social Norms in Tax Compliance Behavior. *Journal of Business Ethics* 115: 451–468.

Braithwaite, Valerie. 2003. "Dancing with Tax Authorities: Motivational Postures and Non-Compliant Actions." In Valerie Braithwaite (Ed.) *Taxing Democracy: Understanding Tax Avoidance and Evasion* (pp. 15–39). Ashgate.

Braithwaite, Valerie, John Braithwaite, Diane Gibson, and Toni Makkai. 1994. Regulatory Styles Motivational Postures and Nursing Home Compliance. *Law and Policy* 16 (4): 363–394.

Burby, R.J., and R.G. Paterson. 1993. Improving Compliance with State Environmental Regulations. *Journal of Policy Analysis and Management* 12 (4): 753–772.

Cialdini, Robert B. 2001. *Influence: Science and Practice.* Boston: Allyn and Bacon.

Cialdini, Robert B. 2007. Descriptive Social Norms as Underappreciated Sources of Social Control. *Psychometrika* 72 (2): 263–268.

Cialdini, Robert B., and N.J. Goldstein. 2004. Social Influence: Compliance and Conformity. *Annual Review of Psychology* 55: 591–621.

Cialdini, Robert B., and Melanie R. Trost. 1998. "Social Influence: Social Norms, Conformity, and Compliance." *Handbook of Social Psychology, 98 Edition*, 151–192.

Cialdini, Robert B., R.R. Reno, and C.A. Kallgren. 1990. A Focus Theory of Normative Conduct: Recycling the Concept of Norms to reduce Littering in Public Places. *Journal of Personality and Social Psychology* 58: 1015–1026.

Cialdini, Robert B., Linda J. Demaine, Brad J. Sagarin, Daniel W. Barrett, Kelton Rhoads, and Patricia L. Winter. 2006. Managing Social Norms for Persuasive Impact. *Social Influence* 1 (1): 3–15. https://doi.org/10.1080/15534510500181459.

Decker, Scott H., Richard Wright, and Robert Logie. 1993. Perceptual Deterrence among Active Residential Burglars: A Research Note. *Criminology* 31: 135–147.

Fine, Adam, Benjamin Van Rooij, Yuval Feldman, Shaul Shalvi, Margerita Leib, Eline Scheper, and Elizabeth Cauffman. 2016. Rule Orientation and Behavior: Development and Validation of a Scale Measuring Individual Acceptance of Rule Violation. *Psychology, Public Policy, and Law* 22 (3): 314–329.

Gino, Francesca, Shahar Ayal, and Dan Ariely. 2009. Contagion and Differentiation in Unethical Behavior the Effect of One Bad Apple on the Barrel. *Psychological Science* 20 (3): 393–398.

Grasmick, Harold G., and G.J. Bryjak. 1980. The Deterrent Effect of Perceived Severity of Punishment. *Social Forces* 59 (2): 471–491.

Grasmick, Harold G., and R.J. Bursik Jr. 1990. Conscience, Significant Others, and Rational Choice: Extending the Deterrence Model. *Law and Society Review* 24 (3): 837–861.

Grasmick, Harold G., and Donald E. Green. 1980. Legal Punishment, Social Disapproval and Internalization as Inhibitors of Illegal Behavior. *The Journal of Criminal Law and Criminology* 71 (3): 325–335.

Gray, W.B., and J.T. Scholz. 1991. Analyzing the Equity and Efficiency of OSHA Enforcement. *Law and Policy* 13 (3): 185–214.

Greenberg, David F. 1981. Methodological Issues in Survey Research on the Inhibition of Crime. *The Journal of Criminal Law and Criminology* 72 (3): 1094–1101.

Gunningham, Neil, Peter Grabosky, and Darren Sinclair. 1998. *Smart Regulation, Designing Environmental Policy*. Oxford: Oxford University Press.

Hanno, D.M., and G.R. Violette. 1996. An Analysis of Moral and Social Influences on Taxpayer Behavior. *Behavioral Research in Accounting* 8: 57–75.

Huisman, Wim. 2001. *Between Profit and Morality: The Backgrounds to Enterprise Compliance and Violation [Tussen Wins ten Moraal, Achtergronden van Regelnaleving en Regelovertreding door Ondernemingen]*. Den Haag: Boom Juridische Uitgevers.

Hutter, Bridget M. 2011. *Managing Food Safety and Hygiene: Governance and Regulation as Risk Management*. Cheltenham: Edward Elgar.

Kagan, R.A., and J.T. Scholz. 1984. The "Criminology of the Corporation" and Regulatory Enforcement Strategies. In *Regulatory Enforcement*, ed. K. Hawkins and J.M. Thomas, 67–95. Boston: Kluwer-Nijhoff Publishing.

Kahan, D.M. 1997. Social Influence, Social Meaning, and Deterrence. *Virginia Law Review* 83: 349–395.

Keizer, Kees, Siegwart Lindenberg, and Linda Steg. 2008. The Spreading of Disorder. *Science* 322 (5908): 1681–1685.

Keizer, Kees, Siegwart Lindenberg, and Linda Steg. 2011. The Reversal Effect of Prohibition Signs. *Group Processes and Intergroup Relations* 14 (5): 681–688.

Kim, Pauline T. 1999. Norms, Learning, and Law: Exploring the Influences on Workers' Legal Knowledge. *University of Illinois Law Review* 2: 447–516.

Klepper, Steven, and Daniel Nagin. 1989. The Deterrent Effect of Perceived Certainty and Severity of Punishment Revisited. *Criminology* 27 (4): 721–746.

Klepper, Steven, and Daniel Nagin. 1989a. "Tax Compliance and Perceptions of the Risks of Detection and Criminal Prosecution." *Law and Society Review*: 209–240.

Klockars, Carl B. 1974. *The Professional Fence*. New York: The Free Press.

Lee, E. 2008. Socio-Political Contexts, Identity Formation, and Regulatory Compliance. *Administration and Society* 40 (7): 741–769.

Leventhal, G. S. 1980. "What Should Be Done with Equity Theory?" K. J. Gergen, M. S. Greenberg, and R. W. Willis (Eds.). *Social Exchange: Advances in Equity and Research* (pp.27–55). Boston: Springer.

Levi, M. 1988. *Of Rule and Revenue*. Berkeley: University of California Press.

May, P.J. 2005. Compliance Motivations: Perspectives of Farmers, Homebuilders, and Marine Facilities. *Law and Policy* 27 (2): 317–347.

McGraw, K.M., and J.T. Scholz. 1991. Appeals to Civic Virtue versus Attention to Self-Interest: Effects on Tax Compliance. *Law and Society Review* 25: 471–493.

Minor, W. William. 1981. Techniques of Neutralization: A Reconceptualization and Empirical Examination. *Journal of Research in Crime and Delinquency* 18 (2): 295–318.

Nagin, Daniel and Alfred Blumstein. 1978. "General Deterrence: A Review of the Empirical Evidence." In A. Blumstein, J. Cohen, and D. Nagin (Eds.), *Deterrence and Incapacitation: Estimating the Effect of Criminal Sanctions on Crime Rates*. Washington DC: National Academy of Sciences.

Nagin, Daniel S., and Raymond Paternoster. 1991. The Preventive Effects of the Perceived Risk of Arrest: Testing an Expanded Conception of Deterrence. *Criminology* 29 (4): 561–587.

Nielsen, Vibeke Lehmann, and Christine Parker. 2008. To what Extent Do Third Parties Influence Business Compliance? *Journal of Law and Society* 35 (3): 309–340.

Paternoster, Raymond. 1987. The Deterrent Effect of the Perceived Certainty and Severity of Punishment: A Review of the Evidence and Issues. *Justice Quarterly* 4 (2): 173–217.

Paternoster, Raymond, Linda E. Saltzman, Theodore G. Chiricos, and Gordon P. Waldo. 1982. Perceived Risk and Deterrence: Methodological Artifacts in Perceptual Deterrence Research. *Journal of Criminal Law and Criminology* 73 (3): 1238–1258.

Paternoster, Raymond, R. Brame, R., Bachman, and L. W. Sherman. 1997. "Do Fair Procedures Matter? The Effect of Procedural Justice on Spouse Assault." *Law and Society Review*, 31(1): 163–204.

Piquero, Nicole Leeper, Stephen G. Tibbetts, and Michael B. Blankenship. 2005. Examining the Role of Differential Association and Techniques of Neutralization in Explaining Corporate Crime. *Deviant Behavior* 26 (2): 159–188.

Van Rooij, Benjamin. 2013a. "Deterrence without Enforcement: Dialogues with Chinese Lawyers about Tax Evasion and Compliance." A paper presented on the Third East Asian Law and Society Conference which was organized by the Collaborative Research Network: East Asian Law and Society (EALS) and the SJTU Law and Society Center in Shanghai on March 22–23, 2013.

Van Rooij, Benjamin. 2016. "Weak Enforcement Strong Deterrence: Dialogues with Chinese Lawyers about Tax Evasion and Compliance." *Law and Social Inquiry*, 41(2): 288–310.

Van Rooij, and Jean Louis Van Geelder. 2012. "Compliance: Bridging Legal and Social Models." On file with the authors.

Van Rooij, Benjamin, Rachel E. Stern, and Kathinka Furst. 2014. "The Authoritarian Logic of Regulatory Pluralism: Understanding China's New Environmental Actors." UC Irvine School of Law Research Paper No. 2014–26. Available at SSRN: http://ssrn.com/abstract=2413872.

Scholz, John T., and M. Lubell. 1998. Trust and Taxpaying: Testing the Heuristic Approach to Collective Action. *American Journal of Political Science* 42: 398–417.

Scholz, John T., and N. Pinney. 1995. Duty, Fear, and Tax Compliance: The Heuristic Basis of Citizenship Behavior. *American Journal of Political Science* 39: 490–512.

Schwartz, S.H. 1977. Normative Influence on Altruism. In *Advances in Experimental Social Psychology*, vol. 10, ed. L. Berkowitz, 221–279. New York: Academic Press.

Spence, David B. 2001. The Shadow of the Rational Polluter: Rethinking the Role of Rational Actor Models in Environmental Law. *California Law Review* 89 (4): 917–998.

Sutinen, J. G., and K. Kuperan. 1999. "A Socio-Economic Theory of Regulatory Compliance." *International Journal of Social Economics* 26(1/2/3): 174–193.

Sykes, Gresham M., and David Matza. 1957. Techniques of Neutralization: A Theory of Delinquency. *American Sociological Review* 22 (6): 664–670.

Thornton, Dorothy, Neil Gunningham, and Robert A. Kagan. 2005. General Deterrence and Corporate Environmental Behavior. *Law and Policy* 27 (2): 262–288.

Tyler, Tom R. 1990. *Why People Obey the Law*. New Haven: Yale University Press.

Tyler, Tom R. 1997. Procedural Fairness and Compliance with the Law. *Swiss Journal of Economics and Statistics* 133 (2): 219–240.

Tyler, Tom R. 2006. Psychological Perspectives on Legitimacy and Legitimation. *Annual Review of Psychology* 57: 375–400.

Tyran, Jean-Robert, and Lars Feld. 2002. "Why People Obey the Law: Experimental Evidence from the Provision of Public Goods." *CESifo Working Papers*, 651.

Vandenbergh, M. 2003. Beyond Elegance: A Testable Typology of Social Norms in Corporate Environmental Compliance. *Stanford Environmental Law Journal* 22: 55–144.

Wenzel, Michael. 2004. Social Identification as a Determinant of Concerns About Individual-, Group-, and Inclusive-Level Justice. *Social Psychology Quarterly* 67 (1): 70–87.

Wenzel, Michael. 2005. Misperceptions of Social Norms about Tax Compliance: From Theory to Intervention. *Journal of Economic Psychology* 26 (6): 862–883.

Winter, Soren C., and Peter J. May. 2001. Motivation for Compliance with Environmental Regulations. *Journal of Policy Analysis and Management* 20 (4): 675–698.

Winter, Soren C., and Peter J. May. 2002. Information, Interests, and Environmental Regulation. *Journal of Comparative Policy Analysis* 4 (2): 115–142.

Yan, Huiqi. 2014. *Why Chinese Farmers Obey the Law: Pesticide Compliance in Hunan Province, China.* Amsterdam University (doctoral dissertation).

Yan, Huiqi, Benjamin van Rooij, and Jeroen van der Heijden. 2015. "Contextual Compliance: Situational and Subjective Cost-Benefit Decisions about Pesticides by Chinese Farmers." *Law & Policy* 37(3): 240–263.

Chapter 9
Conclusion

9.1 Introduction

On March 15, 2016, China's state television (CCTV) broadcast a feature about Ele.me, an online take-out food platform. CCTV did so as part of its annual campaign, known as the "315-Night Party," held in honor of World Consumer Rights Day and broadcasting in a two-hour prime-time slot every March 15 since 1991. Ele.me is one of the three most popular Internet platforms for take-out food. According to the introduction on the Ele.me official website, it covered almost 200 cities and had 180,000 join-in restaurants in October 2014. In June 2015, People.cn reported that Ele.me processed as many as 1.2 million orders per day.[1] In its feature broadcast, CCTV accused Ele.me of collaborating with restaurants that did not have proper legal licenses. The broadcast further exposed several restaurants operating without any legal licenses. The report highlighted how these restaurants served food from small and dirty premises out of residential apartments, but Ele.me had represented them with pictures and information that made them look as big and tidy as restaurants at attractive shopping mall locations. CCTV showed video material shot secretly onsite at these restaurants. Viewers watched as chefs used dirty cloths to wipe their pots and pans, opened ham sausages with their teeth, and picked up cooked food from the floor and put it back in the container.

The exposé sparked sweeping responses from the FDA and the Ele.me website. Before the 315-Night Party was over, the FDA in Beijing had sent out special inspectors to five restaurants operating on the Ele.me website and ordered them to close while seizing cooking equipment and food materials.[2] Ele.me apologized through its official WeChat account and claimed all seven restaurants mentioned had been taken off its site. Moreover, the company informed the public that it had initiated a

---

[1] http://politics.people.com.cn/n/2015/0628/c70731-27219553.html.

[2] http://www.takefoto.cn/viewnews-712067.html.

special working team to verify restaurant licenses throughout the country. Furthermore, Ele.me employed a thousand employees in its customer service department to handle additional customer complaints.

In contrast to the rapid and firm regulatory responses, the public remained surprisingly calm. Only 15 people commented on this broadcast on the official CCTV website,[3] and on one of China's most popular bulletin board system (BBS) websites, *Tianya*, only a few people responded to the news.[4] More responses, over 500, appeared on *Zhihu*, the largest Chinese knowledge discussion platform on the Internet. Among those responses, an unexpected thread of comments appeared: people stated that they did not care or that they considered what exposed quite normal. Some even claimed the exposé was a conspiracy against Ele.me. For instance, someone commented, "I think it is quite normal. It has been like this since ten years ago. If you want to eat clean food, just cook by yourself. (See footnote 3)" Someone else said, "Are restaurants with real storefronts clean? I do not think so. I did not have any discomfort after eating food from the restaurants in the broadcast. I thought it was its competition who exposed them." Another commented noted that "everyone knows that restaurant food is not clean but everyone eats there." After two weeks, a journalist investigated restaurants on Ele.me platform again and found that similar problems mentioned in the 315-Night Party broadcast still existed.[5] Some restaurants on the Ele.me platform still did not have opening licenses or provided fake addresses and restaurant photos, sanitation practices remained worrying, and cooks went on kneading dough without washing their hands after touching cash.[6]

Compliance is still a serious challenge for the construction of a law-based society in China. In this book, I empirically studied compliance behaviors in restaurants and examined how these behaviors take place. Focusing on the elements of a compliance model, with compliance as the interaction between legal norms and regulated behavior, expressed simply as Legal Norms  Regulated Behaviors, compliance behaviors have been discussed, and to explain them, their legal, organizational, and individual processes were investigated. In this chapter, the findings of Part A (on compliance behavior) and Part B (explanations of such behavior) are reviewed before an integrated model of compliance research is proposed. After that, several implications for methodology, regulatory strategy and addressing compliance challenge are explored.

[3] http://www.cntv.cn/pinglun/liuyan/zs/index.shtml?param=cms_jingji*ARTIURYooAKcyQr6KVbMPfTr160315*0*http://jingji.cctv.com/2016/03/15/ARTIURYooAKcyQr6KVbMPfTr160315.shtml*"饿了么"惊现黑心作坊,看完你还会饿么…

[4] http://www.search.tianya.cn/bbs?q=饿了么+315&pn=1.

[5] http://www.news.sina.com.cn/o/2016-03-30/doc-ifxqssxu8567398.shtml?tb3bucjl2n.

[6] http://news.sina.com.cn/o/2016-03-30/doc-ifxqssxu8567398.shtml?tb3bucjl2n.

9.2 Summary Findings

This book is composed of two parts. Part A addressed the main research question: How do selected restaurants respond to relevant regulatory rules, and what variation is there in their responses to different types of such rules and at different points in time in their business cycles? It focused on restaurants' compliance behaviors, offering a description of the compliance behaviors restaurants engage in to respond to relevant regulatory rules both during the period of applying for opening licenses and during daily operation. In addition, the evolving process of changes in compliance behaviors and variations in compliance behaviors were highlighted. To do so, the existing endogenous, exogenous, and process approaches to compliance research, as well as their limitations, were discussed, and an ethnographic approach of describing compliance behaviors was developed, which combined the three approaches to certain extent. This approach was applied to describe compliance behaviors in restaurants. Two in-depth and contrasting restaurant cases were elaborated in Chaps. 3 and 4. Within the two cases, the compliance or noncompliance behaviors that occurred and the development and evolution of these behaviors were described in detail.

This book found that despite the fundamental differences between the Idealistic restaurant and the Profit-Maximizing restaurant, compliance and noncompliance behaviors emerged in both restaurants. The Profit-Maximizing restaurant engaged in symbolic, fraudulent, and fake compliance behaviors, and in noncompliance behaviors, but was still compliant in certain situations. The Idealistic restaurant clearly engaged in many compliance behaviors, and even beyond compliance behaviors, but fraudulent, fake, and symbolic compliance behaviors still occurred. Thus, neither restaurant responded to regulatory rules in a consistent manner; compliance was found to be complex and beyond the dichotomy of compliance and noncompliance.

Furthermore, this book found compliance with one legal norm included a cluster of behaviors. Restaurants responding to one legal norm would engage in multiple substantive behaviors. However, in both cases, restaurants might have fully completed one behavior, or even surpassed requirements, while partially completing the second and cheating on the third. Therefore, one restaurant would respond to the various requirements of one single legal norm differently.

In addition, the types of compliance with the same aspect of the same legal norm changed during the process of business operation. Full compliance at the stage of opening license application might have changed into symbolic or partial compliance during daily operation, and then it could further evolve into fake compliance a year later.

As summarized in Chap. 5, the description of compliance behaviors revealed that compliance in reality was complex and fluid in terms of types of compliance, various compliance behaviors under one legal norms, and changing compliance behaviors during the process related to the same aspect of the same legal norm. The techniques used to label compliance in the existing literature capture one aspect of behavior with one rule at one static point. However, the compliance behaviors of one restaurant involve many rules, behaviors, and static points during the process of responding to legal norms.

Consequently, to understand compliance, this book introduced the concept of compliance pluralism, which refers to the presence of various aspects of compliance in a social field during the process of responding to legal requirements. With this concept, one can broaden one's view when discussing compliance instead of focusing on only one compliance assessment of one static point. It reveals various compliance behaviors throughout the process and the changing compliance processes. In other words, compliance pluralism reminds researchers to pay attention to the contextual situation of compliance, changing nature of compliance, and interaction between different types of compliance when studying compliance.

Part B focused on the second research question: What factors influence the variation in compliance behavior identified through question 1? In this section, the compliance behaviors described in Part A were explained on three levels—the regulatory level, organizational level, and individual level. It contains three chapters, the first discussing how the law and legal rules arrive at restaurants, the second focusing on the transmission of laws within restaurants, and the third addressing the association between variables and compliance behaviors at individual decision-making level. Factors that influence compliance behaviors and the variations were discussed in the three chapters.

This first factor is comprehensive legal knowledge that came out at the regulatory level. Legal knowledge has long been considered only as a capacity for compliance. Although Kim's (1999) research has shown that the legal knowledge of the regulated may differ erroneously from the written law, little attention has been paid to the discussion of legal knowledge in compliance studies. The finding here supports Kim's argument through its discussion of and findings related to the formation of comprehensive legal knowledge. As Kim and this study have shown, legal knowledge deserves greater study and discussion. From a process perspective, what the regulated actors perceived as the "law," or comprehensive legal knowledge, plays an important role in producing compliance. It is far more than a "capacity" or precondition for compliance—it is a variable involved in the process of constructing compliance.

Comprehensive legal knowledge consists of two kinds of knowledge: doctrinal legal knowledge and legal practice knowledge. Doctrinal legal knowledge refers to the regulated actors' knowledge about the content of written legal norms in terms of whether the regulated genuinely know whether specific behaviors set out in the formal laws and regulations are lawful or unlawful. Legal practice knowledge refers to the regulated actors' subjective knowledge about enforcement and others' compliance behaviors. The two kinds of knowledge may differ and become dissonant in terms of showing what "the law" is with which the regulated actors need to comply. The regulated actors develop the two kinds of knowledge to form their comprehensive legal knowledge of what the law is. Through this development process, doctrinal legal knowledge and legal practice knowledge influence each other.

In both restaurants, doctrinal legal knowledge was limited, but legal practice knowledge was abundant. The two kinds of knowledge interacted and formed restaurants' comprehensive legal knowledge of what the law is, which deviated from the original written law that attempted to enter the businesses. For instance, restaurants' comprehensive legal knowledge showed that they perceived the law as.

- Certain legal requirements are not as compulsory in practice as they seem when the actors first learn about them
- Some legal requirements can be dismissed because they are never verified
- Bribing enforcers is easy and a common way to obtain opening licenses
- Enforcers hope to receive personal, private benefits from enforcing laws instead of caring about the aims of the law
- Once restaurants pass the initial inspections and obtain their opening license, several requirements that were previously emphasized can be ignored in daily operation
- Personal relationships and acquaintance may be more important than legal norms
- Complying with the enforcer is more important than complying with the written legal norm.

Consequently, the laws restaurants perceived pointed in a different direction of compliance than the compliance direction indicated by the original written laws. Restaurants' compliance behaviors were situated in the perceived laws, as their comprehensive legal knowledge indicated. Hence, some variations in restaurants' compliance behaviors actually reflect the variations in restaurants' comprehensive legal knowledge or perception of the law. Additionally, the changes in restaurants' comprehensive legal knowledge during this process largely explain the changes in restaurants' compliance behavior.

The second factor is organizational norms that is salient at the organizational level. A restaurant can be viewed as an organization that is not a single person but composed of people at all levels, including employees and employers, or owners or top managers and workers. To reach the very employees some legal norms target, the law must be transmit throughout restaurant internally, and it is simultaneously mediated, either through activation or competition, by organizational norms that guide employees' behavior, as discussed in Chap. 7. Chapter 7 was devoted to discussing how organizational norms influence restaurants' compliance in the process of the transmission of laws within restaurants.

It was found that certain organizational norms activate and promote certain legally required behaviors. For instance, the norm of healthy food at the Idealistic restaurant aligned with the food safety law and activated employees' behavior that complies with food safety law. Likewise, the norm of cleanliness at S restaurant activated compliance with the disinfection norm. At the same time, organizational norms may compete with legal norms in terms of reducing the reasonability of legal norms, rationalizing the low possibility of meeting the legal requirements, reducing the responsibility of ensuring the goal of legal norms, impeding the enforcement of legal norms, and overemphasizing one aspect of behaviors but dismissing others. For instance, the Profit-Maximizing restaurant disregarded the importance of behaviors that did not align with the norm of providing tasty food, despite these behaviors being regulated by legal norms, including obtaining health certificates, washing hands, and cutting nails, and that impeded its compliance with these legal norms. Similarly, the norm of providing clean glassware at S restaurant impeded certain aspects of compliance with disinfection norms.

Furthermore, organizational norms are composed of managerial, injunctive, and descriptive norms, and the three types of norms interact with each other and shape employees' behaviors during the process of socialization, specifically during the management process. Through discussing the organizational socialization and management processes, factors involved in the formation of various organizational norms, and that mediate the function of legal norms and influence compliance, were discovered. Factors discovered in this book include the owners' preferences, personal belief or norms, the structure of and capacity for internal monitoring, the size of the organization, and the characteristics of employees and customers. These characteristics of an organization combined to produce certain organizational norms that activated or competed with legal norms during the socialization and management processes.

Other factors explaining compliance behaviors are examined at individual level with two methods. First, interviewees' subjective explanations for their behaviors were discussed and analyzed, and second, the association between their behaviors and six influential variables selected from the existing literature was analyzed. The six variables are plural subjective deterrence, personal norms, descriptive norms, perceived obligation to obey the law, recognition of legal requirements, and practical constraints. To identify the association between individual factors and compliance behaviors, the compliance behaviors were coded into a dichotomy of compliance behavior and violation behavior in this chapter instead of retaining their complex nature.

When analyzing interviewees' subjective explanations for their behavior, plural subjective deterrence emerged as the main reason provided for both compliance behavior and violation behavior. It was especially prominent in explaining compliance behaviors. Therefore, the majority of interviewees explained most of their compliance by referring to positive plural subjective deterrence. Personal norms were the second important explanation provided by interviewees when they subjectively explained both compliance behavior and violation behavior. Nevertheless, the explanation related more often to violation behaviors.

In addition, operational benefit and recognition of legal requirements were identified by interviewees as reasons for their compliance behaviors, while practical constraints, descriptive norms, not being responsible for actions, and ignorance of legal requirements were mentioned to explain violation behaviors. Although operational benefit as part of operational costs and benefits was not selected as one of the six variables discussed in this book, interviewees mentioned it without prompts from the interviewer, which underscores the usefulness of the variable to explain compliance, as some researchers have argued (Yan 2014). Not being responsible for compliance is a new factor raised by interviewees. It echoes the concept of motivational posture of disengagement proposed by Braithwaite et al. (1994) and is an important factor that calls for additional attention.

During the variable association analysis, descriptive norms, personal norms, and plural subjective deterrence were found to be the variable most significantly associated with compliance behaviors. Although interviewees mentioned descriptive norms only in relation to several violation behaviors, it was found to be clearly associated with compliance behaviors. Descriptive norms were divided into four categories that show an ordinal order, and it indicated that higher levels of positive descriptive norms were accompanied by higher percentages of compliance behaviors. Perceived obligation to obey the law (POOL) was found to be overwhelmingly negative and not obviously associated with compliance behaviors. Moreover, the variable of practical constraints was negatively associated with compliance behaviors, which aligned with the theoretical prediction. However, the association seemed very weak. Finally, individuals' recognition of the legal requirements, in terms of whether they knew specific requirements are law, was overwhelmingly negative, and it did not show association with compliance behaviors.

9.3 An Integrated Model

In addition to describing and explaining compliance behaviors, this book offers an integrated and dynamic approach to studying compliance. Examining the compliance process on three levels, that is, the regulatory, organizational, and individual levels, and studying each component and the internal conjunctions in the compliance model of Legal Norms $\longleftrightarrow$ Regulated Behaviors produced significant understandings of the overall compliance processes. This has enabled me to propose an integrated model for studying compliance.

First, if viewing knowledge of legal norms in a narrow sense, as many compliance researchers have done (Winter and May 2001), compliance behaviors can originate from knowledge of legal norms and without knowledge of legal norms. Thus, knowing legal norms is not a necessary precondition for compliance. This finding challenges the established presumption that legal knowledge as an aspect of capacity is a precondition for compliance (Winter and May 2001). As shown in Chap. 8, only five of 108 responses indicated certainty that the required behaviors were regulated by laws. In a narrow sense, the other 103 responses did not show the capacity of knowing the law. However, 51 of the 103 responses indicated that interviewees complied with laws they did not know, and only one of the five interviewees who knew the laws complied.

Second, if considering legal knowledge in a broader sense, as is the case in this book, and starting from the compliance behaviors instead of legal norms, it becomes apparent that compliance behaviors are responses to "the law" the regulated actors perceiving subjectively, which may differ from doctrinal law. What the regulated actors see as the law can be captured by examining their comprehensive legal knowledge. Comprehensive legal knowledge is composed of doctrinal legal knowledge and legal practice knowledge, and it is the result of interaction between the two kinds of knowledge. Legal practice knowledge provides information about enforcement and others' compliance, which may challenge doctrinal legal knowledge in terms of what is allowed, what is compulsory, and so forth. Hence, the regulated actors always add their own interpretations to the legal norms, and they act according to what they interpret as and believe is the law rather than the objective doctrinal law written in documents. In other words, the law faces challenges related to the regulated actors' experiences with the regulatory system, for instance, interaction with inspectors during enforcement encounters. Therefore, how the regulated actors interpret the law and form comprehensive legal knowledge is one of the compliance processes. The regulated actors' compliance behaviors respond to their comprehensive legal knowledge rather than original legal norms. Consequently, understanding the formation of this "perceived law" and knowing the content of "perceived law" are crucial for understanding and predicting compliance behaviors.

Moreover, examination of the internal process within the regulated organization indicated that legal norms also face challenges from organizational norms before reaching the members of the organization. Organizational norms, including managerial, injunctive, and descriptive norms, may activate or compete with legal norms. Due to competition from organizational norms, the reasonability of legal norms may be reduced, the perceived likelihood of meeting the legal requirements may be reduced, responsibility for ensuring the goals of legal norms are met may be reduced, the enforcement of legal norms may be impeded, and one aspect of legal norms may be overemphasized while other aspects of the same norm are dismissed. Ultimately, members' compliance behaviors are shaped by the combination of legal norms and organizational norms through organizational socialization and management processes. That means, members' compliance behaviors do not actually correspond to legal norms alone but to the outcome of interaction between legal norms and organizational norms.

These points have an important implication for compliance study. While most compliance studies begin with legal norms and assume knowing legal norms is a precondition for compliance, this study shows that compliance behaviors may originate from or respond to a different "law" that is subjective and dynamic. Compliance behaviors are the outcomes of interaction between doctrinal legal knowledge and legal practice knowledge, and the outcomes of interaction between legal norms and organizational norms. From this perceptive, the findings of Kim's (1999) research—that the regulated actors comply with legal norms without knowing them—become clearer. It also explains the interaction illustrated in the compliance scheme Legal Norms $\longleftrightarrow$ Regulated Behaviors: the regulated actors may engage in compliance behavior without knowing legal norms, but their compliance behaviors align with legal norms.

Third, this research examined the regulatory, organizational, and individual levels simultaneously.[7] By integrating the three levels, this research proposed a way to

---

[7]In the area of white-collar crime, Vaughan (2007) suggested integrating multiple levels of analysis for causal explanations, specifically the macro-, meso-, and micro levels. Her aim was to use white-collar crime research and theory as an example for general theory in sociology that empirically merges macro-, meso-, and micro-levels of analysis. However, the three levels discussed in this

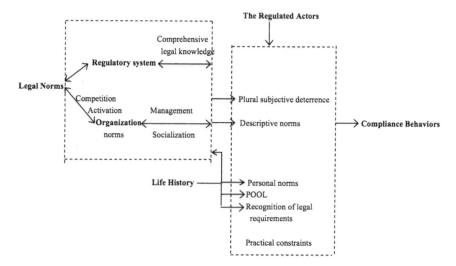

Fig. 9.1 An integrated model of legal norms-compliance behaviors

describe and understand the process of how compliance behaviors take place (see Fig. 9.1).

If the problem is approached from the side of legal norms, as shown previously, the legal norm should be replaced by a combination of at least two processes, comprehensive legal knowledge formation and the interaction between organizational and legal norms. The two processes would reveal several variables that influence individual decision making, such as plural subjective deterrence and descriptive norms. However, some variables at individual level are not only influenced by those on the regulatory and organizational levels but also by the individual's general life history, such as personal norms, POOL, and recognition of law. In turn, these variables influence the regulatory and organizational level processes. Moreover, the variables listed at individual level in this framework are only a fraction of the variables discussed in the literature, and others have been excluded, including procedural justice and cost–benefit calculation. Subsequently, all variables functioning in the two processes and produced by the two processes come together at individual level again and produce the final compliance behaviors in which individuals engage.

In this book, association analysis of these variables at individual level confirmed that plural subjective deterrence, descriptive norms, and personal norms are important factors that associate with individual compliance behaviors in the restaurants studied. This is understandable, as plural subjective deterrence and descriptive norms are the most vital outcomes of the regulatory and organizational processes. In other words, they are directly linked to or part of what "the law" is in the perception of the regulated actors. Personal norms underline the entire process of comprehensive legal

book are not necessarily in the same vertical or hierarchical planes. They simply present three kinds of processes through which compliance behaviors mostly occur.

knowledge formation and keep conflicting with final comprehensive legal knowledge if it deviates from what comprehensive legal knowledge shows is proper. Hence, personal norms are closely linked to comprehensive legal knowledge and the rules regulated actors accept as their guiding law.

Practical constraints seemed to have a weak negative association with compliance behavior, and POOL and recognition of law were not found to be significant variables associated with compliance behaviors. This could be because POOL and the recognition of law are so skewed that most individuals are negative about the two variables, which implies that the two variables are not suitable for explaining compliance behaviors in this context. Alternatively, the effect of recognition of law on compliance may be involved in other variables' effect on compliance in a more specific and subtle way, such as in plural subjective deterrence and descriptive norms.

Fourth, comprehensive legal knowledge is a core concept in this model. Comprehensive legal knowledge consists of both doctrinal legal knowledge and legal practice knowledge. Legal practice knowledge includes knowledge of enforcement and knowledge of others' compliance. When the regulated actors learn how regulatory departments work and how the requirements are enforced, they learn to perceive and understand the deterrence from regulatory departments they face, and this becomes an aspect of subjective deterrence that they consider. Subjective deterrence differs from objective deterrence in that violations will be discovered and punished with certain certainty and severity from the perspective of the regulator or what is written in the legal norm. Subjective deterrence is the outcome of the regulated actors' overall assessment of troubles or risks they face from the regulator. It originates from the regulated actors' knowledge of enforcement, knowledge of other's compliance, and doctrinal legal knowledge. Knowledge of others' response to legal requirements evolves into descriptive norms that provide the regulated actors with important information of efficient and potential behaviors.

The three kinds of knowledge interact with each other and finally provide the regulated actor with comprehensive knowledge of the legal norms or the enforced requirements. Then the "law," or more accurately, the "rules," that regulate their behaviors in reality come into being. These "rules" form the starting point from which the regulated begin the compliance journey. These "rules" also can emerge within organizations in which doctrinal legal norms are more invisible or in which doctrinal legal norms have been replaced by managerial norms. For example, managerial norms may overshadow doctrinal legal norms that have not entered restaurants and been received by the regulated actors in regulating compliance behaviors. Similarly, interaction between managerial norms, injunctive norms, descriptive norms, and internal enforcement institution leads to the formation of comprehensive knowledge of the internal rules of an organization.

Fifth, the regulated actors have been socialized differently throughout their lives and have different personal norms and beliefs. This influences how they form and evaluate their legal knowledge and how they react to comprehensive legal knowledge. As the theory of cognitive dissonance (Festinger 1962) and other research on information processing (see Gilovich 1991) showed, individuals select and accept different information based on their personal preferences and norms. New information that does not fit preconceived notions or patterns will likely be discounted. The regulated actors' personal norms or beliefs may support or contest with their comprehensive legal knowledge and are influenced by their comprehensive legal knowledge.

Personal norms or beliefs have multiple dimensions. Braithwaite (2002) identified three dimensions of belief regarding legal norms when developing the concept of motivational posture, which classifies the attitudes of regulated actors and the ways they interact with regulatory team, namely reasonability, possibility, and responsibility. This research revealed three additional dimensions. The first dimension is that the regulated actors agree with the goal of legal norms but do not fully agree with the execution of the goal that is regulated by legal norms. For example, the owner of the Idealistic restaurant agreed with the food safety norms that the pork quarantine certificate aims to safeguard, but she did not agree that the certification process guarantees the quality of the pork. In addition, she agreed with the importance of disinfecting dishware, but she disagreed with the necessity of keeping a disinfection log. Similarly, several interviewees agreed with the importance of health certificates to safeguard food safety, but disagreed with the necessity of annual health checks or disagreed with the usefulness of health checks to safeguard health.

The second dimension is that the regulated actors do not care about legal norms per se but care about the enforcers who enforce them. For example, the owner of L restaurant paid the prescribed fees when applying for the business license without knowing or wanting to know what the fee covered. She paid tax without knowing or wanting to know how tax is calculated. She claimed, "I do not know about the law things, and I just do what they [inspectors] asked."[8] The third dimension is that the legitimacy of legal norms is not morally considered but linked closely to the regulator or enforcement, and it is largely downplayed. For instance, the owner of the Profit-Maximizing restaurant believed opening licenses were a revenue stream for regulators and that they simply conferred a certain status on restaurants to avoid punishment. These dimensions show that the regulated actors' personal norms and beliefs regarding legal norms are multidimensional.

Personal norms or beliefs regarding legal norms may conflict with legal knowledge if they differ from the supposed belief supporting the written legal norms. For example, the beliefs of the owner of the Idealistic restaurant about good food and the best way to slaughter pigs competed with the legal requirements of obtaining pork quarantine certificates. Based on her comprehensive legal knowledge, she knew that she needed pork quarantine certificates and that inspectors would check them, yet she had a strong inclination to process food in the traditional and ecofriendly manner. She believed pork quarantine certificates could not guarantee that pork was safe but that the pork she sourced and slaughtered was safe. Consequently, her personal norms or beliefs regarding the pork quarantine certificate, which translated to skepticism about the certificates' usefulness to safeguard food safety, conflicted with the legal requirement.

---

[8]Interview with the owner of L restaurant on May 10, 2012.

Moreover, legal practice knowledge may influence personal norms or beliefs regarding legal norms. For instance, the owner of the Profit-Maximizing restaurant had legal practice knowledge that the enforcement of opening licenses was flawed and unjust. Subsequently, he linked the flawed enforcement to the opening licenses and formed the negative personal norms towards the opening license.

Sixth, before compliance or noncompliance behaviors are carried out, other restrictive variables may still exist. For instance, practical constraints may play a role in the compliance process. Although the association between practical constraints and compliance behaviors is very weak, in some case, practical constraints can have a significant influence. For example, in the case of the owner of the Idealistic restaurant and the pork quarantine certificates, she initially did not genuinely comply with this legal requirement, as she bought counterfeit certificates. However, later, she became fully and genuinely compliant because she found it increasingly troublesome and expensive to slaughter pigs in the traditional manner, and the slaughterhouse was an acceptable alternative. Furthermore, the slaughterhouse automatically issued quarantine certificates to her, so she no longer needed to buy counterfeit certificates. In this case, nothing changed except the practical constraints. Therefore, it supports the argument that the practical constraints that cause people to engage in noncompliance behavior play a role in compliance. Thus, it might be necessary to consider practical constraints affecting both compliance and noncompliance when explaining compliance in future research.

9.4 Methodological Implications

This research has relied on combining exogenous, endogenous and processual concerns through a highly detailed ethnographic analysis of a myriad of compliance behaviors relating to a multitude of rules over a longer period in small organizational settings. There are several benefits to this methodology, and it has some implications for general compliance study.

First of all, the methodology allows the researcher to enter the real-life context of the regulated actors and so to better understand what happens in that context. Social behaviors are deeply embedded in their social contexts, as are compliance behaviors. Some researchers have claimed that compliance is situated in specific environments (Aarts and Dijksterhuis 2003) and organizational structures (Vaughan 1998) and that influential variables for compliance are contextual in terms of the type of rules, the type of regulatees, and the type of operations (Yan 2014; Yan et al. 2015). Although numerous studies on compliance have been conducted, such methodology will always be needed and will greatly benefit compliance studies by facilitating the identification of different and changing social contexts for compliance. Furthermore, many compliance researchers are inclined to choose one specific law the regulated face but dismiss other laws with which the regulated deal simultaneously. In reality, one organization deals with numerous kinds of laws at the same time. Compliance with one law is inevitably related to compliance with other laws, and how the organization deals with different laws shapes the organization as a whole. Studying the organization's compliance behavior related to multiple laws could help researchers to capture the characteristics of the compliance actor more fully, and broadens researchers' view when classifying the regulated actors. Capturing the characteristics of the regulated actors by studying their perceptions of and behavior towards only one regulatory system is challenging, because some of their features may not be prominent in that regulatory system at that time. By examining and comparing the regulated actors' perceptions, responses, and behaviors toward multiple regulatory systems, researchers can understand the regulated actors better and classify them in a more appropriate way. It also facilitates the discussion of the interaction between different law enforcement systems and compliance. This could bring a broader view to discussing the regulatory system as a whole as well as the legislation, and it could enable a comparison between different law enforcement systems.

Secondly, conducting ethnographic fieldwork, which combines participant observation and interviews, yielded trustworthy data, as it enabled researchers to observe the regulated actors' behaviors directly or to verify the information regarding behavior collected through interviews with other information collected through fieldwork if direct observation was impossible. By interacting with the regulated for an extended period and developing friendships with them, I could reassure them that the study would not harm them, which motivated the regulated to share genuine experiences and perceptions, show me the reality of daily life.

Thirdly, it facilitates to discover additional influential variables. The perspective of the regulated actor in this method does not use the law for guidance or as a starting point for discussions. It begins from the practical behaviors and the consideration of those behaviors. In doing so, it broadens the view of the research and creates the possibility to include variables that are not used in or are taken for granted in the legal perspective. Furthermore, the perspective of the regulated actor echoes what Gray and Silbey (2011) termed "the other side of the compliance relationship." As found in several other studies, in the real-world situation, the formal agents of law may be absent and its coercive force less visible (Ewick and Silbey 1992; Silbey 2005). It demands examination of the role of the regulated actor in compliance, which draws into focus the frontline workers within organizations who are responsible for enacting compliance daily yet generally are dismissed in compliance studies, thus broadening the discussion of compliance to include more variables and to align more closely with real life.

Fourthly, it revealed possibilities to discover new ways to evaluate compliance. This book has shown that compliance can be evaluated differently in different phases during the process. For instance, during the process of applying for a catering services license, the Profit-Maximizing restaurant was required to provide health certificates for its employees. The owner provided such certificates, and the regulator accepted these as being in compliance. When evaluating compliance at this time point, one may conclude that the Profit-Maximizing restaurant complied with the legal norm of health certificates, as the enforcement records will indicate. Of course, by studying the process of how this compliance behavior was accomplished, it became clear that the certificates had been falsified. This enables me to qualify compliance in this case not simply as compliance but as fraudulent compliance. Similarly, when the owner of the Idealistic restaurant was required to provide the same health certificates while applying for the same catering license, she provided certificates the regulator accepted, which also implied compliance. Yet when the compliance process was traced back, it became apparent that she did not have health certificates for all the workers. Therefore, rather than labeling this compliance, it should be labeled partial compliance. Consequently, measurement of compliance became a sequence of observation and data collection. Compliance should not be measured at a static point but at many time points in the process within which it takes place, develops, and changes.

Overall, this method of describing compliance behaviors is time consuming and limited to a small number of cases. However, it opens many possibilities for penetrating other aspects of compliance that the existing conventional methodologies do not provide.

9.5 Implications for Regulatory Strategies

This book indicates that compliance behavior that occurs in the start-up phase of business is important for later compliance behaviors, and should be paid more attention to in regulatory strategies. The start-up phase refers to the setting up period during which a restaurant enters the market and the regulatory system. Restaurants obtain their legal status during the start-up phase and become legal business organizations. Subsequently, restaurants enter the daily operation phase, during which they are engaging in business activities and maintain their legal status. Due to the difference between the start-up and operations phases and the critical role the start-up phase plays in compliance, it requires further attention.

First, during the start-up phase, the regulated actors are new to the regulatory system, and for them, it is the beginning of learning "the law" of this regulatory system, including doctrinal legal knowledge and legal practice knowledge. Although these forms of knowledge are ever changing, the very knowledge obtained at the beginning has a prolonged influence on the later development of comprehensive legal knowledge and on compliance due to the effects of path dependency or habitus. Hence, the initial actions in forming comprehensive legal knowledge in one direction constrain future choice sets and elicit further moves in that same direction (North 1990, 98–99). In terms of Bourdieu's (1990) concepts of habitus and field, a regulatory system is a social field that exerts force upon all the regulated who come within its range. When the regulated encounter a habitus with which the regulatory field is not familiar, the resulting disjuncture generates change and transformation. During the start-up phase, the regulated must apply for various opening licenses and frequently interact with the regulator to obtain legal status. It provides dense opportunities for the regulated to collect a variety of knowledge in the field and to form their comprehensive legal knowledge and new habitus in this field.

The practice of *Hongbao,* or bribery, at the Idealistic restaurant is an excellent example of how the new habitus formed during the start-up phase, and of how the new habitus predicted the restaurant's comprehensive legal knowledge and subsequent operation and compliance behavior. Initially, the owner of the Idealistic restaurant was morally opposed to bribery, claiming,

> I think it [*Hongbao*] is the reason why the society is not fair. So many people choose to do that [give *Hongbao*]. I feel they [the regulator] just do things for getting *Hongbao*, but not really because this thing is good for the public. Most of time, they will be quite rigorous on you, and you give them *Hongbao*. Money goes to their personal pocket, only then they will do their work. If they really do their work, you do not need to pay so much money.

She did not plan to give *Hongbao* at the beginning when applying for opening licenses. That means the recognition of other people using *Hongbao* as a way to realize compliance was not an option for her at the beginning. She followed the direction of her personal norms when attempting to comply with or even exceed all opening license requirements, including by installing a high-quality disinfection cabinet and by buying more fire extinguishers. However, she encountered problems and faced the risk of not being able to obtain licenses. On several critical occasions— when applying for the fire and catering services licenses—she made a different choice and engaged in giving *Hongbao.*

Ultimately, *Hongbao* was effective and saved a great deal of time and energy while, more importantly, removing the risk of operating illegally. As a result, her determination not to engage in bribery, which was formed before entering the regulatory field and during her socialization, had quietly become shaky and had slowly changed when she entered this new field and began to interact with regulators. Furthermore, giving *Hongbao*, which she knew about before but had not absorbed as her own knowledge, became her own knowledge and a way to deal with problems. Therefore, her comprehensive legal knowledge changed. Later, when she faced challenges in obtaining a drainage license, she knew to invite the inspectors to meals and offer them gifts.

Second, focusing on the start-up phase of compliance develops an understanding of the initial interaction between the regulated and the regulators, which shapes the meaning but also the processes of compliance. As endogenous studies have shown, the meaning of compliance is constructed during interaction between the regulator and the regulated (Lange 1999; Talesh 2009; Huising and Silbey 2011). The initial interaction between the regulated and the regulator is especially vital, because it is the first time the two parties are involved in the regulatory field, and during this interaction, they attempt to establish the right track for later interaction.

Before a new restaurant enters the field, preexisting rules and power structures have set a basic track for the new restaurant to follow. These rules and power structures influence the restaurant, but as a subject of regulation, the new restaurant always brings its own knowledge, resources, attitudes, beliefs, and habitus, to the field. Consequently, while the regulated learn and respond in this field, it also challenges and influences the existing regulatory system. The final behavioral disposition or behavior habitus of the regulated is formed with the interweaving of the two influence

processes. In this sense, both parties, the regulator and the regulated, are new to
each other in this phase. Many things are unknown, fluent, and changeable. For
instance, how does the regulator work with this specific regulated, how does the
regulated interact with the regulator, where is the baseline for their behavior, what
are compulsory requirements, what could be accepted by both parties, and so forth.
It is essential for the regulator to assimilate the new arrivals into its system, while it
is also important for the new arrivals to form new habitus to deal with this system.
Their early experiences are crucial in determining their future responses, as they tend
to react to new experiences by assimilating them into the generative principles they
acquired (Bourdieu 1990: 60).

Furthermore, what the regulated learn in the start-up phase helps them construct
their own discourse of regulation, which helps them to explain what is happening,
predict the outcome of their behavior, and make decision regarding regulatory
matters. In this way, it is significantly easier to perform the enforcement from the
beginning than later. Nevertheless, as shown in the case studies, enforcement at start
up is poor. The regulator does not verify information and fully control the entire
process.[9] The regulated may learn that they can circumvent requirements, which
will erode regulation.

9.6 Implications for Addressing Compliance Challenge

This book aims to offer some new knowledge about overcoming compliance problems in China. While the data from the restaurant case studies cannot directly be
generalized beyond the cases studies, let alone beyond the particular industry, they
do offer some new insights about how to address China's compliance challenges.

Enforcement is certainly a core issue. First, enforcers should pay more attention to
what the regulated actors learn from their enforcement. As this research has shown,
restaurants have their own comprehensive legal knowledge, and they comply with the
"law" they learned from their doctrinal legal knowledge and practical legal knowledge. Doctrinal legal knowledge is always verified, and practical legal knowledge
is changeable. One important way to improve restaurants' compliance is to narrow
the gap between the "law" perceived by restaurants and the law that is enforced. The
start-up phase of the business is a critical time for restaurants in terms of learning
the law. To verify each enforced legal requirement in this phase is valuable, and it
will be a strong signal for restaurants that these requirements matter. As the variable
of plural subjective deterrence shows, perceiving that the requirements are enforced

---

[9]As shown in that case of the Profit-Maximizing restaurant, the regulator did not verify in person
whether the Profit-Maximizing restaurant changed the stone kitchen table to a stainless table but
approved the license application based on a photo. Likewise, the regulator did not verify in person
whether the restaurant bought enough fire extinguishers and exit signs but approved its application
based on photos. In the Idealistic restaurant's case, the regulator at the Fire Department did not
verify in person whether the restaurant's door had been changed approved the application based on
the owner's statement.

accounts for a positive subjective deterrence despite a lack of knowledge of sanction severity or certainty of being caught.

Second, the regulator should pay attention to different organizational norms and use this knowledge to inform their inspection objectives. Organizational norms may compete with or activate legal norms. By studying the organizational norms of specific restaurants, the regulator can learn which organizational behaviors to expect and use these organizational norms to differentiate enforcement objectives, thus making inspections more efficient. For instance, for restaurants such as S restaurant where dishware disinfection is a critical organizational norm, enforcers do not need to inspect whether dishware is being disinfected. Instead, they should educate the manager or employees about disinfectant residues and inspect whether residues exceed standard levels.

Third, responsibilities related to various legal requirements should be clarified during enforcement. For instance, inspectors or regulators should explain whose responsibility it is to obtain a health certificate before an employee begins working in a restaurant, as this seems ambiguous to the regulated actors.

Besides enforcement, existing social norms related to what legal norms aim to regulate, such as social norms related to restaurants' food safety, should receive more attention. As the Ele.me food safety crisis revealed, some social norms related to restaurants' food safety, especially descriptive social norms, are somewhat frustrating, as they imply that it is "normal" that many restaurants do not provide clean and safe food. These negative social norms significantly undermine legal norms, cause deviations in the regulated actors' comprehensive legal knowledge from doctrinal law, and socialize and direct the regulated actors' behaviors in the wrong direction. To promote compliance, great efforts should be made to research existing social norms that compete with legal norms and to find ways to modify and weaken social norms competing with legal norms.

Moreover, descriptive social norms function more unconsciously, but are a critical influential factor for compliance. It is important to avoid repeating and emphasizing descriptive norms that conflict with legal norms and to find ways to change these norms to support legal norms. Finally, personal norms are influenced by how legal norms are implemented, such as in the case of health certificate. Unclear procedures or inadequate information during the health certificate application process arouses the regulated actors' suspicions of the value of health certificates, so the implementation procedure should be carefully designed to promote rather than weaken personal norms.

References

Aarts, Henk, and Ap. Dijksterhuis. 2003. The Silence of the Library: Environment, Situational Norm, and Social Behavior. *Journal of Personality and Social Psychology* 84 (1): 18–28.

Braithwaite, John, Diane Gibson, and Toni Makkai. 1994. Regulatory Styles Motivational Postures and Nursing Home Compliance. *Law and Policy* 16 (4): 363–394.

Braithwaite, Valerie. 2002. "Dancing with Tax Authorities: Motivational Postures and Non-Compliant Actions." In Valerie Braithwaite (Ed.), *Taxing Democracy: Understanding Tax Avoidance and Evasion* (pp. 15–39). Ashgate.

Bourdieu, Pierre. 1990. *The Logic of Practice*. Stanford, CA: Stanford University Press.

Ewick, Patricia, and Susan S. Silbey. 1992. *Conformity, Contestation, and Resistance: An Account of Legal Consciousness*. New England Law Review.

Festinger. 1962. *A Theory of Cognitive Dissonance*. Stanford, CA: Stanford University Press.

Gilovich, Thomas. 1991. *How We Know What Isn't So: The Fallibility of Human Reason in Everday Life*. New York: Free Press.

Gray, and Susan S. Silbey. 2011. "The Other Side of the Compliance Relationship." In Christine Parker and Vibeke Lehmann Nielsen (Eds.), *Explaining Compliance: Business Responses to Regulation* (pp.123–138). Cheltenham: Edward Elgar.

Huising, Ruthanne, and Susan S. Silbey. 2011. Governing the Gap: Forging Safe Science through Relational Regulation. *Regulation and Governance* 5: 14–42.

Kim, Pauline T. 1999. Norms, Learning, and Law: Exploring the Influences on Workers' Legal Knowledge. *University of Illinois Law Review* 2: 447–516.

Lange, B. 1999. Compliance Construction in the Context of Environmental Regulation. *Social and Legal Studies* 8 (4): 549–567.

North, D.C. 1990. *Institutions, Institutional Change and Economic Performance*. Cambridge: Cambridge University Press.

Susan S. Silbey. 2005. After Legal Consciousness. *Annual Review of Law and Social Science* 1:323–368.

Talesh, Shauhin. 2009. The Privatization of Public Legal Rights: How Manufacturers Construct the Meaning of Consumer Law. *Law and Society Review* 43 (3): 527–562.

Vaughan, Diane. 1998. Rational Choice, Situated Action, and the Social Control of Organizations. *Law and Society Review* 32 (1): 23–61.

Vaughan. 2007. Beyond Macro-and Micro-levels of Analysis, Organizations, and the Cultural Fix. In *International Handbook of White-Collar and Corporation Crime*, ed. Henry N. Pontell and Gilbert Geis, 3–24. New York: Springer.

Winter, Soren C., and Peter J. May. 2001. Motivation for Compliance with Environmental Regulations. *Journal of Policy Analysis and Management* 20 (4): 675–698.

Yan, Huiqi. 2014. *Why Chinese Farmers Obey the Law: Pesticide Compliance in Hunan Province, China*. Amsterdam University (doctoral dissertation).

Yan, Huiqi, Benjamin van Rooij, and Jeroen van der Heijden. 2015. "Contextual Compliance: Situational and Subjective Cost-Benefit Decisions about Pesticides by Chinese Farmers." *Law & Policy* 37(3): 240–263.

Appendix A
Laws Concerning Restaurants Involved in This Book

Several laws that apply to restaurants were studied in this book. These laws encompass several regulatory fields, including food safety, environmental concerns, business management, taxation, fire control, city management, and alcohol sales. In this appendix, and brief introduction to the relevant laws is provided, and the specific rules in these laws concerning restaurants are highlighted.

1. **Food Safety Laws**

Several laws about food safety are relevant. The first and most important is the Food Safety Law of the People's Republic of China (the Food Safety Law), which was promulgated on February 28, 2009, and revised on April 24, 2015. It was enacted to ensure food safety and guarantee the safety and health of the public. All food production, processing, circulation, and catering services, as well as food additives and food-related products, including packing materials, containers, detergents, and disinfectants for food and utensils and equipment for food production and operation, are governed by this law. The law makes provisions for food-safety risk inspection and assessment, food safety standards, food production and operation, food testing, food import and export, food-safety incident resolution, and food safety inspection and management.

Rules related to restaurants address licensing, locations, equipment, disinfection, food safety personnel and internal regulations, layout and processing procedures, dishware, food materials, food additives, food storage, food workers' health condition and personal sanitation, washing hands, clothes, water, detergent, and disinfectants. Several of these were studied.

Several complementary implementation regulations and operational norms that regulate restaurants support the main Food Safety Law, including

- Implementation Regulation of Food Safety Law of People's Republic of China (Implementation Regulation),
- Catering Service Food Safety Inspection and Management Measures (Inspection Measures) issued by the Ministry of Sanitation on March 4, 2010, and

- Operational Norms of Catering Services for Food Safety[1] (Operational Norms) issued by the FDA in 2011.

These regulations, measures, and operational norms further refine the general rules set out in the Food Safety Law.

For instance, while article 27 of Food Safety Law mentions that "the persons engaging in the production or business operation of food shall…[wash] their hands clean," the Operational Norms further identify eight conditions under which a food worker should wash his or her hands. They are before processing food; after using the toilet; after touching raw food materials; after touching polluted tools or equipment; after coughing, sneezing, or blowing one's nose; after dealing with animals or garbage; after touching the ears, nose, hair, face, mouth, or other parts of the body; and after any activities that may pollute the hands. Similarly, while article 27 of the Food Safety Law mentions that "persons engaging in the production or business operation of food shall keep personal hygiene," the Operational Norms further detail several substantial aspects of personal hygiene. As article 12 of Operational Norms state, people who work with food "shall keep personal hygiene [and] wear clean working clothes and hats during the processing of food, [and] hair should not be outside of the hat, [and the person] should not have long nails, paint nails, [or] wear accessories."

In this book, six specific requirements from Food Safety Law and its complementary regulations, measures and operational norms were studied. The first was licensing, specifically the catering services license. According to Article 29 of the Food Safety Law, "the state shall adopt a licensing system for the food production and business operation. Those intending to engage in food production, food circulation or catering services shall obtain a license for food production, food circulation or catering services." The second was the regulations related to health certificates. According to article 34 of the Food Safety Law,

> Food producers and traders shall establish and implement an employee health management system. Anyone who suffers from an infectious disease of digestive tract, such as dysentery, typhoid, or virus hepatitis, active tuberculosis, and purulent or weeping skin diseases that adversely affect food safety must not engage in work in direct contact with food for consumption. The personnel involved in food production and trading shall take a medical check-up each year, and can work only after they have obtained a health certificate.

The third was regulations related to raw meat, specifically pork and chicken. According to article 28 of the Food Safety Law,

> it is forbidden to produce or engage in business operation of the following food…meat that has not been quarantined by the animal health inspection institution or has failed the quarantine or meat products that have not been inspected or have failed the inspection.

The fourth was dishware disinfection. Subarticle 5 of article 27 of the Food Safety Law reads, "[E]nsuring that the cutlery, drinking sets and containers for ready-to-eat food are washed clean and disinfected prior to use."

---

[1] Refer to http://www.foodmate.net/law/shipin/173257.html.

The fifth was washing hands, as set out in subarticle 8 of article 27 of the Food Safety Law, which states, "[E]nsuring that the persons engaging the production or business operation of food shall keep personal hygiene, washing their hands clean..." The Operational Norms further identify eight conditions under which a food worker should wash his or her hands, as mentioned preciously in this section. The sixth was cutting nails. Article 12 of Operational Norms highlights "should not have long nails" as one aspect of maintaining "personal hygiene," which is required under article 27 of the Food Safety Law.

2. Environmental Laws

Restaurants are considered polluters of the environment, as they release cooking fumes and oily wastewater, and they contribute to noise pollution, so they should abide by environmental laws. Several environmental laws are relevant, including

- Air Pollution Prevention Law of the People's Republic of China[2] (Air Pollution Law)
- Water Pollution Prevention Law of the People's Republic of China[3] (Water Pollution Law)
- Regulation for Administration of Pollutant Discharge License,[4] issued by the Ministry of Environmental Protection of the People's Republic of China
- Provincial Regulation for Environmental Protection in XX Province
- Provincial Regulation for Administration of Pollutant Discharge License in XX Province
- Local Regulation for Administration of Drainage in XX City.

This research studied the environmental and drainage licenses required in terms of these laws. According to Article 20 of the Water Pollution Law,

> [T]he nation [is to] implement [a] discharge licensing system. Companies and entities that directly or indirectly discharge industrial wastewater and medical wastewater and other companies and entities that should get discharge license before discharging wastewater and polluted water according to regulation, shall get discharge license... Companies and entities [are prohibited from discharging the] above-mentioned wastewater and polluted water without a discharge license or to violate the regulation of discharge license.

According to Article 19 of the Air Pollution Law, "companies and entities that discharge industrial exhaust gas or other poisonous air pollutants listed in article 78...and other implement discharge licensing management units, shall get discharge license." Article 81 of the Air Pollution Law specifically notes that

---

[2]http://www.envir.gov.cn/law/air.htm.

[3]http://www.scio.gov.cn/xwfbh/xwbfbh/wqfbh/2015/20150331/xgbd32636/Document/1397628/1397628_1.htm.

[4]http://www.mep.gov.cn/hdjl/yjzj/zjyj/201411/t20141127_292080.shtml. This regulation is an exposure draft. There is no officially issued national regulation on pollutant discharge. However, many provinces, such as Yunnan, Guangdong, Jiangsu, and Zhejiang, have created their own provincial regulations.

catering service entities giving out oil smoke shall install oil smoke purify equipment and use it normally, or take other purification measure to make sure the oil smoke reach the discharge standard, and prevent from pollution to residents' living environment in vicinity.

Other provincial and local city environmental protection and licensing regulations detail further the license administration. To maintain confidentiality, they are not provided here.

3. **Business Registration and Taxation**

As business organizations, restaurants must abide by the Regulation for Individual Business,[5] issued by the executive meeting of the State Council, and Measures of Administration of Individual Business Registration[6] (Business Registration Measures), issued by the State Administration for Industry and Commerce of the People's Republic of China. Restaurants should obtain business licenses according to these regulation and measures. Article 2 of Regulation for Individual Business points out that "citizens that register in industry and commerce administration bureaus and operation industry and commerce operation are individual business entities." Article 2 of Business Registration Measures states, "citizens shall register in industry and commerce administration bureaus, and get individual business license before operating business." If a restaurant's ownership changes, the former owner should cancel the old business license and the new owner should apply for a new business license, according to article 10 of Regulation for Individual Business:

> [I]f items of the individual business registration change, individual shall apply to change registration. If the individual business changes owner, it shall apply new registration after cancelling the old registration. If individual business that is operated by a family changes the owner within the family, it shall apply to change registration according to the article.

After obtaining a business license, a restaurant should apply for a tax registration license. Taxation is governed by

- The Law of The People's Republic of China Concerning the Administration of Tax Collection[7] (Tax Law)
- Regulation for Implementation of The Law of The People's Republic of China Concerning the Administration of Tax Collection[8] (Regulation of Implementation of Tax Law)

---

[5]This regulation was issued by the 149th executive meeting of the State Council on March 30, 2011, and executed on November 1, 2011.
   http://www.gov.cn/flfg/2011-04/28/content_1854129.htm.

[6]This administrative measure was first issued on September 30, 2011, and revised on February 20, 2014. http://www.gov.cn/flfg/2011-10/08/content_1963965.htm, http://www.chinalawedu.com/fal vfagui/22016/wa201403030919466262060.shtml.

[7]The tax law was first promulgated on September 4, 1992, and revised in 1995, 2013, and 2015. http://www.gov.cn/banshi/2005-08/31/content_146791.htm.

[8]This regulation was first issued on September 7, 2002, and revised in 2012 and 2013. http://www.gov.cn/gongbao/content/2014/content_2695454.htm.
http://www.gov.cn/zwgk/2012-11/16/content_2268184.htm.
http://www.gov.cn/flfg/2013-07/26/content_2477674.htm.

- Administration Measures of Taxation Registration,[9] issued by the State Administration of Taxation.

According to article 15 of the Tax Law,

Enterprises, branches in other jurisdictions established by the enterprises, sites engaged in production or business operations, individual households engaged in industry and commerce as well as institutions engaged in production or business operations (hereinafter collectively referred to as "taxpayers engaged in production or business operations") shall, within 30 days after the receipt of a business license, report to and complete tax registration formalities with the tax authorities on presentation of the relevant supporting documents. Upon examination and verification of the supporting documents, the tax authorities shall issue tax registration certificates.

However, on September 1, 2016, four state departments—the State Administration for Industry and Commerce (SAIC), State Administration of Taxation (SAT), National Development and Reform Commission (NDR), and State Council Legislative Affairs Office (SCLAO)—announced together that China will integrate business licenses and tax registration certificates into one license. Four trial districts, Heilongjiang, Shanghai, Fujian, and Hubei, implemented the system on October 1, 2016, while another 27 provinces, autonomous regions, and municipalities directly governed by the Central Government, and five selected cities implemented it on December 1, 2016. Consequently, since the end of 2016, restaurants need one license for both business registration and tax registration.

In terms of the formal *Fapiao* receipts used to collect tax, Article 20 of *Fapiao* Receipt Management Rule of the People's Republic of China[10] states "a company or individual who sells products, provide services, and other business activities should issue invoice to the customers." Therefore, restaurants pay tax based on the value of the *Fapiao* receipts they buy from the taxation bureau.

4. Fire Control

As a public gathering place, a restaurant needs a fire license, according to article 15 of the Fire Control Law[11] issued in 2008, which states public gathering places should apply for fire control safety assessment before use and opening. Provisions on Administration of Fire Safety in Public Entertainment Location[12] (Provision of Fire Safety), issued by the Ministry of Public Security, states in article 10, "safety exits …shall install light escape direction signs that meet the standards". Furthermore, article 11 of Provision of Fire Safety requires that "public entertainment locations, including restaurants, shall install fire accident emergency lights."

---

[9] http://www.gov.cn/gongbao/content/2004/content_62924.htm.

[10] http://www.chinaacc.com/new/63/67/81/2005/12/dr65075413310321500219845-0.htm.

[11] http://www.gov.cn/flfg/2008-10/29/content_1134208.htm.

[12] http://119.china.com.cn/qwxx/txt/2010-09/22/content_3737835.htm.

5. City Management

Restaurants are also subject to the Urban Management Law Enforcement Bureau that regulates any attachment outside the building such as awnings and light boxes. Relevant laws include Regulation for City Road[13] and Law of the People's Republic of China on Administrative Penalty.[14]

6. Liquor Licenses

Restaurants that sell alcohol must apply for liquor licenses, according to Regulation Rule of Alcohol Circulation[15] that was issued by the Ministry of Commerce in 2005. Article 6 of the regulation requires that "an organization or individual who sells alcohol, including wholesale and retail, should register in commerce administration departments on the same level as the industry and commerce administration bureaus where they registered, within 60 days after getting business licenses."

---

[13]http://www.gov.cn/gongbao/content/2011/content_1860785.htm.

[14]http://www.gov.cn/banshi/2005-08/21/content_25101.htm.
    http://www.gov.cn/flfg/2009-08/27/content_1403326.htm.

[15]http://www.mofcom.gov.cn/aarticle/b/d/200511/20051100748397.html.

Appendix B
The Methodology of Case Study

To describe compliance behavior in a manner that incorporates the process perspective and a subjective perspective of the regulated actor, the methodology of case studies were used in this book.

The term "case study" is a definitional morass. Although the definition seems clear, it can give rise to controversy. Usually, when referring to a work as a case study, several key terms come to mind: (a) small N study (Yin, 2013), (b) application of the qualitative method (Yin, 2013), (c) process tracing (George & Bennett, 2004), and (d) in-depth study and considering the cases as whole entities (Ragin 1987). However, Skinner (1963: p 508) captured the core characteristic of the case study: "instead of studying a thousand rats for one hour each, or a hundred rats for ten hours each, the investigator is likely to study one rat for a thousand hours." Of course, this view does not imply that case study research is limited to a sample of $N = 1$, but it does imply a relatively small sample. Gerring's (2004: p 342) narrow definition further clarifies this view: "the case study as an intensive study of a single unit for the purpose of understanding a larger class of (similar) units."

The case study method has several limitations. Some researchers view the case study as a soft method used in the social sciences and suitable for only descriptive or exploratory research, or in the preliminary stage of theoretical construction research to propose questions and hypotheses. When researchers want to study causal relationships or test hypotheses in a larger population, the case study is viewed as less appropriate than the quantitative survey. Furthermore, the findings of case studies cannot be generalized due to the limited number of cases studied and the typical lack of representativeness of the sample. According to critics, this lack of representativeness is the most significant limitation of case studies. Thus, the case study method does not allow researchers to answer questions related to "how many" or "how much" for the population or to generalize the findings statistically to the entire population. For instance, one cannot answer questions such as how much will X (general deterrence and specific deterrence) influence Y (compliance), or how many people are A (Buddhist)?

Y. Wu, *Compliance Ethnography*, Understanding China, https://doi.org/10.1007/978-981-16-2884-9

However, the case study is the preferred method when (a) "how" or "why" questions are being posed and (b) the focus is on a contemporary phenomenon within a real-life context. While the number of cases studied is small and the breadth of research is limited, cases can be studied in great depth, and researchers can discuss various variables. According to Gerring (2004), while unsuitable for studying the causal effect (How much will X influence Y?), the case study method enjoys a comparative advantage in studying causal mechanisms (How and in what way will X influence Y?). It allows one to peer into the box of causality to the intermediate causes lying between some cause and its purported effect. Ideally, it allows one to see how X and Y interact. Therefore, the case study method was selected for this research, as it would show how compliance behavior takes place and how various factors contribute to the processes.

Moreover, the case study method allows one to test the causal mechanism of a theory, thus providing corroborating evidence for a causal argument, which is referred to as pattern matching. If the existing theory suggests a specific causal pathway, the researcher may perform a pattern-matching investigation, for instance, study a typical case. The findings from the case study are judged according to whether they validate the stipulated causal mechanisms or not. In this way, the case study also can test theory based on cases with the type of test Karl Popper (1959) called "falsification" (as cited in Flyvbjerg 2006). Falsification is one of the most rigorous tests to which a scientific proposition can be subjected: if just one observation does not fit with the proposition, it is considered generally invalid and must therefore be either revised or rejected.

By strategic selection of cases (see Ragin 1987; Rosch 1978), we can increase the generalizability of case studies, for instance, by selecting a typical case, diverse case, extreme case, deviant case, influential case, or most similar or most different cases (Seawright and Gerring 2008).

To describe compliance behavior and capture the complexity of the processes of compliance behavior, the diverse cases technique was used to select cases in this book. Diverse cases encompass maximum variance along relevant dimensions (Seawright and Gerring 2008). Based on a pilot study, two contrasting restaurants were chosen to exemplify how compliance behavior takes place. As the review of the three classification methods of compliance behavior suggests, the nature or ideology of the actors, the attitudinal factor, and the commitment to regulation are useful elements in understanding and classifying compliance behavior. The two restaurants chosen had different operation ideologies. One was health oriented, claiming that it provided only healthy food and that it rejected unhealthy ingredients and cooking methods. This health-oriented ideology aligns with the purpose of food safety laws restaurants have to obey, and which formed the main legal context of this research. During the pilot study, it was found that this restaurant satisfied most legal requirements. Sometimes, it even went beyond the legal requirements. I called this restaurant the Idealistic restaurant. The second restaurant was economy oriented, sold cheap and tasty food, and aimed to get as much profit as possible. It used various, sometimes dishonest, strategies to satisfy legal requirements. In this book, I call it the Profit-Maximizing restaurant.

Although only two types of restaurants are highlighted in the study, more types exist. In fact, in Chap. 5, when including the restaurants studied in less depth, three actual restaurant types and two theoretical types based on the differentiation between dimensions emerge from the findings.

Appendix C
Supplemental Cases

In addition to the two restaurants studied in depth, four restaurants were studied in less depth—L restaurant, W restaurant, H restaurant, and S restaurant. The four restaurants differed in terms of scale, location, and clientele. L restaurant, similar to the Profit-Maximizing restaurant, was located in a residential area and near a fresh food market. It could serve 50 customers, and each customer spent around 30 CNY. W restaurant was located in a village-in-the-city and had only four tables, serving a maximum of 30 customers. Most customers were local residents, and the average cost of a meal was 20 to 30 CNY. H restaurant was located near universities, TV stations, hospitals, and residential areas, and most of its customers lived or worked nearby. At approximately 400 m^2, it could serve 200 customers. The average cost for each customer was about 30 CNY. S restaurant was located in a central business area, and it could seat 300 customers. Its upmarket clientele spent approximately 100 CNY each. The data collected at S restaurant derived mainly from workers, and it was used for variable analysis at individual level. Because of a lack of information about its compliance as an entity and interaction with regulators, it is not discussed in this section. Instead, L restaurant, W restaurant, and H restaurant are introduced.

L restaurant

L restaurant had more difficulty than the Idealistic restaurant and the Profit-Maximizing restaurant to obtain its environmental license. The owner, the owner of L restaurant, had successively established two L restaurants, which shared the same characteristics in terms of location, scale, and customers.[16] The first L restaurant was the first restaurant the owner of L restaurant had opened, and everything was new to her. When she applied for the environmental license, the inspectors announced that they could not issue the license because the restaurant was 25 m from a river,

---

[16] the owner of L restaurant from L restaurant had opened two restaurants. The first was successful and profitable, but she had to close it after the area underwent reconstruction. She chose another site for her new restaurant in another district. In this study, L restaurant refers to both restaurants.

© The Editor(s) (if applicable) and The Author(s), under exclusive license to Springer Nature Singapore Pte Ltd. 2021
Y. Wu, *Compliance Ethnography*, Understanding China,
https://doi.org/10.1007/978-981-16-2884-9

and the regulations stated that it could be no closer than 30 m. However, the owner of L restaurant noticed that a nearby restaurant was located only 20 m from the same river. When she asked the inspectors why that restaurant could operate so close to the river, the inspectors answered they (personally) had not approved that license.

Subsequently, the owner of L restaurant obtained an environmental license by asking an acquaintance in the Sanitation Bureau for help. Through an acquaintance of this acquaintance, who worked in the Environmental Bureau, she obtained a license. In this case, L restaurant had an environmental license, which one could claim showed compliance, but when tracing back the process of obtaining the license, it becomes clear that the restaurant engaged in fraudulent compliance. It did not satisfy the licensing conditions but obtained the license to show it was in compliance.

Furthermore, the environmental license at the new L restaurant revealed another compliance issue. When the owner of L restaurant opened the new L restaurant, she did so in another district, which belonged to a different enforcement bureau. However, it was a restaurant before, and the former restaurant had the required opening licenses. With the lease, the owner of L restaurant received the old environmental license. According to the law, she should have applied for a new license, as ownership had changed, similar to the case of the owner at the Profit-Maximizing restaurant. Nevertheless, in light of her experiences at the first L restaurant, she did not apply for a new license but invited some inspectors for dinner via an acquaintance. She said the enforcement in that district was not strict. The outcome was that she was accepted as being in compliance and experienced no trouble related to that license. This was fake compliance, as shown when examining the process. The environmental license the owner of L restaurant held for the second restaurant was not a genuine license issued to L restaurant.

Moreover, the owner of L restaurant engaged in full compliance at the first restaurant and fake compliance at the second when applying for the fire license. At the first L restaurant, she was asked to buy five fire extinguishers, which she did. Unlike at the Profit-Maximizing restaurant, the inspectors in this district came to verify in person that she had carried out their instructions. In her view, one fire extinguisher was too many if no fires broke out, but once a fire broke out, any number of fire extinguishers would not be enough. At the second L restaurant, she did not apply for a fire license and did not buy any fire extinguishers but invited the inspectors to a meal, as she did when applying for her environmental license. Although faced with the same legal requirements, the owner of L restaurant engaged in completely different compliance behaviors. When she opened her first restaurant, she fully complied with fire license requirements and bought the required number of fire extinguishers, but when she opened the second one, she had learned to play games with legal requirements. If no inspectors questioned L restaurant's license, it did not need to apply for a new one.

For the dish disinfection log, when inspectors told the owner of L restaurant to keep a log showing how many bowls and chopsticks had been disinfected each day, she complied for a month. However, when she realized the inspectors did not check the log, she stopped, and compliance became noncompliance.

These compliance behaviors described at L restaurant show a learning process. In the process of responding to legal requirements, the owner of L restaurant learned the practical rules from her experience of dealing with inspectors. The practical rules she learned guided her responses in return. For example, despite following inspectors' directions to complete a disinfection log, after she learned that inspectors would not check it, she soon stopped complying with this requirement. As a result, compliance behavior turned into noncompliance behavior. When she learned inspectors would check the fire extinguishers before issuing a fire license, she bought the required number of fire extinguishers, but when she found out that inspectors in another district were not strict on this, she did not buy any fire extinguishers and engaged in dishonesty to escape the regulatory encounter. Previous compliance behaviors changed to fake compliance behaviors. Additionally, she learned the practical rules from another restaurant's experience. Although she was told that opening a restaurant within 30 m of the riverside was prohibited, she saw that another restaurant was located within this distance. This showed that the practical rule differed from what she was told. As a result, she found a corrupt way to obtain the license, and compliance became fraudulent compliance.

This learning process also embodies a process of contesting, where the owner of L restaurant's beliefs contest with the legal requirements. For most legal requirements, the owner of L restaurant did not pay much attention to the legal requirements per se, and her belief was not having belief in those legal requirements. Her ideology did not align with the aims of the legal requirements, such as food safety and concern for the environment. In other words, her belief is amoral and pragmatically oriented. She claimed, "I am just an ordinary person and have not studied in school. I do not know about the law things and do not know whether it is rational or not. I just do what they asked." Thus, her belief is, "I do not know what I should or should not do; I just do what the inspectors asked." However, during the process in which she found out what the genuine regulations were that she should follow in practice, she learned to circumvent legal requirements that were not strictly enforced. In this way, her beliefs competed with the law in clarifying what needed to be done and what did not need to be done.

From the perspective of motivational posture, L restaurant showed manly capitulation and game playing. It accepted the regulatory authority as legitimate, and it would have liked to do what it was asked, but in the process of learning practical rules, it tried to falsify those requirements and escape whatever it could manage to escape. In terms of management style, L restaurant showed characteristics of laggards and reluctant compliers. As a laggard, it actively escaped legal requirements whenever it saw the opportunity to do so. As a reluctant complier, it also showed the willingness to comply with the legal requirements set out by inspectors, but only aimed to meet the minimum standards.

W restaurant

W restaurant was located in a "village in a town" in a suburban area. It did not have any opening licenses and seemed to engage in noncompliance behaviors. However, when asked about the process of how the noncompliance behaviors took place, the owner explained that the restaurant actually complied with the norms the local enforcement department required. Inspectors from the local enforcement department, ICB, came to check W restaurant when it first opened. They asked W restaurant to pay 2000 CNY and said after that it did not need to apply for all the licenses. According to the owner, the inspectors said that if restaurant owners wanted to apply for opening licenses, they just applied. If they did not want to apply for opening licenses, they simply needed to pay the 2000 CNY fee. The owner thought,

> They are the same person that I need to resort for if I want to apply opening licenses. They will not give opening licenses to me if I apply. Since they said I can run the restaurant by paying some fee and without opening licenses, I just pay some money and do not need to apply for those licenses. Restaurants in the whole street do not have opening licenses…

Later, the boss bargained with the inspectors and finally handed over 1500 CNY. Subsequently, the restaurant was considered legitimate.

According to the owner, inspectors said it was acceptable to open restaurants there, but it was impossible to obtain opening licenses. When asked why, the owner stated that the inspectors did not explain why. When one considers the letter and the spirit of the laws that regulate restaurant behaviors, it is clear that W restaurant did not comply with either. However, when considered from the oral requirements of the regulatory department, it could be argued that W restaurant complied with the law by negotiating with inspectors. The regulatory department clearly knew it was impossible for restaurants to obtain opening licenses in that street for various reasons, yet it wanted to allow restaurants to operate there. Therefore, it created its own practical rule for these restaurants, that is, to register with a fee. After paying the fee, W restaurant was considered legitimate and in compliance. Although it did not comply with the general laws that apply to ordinary restaurants, it complied with the specific practical rule made by this specific regulatory department. This kind of compliance can be seen as a form of creative compliance.

In addition, this creative compliance behavior at W restaurant involved the learning and contesting processes. The owner of W restaurant actually knew about opening licenses because one of his friends had a restaurant in the city and had those opening licenses. Nevertheless, he also learned that restaurants in the same street did not have opening licenses but paid the regulatory department. Consequently, when the inspectors told him he could apply for licenses or pay the fee, he quickly decided to pay the fee. He learned to follow the practical rule that applied specifically in that area and not to attempt to follow the general laws for restaurants. Furthermore, he learned from other people's experience to bargain with the inspector and finally discounted the fee by 500 CNY.

The contesting process shares some similarities with that of L restaurant, specifically the belief that "I do not know about the law; I just did what they asked." This argument justifies its response to the specific practical rule but not the general law for restaurants. What is different is that the owner W restaurant believed that restaurants should have fire extinguishers. As a result, W restaurant bought two fire extinguishers although it was not required to do so. Considering this behavior falls outside the requirements of the specific practical rule in that area, it can be viewed as beyond-compliance behavior.

While the Profit-Maximizing restaurant showed that the attitude of the regulated toward the regulatory authority and the law could differ, W restaurant showed that the legal requirements might differ when dealing with a specific regulatory authority. From friends, W restaurant knew the general legal requirements for restaurants, that is, to obtain various opening license; however, from the specific regulatory authority, it learned that it needed to follow another kind of specific practical rule but not the general legal requirements. In terms of motivational posture toward the regulatory authority, it clearly showed capitulation. It was inclined to follow inspectors' directions, although they differed from what was known from friends. Again, the motivational posture of capitulation does not forecast positive compliance behaviors toward general laws for restaurants, but a kind of creative compliance behavior. This can be seen as an extreme case where the practical rule enforced by the regulatory authority differs completely from the general laws it should enforce.

In addition to capitulation, W restaurant showed the motivational posture of game playing, as can be seen by negotiating the fee. What the regulatory authority required was not respected as defining the limits of acceptable activity but was viewed as something that could be molded to suit the restaurant's purposes. Although it was inclined to cooperate with the regulatory authority and followed its directions, at the same time, it tried to manipulate the specific practical rule to minimize its cost of compliance. The two kinds of motivational postures were taken and changed in the compliance process of learning the specific practical rule.

In terms of management style, W restaurant was a laggard regarding most general laws for restaurants, a reluctant complier regarding the specific practical rules enforced by the specific regulatory authority, and a strategist regarding the fire-fighting law. The three kinds of management styles were adopted and altered during the contesting process. When it showed a motivation of capitulation toward the specific regulatory authority and did not share the same beliefs as the general laws for restaurants imply, it became a laggard. When it learned the specific practical rule, showed capitulation toward the authority and game playing toward the specific practical rule, it became a reluctant complier. When it shared the beliefs implied in the fire-fighting law and bought fire extinguishers without enforcement, it became a strategist.

H restaurant

Previously, H restaurant used prepacked tableware, as was the case at the Profit-Maximizing restaurant. However, it stopped after a nearby TV station filmed a TV program in the restaurant. Customers were interviewed about their opinions of the prepacked tableware, and they complained that the restaurant, not customers, should bear the costs of washing the dishes. Subsequently, the owner stopped using prepacked tableware because of the TV program, the complaints, and the questionable cleanliness of the prepacked tableware.

H restaurant tried to make its dishware acceptable for customers, and one of its internal standards was dryness. It did not use a high-quality disinfection cabinet like the one at the Idealistic restaurant but partially dried the dishware with a cloth after washing it. The cloths were not disinfected every time before drying dishes. However, the owner H restaurant believed that wet dishes equated to dished that had not been disinfected. The owner state, "Sometimes I eat outside [at another restaurant]. I will not use dishware that is wet. Why? If the dishware has been disinfected, [where does] the water come [from]?" As a result, she required servers to wipe the dishware after washing, even though items were not disinfected every time. According to the dishwasher, the dishware was disinfected with disinfection fluid at random interval. Nevertheless, disinfection was rare, as I did not see this practiced once during the two-week observation period. Therefore, H restaurant only partly complied with the disinfection legal requirements.

Handwashing was not regulated by internal rules at H restaurant. According to my observations, servers would not wash their hands unless they were too oily, and every server had her own handwashing habits. When asked about handwashing, the manager and chef stated,

> It is enough that workers wash their hands before starting doing their work [this means once in the morning and once in the afternoon when workers come to work]. It is impossible to wash hands every time you touch or scratch your body in the middle of doing kitchen work…Such small detail will not have any big influence. …In our village, people cook even without wash the vegetable, not mention about washing hands. The hands of the cook look almost black, but the cook grab some vegetable and throw into the pan to fry. However, people in our village are healthier than people in the city. The most important is the big issues such as chemicals.

Consequently, H restaurant did not comply with handwashing requirements.

Examining compliance behavior at H restaurant showed that learning and contesting processes occurred. H restaurant learned that prepacked dishware was unacceptable to its customers and consequently stopped using prepacked dishware, despite its benefits of convenience and profitability. It disinfected dishware occasionally with disinfectant, which led to partial compliance. From experience, it learned that one standard for identifying disinfected dishware is dryness. As a result, to meet that standard, it ensured that dishes were wiped after washing, as it did not disinfect its dishware with a heated disinfection cabinet. However, these actions did not truly comply with disinfection legal norm. Moreover, contesting was present in the process, as the manager's argument about handwashing shows.

Due to a lack of data about the interaction between H restaurant and the regulatory authority, the restaurant's motivational posture is unclear. In terms of management style, it shows characteristics of both laggard and strategist. As laggard, it had a negative attitude toward the legal requirement of handwashing and engaged in noncompliance behavior. As a strategist, it voluntarily abandoned the use of prepacked dishware to retain its customers and realize economic benefit, although the prepacked dishware was acceptable for meeting legal requirements. The restaurant learned from customers' responses that while using prepacked dishware was convenient, it might lose customers by doing so, which would influence its business. For the sake of the business, it preferred to give up the prepacked dishware despite not being required to do so by law. Nevertheless, abandoning the prepacked dishware did not mean it was concerned about the disinfection promoted by the legal requirement. As its disinfection practices showed, it paid scant attention to disinfection. In addition, the

Table C.1 Compliance behaviors, motivational postures, and management styles in the three restaurants

Restaurant	Behaviors	Types of compliance	Motivational posture	Management style
L restaurant	Obtained environmental license at first restaurant but did not satisfy requirements	Fraudulent	Game playing	Laggard Reluctant complier
	Invited inspectors for dinner and did not apply for new license at second restaurant	Fake		
	Did not maintain disinfection log	Noncompliance		
	Bought enough fire extinguishers and obtained fire license at first restaurant	Full	Capitulation	
W restaurant	Did not apply for opening license but paid fee to regulatory authority; negotiated 500 CNY discount	Creative	Capitulation, Game playing	Laggard, Reluctant complier
	Bought fire extinguishers despite no instruction from regulatory authority to do so	Beyond		Strategist
H restaurant	Give up packed dishware, disinfect dishware with disinfectant occasionally	Partial		Strategist
	Did not have handwashing rules and workers did not always wash their hands	Noncompliance		Laggard

restaurant's belief about wet dishes indicating its ignorance regarding disinfection. As to handwashing, it strongly believed that this requirement was not necessary. This belief competed with the legal requirement and result in noncompliance with the requirement.

Uncited References

Cao, Gang, and Xiaorong Wu. 2009. Necessity and Oughtness of Compliance: A Perspective of Moral Psychology [*Shou fa de bi ran he ying ran: yi ge dao de xin li xue de shi jiao*]. *Journal of Henan Normal University (Philosophy and Social Sciences Edition) [Henan Shifan Daxue Xuebao]*, 2.

Ding, Yisheng, and Qingchun Li. 2004. Why Citizens Comply with the Law: Comments on Theories of Citizen Compliance in Western Academy [*Gongmin weishenme zunshou falv?*]. *Law Review [Faxue Pinglun]*, 1.

Ding, Qiming, and Jing Zhao. 2011. Constructing Motivations for Corporate Environmental Compliance [*Lun qiye huanjing shoufa jili jizhi de jiangou*]. *Academic Exchange [Xueshu jiaoliu]*, 3: 75–77.

Fang, Jiancun, Dawei Xi, Xiaoyun Liu and Xinxiu Liu. 2008. Analysis of a Case that Fake Health Certificate for Public Business Place Workers [*1 qi gonggong changsuo congye renyuan weizao jiankangzheng anli fenxi*]. *Preventive Medicine Tribune [Yufang yixue luntan]*, 14(11): 1042.

Feng, Yu, and Bing the Owner of L Restaurant. 2008. Compliance as a Road to Bridge Morality and Well-Being [*Defu xiangtong de shoufa zhilu*]. *New Vision of Future [Xin Yuan Jian]*, 7: 119–124.

Flyvbjerg, B. 2006. Five Misunderstandings about Case-Study Research. *Qualitative Inquiry* 12 (2): 219–245.

George, Alexander L., and Andrew Bennett. 2004. *Case Studies and Theory Development*. Cambridge, MA: MIT Press.

Gerring, John. 2004. What is a Case Study and what is it good For? *American Political Science Review* 98 (2): 341–354.

Gerring, John. 2007. *Case Study Research: Principles and Practices*. Cambridge, UK: Cambridge University Press.

Gong, Guangming. 2008. Factors Influencing Hand-washing Compliance among Clinic Nurses and Countermeasures. *Chinese Journal of Nosocomiology* 18 (10).

Gunningham, Neil, Peter Grabosky, Darren Sinclair, Dorothy Thornton, and Robert A. Kagan. 2005. Motivating Management: Corporate Compliance in Environmental Protection. *Law & Policy* 27 (2): 289–316.

Hou, Meng. 2014. The Traditions and Challenges for Social Science of Law [*Sheke faxue de chuantong yu tiaozhan*]. *Studies in Law and Business [Fashan Yanjiu]*, 163 (5): 74–80.

Li, Na. 2015. Compliance as Individual Choice: Based on Empirical Research of Construction Worker's Work Safety Compliance Behaviors. *Thinking* 41 (6): 112–119.

Li, Na. 2016. Compliance as Process: Work Safety in the Chinese Construction Industry. Ph.D. Thesis, Faculty of Law, Amsterdam University. http://dare.uva.nl/document/2/176952.

Li, Wanxin, and Krzysztof Michalak. 2008. Environmental Compliance and Enforcement in China. In *Governance, Risk, and Compliance Handbook: Technology, Finance, Environmental, and*

271

Y. Wu, *Compliance Ethnography*, Understanding China, https://doi.org/10.1007/978-981-16-2884-9

International Guidance and Best Practices, ed. Anthony Tarantino, 379–391. Hoboken, NJ: Wiley.

Liu, Tongjun. 2005. *The Theoretical Logic of Ethics of Compliance [Shou Fa Lun Li de Li Lun Luo Ji]*. Jinan: Shandong People's Press.

Liu, Yang. 2010. Systematic Theory among Morals, Laws, Duty of Compliance [*Dao de, fa lv, shou fa yi wu zhi jian de xi tong xing li lun*]. *Chinese Journal of Law [Fa Xue Yan Jiu]*, 2: 3–22.

Liu, Nicole Ning, Carlos Wing-Hung Lo, Xueyong Zhan, and Wei Wang. 2014. Campaign-style Enforcement and Regulatory Compliance. *Public Administration Review*, 75 (1): 85–95.

Lu, Yilong. 2005. Factors Affecting Peasants' Legal Behavior: A Positivist Test on Two Classical Paradigms. *Journal of Renmin University of China* 4: 91–97.

Luo, Yang, Guo-Ping He, Jijan-Wei Zhou, and Ying Luo. 2011. Factors Impacting Compliance with Standard Precautions in Nursing China. *International Journal of Infectious Diseases*, 14: 1106–1114.

Ma, Xiaoying, and Leonard Ortolano. 2000. *Environmental Regulation in China: Institutions, Enforcement, and Compliance.* Lanham, England: Rowman & Littlefield Publishers.

Murphy, Kristina, and Tom Tyler. 2008. Procedural Justice and Compliance Behavior: The Mediating Role of Emotions. *European Journal of Social Psychology* 38: 652–668.

OECD. 2006. Environmental Compliance and Enforcement in China: An Assessment of Current Practices and Ways Forward. http://www.oecd.org/env/outreach/37867511.pdf.

OECD 2009. Ensuring Environmental Compliance: Trends and Good Practices. http://www.oecd-ilibrary.org/environment/ensuring-environmental-compliance_9789264059597-en.

Popper, K. 1959. *The Logic of Scientific Discovery*. New York: Basic Books.

Potter, Pitman B. 2002. *Guanxi* and the PRC Legal System: From Contradiction to Complementarity. In *Social Connections in China: Institutions, Culture, and the Changing Nature of Guanxi*, ed. Thomas Gold, Doug Guthrie, and David Wank, pp. 178–196. Cambridge University Press.

Ragin, Charles C. 1987. *The Comparative Method: Moving beyond Qualitative and Quantitative Methods.* Berkeley: University of California.

Rosch, E. 1978. Principles of Categorization. In *Cognition and Categorization*, ed. E. Rosch and B.B. Lloyd, 27–48. Hillsdale, NJ: Lawrence Erlbaum.

Shang, Shao-mei, Yi-zhi Wang, Xiu-xia Zheng, Yu-mei Sun, Jing-xiong Huang, and Yuan-ru He. 2003. Effective Program of Compliance with Handwashing [*Cujin huli renyuan xishou xingwei yicongxing de yanjiu*]. *Chinese Journal of Nosoconmiology [Zhonghua yiyuan ganranxue zazhi]*, 13 (6): 507–510.

Skinner, Burrhus F. 1963. Operant Behavior. *American Psychologist* 18 (8).

Sun, Yufeng. 2009, January. On significance of compliance ethic education [*Lun shoufa daode jiaoyu de biyao xing*]. Internet Fortune [*Wangluo caifu*] (January 2009): 18–19.

Van der Meer, Cornelius. 2006. *China's Compliance with Food Safety Requirements for Fruits and Vegetables: Promoting Food Safety, Competitiveness, and Poverty Reduction.* Washington, DC: World Bank.

Van Rooij, Benjamin. 2006a. "Implementation of Chinese Environmental Law: Regular Enforcement and Political Campaigns." *Development and Change* 37 (1): 57–74.

Van Rooij, Benjamin. 2006b. *Regulating Land and Pollution in China, Lawmaking, Compliance, and Enforcement; Theory and Cases.* Leiden: Leiden University Press.

Van Rooij, Benjamin. 2012. "The People's Regulation: Citizens and Implementation of Law in China." *Columbia Journal of Asian Law*, 25: 116.

Van Rooij, Benjamin, Adam Fine, Zhang Yanyan, and Yunmei Wu. 2016. Comparative Compliance: Digital Piracy, Deterrence, Social Norms, and Duty in China and the United States. *Law & Policy* 39 (1). https://doi.org/10.1111/lapo.12071.

Van Rooij, Benjamin, Margarita Leib, Shaul Shalvi, Yuval Feldman, Eline Scheper, Qian Zheng, and Zhang Wanhong. Forthcoming. The Exogenous Rule of Law: Comparative Evidence about the General Duty to Obey the Law amongst Law Students.

Wang, Feng. 2009. Economic Analysis of Compliance [*Shoufa de jingji fenxi*]. *Journal of Hubei Institute for Nationalities (Philosophy and Social Sciences)* [*Hubei minzu xueyuan xuebao*] 27 (4): 140–145.

Wang, Xiaoshuo. 2009. On Formal Justice of Laws and Compliance [*Lun fa de xingshi zhengyi yu shoufa*]. *Journal of Hebei University (Philosophy and Social Sciences Edition)* [Hebei daxue xuebao] 4: 42–45.

Wang, Xiaoshuo, and Qingshun Liu. 2010. An Analysis of Psychological Factors of Law-Abiding Behavior [*Shoufa xingwei de xinli yinsu fenxi*]. *Journal of Hebei University (Philosophy and Social Science)* [*Hebei daxue xuebao (zhexue shehui kexue ban)*] 35 (6): 73–80.

Wang, Shitong, Xiangxia Wang, and Aiting Wang. 2009. Analysis of a Case That Fake Health Certificate and Training Certificate [*Yiqi weizao jiankangzheng he peixun hegezheng anli fenxi*]. *Henan Journal of Preventive Medicine* [*Henan yufang yixue zazhi*] 20 (2): 153–154.

Wei, Shouyu. 2008. On Moral Construction and Formation of Compliance Consciousness [*Lun daode jianshe yu shoufa yishi de xingcheng*]. *Journal of Xingtai University* [*Xingtai xueyuan xuebao*] 23 (3): 32–33.

Wu, Yahui. 2011. The Logic of Compliance: Based on Legal Economy Analysis Paradigm [*Lun shoufa de luoji: ji yu fa jingjixue fenxi fanshi*]. *Journal of Guangdong University of Business* [*Guangdong Shangxueyuan xuebao*] 2: 83–90.

Xiang, Shiming. 2009. On the Ethic Base of Compliance [*Lun shoufa de daode jichu*]. *Legal System and Society* [*Fazhi yu shehui*] 3: 10–11.

Yao, Junting. 2009. Compliance Possibility and Limitations with Perspective of Emotional Choice [*Ganxing xuanze yu zhong de shoufa kenengxing jiqi xianduyu*]. *Weishi* 7: 58–61.

Yin, Robert K. 2013. *Case Study Research: Design and Methods.* London: Sage Publication.

You, Quanrong. 2006. On Law Abiding Cost and Its Control [*Shoufa chengben jiqi kongzhi*]. *Journal of National Prosecutors College* [*Guojia jiancH restaurant xueyuan xuebao*] 14 (5): 77–80.

Yu, Weijian, Shuixin Deng, and Yonghong Lu. 2014. Compliance Behaviors in Fragile Legal Environment [*Cuiruo fazhi xia de shoufa xingwei*]. *Journal of Public Administration Research and Theory* [*Zhongguo zhili pinglun*] June 12, 2014: 1–28.

Zhan, Maohua. 2013. Compliance Concept Interpretation under the Perspective of Jurisprudence [*Falixue shijiao xia de shoufa gainian jiedu*]. *Hunan Social Sciences* [*Hunan shehui kexue*] z1: 261–264.

Zhao, Yuxi, and Ran Jie. 2011. Reasons and Suggestions on the 'Labor Shortage' of Catering Industry [*Can yin qi ye yong gong huang de yuan yin ji dui ce fen xi*]. *Economic Research Guide* [*Jingji yanjiu daokan*] 141 (31): 108–109.

Zhao, Zu'an. 2011. Company Pay Salary, Workers have to Submit *Fapiao* Receipt? [*Qiye fa gongzi, yao pin fapiao baoxiao?*] *Employment and Safeguard* [*Jiuye yu baozhang*] 11: 22–23.